COMPUTER-AIDED SOFTWARE ENGINEERING (CASE)

SECOND EDITION

COMPUTER-AIDED SOFTWARE ENGINEERING (CASE)

SECOND EDITION

ELLIOT CHIKOFSKY

IEEE Computer Society Press
Los Alamitos, California

Washington • Brussels • Tokyo

IEEE COMPUTER SOCIETY PRESS TECHNOLOGY SERIES

Library of Congress Cataloging-in-Publication Data

Chikofsky, Elliot J.
Computer-Aided Software Engineering (CASE) / Elliot J. Chikofsky. — 2nd ed.
        p. cm. — (IEEE Computer Society Press technology series)
    Includes bibliographical references.
    ISBN 0-8186-3590-8 (pbk.). — ISBN 0-8186-3591-6 (fiche).
    1. Computer-aided software engineering. I. Title. II. Title: CASE. III. Series.
QA76. 758.C5 1992
005.1 — dc20   92-41057
                                                                                        CIP

Published by the
IEEE Computer Society Press
10662 Los Vaqueros Circle
PO Box 3014
Los Alamitos, CA 90720-1264

IEEE Computer Society Press Order Number 3590-05
Library of Congress Number 92-41057
ISBN 0-8186-3590-8 (paper)
ISBN 0-8186-3591-6 (microfiche)

Additional copies can be ordered from

IEEE Computer Society Press
Customer Service Center
10662 Los Vaqueros Circle
PO Box 3014
Los Alamitos, CA 90720-1264

IEEE Computer Society
13, avenue de l'Aquilon
B-1200 Brussels
BELGIUM

IEEE Computer Society
Ooshima Building
2-19-1 Minami-Aoyama
Minato-ku, Tokyo 107
JAPAN

Technical Editor: Rao Vemuri
Production Editor: Lisa O'Conner
Copy Editor: Henry Ayling
Cover artist: Joe Daigle
Printed in the United States of America by KNI, Incorporated

THE INSTITUTE OF ELECTRICAL AND ELECTRONICS ENGINEERS, INC.

TABLE OF CONTENTS

INTRODUCTION

Computer-aided software engineering (CASE) is the name used for both a technology and a marketplace. Despite marketing hype and over promotion, CASE technology has continued to move forward. This book addresses that technology, its background, and its evolution. The papers presented in this volume illustrate the present state of CASE, how its key concepts have fared over time, and how it looks as a technology for the future.

Since the inception of CASE in the 1970s, its gross objective has remained stable (but not static) — to utilize computer and software technology for improving the systems development process and the products of that process. These are moving targets; the products that must be produced, and what it means to improve the production process, are evolving entities. As users of the technology have become more sophisticated and more practiced, their needs and their demands have increased. CASE has adherents and detractors. And, like many technologies that organizations have introduced as panaceas, the CASE technology has had vibrant successes and flaming failures. Its truth and its value lie somewhere in between.

Since the mid 1980s, CASE has introduced automated tools, environments, and software development workstations into many organizations. This has made the widespread application of system development methods practical and economical. CASE environments provide a mechanism for systems and software developers, on both small and large projects, to document and model an information system from its inception as user requirements through its design and implementation. CASE environments provide the project team with powerful analytic tools to ensure consistency, completeness, and conformity to standards. They also enable organizations to introduce and support process-based management, software reuse, design reuse, metrics, reverse engineering, and other techniques to make development and maintenance more effective.

THE SELECTED PAPERS

In Part I of this volume, three papers introduce the CASE technology — CASE and I-CASE — and issues involved in forming comprehensive environments. Part II shows how environmental concepts have been refined over the last decade. Dart et al., and Wasserman, provide background on the general concepts of software development environments and their evolution. The three papers from 1992 show these concepts in action and where they lead us now.

Parts III through V highlight three technologies being applied to provide advanced user functionality in CASE environments: the data-browsing technology, including hypertext and database query; assistants and expert-system approaches; and the application of prototyping and transformational techniques to change the software development paradigm through automation.

Part VI illustrates issues involved in tailoring environments — one of the most important areas for the future of CASE. As the needs and sophistication level of CASE users grow, fixed environments become too limiting and are unable to meet the changing world of software development. Concepts of extension, metaspecification, and the generation of environments will be critical to the success of CASE over the next decade. Part VII describes key issues in evaluating the CASE technology, handling its introduction, and managing it effectively. CASE does not replace good management practices in software development. On the contrary, it requires them.

One well-advertised CASE topic is not called out in this volume; namely, repositories — the accepted term for the integrated databases of CASE environments. Considerable effort and attention have been put into repository technology over the last few years of CASE, including large-scale developments such as IBM's Repository Manager and Digital's CDD/Repository. But it is important to recognize that repositories are only an enabling technology for CASE. Repository requirements and examples abound in the papers presented herein. CASE environments must have an integrated datastore, but having a great repository is not sufficient. A meaningful software process, effective tools, usable methods, and adequate support for people are critical to making CASE work.

Elliot Chikofsky
January, 1993

PART I: CASE ENVIRONMENTS AND TOOLS — OVERVIEW

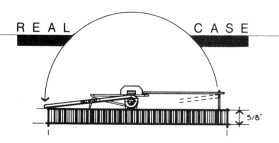

CASE: Reliability Engineering for Information Systems

Elliot J. Chikofsky and *Burt L. Rubenstein*, *Index Technology*

You can use CASE environments in new ways to support the entire software life cycle, including reliability engineering, maintenance, documentation, and auditing.

Developers of information systems have historically been the last to apply computer-based tools to improve the quality, reliability, and productivity of their own work — a phenomenon known as the "shoemaker's children" syndrome, from the story of the shoemaker whose children never had new shoes because all new shoes were made for others. This tradition is changing as organizations involved in both commercial data processing and embedded real-time applications review their heavy investment in software and information systems. Having recently identified information systems as a capital resource, they now realize their need for surer design and reliability. By introducing new CASE technology, they can achieve greater system development productivity while providing a new approach to engineering information systems reliably.

As early as 1973, Barry Boehm projected that software costs would, by 1985, reach or exceed 90 percent of the total cost of data processing (the combined hardware and software costs),[1,2] as Figure 1 shows. It was clear that hardware costs were rapidly falling and that personnel costs in the labor-intensive software development arena were rising. The projection has turned out to be all too true.

Today, the rapid pace at which hardware innovations are announced, particularly in the area of microprocessor technology, now well exceeds the capabilities of our software-development technology. Consider, for example, the Intel 80286 processor, which can support multitasking operations. At the time of its introduction, the existing general-purpose operating systems for IBM PCs (such as MS-DOS and Xenix) had no way to use its capabilities. And then, before the first operating system (OS/2) was available to take full advantage of the 286, the 80386 processor made its debut with even greater capabilities. An entire generation of processor hardware technology has arrived and been superseded without any

Reprinted from *IEEE Software*, Vol. 5, No. 2, March 1988, pp. 11-16. Copyright © 1988 by The Institute of Electrical and Electronics Engineers, Inc. All rights reserved.

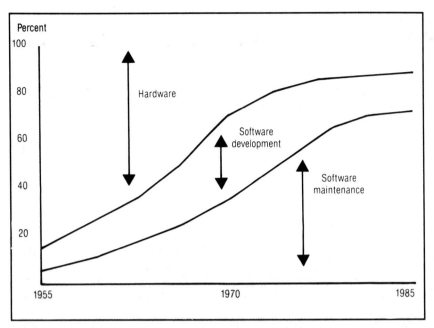

Figure 1. Evolution of system-development costs (*y*-axis is percent of total cost).

software to support it reaching the marketplace!

Further, the ability to develop software to meet new needs is rapidly losing ground to software maintenance. The US Air Force's F-16 jet fighter, for example, has an $85-million budget for software development. On top of this, the Air Force is expecting to spend about $250 million in software maintenance — almost three times the development cost.[3]

Organizations are now recognizing how the software crisis affects them. Randall Jensen of Hughes Aircraft, for example, has identified six key software problems resulting from systems-development approaches as commonly applied:[4]

- products exceeding cost estimates,
- late delivery,
- inadequate performance,
- impossible maintenance,
- prohibitive modification costs, and
- unreliability.

More than ever before, organizations are looking for workable solutions to increase the productivity of their systems-development staff, to improve the cost-effectiveness of the development process, and to ensure the reliability and quality of systems produced.

Development approaches

Since the mid-1970s, the approach to developing information systems has evolved with the growth of methods to aid

both project management and specification. Organizations have turned to more formal methods of system development and, most recently, to automated tools to support these methods.

Classical methods. The development of information systems and software has long been viewed as an art rather than a science. The programmer or analyst would wade through a loose collection of user wants and needs. Some time later, through some arcane and mystical process, a system would appear that, even though it did not meet all the user's needs, was usually considered better than what existed before. This classical approach was characterized by informal guidelines, lack of standardization, and minimal documentation (usually produced as an afterthought).

Some order was introduced in the early 1970s in the form of project-management methods based on models of the system-development life cycle. Since then, many packaged life-cycle methods — incorporating directions, forms, and acceptance standards — have been marketed commercially. Military standards for specification and documentation practices in use today are examples of content-based life-cycle methods. These methods try to manage the development process by requiring that documents be produced at specific checkpoints, according to prescribed forms or document-content guidelines.

The effectiveness of life-cycle methods

has been limited by two key problems: lack of formality, resulting in inconsistency, and lack of maintainability. Most life-cycle methods stress the capture of documentation during the development process but do not adequately provide for the continued usefulness of the documents produced. The result is often notebooks full of completed forms or a set of Victorian novel-like narrative specifications, both of which are destined to sit on bookshelves gathering dust. The specifications produced are often incomplete, inconsistent, and incorrect, and are seldom updated with changes to the system.

Formal methods. The need for greater productivity in the system-development life cycle led to the introduction of more formal methods in the late 1970s and early 1980s. Most methods were aimed at specific stages of the life cycle and were based on different user viewpoints about the target information systems.

Structured analysis, introduced popularly by Tom DeMarco,[5] applied some of the decomposition techniques that improve programming to the front-end requirements and analysis phases of the systems life cycle. Structured analysis grew out of structured design, which itself had grown out of structured programming. Through the use of structured dataflow diagrams and descriptions of data, the analyst could build up a systematic description of the information system's logical (functional) and physical (implementation) aspects. Management procedures provided manual validation of the dataflow diagrams via walkthroughs, and diagrams and data descriptions became deliverable parts of system documentation.

Many variations of formal methods now exist. Well-known versions of structured analysis include the Yourdon/DeMarco and Gane/Sarson methods. Recent adaptations of structured analysis to specific needs of real-time systems development include the Ward/Mellor and Hatley methods. Data-oriented methods, applying similar principles to both data-centered design and data administration, include the Warnier/Orr, Holland, Bachman, and Martin's information-engineering approaches. The realm of structured design has the Yourdon/Constantine and Jackson methods.

Much fanfare accompanied the introduction of formal methods, but their manual nature has limited their general use and acceptance. Dataflow diagrams developed manually are difficult to modify and are seldom maintained with the system they represent. The effort and cost to develop complete and useful descriptions of an evolving system are hard to justify when the information is clearly not a lasting part of maintenance.

What CASE offers

With the spread of desktop computers, the mid-1980s have seen the introduction of automated environments and tools that make it practical and economical to use formal system-development methods. This technology, known as CASE, lets systems analysts document and model an information system from its initial user requirements through design and implementation and lets them apply tests for consistency, completeness, and conformance to standards.

These techniques for software engineering apply equally well to modeling hardware and human interfaces, so the acronym also refers to computer-aided *systems* engineering. Integrated in this field are models, tools, and techniques that open new areas for applying reliability engineering to information systems.

Much like the children of the shoemaker who were always the last to get new shoes, computer professionals have traditionally been the last ones to apply the benefits of computer technology to the improvement of their own work. Now, however, with personal workstations becoming a common resource, CASE environments let computer professionals develop and validate system designs and specifications, automating and enhancing the manual methods of the 1970s and 1980s.

Features. A CASE environment provides the analyst or systems developer with facilities for drawing a system's architectural diagrams, describing and defining functional and data objects, identifying relationships between system components, and providing annotations to aid project management.

The user's various work products are stored in an integrated, nonredundant form in a central repository or dictionary on the workstation or on a central server or host system. The system definition as a whole can be checked for consistency and completeness. Analysis can be performed on the information collected or defined to date, thus supporting incremental development and the detection of inconsistencies and errors early in the life cycle. Documentation required by organiza-

---

Computer professionals are usually the last to apply the benefits of computer technology to their own work. CASE is one of those benefits.

---

tional or deliverable standards, such as DoD-Std 2167, can be generated from the system description in the dictionary. Also, generators for database schemas and program code are being incorporated in, or interfaced to, CASE environments to provide a step toward automated system generation. Figure 2 shows key elements in a CASE system.

Tools. A comprehensive CASE development environment for the front end of the life cycle integrates several component tools and facilities:

• The system developer can choose from at least seven basic diagram types, including dataflow diagrams (Yourdon/DeMarco or Gane/Sarson notations), structure charts (Yourdon/Constantine or Jackson), entity-relationship diagrams, logical data models, and presentation graphs. Additional diagram types are available for real-time system development, including transformation graphs, state-transition diagrams, and decision matrices. The user can directly create dia-

grams with the graphics-editing facilities on the workstation and then produce those diagrams for system documentation. Figures 2 and 3 demonstrate these graphics capabilities.

• Information about the user's target system, entered incrementally via diagrams and form screens, is integrated in a central dictionary.

• End-user screens and reports can be developed for the system under design with screen-paint facilities tied to the central dictionary. These form functional prototypes on the workstation that can be demonstrated to end users for evaluation and validation.

• Analysis facilities provide checks for consistency and completeness. Entity-list query capabilities combined with a general report writer allow user-definable analysis that can be tailored to meet project or organizational needs. Extended analysis utilities provide advanced conclusions about the integrity of a proposed design, including validation of data normalization and traceability of data elements through activities in the target-system description.

• Deliverable documentation can be organized graphically and can incorporate diagrams and text from the central dictionary. This facility lets the user generate documentation that is internally consistent and true to the system design. The environment provides links to desktop-publishing, page-layout, and Postscript output facilities.

• An open architecture for access to the central dictionary allows the integration of the CASE environment with other tools of the project or the organization. Import/export facilities let you bridge to other programs, transfer information among multiple analysts, and access other information resources, such as the corporate data dictionary (Figure 3 shows data-dictionary integration). In addition, a programmer interface lets you access the system description in the central dictionary from application programs to allow transfer of data, broader analysis, and specialized documentation.

• Established bridges and integrated packages connect the front-end environment to many tools used in later stages of the life cycle. Links to code-generation

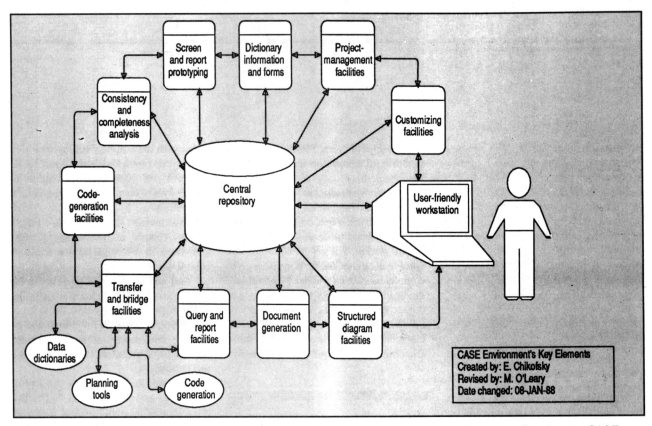

Figure 2. Key elements in a CASE system. This figure was generated from Index Technology's Excelerator CASE system and represents current CASE graphics capabilities.

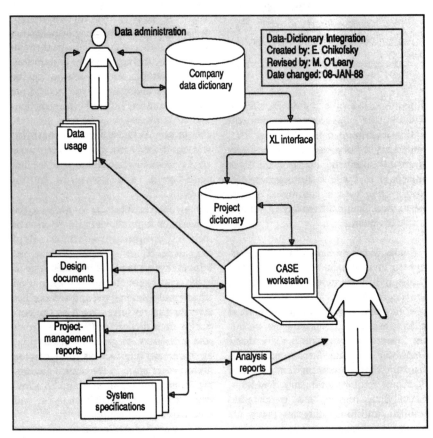

Figure 3. Data-dictionary integration. This figure was generated from Index Technology's Excelerator CASE system and represents current CASE graphics capabilities.

tools and fourth-generation languages, as well as to other types of development tools, give users a wide variety of options.

Adaptability. A key feature of a well-developed CASE environment is adaptability. To be successful in a wide range of organizations and projects, the environment must be able to operate on many hardware configurations in a consistent and user-friendly manner. To serve today's development organizations, the same base environment should be available on IBM PC-class and PS/2-class machines, on engineering workstations from Sun, Apollo, and Digital Equipment Corp., and on a variety of local-area networks.

Another important aspect of adaptability is how well the CASE environment can conform to an organization and project, rather than how much it makes the project conform to the idiosyncrasies of the tool. The CASE environment needs to be customizable so the user can adapt it to closely fit the organization's development method, project-management standards, and information requirements. This versatility lets a single CASE environment support the organization even as projects, standards, and contractual obligations change.

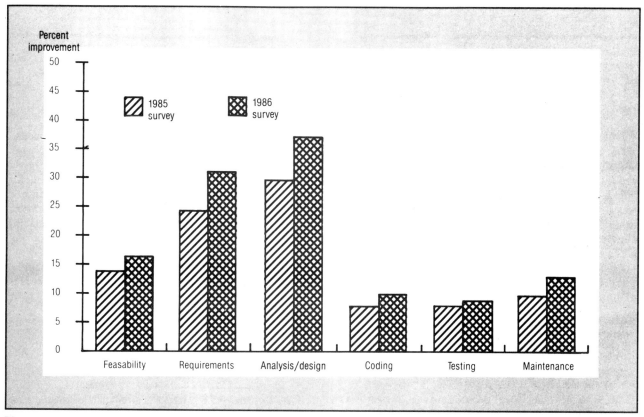

Figure 4. Productivity improvement in a system's life-cycle phases when using a CASE tool (sources are two surveys of users of Index Technology's Excelerator product).

Benefits. Organizations using CASE environments have experienced various degrees of improvement in productivity. Users of Index Technology's Excelerator environment, for example, have reported in surveys an average of 30- to 40-percent improvement in the life cycle's analysis and design phases (see Figure 4). But many of the user organizations also report that their key gain is in the quality of the systems being developed, principally because they can detect errors and inconsistencies and refine specifications easily to reflect their own customer's needs.

Reliability engineering

Besides serving as productivity aids to support the capture of system-design information, CASE environments provide new opportunities to use analysis techniques to assess the reliability of information systems before they are implemented. They also help audit a completed system against its design and maintain the system description as accurate documentation.

Analysis. A CASE environment stores the systems description in an integrated form in a central repository or dictionary. It provides native facilities for inspecting and analyzing aspects of the system description, particularly in support of standard development methods such as structured analysis.

With the system description in the dictionary, other forms of inspection can be made using database query techniques. For example, if the correctness of timing factors is important to a system's success, an analyst can target those portions of the description that affect timing. The dictionary can provide information not only about the specific timing attributes but also about all other components that affect these attributes.

An analyst can also discover secondary effects, where the impact of an attribute was not explicitly defined but was implicit in the design of other parts of the system. The CASE environment thus forms a vehicle for reliability assessment as well as for system description.

The CASE environment can help standardize quality assurance and test processes for systems under development. By using the available system description for test planning, aided by automated CASE facilities, an organization can develop more rigorous coverage for test cases and can better determine if the features and components being tested match important paths in the system.

Maintenance. When a system description has been completed, the CASE environment can continue to serve as an active repository and reference encyclopedia for the system's builders and maintainers. The ease of making changes to the system description lets the documentation be maintained with the system. When maintenance staff can use an up-to-date system description as a source of information on the system architecture, they are encouraged to update it for their own benefit as they make system modifications. The result is more shoemaker's children with new and valuable shoes.

Audit. The same principle applies to auditing. With an up-to-date system description supported by a CASE environment, the dictionary can serve as a key resource and record-keeping vehicle. Various system components and their operation can be compared to their intended function in the system description, and notes can be made in an auditor's copy of the dictionary. The completed system can be more effectively evaluated against its design, and automated assistance can be provided to trace requirements through design and into the finished system. Thus, the CASE environment also becomes an auditor's tool. This advantage can be further enhanced by customizing the CASE environment to handle the specific attributes required of the auditing or reliability evaluation task at hand.

Emerging technology in CASE provides new and potentially invaluable support to aspects of systems work throughout the systems life cycle. There are broad opportunities for automating reliability-engineering tasks for information systems. As this technology matures, we can look forward to the incorporation of meaningful expert-system and artificial-intelligence capabilities to help the systems analyst, libraries of reusable system designs, and automated prototyping of systems to help determine reliability.

Existing developments in CASE put these possibilities within our grasp and offer a bright future for the entire area of information-systems reliability.   -◊-

References

1. B. Boehm, "Software and Its Impact: A Quantitative Assessment," in *Writings of the Revolution*, Yourdon Press, New York, 1982, pp. 267-289.

2. B. Boehm, *Software Engineering Economics,* Prentice-Hall, Englewood Cliffs, N.J., 1981.

3. W. Suydam, "CASE Makes Strides toward Automated Software Development," *Computer Design*, Jan. 1, 1987, pp. 49-70.

4. R. Jensen, "Predicting and Controlling Software Development Costs: Metrics for Managers," *Proc. Second Ann. Excelerator Users' Conf.*, XL Group, Cambridge, Mass., 1986.

5. T. DeMarco, *Structured Analysis and System Specification*, Yourdon Press, New York, 1978.

Elliot J. Chikofsky is director of research and technology at Index Technology and teaches graduate courses in software engineering and database management at Northeastern University. Before joining Index Technology, he worked on the University of Michigan's ISDOS project.

Chikofsky received a BS in computer and communication science and an MS in industrial and operations engineering, both from the University of Michigan.

Burt L. Rubenstein is a vice president of research and technology at Index Technology. He was the original architect of the Excelerator CASE system. He has also worked at Index Systems and Digitial Equipment Corp.

Rubenstein received a BS in management and computer science from the Massachusetts Institute of Technology, where he also did systems research in the Laboratory for Computer Science.

Reprinted from *IEEE Software*, Vol. 9, No. 2, March 1992, pp. 18-22. Copyright © 1992 by The Institute of Electrical and Electronics Engineers, Inc. All rights reserved.

A Framework for Integrated CASE

Minder Chen, *George Mason University*
Ronald J. Norman, *San Diego State University*

◆ *CASE technology has made significant advances recently, but its potential is limited by integration difficulties. The authors propose an organizational framework to guide integrated CASE development and research.*

Today's information-based organizations need comprehensive information systems to support their business. Products and services are often information-intensive and must be brought to market faster if the organization intends to compete globally.

The dual trend of distributing the information-systems function into business areas and outsourcing systems-development work has increased the pressure on IS organizations to enhance their credibility. Integrated CASE environments are becoming a key strategic component in IS organizations' attempts to meet these new challenges.

Although CASE has significantly affected the practice of systems development (the article on pp. 12-16 explains the evolution of CASE), its potential is limited by the difficulties involved in integrating tools into a cohesive environment. There is growing interest in the research,

development, and deployment of integrated CASE environments, as evidenced by

◆ the announcement of comprehensive CASE product strategies by hardware and software vendors (including IBM's AD/Cycle, Digital Equipment Corp.'s Cohesion, and Hewlett-Packard's SoftBench product lines),

◆ the increasing market acceptance of integrated CASE products (including Atherton Technology's Software BackPlane, Interactive Development Environments' Software through Pictures, KnowledgeWare's Application Development Workbench, and Texas Instruments' Information Engineering Facility).

◆ recent efforts in CASE standards and frameworks (including the American National Standards Institute's Information Resource Dictionary Systems, IEEE's work on tool interconnectivity, and the Electronic Industries Association's interim standard CASE Data Interchange Format).

However, there is as yet no coherent strategy for building and using integrated CASE. Technical frameworks exist but they do not put tools in the context of the development organization. Therefore, any comprehensive integrated CASE development and implementation strategy must have an organizational framework as well.

We propose such a framework, based on the reference model for integrated software-engineering environments being developed by the National Institute of Standards and Technology and European Computer Manufacturers Association[1] and Anthony Wasserman's work on CASE tool integration.[2]

> There is as yet no coherent strategy for building and using integrated CASE. Technical frameworks exist but don't put tools in the context of the development organization.

TECHNICAL FRAMEWORK

An integrated CASE environment must be as adaptable, flexible, and dynamic as the enterprise, projects, and people it supports. In such an environment, users can coherently mix and match the most suitable tools that support selected methods. They can then plug those tools into the environment and begin working with them.

We have adapted the NIST/ECMA reference model, shown in Figure 1, as a basis for describing the technical aspects of integrated CASE environments. Services defined in the reference model enable three forms of integration:

♦ *data* integration, which is supported by repository and data-integration services;

♦ *control* integration, which is supported by process-management and message services; and

♦ *presentation* integration, which is supported by user-interface services.

This reference model, which describes a wide range of CASE environments and frameworks, can guide standards development and serve as a basis for educating software engineers.

Data integration. The ability to share design information is key to integrating tools. According to the IEEE draft standard for tool interconnection (P1175),[3] there are four information-sharing methods:

♦ *Direct* transfer of design information between two tools is most efficient when real-time integration is required. However, it is very difficult to implement direct transfer when many tools must be integrated.

♦ *File-based* transfer is the simplest to implement. The CASE Data Interchange Format developed by the EIA is the most mature file-based transfer standard.[4]

♦ *Communication-based* transfer is appropriate for open systems and distributed environments.

♦ *Repository-based*[5] transfer supports a tightly coupled, consistent environment and is the cornerstone of several integrated CASE products. A (data) repository provides many basic services, including storage and management of objects/entities and links/relations; version and configuration control; naming services; security; and transaction control.[1]

Repository requirements. Data-integration services provide several high-level functions that tightly integrate tools and the repository, including

♦ a *metamodel* service, which defines, controls, and maintains a metamodel;

♦ a *query* service, which supports the retrieval of the metamodel and metadata from the repository;

♦ a *view* (or subenvironment) service, which lets developers define a subset of objects and operations in the repository and maintains consistency between the environment and this subenvironment; and

♦ a *data-interchange* service, which sup-

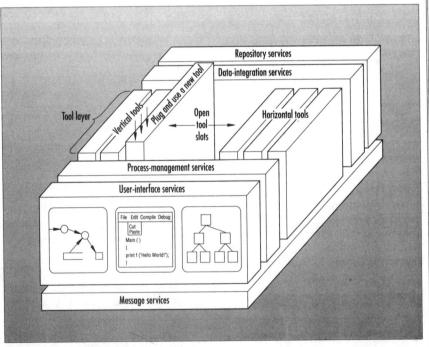

Figure 1. *The NIST/ECMA reference model.*

ports two-way translation between flat-file and repository data.

A repository should also offer pragmatic interfaces, including command- and menu-driven interfaces, and provide application-program interfaces for CASE tool builders.

Metamodels. In a CASE framework, a comprehensive metamodel is necessary to achieve a higher degree of data integration. Examples of metamodels include the Information Model of AD/Cycle, the Basic Functional Schema of IRDS, the semantic model of CDIF, and the Software Concepts defined in the IEEE P1175.

In ANSI's standard, X3.138, IRDS structures are described with an entity-relationship model.[6] Many CASE products support the IRDS standard; others use proprietary object-management systems to manage their repositories.[5]

An enterprise-wide repository makes it easier for systems projects to share information. For example, repository functions like metadata sharing and distribution, merging of actual and trial metadata, version control, downloading and uploading, and concurrency and security controls can facilitate integration across and among large project teams.

Control integration. Tools must be able to notify each other of events, activate other tools under program control, and share functions.[2]

Control-integration mechanisms include explicit message passing, time- or access-activated triggers, and message servers. To achieve control integration, tools call on message services to provide three types of communication: tool-to-tool, tool-to-service, and service-to-service.

Process-management services can explicitly represent tool-invocation sequences and policies, so users are insulated

from the tools' details and are free to deal with the abstraction of tasks and processes. Processes are related to the overall enterprise-wide systems development processes and are considered to be an abstraction of tasks.[1]

Because improved control integration can increase the degree of automation, the environment can support global process management, project-level task management, and tool invocation.

Early implementations of integrated project-support environments focused on control integration to coordinate teams through facilities like electronic mail, configuration management, and context management. (Context management controls what is visible to each tool and each user, simplifying the user's interactions with tools and other users.)

The Portable Common Tool Environment is a tool-interface standard adopted by ECMA to support tool portability. Under PCTE, tools are stored in the repository and executed as processes, making it possible to improve tool execution, composition, communication, and synchronization.[7]

Presentation integration. User-interface services let CASE users interact with tools consistently, making new tools much easier to learn. Window-based tools have four levels of presentation integration:[2] the window system, the window manager, the user-interface-development tool kit, and the look-and-feel guidelines.

Most CASE frameworks and environments have adopted generic standards for the user-interface services. For example, Motif is the presentation standard used by most CASE tools in the open-systems world. Individual environments extend these presentation standards with sets of presentation and dialogue design guidelines for displaying and manipulating structured texts, structured graphics, and

matrices common across the methods supported.

Other dimensions. The NIST/ECMA reference model addresses other dimensions of CASE integration indirectly through a tools layer. Vertical and horizontal tools can be configured and plugged into the tools layer to support vertical and horizontal integration:

♦ *Vertical* (full life-cycle) integration ensures the completeness and consistency of information generated in various life-cycle phases. Mechanisms that support vertical integration include forward and reverse engineering, configuration and change management, and requirements-tracing tools.

♦ *Horizontal* (methodological) integration maintains the integrity of design information within each life-cycle phase when many modeling methods are used (such as data, process, event-driven, and object-oriented). Mechanisms that support horizontal integration are a comprehensive repository metamodel, integrity-checking rules, and hypertext-like navigation across multiple modeling perspectives.

ORGANIZATIONAL FRAMEWORK

A tool is most effective when it works within an organizational context.[3] The technical framework just described does not consider specific tools' functions. Instead, as Figure 1 shows, tools are plugged into a tools layer, which calls on the framework services to support a particular systems-development function.[1]

The organizational framework shown in Figure 2 seeks to place CASE tools in a development and management context.[8] On the left side of the figure, we group an environment's services and tools into three levels. Components at each level support the corresponding activities on the right side.

On the right side of the figure, the framework divides systems development and management into three activity levels:

♦ IS infrastructure planning and design is undertaken at the enterprise level.

♦ Systems project management and decisions are made at the project level.

> This organizational framework complements the technical framework to guide development and deployment, direct future research, and help users select and configure tools.

♦ Software-development processes are carried out at the individual and team level.

Higher level activities can control lower level activities; lower level activities can influence higher level activities. An integrated CASE environment must support activities at all levels.

This organizational framework, which complements the technical framework, can guide the development and deployment of integrated CASE environments, direct future research, and help CASE users select and configure tools in an integrated CASE environment.

Planning and design of IS infrastructures. Activities at the highest level determine how development processes should be managed. The major concern at this level is building the enterprise-wide IS infrastructure. Activities at this level include

♦ establishing guidelines for the deployment of computing platforms,

♦ evaluating and adapting methods and process models, and

♦ formalizing procedures and policies for project management and coordination.

Several organizations have set up development or productivity centers within their IS organizations to perform these functions. The decision to introduce new tools and the evaluation of the integration effort involved are usually made at this level. The introduction of new methods, development standards, and tools is aided by the tool-integration mechanism and the repository services.

Integrated frameworks, which provide an infrastructure for data, tool, and process integration at the enterprise level, should be independent of languages, methods, tools, and platforms so that they can accommodate existing and future tools.

Management of systems projects. The second level includes the management and decision processes that extend across many or all life-cycle phases. These activities include project and process management, impact analysis and change management, documentation, and reuse. Examples of project-management activities supported by tools are scheduling and tracking, personnel assignment, cost esti-

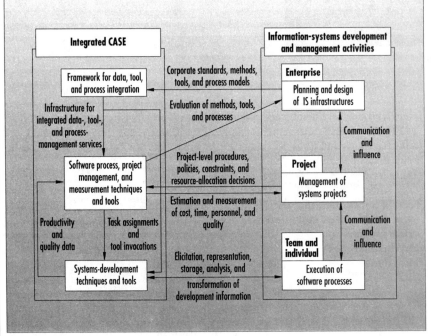

Figure 2. Organizational framework to place CASE tools in a development and management context. On the left side, an environment's services and tools are grouped into three levels. Components at each level support the corresponding activities on the right side, which divides systems development and management into three activity levels.

mation, and coordination.

Process-management tools can invoke appropriate CASE tools and retrieve design objects according to defined process models in a way that enforces development disciplines and policies. Communication tools, such as electronic mail, can also be used to coordinate project teams.

Design information captured by CASE tools and stored in a repository contains many attributes about the process and products. In an integrated CASE environment, measurement tools can generate productivity and quality metrics using this information. Several CASE products collect data and calculate metrics automatically. It is very important to develop a historical project database to calibrate existing metrics and models and derive new models. These metrics can provide feedback for scheduling, cost and staff estimation, and quality control of both the process and the product.

IS personnel can also use measurement results to evaluate tools, methods, and process models and to ensure that ongoing process monitoring and improvement is successful.

Execution of software processes. At the lowest level, integrated CASE should support activities for each life-cycle phase: planning, analysis, conceptual design,

technical design, programming, testing, production, and maintenance.

Upper, or front-end, CASE tools assist upstream activities; lower, or back-end, CASE tools assist downstream activities. These vertical tools can support the elicitation, representation, storage, analysis, and transformation of development information.

Requirements-elicitation tools can make it easier for developers and users to interact as they define system specifications. These tools can elicit and represent information in various formats and store it in local or enterprise-wide repositories. The consistency and completeness of the specifications are checked against a set of integrity rules specific to the method used.

To further assist the mapping of design information, some CASE tools include a transformation function that converts specifications from one life-cycle phase to the next. Automatic two-way transformation between phases is essential to achieve vertical integration. Transformation tools can be used for forward and/or reverse engineering. Reverse-engineering tools are useful when development information is available only in a low-level form (like code), but in the long run they will be less useful because systems developed in integrated CASE environments are maintained through high-level specifications.

Different CASE environments require different forms and levels of integration. Science and engineering applications, for example, require more control integration, while business applications tend to require more data integration. CASE users should choose or implement appropriate forms of integration according to the characteristics of their own development infrastructure and practices.

Tomorrow's complex, integrated applications will be developed using a combination of several enabling technologies (database- and knowledge-based systems, object-oriented technology, and hypermedia). Today's CASE environments support application development in limited domains using one or two specific enabling technologies. Future integrated CASE environments will support a wider range of applications in an open-systems environment.

Current CASE technology still encourages an individual approach to development, although mechanisms like version- and configuration-control and multiuser repositories do support programming in the many. In the future, gains in quality and productivity may come from improved, direct human interaction — both between developers and users and among developers. Future CASE environments will incorporate collaborative tools (groupware) to support cooperative development.[9]

The repositories of today's CASE environments are used only by IS personnel for systems development, even though the data and process models they contain — information about the organization's structures, business goals, and processes — are valuable to managers. Future CASE environments will support both systems development and information delivery. Guided by metadata stored in the repository, users and managers will have a context for the application data they access.

The key issue in designing and selecting an integrated CASE environment is how to strike a balance between integration and flexibility: Tighter integration usually means less openness. CASE shells (also called metasystems, CASE tool generators, and metaCASE) are an emerging class of CASE environments that let CASE developers or users customize CASE tools and environments to their new or unique methods. Examples of CASE shells are CADWare's Foundry, Intersolv's XL/Customizer, and Systematica's Virtual Software Factory.

Reuse is one of the most promising approaches to achieving significant productivity gains. Using reusable components not only reduces development cost, but also increases development speed and product quality. The reuse concept should be extended from code to high-level specifications and processes. Object-oriented technology offers effective mechanisms, inheritance and encapsulation, for creating and adapting reusable components. Artificial-intelligence techniques, such as analogical and case-based reasoning, can help identify and select components for reuse.

CASE standards have played a major role in the development of open CASE systems. Integrated CASE environments should be based on these standards. However, many CASE standards overlap and conflict. If we are to realize useful CASE standards, we must harmonize the efforts of formal standards organizations, gain support from vendors and users, and develop CASE standards based on other relevant standards.

Technology transfer and the study of organizational behavior is another fertile, essential research area that is relevant to integrated CASE.[10]

Finally, AI techniques may enable integrated CASE environments to incorporate domain-specific knowledge that can help end users develop and maintain their own systems using high-level languages or diagramming tools. Eventually, end users may be able to retrieve or purchase high-level reusable business models, modify them, plug them into an integrated CASE environment, and generate their own applications. What a day that will be! ◆

ACKNOWLEDGMENTS

Several important ideas in this article were generated from discussions with Tsang-Hsiung Lee, Edgar H. Sibley, and William Wong. We also thank Jay F. Nunamaker, Jr. and Anthony I. Wasserman for their comments on an early draft of this article.

REFERENCES

1. *Reference Model for Frameworks of Software Engineering Environments*, Draft Version 1.5, Nat'l Inst. Standards and Technology, Gaithersburg, Md., 1991.
2. A.I. Wasserman, "Tool Integration in Software Engineering Environments," in *Software Engineering Environments*, Fred Long, ed., Springer-Verlag, Berlin, 1990, pp. 137-149.
3. *A Reference Model for Computing System Tool Interconnections*, Draft of IEEE P1175/D11, IEEE CS Press, Los Alamitos, Calif., 1991.
4. *CDIF - Framework for Modeling and Extensibility*, EIA/IS-81, Electronic Industries Assoc., Washington, D.C., 1991.
5. M. Chen and E.H. Sibley, "Using a CASE Based Repository for Systems Integration," *Proc. Hawaii Int'l Conf. System Sciences, Vol II*, IEEE CS Press, Los Alamitos, Calif., 1991, pp 578-587.
6. *American National Standard X3.138, Information Resource Dictionary System*, American Nat'l Standards Inst., New York, 1988.
7. I. Thomas, "PCTE Interfaces: Supporting Tools in Software-Engineering Environments," *IEEE Software*, Nov. 1989, pp. 15-23.
8. T. Lee, M. Chen, and R.J. Norman, "Computer-Aided Software Engineering Adoption and Implementation: A Theoretical Analysis from an Organizational Innovation Perspective," *Proc. Hawaii Int'l Conf. System Sciences, Vol. III*, IEEE CS Press, Los Alamitos, Calif., 1991, pp 3-17.
9. M. Chen and J.F. Nunamaker, Jr., "The Architecture and Design of a Collaborative Environment for Systems Definition," *Data Base*, Winter/Spring 1991, pp. 22-29.
10. R.J. Norman and J.F. Nunamaker, Jr., "CASE Productivity Perceptions of Software-Engineering Professionals," *Comm. ACM*, Sept. 1989, pp. 1102-1108.

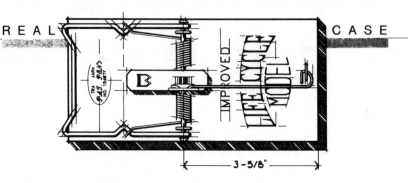

Looking Beyond CASE

Ed Acly, *International Data Corp.*

Traditionally, new software tools have contributed to instability and incompatibility. For the CASE market to evolve, the user's need for stability and integration must be addressed.

The year 1983 witnessed the emergence of a new family of products for the development and maintenance of commercial information systems. These products were designed to use the power of the computer to support systems analysis and, to a lesser extent, design and strategic planning. For the first time, computer aid was extended to development tasks such as strategic planning and enterprise modeling. This family of products has come to be called CASE.

Although computer support for analysis, design, and planning is certainly important, research done in early 1986 at International Data Corp. revealed that these products are only the tip of the iceberg, part of a far more significant long-term direction.

While CASE may be an appropriate name for the family of products (or tools) now on the market, it does not adequately describe the direction in which these products will evolve. This direction embodies far more than computer-aided support for the concepts of software engineering. IDC research shows that the majority of vendors providing CASE products today will eventually provide, either on their own or through ties to other vendors, application-development and maintenance environments that address all phases of the systems development life cycle in a top-down, integrated fashion.

IDC coined the term "computer-aided development and maintenance environments" to describe and model the direction of the product evolution that will be followed by today's CASE products. CADME places emphasis on the fact that users will look for increased productivity by building integrated environments to support all aspects of application development and maintenance rather than merely using stand-alone tools to implement the concepts of software engineering at discrete points within the software development life cycle.

No matter how advanced CADMEs become there will continue to be a place for third-generation and fourth-generation languages and products. I see CADME as an evolution into fifth-generation application-development and maintenance technology. As an evolution, it will not replace third- and fourth-generation technology, which will continue to be used to a lesser degree where appropriate. The challenge for CADME will be to integrate itself with third and fourth-generation technology rather than to try present a revolutionary new way of doing things.

Reprinted from *IEEE Software*, Vol. 5, No. 2, March 1988, pp. 39-43. Copyright © 1988 by The Institute of Electrical and Electronics Engineers, Inc. All rights reserved.

User needs

Vendors of today's CASE products should be concerned about how their products will be positioned for the transition into the CADME products of tomorrow. In mapping out a transition strategy, vendors should consider two fundamental needs that commercial application-development and maintenance organizations have:

• The need for stability. How can you build a stable platform for development and maintenance in a world where technology and products are constantly changing? Without a stable platform, any integrated application and development environment you build is likely to crumble.

• The need for systems integration. How can you integrate the many development and maintenance tools into one environment? It is highly unlikely that any one vendor will ever be able to deliver a total solution. As a result, users who seek optimal solutions will always have to act as their own systems integrator.

Industry trends

Two industry trends are emerging, the three-schema data architecture and the information-resource dictionary system. In the world of commercial information systems, these two trends may go a long way toward

• helping meet these two fundamental needs and

• deciding the architecture on which tomorrow's successful CADMEs will be built.

This article focuses on the mainstream world of commercial information systems — it does not address technical or real-time computing. Although there are many parallels between these worlds, the needs and priorities of the user groups are different enough to consider them separately.

Three-schema architecture

The software industry has not matured to the point where software products from one vendor can be integrated easily with those from another. Organizations that expend the (often considerable) effort to handcraft integrated development and maintenance environments find that new products and technologies frustrate and make obsolete their efforts.

The introduction of new products runs contrary to the goal of stable environments. The three-schema data architecture will let organizations build stable development and maintenance environments that are shielded from rampaging technology.

The technology. The three-schema architecture was proposed by an American National Standards Institute study group (ANSI/X3/Sparc Database Study Group) in 1977. As Figure 1 illustrates, it supports three independent models (schemas) of data.

At the highest level is the conceptual

IDC coined the term CADME to describe the direction of the product evolution that today's CASE products will follow.

---

model. It supports the organization as a whole and embodies specifications of data (and processes) from a business viewpoint. At the intermediate level is the external model. It supports the requirements of an individual or function that wants to use a logical subset of the data described in the conceptual model — separately stored pieces of data can be joined into one logical user view. At the lowest level is the internal model. It supports the physical definition of the data structures and access methods.

A key advantage of the three-schema architecture is that the specifications for each data (and process) model are independent. Consequently, changes can be made to the specifications at one level without affecting the specifications at the other levels. To be effective, software must be able to automatically translate specifications made in the conceptual model to the external model and in the external model to the internal model.

User payback. Adopting the three-schema architecture would let users engineer an environment where development of system specifications at one level is independent of specifications created at the other two levels. This capability, along with the proper translation mechanisms, gives users the flexibility to integrate application development and maintenance products from different vendors, basing their choice on merit and need.

In addition, developers working at different stages of the development life cycle are better insulated from each other. This will allow a more stable development and maintenance environment. For example, planners and analysts would be free to concentrate their work at the conceptual (enterprise) model. They would no longer need to change their conceptual model because of new data-processing products or technology that affects the external or internal models.

Vendor payback. Adopting the three-schema architecture would let vendors specialize in certain areas of the life cycle. Accordingly, those vendors who introduce products for planning and analysis could gravitate toward serving the needs of the conceptual model. Vendors who specialize in application generators and fourth-generation languages could gravitate toward the external model. Vendors of physical data managers could gravitate toward the internal model. Of course, this is a simplistic segmentation of the market. Some vendors would choose to market products to serve all three models.

The three-schema architecture would also give vendors a competitive edge in their chosen area of specialization. Users would recognize this excellence by mixing and matching products from more than one vendor in an integrated development and maintenance environment.

Market acceptance. The Supra database-management system, announced by Cincom Systems in 1986, was the first commercial product founded on the three-schema architecture. Computer Associates later announced support of the three-schema architecture for its CA-Universe database-management system. IBM has announced that all future IBM CASE products will be based on the three-schema data architecture.

In the future, CADME products will be absolutely vital to vendors of mainframe database-management systems. I believe the three-schema architecture is a good way for these vendors to extend their product lines to support the more logical, enterprise modeling capabilities inherent in CADME.

Information-resource dictionary system

Developers of commercial information systems use many development and maintenance tools that have proprietary data dictionaries. Traditionally, the industry has called the information stored in these dictionaries metadata. Generally, these proprietary dictionaries have prevented individual tools from sharing the metadata each relies on.

The technology. For the last six years, a committee sponsored by the National Bureau of Standards, through its Institute for Computer Sciences and Technology, has been developing a federal information-processing standard for data-dictionary systems. The committee has included representatives from NBS, many federal agencies, several data-dictionary vendors, users with no vested interest, and other consultants. In 1980, ANSI also formed a committee (X3H4) to develop a standard IRDS. The committees merged in September 1983 — under the ANSI X3H4 banner — with the combined mission to develop both an ANSI and FIPS standard.

The design objectives for the IRDS are:[1]

• It should contain the major features and capabilities of current dictionary systems.

• It should be modular, to support many user environments and cost-effective procurement.

• It should support portability of skills and data.

Portable skills and data will be promoted through three interfaces, which the IRDS draft standard currently specifies:

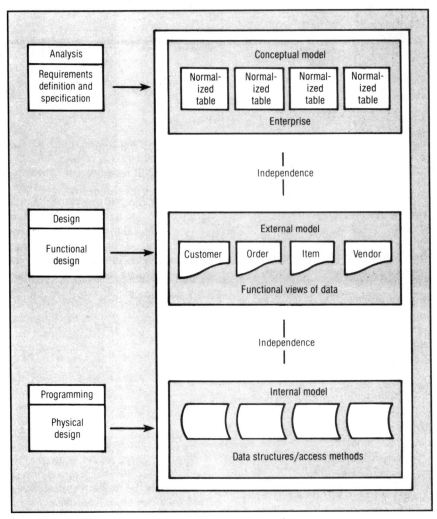

Figure 1. The three-schema data architecture has three independent models.

• a standard command-language interface that is available to both batch and online users,

• menu interfaces, available only to online users, and

• an IRD-IRD interface, to move metadata from one IRDS to another.

The IRDS standard can be extended to describe any entities, attributes, or relationships it does not include.

Road to a standard. The IRDS standard has taken several steps toward adoption by ANSI, NBS, and the International Standards Organization:

• A common specification document was completed as a draft proposal for an ANSI standard in 1985.

• The first public review of this draft proposal was completed in October 1985. Eight comments were received — six from US sources, five of whom were vendors.

• During the winter of 1985-86, the ANSI committee resolved all the comments and finalized a change document to the draft proposal in the spring of 1986.

• The public review of the change proposal ended in November 1986. This review attracted one set of comments that resulted in another small change document. Because of the new change document was small, no public review was held.

• During this time, the ISO was working on the specifications for consideration as an ISO standard. The IRDS specifications were accepted by the ISO in January 1987 as a draft proposal.

• The plan is to forward the IRDS specifications, with all comments satisfied, to the parent ANSI committee for approval as an ANSI standard in July 1988. Waiting until July will allow the revised specifications document to circulate in the international community, which is essential because it is being considered as an ISO standard. Any unfavorable comments that result from the review by the international community could postpone forwarding the specifications to the parent ANSI committee. However, members of the combined ANSI/NBS committee feel that a holdup is not likely.

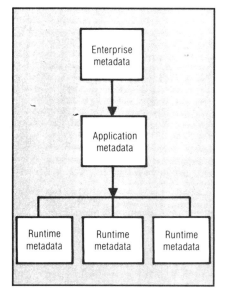

Figure 2. The global, enterprise metadata system that describes the whole organization feeds the application-generation and runtime dictionary systems below.

• Once the IRDS specifications are approved as an ANSI standard, they should become an official ANSI standard two to five months later.

• Once the IRDS specifications become an official ANSI standard, they are expected to almost immediately become a FIPS standard.

• Finally, the IRDS specifications could become an ISO standard during the second half of this year.

A standard bus. Once approved, the IRDS standard will not be static. Already, NBS and ANSI are working to extend it.

The first major item being worked on is a fourth interface, for services. This interface will provide a common protocol so software external to an IRDS dictionary can interface and communicate with that dictionary. This interface will be programmed through the standard call routine functionality. As a result, products such as database-management systems, fourth-generation languages, and compilers can be integrated with an IRDS standard dictionary.
tionary.

This full-blown software interface will turn the IRDS dictionary into an active dictionary.

User payback. A way to store and manage all the components of application development in one logical dictionary system is the cornerstone for automation and reusability in the future. Figure 2 shows how global, enterprise metadata systems that describe the whole organization will, in turn, feed the application-generation and runtime dictionary systems that have

come into widespread use under fourth-generation technology.

For integrated environments to be built, it is essential that dictionary systems, which have traditionally been embedded in proprietary systems, be shared. Likewise, it is essential that metadata be easily migrated from one dictionary system to another, to provide stability for future user requirements. The IRD-IRD interface in Figure 3 illustrates how the IRDS standard supplies these capabilities.

Vendor payback. Vendors can look to the market performance of fourth-generation languages to see why the IRDS is so important. Fourth-generation languages have too often been sold to users who believe that they will provide a complete solution to the application-development backlog. In reality, the fourth-generation languages can be no more than a part of the solution — sometimes just a small part. Also, this partial solution is proprietary and does not integrate well with the user's environment. So today the vast majority of the mainframe application development and maintenance

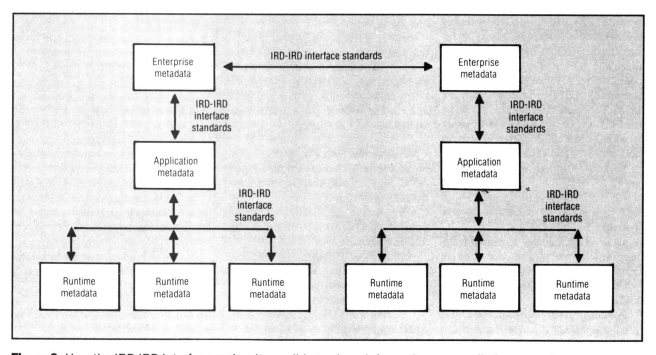

Figure 3. How the IRD-IRD interface makes it possible to share information among dictionary systems.

is still done with Cobol.

If development and maintenance technology is to move forward — if today's CASE products are to sell like hotcakes — these barriers must be overcome with totally integrated solutions. The IRDS provides the standard mechanism to let vendors' products be engineered together into total solutions.

Market acceptance. Pansophic Systems was the first, and is the only, commercial backer of the IRDS standard, with the ongoing development of its Pan/RD product. Pan/RD (Pansophic Resource Dictionary) is being developed as a full-function resource dictionary in compliance with the evolving IRDS standard. In about a year, Pansophic hopes to include Pan/RD in one of its other commercial products. Subsequently, other Pansophic products will be migrated to use Pan/RD and eventually Pan/RD will become the metadata server for the entire family of Pansophic application development and maintenance products.

IDC predicts that Pansophic's effort will go a long way toward legitimizing the IRDS standard, and that Pansophic will be followed by many other vendors during the next two years.

Pansophic made the request for the addition of the services interface after working on the X3H4 committee. My educated guess would be that the specification for the services interface will be released for public review in six to 12 months, and will become an ANSI standard in two years.

In the long term, application development and maintenance products in the commercial information systems market will migrate to the CADME concept. Vendors who want to succeed in this market must realize that they need to fit into a larger environmental solution that transcends their products.

Environments that evolve in line with emerging industry trends hold promise to address long-standing user needs. At the same time, these trends will provide a realistic way for vendors to segment the market for application development and maintenance products.   -◊-

Reference
1. *A Technical Overview of the Information Resource Dictionary System*, Tech. Report NBSIR 85-3164, Nat'l Bureau of Standards, Gaithersburg, Md., 1985.

Ed Acly is the program manager for the Software Technology Service at International Data Corp. The STS provides research and consulting on issues such as application-development and maintenance, database management and administration, and centralized computing services.

Before joining IDC, he was a project manager for Simplex Time Recorder, a systems and programming manager for Dresser Industries, and a programmer analyst with Norton Co.

Acly received the BA in economics from Bucknell Univ. and is an MBA candidate at Nichols College.

Questions about this article can be addressed to the author at IDC, 5 Speen St., Framingham, MA 01701.

PART II: THE EVOLUTION OF SOFTWARE DEVELOPMENT ENVIRONMENT CONCEPTS

Software Development Environments

Susan A. Dart, Robert J. Ellison, Peter H. Feiler, and A. Nico Habermann

Carnegie Mellon University

"**E**nvironment" refers to the collection of hardware and software tools a system developer uses to build software systems. As technology improves and user expectations grow, an environment's functionality tends to change. Over the last 20 years the set of software tools available to developers has expanded considerably.

We can illustrate this change by observing some distinctions in the terminology. "Programming environment" and "software development environment" are often used synonymously, but here we will make a distinction between the two. By "programming environment" we mean an environment that supports only the coding phase of the software development cycle—that is, programming-in-the-small tasks such as editing and compiling. By "software development environment" we mean an environment that augments or automates *all* the activities comprising the software development cycle, including programming-in-the-large tasks such as configuration management and programming-in-the-many tasks such as project and team management. We also mean an environment that supports large-scale, long-term maintenance of software.

The evolution of environments also demands that we distinguish basic operating system facilities—fundamental services such as memory, data, and multiple-program management—from the enhanced functionality that characterizes state-of-the-art environments. This enhanced functionality is typically achieved through tools such as browsers, window managers, configuration managers, and task managers. In a sense, environments have evolved in concert with the software engineering community's understanding of the tasks involved in the development of software systems.

To better understand the technological trends that have produced state-of-the-art environments, we here present a taxonomy of these trends. We cite examples of research and commercial systems within

---

A taxonomy of software development environments reveals trends in their evolution.

---

each class. We intend the taxonomy to show the direction of the trends and to suggest where more work needs to be done.

The taxonomy comprises four categories, each representing trends having a significant impact on environments—on their tools, user interfaces, and architectures. The four categories are

• *Language-centered environments.* These are built around one language, thereby providing a tool set suited to that language. These environments are highly interactive and offer limited support for programming-in-the-large.

• *Structure-oriented environments.* These incorporate techniques that allow the user to manipulate structures directly. The language independence of the techniques led to the notion of generators for environments.

• *Toolkit environments.* These provide a collection of tools that includes language-independent support for programming-in-the-large tasks such as configuration management and version control. There is little, if any, environment-defined control and management of tool usage.

• *Method-based environments.* These incorporate support for a broad range of activities in the software development process, including tasks such as team and

Reprinted from *Computer*, Vol. 20, No. 11, November 1987, pp. 18-28.

project management (programming-in-the-many). These environments also incorporate tools for particular specification and design methods.

We could discuss the trends from several perspectives. For example, we could take a tool builder's perspective, focusing on techniques for tool integration. We could take an expert system builder's perspective, focusing on the automation of the software development process by means of a programmer's assistant that uses knowledge-based concepts. However, we discuss the trends from the user's perspective; that is, we examine how the trends affect the user's perception of, and interaction with, an environment.

User requirements for environments cover a broad spectrum. The functionality of environments includes support for a single user for programming-in-the-small, coordination and management of multiple users for programming-in-the-large, and management of the software development cycle. The nature of the user interface is of considerable importance. Undoubtedly, the user of an environment needs to be able to customize it, either by tailoring or extending a particular tool or by creating specialized tools via generation facilities. To support this, the environment must be implemented so as to allow tools to be easily integrated into it. The user also needs facilities to support incremental development of software to aid prototyping. In essence, the user requires support for the entire software development cycle—from specification through coding to maintenance—including the ability to trace information across phases. This spectrum of needs is addressed across all the categories of our taxonomy, though no single category deals with them all.

We do not attempt to survey all existing environments nor do we provide detailed descriptions or evaluations of them. Neither do we advocate any particular environment. In fact, because users have varying levels of expertise, different application requirements, and different hardware, no single environment can satisfy all users.

The significance of our taxonomy is in its clarification of trends rather than in categorization of particular environments. A particular environment may fit into a number of categories. These categories do not represent competing viewpoints; instead, they represent areas of effort that have provided fertile feedback and inspired further research and development.

Language-centered environments

Language-centered environments are those in which the operating system and tool set are specially built to support a particular language. Examples of language-centered environments are Interlisp for the Lisp language, Cedar for Mesa/Cedar, Smalltalk for Smalltalk, and the Rational Environment for Ada. Initial implementations of Lisp environments emerged in the late 1960s. Researchers at Xerox worked concurrently on the Cedar, Smalltalk, and Interlisp environments in the mid-1970s. The Lisp activities culminated in the early 1980s with the definition of the Common Lisp language. The Rational Environment emerged in the early 1980s.

Lisp environments were the most influential in the development of techniques suited for language-centered environments. They contributed the notion of an exploratory style of programming and demonstrated the benefits of making semantic information available to the user. Subsequent environments for imperative languages extended these notions toward supporting programming-in-the-large to meet large-scale software development requirements.

Exploratory style. Environments in the language-centered category encourage an exploratory style of programming to aid rapid production of software. The development environment and the runtime environment are the same. Code can be developed, executed, tested, debugged, and changed quickly; small code changes can be made executable in a matter of seconds. Programs can be built interactively in increments, allowing the user to experiment with software prototypes. Implementation techniques for these environments result in a coupling between the application program and the environment. This coupling makes all the facilities of the environment available to the user building an application.

Language-centered environments use language-specific implementation techniques. To support the rapid production of software for research prototypes, Interlisp uses a large virtual memory space, for example. The tools are engineered as a monolithic system in one address space, and the application program is embedded in the same address space. Thus, the environment does not need to context-switch between tools and the application program. Execution of the application program can be halted, and changes can be made to sources that are then dynamically linked into the executable image. Such use of memory created the need for garbage collection of unused, expired objects.

The embedding of the application in environment code allows the application writer to use all the facilities in the environment when constructing an application. Since the environment and the application program share the same language, the application has all the features of the environment available to it as building blocks. For example, Interlisp is a "residential system" in which the Lisp program resides in the runtime system as a data structure.[1] As a result, the user is able to quickly prototype an application by reusing code available as part of the environment. In the same manner, the user is able to extend the environment with tools to satisfy specific needs. This approach is particularly evident in Smalltalk, in which the user can create objects and operations that default to or inherit the properties of other objects.

Since the close coupling of application and environment results in a lack of clear separation between the host environment and the target runtime environment, in cases such as cross-machine development special efforts have to be made to deliver an application program without the full development environment.

Semantic information. Language-centered environments support the exploratory, interactive mode of programming by recording and making available semantic information. Language-centered environments maintain syntactic and semantic information about programs in a particular program representation format. For example, the Rational Environment uses a DIANA format to represent Ada programs. It creates this structure when parsing program text and attaches semantic properties to the structure. Semantic information is typically symbol-table information such as information about the definition and use of variables and procedures and information about types. By making this information available through such tools as browsers, the environment helps the user understand the status and structure of code under development. Browsing involves navigating through the set of program objects (functions or modules, for example) and making queries about the objects and their relationships. Interlisp's Masterscope was one of the first browsers to make semantic information available to the user during program development.

Browsers have been accepted as fundamental, powerful tools for exploratory program development. They also have the potential of being very effective during program maintenance. Maintainers are usually not the original developers of a program and often can depend only on the source code as the up-to-date documentation. Before making changes to a large, unfamiliar program, maintainers usually spend considerable time understanding the program structure and the interconnection of its components. Browsers help maintainers determine the scope of a change by allowing them to interactively examine the program structure and ask which components may be affected by a change.

Programming-in-the-large. High-level programming languages do not adequately support the activities involved in constructing large systems. For example, Ada provides packages to support modularization, but it does not permit alternative implementations or successive versions of code to be attached to a package specification. For that reason, language-centered environments have added facilities to support programming-in-the-large.

Techniques for controlling and managing multiple versions of modules among multiple users have also been developed. These techniques inspired more formal definitions of version control and configuration management. For example, Cedar pioneered a paradigm for system modeling. It allows the user to define a blueprint—that is, a system model. The model is a description of the modules that make up a program. Given the model, the environment can maintain a history of the versions of the modules and can assist the user's selection of various versions in forming a program. The environment can also determine the recompilation needs of a program and can recompile modules to maintain consistency among them.

The Rational Environment supports multiple users. It provides facilities for building and maintaining versions of groups of modules (subsystems). It can enforce a check-in/check-out procedure that prevents programmers from overwriting each other's modifications. It also controls access to program components.

Observations. Language-centered environments give the user a one-language uni-

> **Language-centered environments give the user a one-language universe of discourse and well suit the coding phase of the software development cycle.**

verse of discourse. These environments are well-suited to the coding phase of the software development cycle. They provide incremental compilation or interpretation techniques to help reduce the impact of small code changes during maintenance. The exploratory style of programming they support helps the user experiment with software prototypes. Tools such as browsers not only are extremely helpful to the user during exploratory program development but can be quite effective for maintenance of large software systems.

Because of the specialized techniques used to implement them, these environments generally do not support multiple languages and, in some cases, do not facilitate the porting of application programs. Also, language-centered environments can become too large for one person to comprehend and extend.

The environments for imperative languages support programming-in-the-large facilities such as version control. But they do not currently support programming-in-the-many tasks such as project management nor do they provide support for development tasks other than coding. It is not clear whether such environments can scale up their facilities to fulfill these requirements, but they will probably form one component of future environments that will support the entire software life cycle. The specialized, handcrafted nature of these environments makes it difficult to adapt them to phases other than coding.

Developers of commercial software systems are trying to refine their implementation techniques to improve performance. They are building language-centered environments for imperative languages such as C and Modula-2 and are attempting to scale up these environments to support the design phase and to incorporate some project management techniques. The research community is applying language-centered techniques to languages such as Prolog and to specification languages. Commercial application builders so far have used language-centered environments mainly for developing prototype systems.

Structure-oriented environments

The initial motivation for structure-oriented environments was to give the user an interactive tool—a syntax-directed editor—for entering programs in terms of language constructs. This capability was extended to provide single-user programming environments that support interactive semantic analysis, program execution, and debugging. The editor is the central component of such environments; it is the interface through which the user interacts and through which all structures are manipulated. Efforts were continued to support programming-in-the-small and programming-in-the-large and to support structures such as history logs and access control lists. Thus the term "syntax-directed" has gradually been replaced by "structure-oriented."

Structure-oriented environments have made several contributions to environment technology—they have provided direct manipulation of program structures, multiple views of programs generated from the same program structure, incremental checking of static semantics and semantic information accessible to the user, and, most important, the ability to formally describe the syntax and static semantics of a language from which an instance of a structure editor can be generated.

Manipulation of structure and text. Structure-oriented environments support the concept of direct structure manipulation. The user interacts directly with program constructs and avoids the tedium of remembering the details of the syntax. While program text is displayed on the screen, the user directly modifies the underlying structure. Early environments such as Emily used parse trees as program structures. Most current environments use abstract syntax trees, which were introduced in the Mentor environment.

Structure-oriented environments take several approaches to the manipulation of structures. One involves purely structural editing; it can be viewed as primarily template-driven editing. An example of this approach is the Aloe editor in the Gandalf project. Aloe provides editing operations only on structural elements and does not permit the user to construct syntactically incorrect programs. To overcome the difficulties in entering and modifying language expressions, some environments such as the Cornell Program Synthesizer represent expressions as text.

Another approach is mixed-mode operation, which is being used in several commercial structure-oriented environments. For example, in the Rational Environment the user can operate on the textual representation and on the structure. The user enters program fragments as text and asks the environment to complete the processing as far as possible. Using incremental parsing techniques,[2] the environment converts the text fragment into a program structure. The user can edit the program using commands applied to both the program structure and the program text. The environment keeps the two representations consistently updated.

Multiple views of program structures. Structure-oriented environments generate the textual representation of a program from its structure. Thus, different representations can be generated from the same structure. This property allows users of structure-oriented environments to view programs at different levels of abstraction and detail. Browsing of large program structures is provided by showing views of different levels of detail in different display windows. The user can select a program component in one window and have it displayed in more detail in another. This capability can be found in research environments such as the Gandalf prototype and in commercial products such as the Rational Environment. Moreover, research prototypes such as the Pecan environment have demonstrated that it is feasible to produce graphical representations from program structures.

Semantics and incremental processing. After the first syntax-directed editors were built, it was quickly recognized that enforcing correct syntax is only one way of supporting the programmer. Analysis of static semantics was added to editors. The semantic analyzer processes the program structure and decorates it with semantic

information. The user can access the semantic information—such as the definition of identifiers and the locations of their use—and type information through the editor. For example, as the user programs a procedure call, the editor can display the specification of the procedure and, as soon as the procedure name has been entered, provide a template for the procedure parameters.

A structure-oriented environment is an interactive tool. Therefore, it should not only give the user immediate feedback on syntax errors but also report static semantic errors before the user moves on to edit other parts of the program. This means that the environment must track the user's changes to the program (that is, know its structure) and reanalyze only those parts that are affected, doing this upon explicit user request or when the user leaves the modified program unit. Proven compiler technology, such as attribute grammars, has been successfully extended to support such incremental processing. Environments such as LOIPE demonstrate that the notion of incremental processing can also be applied to code generation and linking. There is a trade-off between processing as small a unit as possible and the complexity of the algorithm for doing so. Different types of processing can be done at different levels of granularity. For example, syntactic correctness can be enforced at the language construct level while static semantics is checked at the program unit level (at the level of a procedure, for example) and code is generated at the module level.

Generation of structure-oriented environments. One of the major contributions

of structure-oriented environments is their ability to support manipulation of program structures in a language-independent manner. The environment developer achieves this by encapsulating the syntactic and semantic properties of a language in a grammar. Given this declarative description of the language, generation tools can automatically produce instances of structure-oriented environments. This is more efficient than building an environment from scratch. Proven compiler technology such as parser generation has paved the way for progress in this area. The Aloe editor introduced the capability of describing the syntax of a language. The Cornell Synthesizer Generator is a well-known example of supporting the description of semantic properties in terms of attribute grammars, and of providing incremental analysis algorithms as part of the generated structure-oriented environment instance.

The language-specific information can be kept in a form that can be loaded into the language-independent environment kernel at runtime, permitting one instance of the structure-oriented environment to understand several program structures simultaneously. The environment can be adapted and tailored through changes in the declarative description.

Observations. Structure-oriented environments support direct manipulation and multiple textual views of program structures. Research has shown how static semantic information can be attached to program structures and made available to the user. Algorithms that can incrementally analyze this information have been developed. Instances of structure-oriented environments can be generated automatically from descriptions of the language to be supported. These descriptions specify both syntactic and static semantic information in a declarative manner.

Structure-oriented environments have become mature enough that they are becoming available in commercial products. Environment builders can generate instances of structure editors for different languages with little effort. In many cases, the capabilities of these generated editors are restricted to syntactic checking. Semantic analyzers are often constructed manually.

Structure-oriented environments have been accepted primarily as teaching aids. Universities have been using them to teach introductory programming courses. Despite their availability, they have found

> **Structure-oriented environments support manipulation of program structures in a language-independent manner.**

A sampler of software development environments

Listed here are the languages, methods, and environments discussed in this article. They are grouped into the four categories of our taxonomy; a citation to the literature appears for each.

Language-centered environments

Ada
Ada Programming Language, American National Standards Institute, New York, 1983.

Cedar
D.C. Swinehart, P.T. Zellweger, and R.B. Hagmann, "The Structure of Cedar," *SIGPlan Notices* (Proc. ACM SIGPlan Symp. Language Issues in Programming Environments), July 1985, pp. 230-244.

Common Lisp
G.L. Steele, Jr., *Common Lisp—The Language*, Digital Press, Burlington, Mass., 1984.

DIANA
G. Goos et al., eds., *DIANA—An Intermediate Language for Ada* (*Lecture Notes in Computer Science*, Vol. 161), Springer-Verlag, Berlin, 1983.

Interlisp
W. Teitelman and L. Masinter, "The Interlisp Programming Environment," in *Tutorial: Software Development Environments*, Computer Society Press, Los Alamitos, Calif., 1981, pp. 73-81.

Rational Environment
J.E. Archer, Jr., and M.T. Devlin, "Rational's Experience Using Ada for Very Large Systems," *Proc. First Int'l Conf. Ada Programming Language Applications for the NASA Space Station*, NASA, June 1986, pp. B2.5.1-B2.5.12.

Smalltalk
A. Goldberg, "The Influence of an Object-oriented Language on the Programming Environment," in *Interactive Programming Environments*, D.R. Barstow, H.E. Shrobe, and E. Sandewall, eds., McGraw-Hill, New York, 1984, pp. 141-174.

Structure-oriented environments

Aloe
P.H. Feiler and R. Medina-Mora, "An Incremental Programming Environment," *IEEE Trans. Software Engineering*, Sept. 1981, pp. 472-482.

Cornell Program Synthesizer
T. Reps and T. Teitelbaum, "The Synthesizer Generator," *SIGPlan Notices* (Proc. ACM SIGSoft/SIGPlan Software Engineering Symp. on Practical Software Development Environments), May 1984, pp. 42-48.

Emily
W.J. Hansen, "User Engineering Principles for Interactive Environments," in *Interactive Programming Environments*,

D.R. Barstow, H.E. Shrobe, and E. Sandewall, eds., McGraw-Hill, New York, 1984, pp. 217-231.

Gandalf
A.N. Habermann and D. Notkin, "Gandalf: Software Development Environments," *IEEE Trans. Software Engineering*, Dec. 1986, pp. 1117-1127.

LOIPE
D. Notkin, "The Gandalf Project," *J. Systems and Software*, May 1985, pp. 91-105.

Mentor
V. Donzeque-gouge et al., "Programming Environments Based on Structured Editors: The Mentor Experience," in *Interactive Programming Environments*, D.R. Barstow, H.E. Shrobe, and E. Sandewall, eds., McGraw-Hill, New York, 1984, pp. 128-140.

Pecan
S.P. Reiss, "Graphical Program Development with PECAN Program Development Systems," *SIGPlan Notices* (Proc. ACM SIGSoft/SIGPlan Software Engineering Symp. on Practical Software Development Environments), May 1984, pp. 30-41.

Toolkit environments

Apollo DSEE
D.B. Leblang and R.P. Chase, Jr., "Computer-aided Software Engineering in a Distributed Workstation Environment," *SIGPlan Notices* (Proc. ACM SIGSoft/SIGPlan Software Engineering Symp. on Practical Software Development Environments), May 1984, pp. 104-112.

Arcadia
R.N. Taylor et al., *Arcadia: A Software Development Environment Research Project*, tech. report, Univ. of California, Irvine, Mar. 1986.

CAIS
Military Standard Common APSE Interface Set, Proposed MIL-STD-CAIS, Ada Joint Program Office, Washington, D.C., Jan. 1985.

PCTE
F. Gallo, R. Minot, and I. Thomas, "The Object Management System of PCTE as a Software Engineering Database Management System," *SIGPlan Notices* (Proc. Second ACM SIGSoft/SIGPlan Software Engineering Symp. on Practical Software Development Environments), Jan. 1987, pp. 12-15.

Unix/PWB
T.A. Dolotta, R.C. Haight, and J.R. Mashey, "Unix Time-sharing System: The Programmer's Workbench," in *Interactive Programming Environments*, D.R. Barstow, H.E. Shrobe, and E. Sandewall, eds., McGraw-Hill, New York, 1984, pp. 353-369.

VMS VAXset CMS
User's Introduction to VAX DEC/CMS, Digital Equipment Corp., Maynard, Mass., 1984.

Method-based environments

Anna

D. Luckham and F.W. von Henke, "An Overview of Anna, A Specification Language for Ada," *IEEE Software*, Mar. 1985, pp. 9-22.

CORE

G.P. Mullery, "CORE—A Method for Controlled Requirement Specification," *Proc. 4th Int'l Conf. on Software Engineering*, Computer Society Press, Los Alamitos, Calif., 1979, pp. 126-135.

DCDS

G.E. Sievert and T.A. Mizell, "Specification-based Software Engineering with TAGS," *Computer*, Apr. 1985, pp. 56-66.

Entity-relationship (ER-Chen) diagrams

P. Chen, "The Entity-Relationship Model—Toward a Unified View of Data," *ACM Trans. on Database Systems*, Mar. 1976, pp. 9-36.

Excelerator

Index Technology Corp., "Excelerator," *Proc. Computer-aided Software Engineering Symp.*, Digital Consulting Inc., Andover, Mass., June 1987.

Genesis

C.V. Ramamoorthy et al., "Genesis: An Integrated Environment for Supporting Development and Evolution of Software," *Proc. Compsac 85*, Computer Society Press, Los Alamitos, Calif., 1985, pp. 472-479.

GIST

S.F. Fickas, "Automating the Transformational Development of Software," *IEEE Trans. Software Engineering*, Nov. 1985, pp. 1268-1277.

IORL

G.E. Sievert and T.A. Mizell, "Specification-based Software Engineering with TAGS," *Computer*, Apr. 1985, pp. 56-66.

IPSE 2.5

D. Morgan, "The Imminent IPSE," *Datamation*, Apr. 1987, pp. 60-64.

ISTAR

M. Dowson, "ISTAR—An Integrated Project Support Environment," *SIGPlan Notices* (Proc. Second ACM SIGSoft/SIGPlan Software Engineering Symp. on Practical Software Development Environments), Jan. 1987, pp. 27-33.

PSL/PSA

D. Teichroew and E.A. Hershey III, "PSL/PSA: A Computer-aided Technique for Structured Documentation and Analysis of Information Processing Systems," *IEEE Trans. Software Engineering*, Jan. 1977, pp. 41-48.

Leonardo

W. Myers, "MCC: Planning the Revolution in Software," *IEEE Software*, Nov. 1985, pp. 68-73.

Merise diagrams

Pham Thu Quang, "Merise: A French Methodology for Information Systems Analysis and Design," *J. Systems Management*, Mar. 1986, pp. 21-24.

Nastec CASE 2000

Nastec Corp., "Nastec CASE 2000," *Proc. Computer-aided Software Engineering Symp.*, Digital Consulting Inc., Andover, Mass., June 1987.

PMA

L.M. Gilham et al., *Project Management in a Knowledge-based Software Environment*, tech. report KES.U.87.2, Kestrel Institute, Palo Alto, Calif., 1987.

Petri nets

J.L. Peterson, *Petri Net Theory and the Modelling of Systems*, Prentice-Hall, Englewood Cliffs, N.J., 1981.

Prospectra

B. Krieg-Brueckner et al., "PROgram Development by SPECification and TRAnsformation," in *Esprit 86: Results and Achievements*, Elsevier Science Pub. Co., New York, 1987, pp. 301-311.

Refine

D.R. Smith, G.B. Kotik, and S.J. Westfold, "Research on Knowledge-based Software Environments at Kestrel Institute," *IEEE Trans. Software Engineering*, Nov. 1985, pp. 1278-1295.

SADT

D.T. Ross, "Applications and Extensions of SADT," *Computer*, Apr. 1985, pp. 25-35.

Schematic design methods

J. Martin and C. McClure, *Diagramming Techniques for Analysts and Programmers*, Prentice-Hall, Englewood Cliffs, N.J., 1985.

SDL

A. Rockström and R. Saracco, "SDL—CCITT Specification and Description Language," *IEEE Trans. Communications*, June 1982, pp. 1310-1318.

Software Through Pictures

A.I. Wasserman and P.A. Pircher, "A Graphical, Extensible Integrated Environment for Software Development," *SIGPlan Notices* (Proc. Second ACM SIGSoft/SIGPlan Software Engineering Symp. on Practical Software Development Environments), Jan. 1987, pp. 131-142.

SREM

M. Alford, "SREM at the Age of Eight: The Distributed Computing Design System," *Computer*, Apr. 1985, pp. 36-46.

Teamwork

Cadre Technology, "Improved Quality and Productivity with Teamwork/SA," *System Development*, Oct. 1985.

TAGS

G.E. Sievert and T.A. Mizell, "Specification-based Software Engineering with TAGS," *Computer*, Apr. 1985, pp. 56-66.

VDM

D. Bjorner, "On the Use of Formal Methods in Software Development," *Proc. 9th Int'l Conf. on Software Engineering*, Computer Society Press, Los Alamitos, Calif., 1987, pp. 17-29.

little acceptance in industry. Structure editors are being used to support only the coding phase and are being viewed as tools for programming-in-the-small. So far, little empirical data has been collected to indicate whether structure-oriented environments actually increase productivity.

Initial attempts to scale up structure-oriented environments to support programming-in-the-large and programming-in-the-many have encountered difficulties. Techniques currently used in many structure-oriented environments have shortcomings in terms of providing efficient, persistent storage for large structures and in coordinating concurrent access to the structures for multiple users or tools. Furthermore, for different tools to be integrated in a structure-oriented environment, they must either be adapted to understand a common structural representation or there must be mechanisms for consistent updating of structures through multiple views.

Toolkit environments

Toolkit environments consist of a collection of small tools and are intended primarily to support the coding phase of the software development cycle. They provide little environment-defined control or management over the ways in which the tools are applied. The toolkit approach starts with the operating system and adds coding tools such as a compiler, editor, assembler, linker, and debugger, as well as tools to support large-scale software development tasks such as version control and configuration management. The toolkit approach was motivated by the need to be language-independent while supporting programming-in-the-large facilities. The toolkit approach uses simple data modeling to aid the extensibility and portability of tools. Examples of commercial toolkit systems are the Unix Programmer's Workbench (Unix/PWB), the DEC VMS VAX-set, and the Apollo Domain Software Engineering Environment (DSEE). Examples of prototype toolkit environments are the Portable Common Tool Environment (PCTE) and the Common APSE Interface Set (CAIS).

Extensibility and portability. Unix is an operating system that has encouraged extensions. It has a very simple data model for tool interaction and persistent data storage: an ASCII byte stream. This uni-

> **Commercial environment builders are placing higher-level interfaces on top of the normal operating system user-command interface.**

form model enables the user to tailor the Unix environment by adding new tools or modifying existing ones. Tools interact via ASCII files or communication channels called pipes, which encourages reuse of existing tools and tool fragments. Each tool or tool fragment must parse the text stream to extract a structured representation of the data; that is, no structure or semantic information is recorded with the data. This results in tools with few incremental processing capabilities. The Unix/PWB places few, if any, restrictions on when and how tools can be used. Such a model gives the user considerable latitude but provides little support in terms of consistently and automatically managing user activities. The simplicity of the tools and their interactions makes them portable across similar environments.

The simple ASCII model lacks support for typing stored data and for uniformly describing and processing the structure of data. It provides very limited typing of objects other than the use of file name extensions. Developments are in progress to extend file systems to include some of this support. Apollo's Extensible Stream package provides a mechanism that supports typed files and permits the introduction of user-defined file types. DSEE has facilities embedded in its file system to provide a version control mechanism that is transparent to the environment user and the tools. Environments such as PCTE and CAIS support persistent, typed objects with an extensible set of object attributes, while the Arcadia research project addresses tool integration and extensibility as well as object management.

Operating system extensions. To provide more environment-defined control facilities while retaining tailorability fea-

tures, commercial environment builders such as Atherton Technology are placing higher-level interfaces on top of the normal operating system user command interface. Such environments allow the user to work within the context of the high-level functions of the environment, such as those for project management, but also to jump into the native operating system command level, such as that for Unix or VMS, when needed. These higher-level "shells" try to place more controls on tool usage in toolkit environments. They can also provide a uniform interface independent of the underlying operating system. Not only can the user be shielded from the operating system itself but he or she can have transparent access to distributed computing facilities. Similarly, the user can add new tools to the toolkit environment without needing to have a knowledge of the underlying hardware and operating system.

Programming-in-the-large. Toolkit environments provide programming-in-the-large tools that are independent of a particular programming language. These tools try to ease the programmer's managing of code by providing mechanisms for recording version numbers for source code. Some file systems append a version number to a file name and increment it each time the file is rewritten. The Unix/PWB and VMS VAXset provide explicit tools—the SCCS (Source Code Control System) and the CMS (Code Management System), respectively—to perform version control. Such tools simply record versions and coordinate access to them; the user must decide how to use the version information. For configuration management, systems such as DSEE build a consistent software system as described and requested by the user.

Observations. Toolkit environments use operating system facilities to "glue" tools into a collection. The intent is to provide a language-independent environment that supports multiple languages with appropriate tools. Such environments allow a high degree of tailoring but provide few environment-defined management or control techniques for using the collection of tools. The user must establish management policies to ensure that tools will be used correctly. Although very popular because of the tailorability and portability of their tools, toolkit environments do not greatly assist the maintenance of large software systems.

The current generation of toolkit environments uses a fairly mature technology. Research on extensions to operating systems is continuing. Extensions include a better data model to support persistent storage and distributed data access, and uniform operating-system-independent user interfaces.

Method-based environments

Method-based environments each support a particular method for developing software. The methods fall into two broad classes: development methods for particular phases in the software development cycle, and methods for managing the development process. Development methods are those used by individual developers in phases such as requirements analysis, system specification, and design. Methods for managing the process are those that support orderly development of a software system via product management procedures for consistent evolution of the product by a number of developers, and via models for organizing and managing people and activities.

Support for development methods. Development methods address various steps in the software development cycle. They include but are not limited to methods for specification, design, validation and verification, and reuse. Different methods exhibit various degrees of formality: a method may be informal, as in written text; semiformal, as in textual and graphical descriptions with limited checking facilities; or formal, with an underlying theoretical model against which a description can be verified. Examples of semiformal methods for specification and design are SREM, IORL, CORE, SADT, SDL, PSL/PSA, variations of data flow diagrams and control flow diagrams, and entity-relationship (ER) diagrams. Examples of more formal methods for specification are Petri nets, state machines, and specification languages such as GIST, Refine, VDM, and Anna. While several of the semiformal methods have been practiced to some degree since the mid-1970s, formal methods are less used. In many cases, they were initially practiced with paper and pencil.

Originally, tools for development methods were provided on mainframes and textual notations or special graphics terminals were used. Examples of such sys-

Method-based environments support particular development methods and the management of the development process.

tems are TAGS and DCDS. The availability of computers to a larger number of developers and the advent of affordable graphical facilities on personal computers and workstations have encouraged the development of a large number of commercial tools—especially for semiformal methods of schematic design—often called computer-aided software engineering, or CASE, tools. Examples of such products are Index Technology's Excelerator, Nastec's CASE 2000, Cadre's Teamwork, and Interactive Development Environments' Software Through Pictures. Such tools support individual users in drawing and updating graphical designs interactively, help organize the design into a hierarchy of abstraction levels, and perform certain consistency checks. Users can invoke analyzers such as level checkers that check for consistent use of names and for connections between levels of the design. Cross-reference information is derived by the analyzer (in most cases not incrementally) and is stored in data dictionaries that can be queried interactively.

Many CASE vendors have realized that it is desirable for their tool to support more than one design method and for customers to adapt the tool to their own methods. Recent releases of commercial tools allow users to define their own graphical symbols for the graphical editor and to write and interface their own analyzers. In some cases, instances of a tool can be generated for different methods. Integration of different methods is limited to instances of graphical editors and analyzers that can be invoked from the same system menu. For methods that differ only in the shape of symbols, such as Merise diagrams and ER-Chen diagrams, a tool can display the design with either set of symbols. All instances of the tool store the cross-

reference information in the same data dictionary.

Support for managing the development process. Managing software development consists of managing the product under development as well as managing the process for developing and maintaining the product. Support of product management includes facilities for version, configuration, and release management along with procedures and standards for performing these tasks consistently. Support for managing the development process includes facilities for project management (project planning and control), task management (helping developers organize and track their tasks), communication management (knowing and controlling the communication patterns in the project organization), and process modeling.

Initially, tools to support particular management functions such as scheduling, cost estimation, or change request control were built in isolation. Recently, research has tried to take a more global approach to understanding and formalizing the software development process and its management. This is evidenced in the literature.[3-5] Research prototypes of environments such as IPSE 2.5, Genesis, and PMA investigate the feasibility of supporting various aspects of encoding and supporting a process model. ISTAR, a commercial development, centers the environment around a particular model—the contract model—rather than around a particular tool. The environment supports planning and management of tasks and management of products as they are being built by teams of developers. It also provides facilities to integrate specification, design, coding, testing, and documentation tools. One of the challenges for such environments is to support process models and management styles without disturbing those in place at a particular organization. The practicality of such environments has yet to be shown.

Observations. Method-based environments support particular development methods and the management of the development process. A number of tools for single users that support semiformal graphical development methods have become available. Instead of encoding particular methods in these tools, their developers have engineered them to be more general purpose. Instances of design tools can be created through a tailoring and generation process. Generally, isolated tools are available to support version and configuration management and project management.

The distance between existing tools and those of an ideal software development environment is great. Progress must occur in several areas and these are the target of long-term research activities. Research efforts such as MCC's Leonardo project are investigating the feasibility of bringing the exploratory style of language-centered environments to specification and design environments. This requires a better understanding of the specification and design process and the development of formal methods that appropriately capture information and decisions. A supportive environment must capture and reason about the semantics embedded in the method, and must process information incrementally to assist the designer in exploring design alternatives. A better formal understanding of the derivation of efficient implementations from a specification permits more automation of this process. Research in formal and executable specifications, program transformations, and program synthesis is making progress, but solutions can be expected initially only in particular application domains. Examples of such research efforts are the Prospectra project sponsored by Esprit and projects at USC/ISI[6] and Kestrel Institute.[7] Finally, an envi-

User interfaces

Major developments in hardware technology such as bit-mapped displays and mouse devices have made novel user interfaces possible. It seems quite natural to use a pointing device as the user interface for object-oriented languages such as Smalltalk. The Smalltalk language-centered environment replaces the textual user interface—command lines—with pop-up menus, a window manager, and a pointing device, thereby providing a very "friendly" interface. On-line tutoring is provided by means of tools such as "explain" and "example" facilities and through on-line documentation.

Cedar is also recognized for its user interface, which uses techniques similar to those of Smalltalk and incorporates icon management. Cedar provides a level of abstraction by defining an imaging model to handle complex graphics on different hardware. This model defines graphic objects by their semantics rather than by their representation. The implementation then maps these graphic objects onto the hardware constraints. Cedar demonstrates how a nontextual interface can be abstracted from the operating system functions.

In structure-oriented environments, the user interface is ruled by the semantics of the language being edited. The Aloe editor of the Gandalf project is a prime example of a pure structure-oriented editor. For example, when the user gives the command *if*, the editor constructs the *if* node in the structure, displays the template for the *if* construct in the program, and places the cursor at the condition of the construct. The syntax is enforced because the user can only apply the *if* command when the placement of the construct is syntactically correct. The user moves the cursor according to the structure. The cursor is shown on the screen as a highlight of the textual area that represents the substructure to which the cursor refers. For example, moving the cursor up from the condition of an *if* construct highlights the text of the whole *if* construct. To modify existing programs, editing operations such as cut and paste and structural transformation operations are provided. This allows the user to change, delete, or move syntactic program fragments rather than single characters or lines of text. Transformation operations allow the user to convert, for example, an *if* statement into a *while* loop or to nest a sequence of statements into a *for* loop. Despite these editing operations, using a purely structural editor to modify expressions is awkward. Therefore, some structure editors (the Cornell Syn-thesizer, for example) treat expressions as text rather than as structure—that is, they allow the expressions to be entered and edited as text and then they parse them.

The Rational Environment works in a mixed mode that allows the user to edit a program both structurally and textually. After the user enters a program fragment in text form, the environment constructs a structure representing the text entered and places the cursor at the first place to be completed. For example, asking the editor to complete the "if" results in the construction of the *if* statement presented. The user can move the cursor and edit according to the structure (for example, move to the next statement or delete a statement) and according to the text (for example, move down a line or delete the rest of the line).

A technique known as elision displays a marker such as . . . (three dots) or a label instead of the actual program. Elision markers are used to compact source code below a particular nesting level. For example, when the user places the cursor at the first statement of a procedure, only the specification and not the body of the procedure is seen. Constructs such as *for*, *while*, or *if* may be similarly compacted. However, when the user moves the cursor to the vicinity of an elision marker, the text is automatically expanded.

Browsing is provided in a similar manner. In one window, the user sees a high-level view of a program, for example, a list of all Ada package names in a program library. The details of the packages are hidden. The user can select a package and open it for viewing. This results in a textual representation of the selected component in more detail in a separate window. The user may see, for example, a list of procedure specifications contained in the package. As before, the user can select one of the structural elements and examine it in more detail or modify it.

Method-based environments consisting of CASE tools have powerful graphics editing facilities. Interfaces appear similar to the menu-based ones for language-centered environments. The difference lies in the manipulation of graphical symbols based on the syntactical constraints of a particular diagramming technique. Symbols and links can be created, deleted, and changed. This is done by positioning the cursor with a pointing device and selecting a particular item from the available menu.

ronment that helps manage the development process requires research into formal models for capturing the process, reasoning about it, and supporting the dynamics of its execution.

Conclusions

The four types of environment in our taxonomy represent the major technical directions that software development environments have taken. We have discussed the work in each area primarily from the user's perspective. Language-centered environments are interactive, incremental environments suited to an exploratory style of programming. Structure-oriented environments generalize and formalize these techniques and provide generators. Both types of environments show the advantages of making semantic information available. Toolkit environments stress user tailorability and the reuse of a fairly generic tool set, while method-based environments concentrate on providing support for development activities such as requirements analysis and design, and management activities such as guiding a team of programmers during the development process. While it would seem straightforward to merge these capabilities to achieve a highly interactive, tailorable, multiple-user, full-life-cycle environment, the implementation strategies used for each type of environment cannot be easily combined to produce such a result. We conclude by examining what we consider to be the primary issues when we try to combine or extend the advantages offered by each category.

Data management. Language-centered and structure-oriented environments can incrementally maintain executable objects and static semantic information about program units. This functionality is very dependent on the underlying programming-language foundations. There are formal means to define the language units, the constraints on those objects, and the relationships between them. Such information is used to maintain a consistent state after a modification (such as the changing of a variable name or the deleting of a statement).

Method-based environments do not yet support such incremental analysis and do not seem to have theoretical foundations as mature as those of language-centered and structure-oriented environments. The development methods they support often

take an operational or control-flow approach to the development process. Most process models are more oriented to managing user activity rather than to managing objects. The object management architecture used by structure-oriented environments is not directly applicable to method-based environments. It is a research question as to whether it should or can be applied.

The kind of tool integration and incremental processing found in structure-oriented environments and in many language-centered environments depends on using a shared data store. The underlying representations for those environments, and for the tools found in the method-based environments, are very specialized. A generalization of a shared data store is a database management system. Commercial databases have been used to support configuration and project management information, but typically have not been used for tool-related data management. Generalization of the features that users like in individual tools in the language-centered and method-based environments requires a solution to the shared data storage problem. The file system extensions discussed earlier may offer a partial solution to this problem.

Programming-in-the-large/programming-in-the-many. As tools for supporting development methods become more readily available, they are being applied to larger projects. This requires scaling up a method—that is, incorporating into its notation and supporting tools techniques for managing large descriptions. Techniques for scaling up are well known in the programming language field and appear in both the toolkit and language-centered environments. They include partitioning mechanisms (such as modularization, data encapsulation, and interface checking) and management mechanisms (such as version control). These concepts are not used as extensively by the method-based environments, which concentrate on the operational aspects of the development process. The subtasks of the programmer are described primarily in terms of actions in which information hiding and data dependencies play no significant role. The issue here may be a simple one of maturity, since there is considerable commercial activity in this area.

Tailorability. There are a variety of ways to achieve tailorability. Toolkit environments take advantage of generic tools

defined on relatively unstructured data. In the other categories, the information maintained is much more complex. Thus, tailorability is more likely to be achieved by tool generators. For method-based environments, we need to consider the tailorability of individual tools (such as editors) for a specific design method, and the tailorability of project or configuration management policies. Structure-oriented environments provide generators for tools such as semantically based editors. Generators are also appearing in method-based environments, where they have been used to build graphical editors for a variety of design methods. Tailoring the environment to a specific management policy or process development model is more difficult than tailoring a specific tool and will depend on better formalisms for describing the software process.

There has been progress in software development environments—their support of coding is particularly well understood. Environments are slowly improving, but combining technologies to better address the entire software life cycle remains an area for active research. □

Acknowledgments

We thank the reviewers and our colleagues at the Software Engineering Institute for their invaluable contributions to the final editing and production of this report.

Work on this article was sponsored by the Department of Defense.

References

1. E. Sandewall, "Programming in an Interactive Environment: The Lisp Experience," in *Interactive Programming Environments*, D.R. Barstow, H.E. Shrobe, and E. Sandewall, eds., McGraw-Hill, New York, 1984, pp. 31-80.

2. C. Ghezzi and D. Mandrioli, "Incremental Parsing," *ACM Trans. Programming Languages and Systems*, July 1979, pp. 58-70.

3. M.M. Lehman and L.A. Belady, *Program Evolution—Processes of Software Change*, Academic Press, Orlando, Fla., 1985.

4. M. Dawson, "Iteration in the Software Process: Review of the 3rd Int'l Software Process Workshop," in *Proc. 9th Int'l Conf. on Software Engineering*, Computer Society Press, Los Alamitos, Calif., 1987, pp. 36-41.

5. *Proc. 9th Int'l Conf. on Software Engineering*, Computer Society Press, Los Alamitos, Calif., 1987.

6. R. Balzer, "A 15 Year Perspective on Automatic Programming," *IEEE Trans. Software Engineering*, Nov. 1985, pp. 1257-1268.
7. D.R. Smith, G.B. Kotik, and S.J. Westfold, "Research on Knowledge-based Software Environments at Kestrel Institute," *IEEE Trans. Software Engineering*, Nov. 1985, pp. 1278-1295.

Peter H. Feiler is a senior computer scientist for the Software Engineering Institute, where he is a member of the Evaluation of Environments Project. His interests include software development environments for large software systems, interactive development tools, application of AI technology to software engineering problems, and support for concurrent applications.

Feiler earned a Vordiplom in mathematics and computer science from the Technical University of Munich, West Germany, and received a doctorate in computer science from Carnegie Mellon University for his work on LOIPE—the Language-Oriented Interactive Programming Environment—in support of the Gandalf project. He is a member of the ACM, the Computer Society of the IEEE, and the American Association for Artificial Intelligence.

Susan A. Dart is a computer scientist at the Software Engineering Institute of Carnegie Mellon University and is currently involved with the institute's Evaluation of Environments Project. Prior to joining the SEI, she was a member of the technical staff at Tartan Laboratories in Pittsburgh. Besides software development environments, her interests include compiler development for concurrent programming languages and protocols for telecommunication systems.

Dart received a bachelor's degree in computer science from the Royal Melbourne Institute of Technology, Australia. She is a member of the ACM, the Computer Society of the IEEE, and the Australian Computer Society.

A. Nico Habermann is a professor of computer science at Carnegie Mellon University. He was instrumental in establishing the Software Engineering Institute at CMU and served as its acting director in 1985. He has been chairman of CMU's computer science department since 1979. His interests include programming languages, operating systems, software engineering, and programming environments.

Habermann has contributed to the design and implementation of Algol 60, Bliss, Pascal, Ada, and various special-purpose languages and has worked on several operating systems, including Famos—the Family of Operating Systems, DAS—the Dynamically Adaptable System, and Unix. He worked with E.W. Dijkstra on the THE System, for which he wrote the Algol 60 interface.

Habermann received a master's degree in mathematics from the Free University of Amsterdam, The Netherlands, and a doctorate in applied mathematics from the Technological University of Eindhoven, The Netherlands. He is a member of IBM's Scientific Advisory Committee and the National Science Foundation's Advisory Committee for Computer Science, and is an editor for *Acta Informatica* and the *ACM Transactions on Programming Languages and Systems*.

Robert J. Ellison is a senior computer scientist for the Software Engineering Institute and is leader of the Evaluation of Environments Project. His interests include software tool and environment generation and environment frameworks. From 1981 to 1985 he was a research associate at Carnegie Mellon University, where he headed the Gandalf programming environment project.

Ellison holds a bachelor's degree in mathematics from Lewis and Clark College and master's and doctor's degrees in mathematics from Purdue University. He is a member of the ACM and the Computer Society of the IEEE.

Questions about this article can be directed to Robert J. Ellison at the Software Engineering Institute, Carnegie Mellon University, Pittsburgh, PA 15213.

The Ecology of Software Development Environments

Anthony I. Wasserman
University of California, San Francisco

Introduction

An environment is the aggregate of surrounding things, conditions, and influences that affect the existence or development of someone or something. It is well understood that changes in the environment can have significant and potentially drastic effects. It is equally well understood that differences in environment can have major effects; individual development, for example, has been shown to have both genetic and environmental components. The field of ecology deals with relationships between organisms and their environment.

We can apply ecological concepts to people engaged in producing computer programs. In such an application, we are concerned with identifying the environmental factors that affect such people, with the interrelationships among these factors, and with the effects on people of modifications to their environment. These last two items, in particular, are ecological concerns.

From that perspective, the notion of a software development environment is quite old, going back to the first programmer for the first computer. In many respects, of course, the environment of the modern software developer is quite different from that of the early programmers; in a fundamental sense, however, they are quite similar.

Components of a software development environment

This similarity becomes more apparent when we identify the most significant factors in the programming environment. The following aspects of the environment seem to have affected both the early programmers and modern software developers:

- the computer system itself, including the processor, its memory, and any peripheral devices for storage or input/output
- the availability of the computer system, including the time it takes to gain access to the system and the time it takes for a job or request to be completed, as well as the physical proximity of the locations for submission of input and receipt of output
- the support personnel for the computer system, including operators and maintenance staff available

- systems programs, especially an operating system, possibly including a file system, linker, loader, and other utility programs
- available languages in which the programmer/developer can express the solution to a problem, along with translators (compilers, assemblers, interpreters) that cause the program to be executed
- software tools, including editors, debuggers, test drivers
- text and program preparation facilities, e.g., keypunches, CRT's, etc.
- project management practices, including team or project organizations, project review methods, documentation and coding standards, and methods for budgeting and predicting costs and schedules
- organizational aspects, including the source(s) of requests for programs, integration of programs with other products in the organization, funding for software development, and product quality assurance
- external constraints, e.g., government directives, upon the programming process, physical workspace factors, including noise levels, office placement and size, and air pollution (smoke)

This list makes it clear that a vast number of factors have an effect on the individual developer within a software development environment. Changes in the available operating system, the programming language, the project organization, the format of specifications, the type of terminal, or project reporting standards can all affect how the developer works and the amount of work that can be done.

Productivity, as a quantitative measure of the amount of work that can be performed by a developer, can be altered in a number of ways; teaching all developers the skills of touch typing, for example, might have a greater impact upon productivity than would the introduction of new software tools or design techniques. Productivity alone, however, does not tell us enough about particular software development environments, since it does not take product quality into consideration. For example, workers in an automobile assembly plant may produce 60 cars per hour, but this measure is not useful if a fourth of the cars require additional work to correct problems. Much of the same applies in software development: the goal is to create an environment that not

Reprinted from *Software Development Environments*, pp. 47-52.

only enhances developer productivity but also supports the creation of superior products.

Software development methodologies

At the heart of the environment is a software development *methodology,* a process for software production. The methodology typically consists of a sequence of steps combining management procedures, technical methods, and automated support to produce software products.

The relationship between a methodology and the development environment is illustrated in Figure 1. It can be seen that a number of software developers, formed into an organization, exist within the software development environment. This organization uses a particular methodology. Management procedures determine the nature of the automated support that is provided, both in terms of the computer system to be used and the languages and tools that support the software development effort. Management procedures also coordinate and guide the technical methods the developers employ. Management is made more effective by the use of technical methods that provide intermediate data, such as specification and design documents, for management review. Automated support enhances the effectiveness of the developer, whose technical needs drive the development of new automated tools and the acquisition of new computer systems.

The software development organization must select among an almost limitless number of possibilities and combinations of management practices, development techniques, and automated support in order to create and evolve the software development methodology. This methodology is also influenced by a wide variety of other considerations, including the size and skills of the software development organization and the intended applications of the programs being developed, the number of places in which they will be used, their criticality to their applications, and the projected needs for maintenance and modification.

Because of the large number of possibilities and the great variations in uses and applications of software, it is not reasonable to expect different organizations to use the same software development methodology. Even groups that follow a recommended methodology for software development will modify it to adapt to the particular characteristics of their organization and their projects. Furthermore, methodologies will be changing constantly to reflect new developments in hardware and software and new staffing and management structures.

An example of different methodologies may be seen in automobile production, which, like software development, is governed not only by the technical aspects of manufacture and assembly, but also by the nature of the work force. Volvo adopted a team organization to car production as their approach to enhancing worker satisfaction; they found that their workers could work effectively together, share responsibilities, and vary tasks. Bayerische Motor Werke (BMW) found that such an organization could not be applied in their environment because language differences made it difficult, if not impossible, for their workers to communicate. Volvo and BMW produce cars at roughly the same rate, and in the same general price range; but differences in their developers—their workers—cause them to use different methodologies.

Characteristics of a methodology

The desirable characteristics of a methodology for software development include the following:

1. The methodology should cover the entire software development cycle. It does relatively little good to have a methodology for software design if there is no systematic procedure to produce the specification used for the design and/or the executable program that must be created from the design. Thus, a methodology must assist the developer at every stage of the development cycle.

2. The methodology should facilitate transitions between phases of the development cycle. When a developer is working on a particular phase of a project (other than requirements analysis), it is important to be able to refer to the previous phase and to trace one's work. At the design stage, for example, one must make certain that the architecture of the software system provides for all of the specified functions; one should be able to identify the software modules that fulfill specific system requirements. During implementation, it should be easy to establish a correspondence between modules in the system design and program units, and between the logical data objects from the design stage and the physical data objects in the program. It is important to note that one must be able to move not only forward to the next phase of the life cycle, but also backward to a previous phase, so that work can be checked and corrections can be made. This phased approach to software development makes it clear that information lost at a particular phase is generally lost forever, with an impact on the resulting system. For example, if an analyst fails to document a requirement, it will not appear in the specification. Eventually, during acceptance testing (or perhaps during system operation), that failure will be recognized, and the system willl have to be modified.

3. The methodology must support determination of system correctness throughout the development cycle. System correctness encompasses many issues, including not only the correspondence between the system and its specifications, but also the extent to which the system meets user needs. Accordingly, those who devise the methodology must not only be concerned with techniques for validating the com-

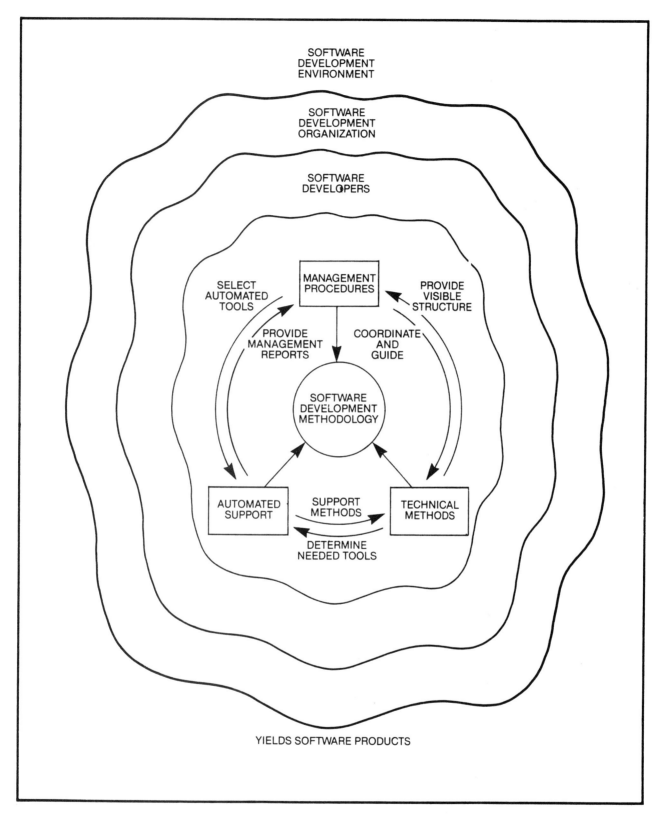

SOFTWARE
DEVELOPMENT
ENVIRONMENT

SOFTWARE
DEVELOPMENT
ORGANIZATION

SOFTWARE
DEVELOPERS

MANAGEMENT
PROCEDURES

SELECT
AUTOMATED
TOOLS

PROVIDE
VISIBLE
STRUCTURE

PROVIDE
MANAGEMENT
REPORTS

COORDINATE
AND
GUIDE

SOFTWARE
DEVELOPMENT
METHODOLOGY

AUTOMATED
SUPPORT

SUPPORT
METHODS

TECHNICAL
METHODS

DETERMINE
NEEDED TOOLS

YIELDS SOFTWARE PRODUCTS

FIGURE 1. THE SOFTWARE DEVELOPMENT ENVIRONMENT

33

plete system but must also give attention to obtaining the most complete and consistent description of user needs during the early stages of the project. For example, the methods used for analysis and specification of the system should aid problem understanding by the developers, the users, and other concerned parties, and make it possible to trace later system development back to the requirements and specification.

4. The methodology must support the software development organization. It must be possible to manage the developers, and the developers must be able to work together. This requirement implies the need for effective communication among analysts, developers, and managers, with well-defined steps for making progress visible throughout the development activity. The intermediate products generated by the methods and tools, such as a detailed design or an acceptance test plan, can be reviewed by the organization so that progress can be effectively measured and quality assured.

5. The methodology must be repeatable for a large class of software projects. While different methodologies will be needed for different classes of systems and for different organizational structures, an organization should be able to adopt a methodology that will be useful for a sizable number of programs that they will build. Certainly, it makes little sense to develop a methodology for each new system to be built.

6. The methodology must be teachable. Even within a single organization, there will be many people who must use the methodology. They include not only those who are there when the methodology is first adopted, but also those who join the organization later. Each person must understand the specific techniques of the methodology, the organizational and managerial procedures that make it effective, the automated tools that support the methodology, and the underlying motivations for the methodology. Since software engineering education is not yet very well advanced, much of the responsibility for teaching a methodology lies with the development organization.

7. The methodology must be supported by automated tools that improve the productivity of both the individual developer and the development team. This collection of tools, and the way in which they are used, constitute what has been called a "programming environment," since most automated tools are aimed at the coding and implementation phases of software development. In considering the future nature of such tools, it is perhaps better to use the term "automated program development environment" or "automated development support system."

8. The methodology should support the eventual evolution of the system. Systems typically go through many versions during their lifetimes, which may last eight to ten years or more. New requirements arise from changes in technology, usage patterns, or user needs, and these changed or additional requirements must be reflected in a modified system. The development methodology can assist this evolutionary activity by providing accurate external and internal system documentation and a well structured software system that is easily comprehended and modified by those making the system changes.

The software development environment, then, which provides a framework for describing how software developers make use of a software development methodology, can be seen to be different for each organization since it depends on who is working in that organization. More importantly, it can be seen that the environment is affected by every change, no matter how minor, ranging from the use of new computer equipment to new hirings.

Ecological considerations in the development environment

A principal concern of those who study software development environments is to optimize the effectiveness of the software development organization for the production of superior software products. This involves, among other things, selecting the appropriate software development techniques, using developers and support staff effectively, designing the physical workspace, and choosing suitable computing equipment.

This optimization process frequently involves trade-offs, and changes to one aspect of the environment may have not only first-order, but second-, third-, and higher-order effects. It is at this point that the concept of ecology comes into play.

Consider, for example, the likely effects of changing from a batch-oriented development environment to an interactive one. The changes include, among others, reconfiguring the computer system to accommodate terminals; changing the operating system to support interactive users—changes that may conceivably involve use of a completely different operating system or operating-system interface; teaching developers to use new tools in the interactive environment and to adapt to terminals (which in turn may change communications patterns within the development group). Even if the total development time is reduced, some members of the development team may take longer to do their particular jobs.

Although this list is far from complete, it gives some indication of the likely effects of a simple change in technique. As noted, these effects may cascade and multiply. A similar situation can be expected to result from the adoption of new management structures or technical procedures. Change in management of a software development group frequently causes people to alter their work patterns, as does a change from assembly-language to high-level-language programming. Some people will perform better in the new setting, while others may not perform as well. The overall impact on the software production process is not immediately clear.

What *is* clear, though, is that there is an ecology of software development environments. Changes in the environment usually have measurable direct and indirect effects. The challenge is to understand these effects and to create environments that have certain properties that promote cooperative and creative effort. These environments should be pleasant, comfortable work settings. The cost of the environment should be reasonable by some measure. Tools and procedures must exist for ensuring that software products perform efficiently, reliably, and correctly. The environment should be flexible enough that it can continue to support developers and programs even as changes occur in staffing and in the software development methodology. Finally, the environment should be instrumentable; it should be possible to obtain measure of the quality of the software development process and of the productivity of the software development organization to serve as the basis for making changes in the environment.

In short, advances in software engineering need to be integrated into software development methodologies, which are, in turn, part of specific development environments within organizations. There must be a means for determining whether or not a new technique improves the software development process in specific cases, in general, or not at all. This perspective leads to two additional key observations, one concerning the role of automated environments and one concerning the need to develop measures and metrics for software engineering techniques.

Automated development environments

The notion of an automated development environment, an integrated collection of computer-based tools that support software development, is subsumed within the notions of a software development methodology and a software development environment. This is as it should be, since automated tools do not normally exist as ends in themselves, but rather as means to an end.

Even though much effort has been put into the design, development, enhancement, and evolution of tools, it should be remembered that the purpose of a tool is to support or facilitate some other activity. (In some cases, the availability of a tool makes an activity practical that might not have been in the absence of that tool.) Tools are developed in response to perceived problems; it is rarely the case that one invents a tool and then searches for a practical application for it.

The inventor and developer of new and/or improved tools must have a solid understanding of the activities carried out by developers *and* must be able to produce tools that fit into these activities. While there has been considerable interest in concepts of "programming en-

vironments," it should be recalled that this automated support is merely part of a larger set of issues. One way to fix this idea in mind is to again use an analogy with automobile manufacturing. A Ferrari or a Rolls-Royce is produced with relatively little automated support in comparison to that available in the production of a Toyota; yet both types of production yield cars that meet the requirements of the automobile manufacturer and for which there is a well-identified market. The automation used in the production of the Toyota is intended to improve the quality of the car and to reduce the cost of production (and hence the selling price); it does not fundamentally change the end product. The use of automation is also intended to foster worker satisfaction, by relieving workers of the most mundane and repetitive tasks associated with automobile production.

Evaluation of software development environments

Along with all of the work in the development and enhancement of software development methodologies, it is necessary to work on the evaluation of environments and on how individual developers use these methodologies and their associated automated support systems.

The field of ergonomics is relevant to this study; it has been suggested[1] that there is a need for "ergonomics of software engineering." Such a field is needed to assist in obtaining data concerning how tools are used and on how they affect the quality of software development.

Ergonomics deals with the mutual adjustment of humans and machines. In the past, humans have done most of the adjustment. Now, however, new advances in hardware technology make it technically and economically possible to explore the ways in which machines can adjust to human needs.

The ergonomics of software engineering, then, is the discipline of analyzing and understanding the requirements for high-quality software development environments, and of translating this understanding into innovative design for management procedures, technical methods, and automated support systems. The major activities of this field include:

- collecting engineering and performance data about the use of tools
- collecting human factors data about programming habits and practices
- collecting data about the psychological impact of tools
- measuring the professional quality and productivity of the software engineer
- measuring the quality and performance of the software product
- translating these data into improvements in the software development process and the software development environment

Conclusion

In summary, then, the development of suitable environments for software development involves awareness of a number of different aspects of the software development organization, including its structure, and development tools, *and* of the interdependencies between organization and tools. Changes in one aspect of the environment will have impacts on other aspects, and it will be necessary to perform extensive experimentation and continuous modification in most settings to make certain that the environment is as supportive as possible. ∎

Reference

1. Spier, M. J., S. Gutz, and A. I. Wasserman, "The Ergonomics of Software Engineering—Description of the Problem Space," in *Software Engineering Environments,* ed. H. Hunke. Amsterdam: North Holland, 1981, pp. 223-234.

Past and Future Models of CASE Integration

Alan W. Brown, Peter H. Feiler and Kurt C. Wallnau

Software Engineering Institute*
Carnegie Mellon University
Pittsburgh, PA 15213
email: awb@sei.cmu.edu

Abstract

Computer-Aided Software Engineering (CASE) tools have revolutionized the way in which much of our software is currently developed. However, automated computer support for large-scale software production involves the use of a software development environment (SDE) that provides coordinated services for groups of users involved in many different tasks within the software life cycle. As a result, users of CASE tools are hearing more and more about the benefits of adopting an integrated approach to CASE. Unfortunately, no consensus has emerged regarding what integration means, or how to achieve it (CASE vendor claims notwithstanding).

The focus of this paper is an analysis of two key approaches to building integrated SDEs: the integrated project support environments (IPSE) approach, developed as part of largescale research and development efforts, and CASE Coalitions approach, resulting from strategic alliances among CASE vendors. The strengths and limitations of these approaches to integration are discussed, leading to a definition of a model of integration. This new model provides the basis for a deeper understanding of integration issues within a SDE, and points the way towards an architecture for future SDEs that combines the benefits of the IPSE and CASE Coalition approaches.

1 Introduction

Computer-Aided Software Engineering (CASE) tools have revolutionized the way in which much of our software is currently developed. CASE tools, typically supporting individual users in the automation of some task within the software development process, have undoubtedly helped many organizations in their efforts to develop better quality software to budget, within predicted timescales. However, automated computer support for large-scale software production involves the use of a software development environment that provides coordinated services for groups of users involved in many different tasks within the software life cycle. As a result, users of CASE tools are hearing more and more about the benefits of adopting

an integrated approach to tool support through the use of a central data repository such as the Information Resource Dictionary System (IRDS), integration products such as Hewlett-Packard's SoftBench and Atherton Technology's Software BackPlane, and standard tool interfaces and data interchange formats such as the Portable Common Tool Environment (PCTE) and the CASE Data Interchange Format (CDIF). Environments based on these ideas, most often called Integrated Project Support Environments (IPSEs), are likely to be a major factor in the future of computer-aided support for software development.

With the attention that IPSE technology is currently enjoying, it is important to be able to analyze the main elements of this integrated approach with the aim of providing a better understanding of what the technology will provide CASE users, and (perhaps more importantly) what it lacks. Hence, the focus of this paper is an analysis of past trends in the area of integrated support for software development, leading to the definition of a model, or paradigm, that provides the basis for a deeper understanding of integration issues within a software development environment, helps in the analysis of past and current CASE and IPSE trends, and points the way to an architecture for future IPSEs that brings together the main advantages from both the CASE and IPSE approaches.

The remainder of this paper is organized as follows. Section 2 introduces some of the history of past work on CASE and IPSE technology. Sections 3 and 4 discuss IPSE and CASE technology, concentrating on their limitations in terms of their environment architecture, integration model, and process support. Section 5 develops a model for understanding past and current CASE and IPSE trends based on the earlier analyses. This model is expanded in section 6, discussing the advantages and application of the model, and its usefulness as a basis for future implementations. The paper is concluded with some final observations in section 7.

2 Evolution of Integration Framework Architectures

The fast-developing CASE market has forced a re-evaluation of long-standing assumptions concerning

---

*Sponsored by the U.S. Department of Defense.

Reprinted from *Proceedings Fifth International Workshop on Computer-Aided Software Engineering*, pp. 36-45. Copyright © 1992 by The Institute of Electrical and Electronics Engineers, Inc.

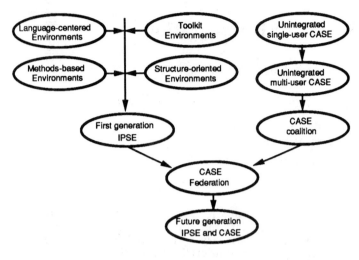

Figure 1: Evolutionary Path Toward CASE Federation.

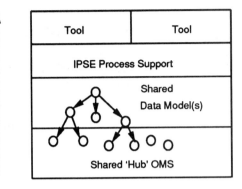

IPSEs are characterized by centralized object management services and centralized support for software process management. IPSEs evolve vertically through OMS development, data model specification and, lastly, integration of tools. Software process support can be in the form of dynamic process control, as found in ISTAR contracts, or static process control, as found in the SLCSE data model.

Figure 2: Integrated Project Support Environments.

architectures for integrated software development environments. The most significant development has been a trend away from monolithic, centralized environments toward more loosely coupled, tool-centered environments. Figure 1 depicts this trend as being driven by two independently-developed technology paths, the software environment path and the CASE tool path.

The software environment path is concentrated on the development of generic environment infrastructure technology (a.k.a. "frameworks") to provide strong software process support for large-scale software development efforts. The environment path draws upon many models of a software environment, including but not limited to those shown in Figure 1. The environment taxonomy provided in Dart *et al* [8], shown in Figure 1 as the antecedents to IPSE, provides some insight into the historical and conceptual basis of the first generation IPSE concept. In terms of commercial impact, the environment technology path culminates in the Integrated Project Support Environment (IPSE), which reflects the vision of integrated environment that formed in the early 1980's.

The CASE tool path began with the development of single-user tools that exploited graphical workstation technology. Early CASE offerings were primitive by today's standards, but evolved to support a wider range of engineering activities, including support for multiple users. Gradually, CASE vendors began to realize that no single tool could encompass all the engineering and management tasks involved in building software systems. As a result, CASE vendors are banding together and producing multi-vendor CASE coalition environments.

Unfortunately, coalition environments are composed of tools that were developed in isolation, and these tools project their own idiosyncratic views of

the software development process. The key problems with coalition environments are a lack of generality, poor evolvability, and residual egocentrism of tools, as reflected in uneven, *ad hoc* software process support. On the other hand, IPSE frameworks are highly generalized and provide strong architectural support for software process, yet suffer from a lack of CASE vendor buy-in to IPSE framework technology.

In the following two sections we examine the IPSE and CASE trends in more detail. While there are clearly benefits associated with each approach, the discussion concentrates on the limitations and pitfalls of these approaches. The table shown in figure 3 summarizes the essential characteristics of IPSE and CASE environments, and predicts the results of merging these characteristics in a Federated environment, whose details are discussed later in this report.

3 First Generation IPSE

The IPSE can be seen as an attempt to synthesize key aspects of language-centered, structure-based, methods-based and toolkit environments into an organic whole. The IPSE concept, depicted in Figure 2, is best characterized by the Stoneman reports [4], which described the requirements and architecture of Ada Programming Support Environments (APSE).

Although the Stoneman requirements were couched in terms of software environment support for Ada software development, the pedigree of these APSE concepts can be found in earlier language ¡and structure-oriented environments such as Gandalf [13] and InterLisp [23]. However, Stoneman went beyond these environment efforts to also address the important issues of scale and complexity that characterize mod-

	First Generation IPSE	CASE Coalition	CASE Federation
Environment Architecture	Central OMS Large-grained tools	multiple private OMSs Tool-function access	Cooperating service domains
Integration Model	Data-oriented integration	Control-oriented integration	Flexible control and data integration
Process Support	Centralized, explicit, large-grained process support	Localized, implicit, fine-grained process support	Service domains as process enaction virtual machines

Figure 3: Three Aspects of Environment Evolution.

ern software-intensive systems. Thus, Stoneman, and the environments that followed the Stoneman architectural vision such as SLCSE [20], ISTAR [10], PACT [25] and EAST [3] all include a strong element of software process support.

Though the implementation details vary considerably among IPSEs such as those listed above, they all share some fundamental characteristics. These architectural, integration and process characteristics of IPSEs, highlighted in Figure 3 and illustrated in Figure 1, are discussed in the following sections.

3.1 IPSE Architectures: Engineered Solutions

First-generation IPSE efforts such as CAIS [9],PCTE [2] and SLCSE [20] were undertaken by large organizations with substantial financial and technical resources at their disposal. Thus, these efforts were able to mount a full frontal assault on the IPSE problem, and resulted in engineered, fully-specified IPSE interface definitions, i.e., a set of interface specifications to a complex software system known as an IPSE framework. However, it is precisely this comprehensiveness that has been a major obstacle in gaining widespread acceptance of IPSE framework technology. There are a number of factors contributing to this ironical outcome.

First, the often-stated IPSE goal of achieving transportability[1] of tools across different IPSE installations led to IPSE framework definitions spanning all infrastructure services that may be required by tools. In the limit, this requires the definition of a virtual operating system interface. This has adverse consequences on the cost and complexity of IPSE frameworks, as well as the ultimate performance of the IPSE in its target setting. Additionally, IPSE users would be confronted with an unfamiliar interface to computer services, which implies the need for significant training, overcoming of cultural biases, and other major technology-transfer problems.

Second, the problem of managing persistent data in an IPSE raised challenging questions regarding data management technology. While conventional file systems provided support for important services such as

data distribution and versioning, they did not support associative naming schemes and data structuring techniques to capture semantic relationships among data. Database technology, however, supported associative naming and capture of semantic information, but did not adequately support distribution, versioning and long-transactions. Thus, several first-generation IPSE efforts defined a new class of data management systems, popularly called object management systems (OMSs), which blurred the distinction between database and file system. However, this new technology area proved remarkably difficult, both at the level of understanding essential OMS requirements [7], as well as in achieving adequate performance.

Third, IPSE frameworks, above all else, needed to be made sufficiently generic to suite the requirements of vastly different users. This includes support not just for the range of potential user roles which exist in the development of any one system, but support for the development of systems across different application domains. The desired degree of genericity resulted in the specification of IPSE frameworks that still required substantial tailoring on the part of customer organizations. This tailoring is most evident in the area of IPSE support for software development processes – a key requirement of IPSEs. Since processes vary across corporate-level organizations, across organizations within corporations, and even across projects, process support provided by IPSEs tended to be far shallower than that which could ultimately be supported by IPSE technology.

In combination, these IPSE framework limitations resulted in slow uptake of IPSE solutions by potential customer organizations. The high-cost, technology instability and need for tailoring proved sufficient disincentives for even large organizations. This resulted in sluggish buy-in by CASE vendors to target their software to IPSE framework specifications which after all would require significant effort given the breadth and complexity of IPSE interfaces. The lack of CASE tool support in IPSEs, particularly when measured against the proliferation of tools in the non-IPSE CASE market, further reinforced customer reluctance regarding IPSEs, resulting in a kind of "catch-22" for would-be IPSE vendors.

3.2 IPSE Integration Models – Data Orientation

IPSE frameworks designed along the model of Stoneman exhibited a prominent, central OMS. Centralized data repositories are heralded as crucial IPSE components even in more recent CASE environment developments [17] [26]. Not surprisingly, tool integration in such environments is seen largely in terms of data sharing,[2] also commonly known as data integration. However, the conceptually simple Stoneman model of data integration via a shared OMS has significant pitfalls which in practice (if not in theory)

---

[1] Often referred to colloquially as "portability".

[2] Data interchange has similar goals but different underlying mechanisms. In this paper we refer to data sharing only, as this is more in keeping with first-generation IPSE use of OMSs. Clearly, data intechange standards and data sharing standards can be seen as complementary.

provide significant obstacles to achieving IPSE integration goals.

First, there are substantial implementation questions regarding whether current-generation OMS technology can adequately support the diverse needs of CASE tools. For example, object granularity (OMS tend to support course-grained objects at the size of files) is often cited as a reason why OMSs do not provide sufficient value-added to entice CASE vendors to make use of OMS services. That is, the potential for using the OMS to achieve effective data integration among tools is substantially reduced if tool vendors make only minimal use of OMS services, for example by writing tool data to a small number of large OMS objects rather than the other way around (referred to as "nested OMSs" in [7]). In addition there are concerns about OMS performance. CASE vendors are loathe to make use of services which make their tools unattractive to end users, and poor performance is a notorious disincentive for end users.

Beyond mechanistic issues such as these, however, are far more substantial and fundamental issues relating to the practical use of OMSs even under ideal OMS implementations. These issues relate to the use of data models to describe the logical, or semantic interface to environment data. That is, the data model which describes the data in the OMS is just as much an OMS interface as the programmatic interfaces defined by IPSE framework builders. Unfortunately, in order to attain genericity of the IPSE across multiple customer sites and projects, these data model interfaces are seldom defined in any depth. In fact, one can view efforts such as [17] as attempts to address this more fundamentally important form of data repository interface, even while sacrificing some of the more advanced features of OMSs in favor of traditional relational database management services.

There are several reasons why the data model interface to the repository is so important, and why it has proven to be difficult to attain consensus on a standard data model, and difficult to use even prototypical data models.

First there is the question of complexity. As found in the pioneering PMDB [18] work, a monolithic data model of software engineering processes required the definition of many entity and relationship types. The definition of these types constitutes, in effect, a modeling of crucial aspects of the software development process (i.e., those aspects that result in the production of data). This design simultaneously imposes constraints on the process, and also requires a substantial maintenance effort to keep the data model in-tune with changes to, and enhancements of, the real world processes. Unfortunately, given the known difficulties of schema evolution (since schema changes may invalidate existing database contents) the data model acts more as an inhibitor than a support for IPSE management of software processes.

Second, from the perspective of data integration among tools, the data model represents a semantic interface to tool data. That is, the relations among tool data are interpreted by the tools to achieve communication of data – indeed, that is the whole point of the OMS. Unfortunately, there is no standard set of tools, nor do tools in the marketplace share a substantial enough base of conceptual models of tool data to allow the definition of a detailed schema to support effective data integration. Put another way, no schema is as yet definable to support data integration among already existing CASE tools in a way that cannot be achieved more simply, and more economically, through the use of conventional file systems.

The schema evolution problem is also related to the definition of data model interfaces to tools. Fixing the semantic interface of tool data in a data model constrains both the future evolution of tools (or at least their insertion into an already-populated IPSE OMS). This also limits flexibility in inserting new tools into the IPSE framework since substantial effort is required to discern and describe a data model for tool data especially for third-parties such as IPSE customers who are not themselves vendors for the inserted CASE tools.

The above are, of course, pragmatic limitations, not theoretical limitations, on data integration in IPSEs. However, pragmatics tend to be dominant issues in the success of new technologies such as IPSEs.

3.3 Centralized, Explicit Large-Grained Process Support

As discussed in the previous section, data modeling has important pragmatic limitations as a vehicle for describing and supporting software processes. While the techniques of data modeling are well understood, in-depth data modeling conflicts with the goal of achieving IPSE genericity across organizations and projects. For example, SLCSE provides an in-depth data model of the DoD-STD-2167 life-cycle process. However, SLCSE typically does not appeal to IPSE customers who do not develop software in the DoD-STD-2167 tradition.

A second aspect of IPSE process support concerns process enaction, that is, the use of an IPSE to carry out the execution of process models. The ISTAR environment is an example of an IPSE which supports process enaction, in this case through the use of ISTAR contracts which serve to model and execute work- flow aspects of project management. However, the contract mechanism provides only a limited form of process enaction, one which supports only large-grained processes (e.g., the completion of a work statement) as opposed to fine-grained processes (e.g., notifying team members of a change in status of an attribute of an object in the repository).

Fine-grained process enaction can be achieved in the context of IPSE-style data modeling provided that two technologies, or technology advances, are combined: the use of sophisticated data models which support the specification of active data values, e.g., attribute monitors and triggers, and the coupling of these active data models with tools which provide programmatic interfaces to specific tool services. While there have been some advances in the opening-up of CASE tool interfaces (see next section) there has not been much progress in combining these technologies. Further, there are many research issues which remain

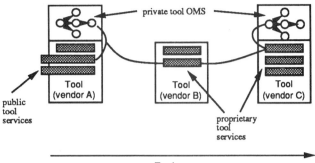

private tool OMS

public
tool
services

Tool
(vendor A)

Tool
(vendor B)

Tool
(vendor C)

proprietary
tool
services

Evolves...

*Coalition environments are characterized by specialized
"point" integration of tool services offered by coalition participants. Coalition environments evolve laterally through
integration of new tools. Difficulties in achieving data interoperability among multiple tool OMSs has resulted in
a proliferation of integration techniques, with emphasis
on control-oriented programmatic tool interfaces. Process
models supported by CASE coalitions are implicit and embedded in the hard-wired integration of tool services.*

Figure 4: CASE Coalition Environments.

open regarding fine-grained process specification and
enaction, such as how to support process dynamism
and evolution [16], how to separate process planning
from process enaction [14], at what level tasks should
be automated, and how such tasks should be specified.

Thus, while IPSEs support the formal specification of certain aspects of software processes, they also
tend to support only large-grained, static (i.e., non-
enacted) processes if they support any processes at
all.

4 CASE Coalition Environment

CASE coalition environments are being produced
as a reaction to customer demand for integrated CASE
solutions, and as a reaction to the CASE vendor realization that no individual vendor can produce all
the tools necessary to support modern software engineering processes. Although coalition environments
are not perfect, they provide a near-term pragmatic
bridge between customer demands and the ideal integrated CASE solutions. An example of a vendor coalition is the Interactive Development Environment's
Software Through Pictures, Sabre Software's Sabre-C
and Frame Technology's FrameMaker coalition integration.

Figure 4 depicts coalition environments as consisting of multiple vendor tools integrated with each
other, and making use of both public and proprietary
tool interfaces.

The key characteristic of coalition environments is
the degree to which the coalition member tools continue to behave in an egocentric manner. That is,
tools developed in isolation have evolved idiosyncratic

concepts that have an impact on software development
processes, e.g., multi-user support and version control.
In coalition environments, the tools do not surrender
such concepts in favor of common process models, but
instead continue to project their own process models.
Further, tool egocentrism is revealed in integrations in
which one or more tools act as the central integration
element, or environment driver. This tendency exag-
gerates the idiosyncratic differences between tools.

CASE coalitions are in many ways the inverse of
IPSEs. Where IPSEs provide a central database and
monolithic tools, coalition tools provide their own
databases, and tool services are becoming separately
accessible; where IPSEs support data-oriented integration via OMS services, coalition tools define their
own integration models and services, frequently rely-
ing on remote execution and other forms of control-
oriented integration; where IPSEs provide explicit
support for software process, especially large-grained
processes such as life-cycle process, coalition tools support finer-grained processes in an implicit, localized
fashion. These characteristics of coalition environments are discussed in the following sections.

4.1 Coalition Architectures: *Ad Hoc* Solu-
tions

The CASE tool industry evolved coincidentally to
(and in isolation from) the IPSE framework efforts described earlier in this paper. The lack of a widely available tool integration framework standard (a la IPSE
framework) has significantly shaped the tool technology underlying the emerging CASE industry.

Due to the relatively limited resources of typical
CASE vendors and the high rate of change in the operating system and workstation marketplaces, vendors
must balance the depth and breadth of services provided against the availability of their tools on various
popular computer platforms. The pressure to maximize product availability across a variety of hardware
platforms has produced two tendencies: use of least-
common-denominator platform services, and a high
degree of tool independence.

The least-common-denominator tendency reduces
dependencies on high-level services (such as object
management) that may not be available on a sufficiently large base of installations. A consequence of
this is that each tool tends to re-implement critically
important services, such as data and configuration
management, in ways that are not standard across
tools, and not accessible by other tools.

The isolationist tendency reduces dependencies on
the presence of other CASE tools. A consequence of
this is that tools tend to become egocentric.

The least-common-denominator and isolationist
tendencies combine to present a chaotic image of potential CASE environments. Tools implement duplicated services, rely on a non-standard set of platform
services, and provide non-standard, idiosyncratic services to the end-user. It is not surprising, then, that
the CASE vendors themselves must become intimately
involved in the integration of their tools not with other
tools in general, but with specific selections of tools,
leading to the so-called *strategic alliance.*

Thus, in contrast to the IPSE engineered environment solution, CASE coalitions are *ad hoc* in the sense that there is:

- no unifying underlying environment framework, but rather point-to-point integration solutions to specific versions of specific tools

- a collection of individual tools, each acting in an egocentric fashion

- a collection of end-user services that were designed and implemented in isolation of each other, and in the absence of a conceived process model

These characteristics of coalition environments raise troubling questions regarding the scalability of these environments to large-scale development efforts and their evolvability over time to include new tools or new versions of old tools.

4.2 Control-Oriented Tool Integration Medium

CASE tools providing complex services, such as those services offered by design and programming tools, are likely to rely on tool-specific object management services. As a result, coalition environments introduce multiple repositories, each potentially providing proprietary, tool-specific data models and data management facilities. Coalition integrations of tools with private OMSs raise issues of repository access methods, duplicated data management services and consistency maintenance across multiple tool OMSs.

The difficulties in achieving data integration in multi-OMS coalition environments is resulting in a technology push on control integration techniques. That is, rather than attempting to migrate data to the functions operating on this data (the idea underlying data integration, whether it is data sharing or data interchange), control integration migrates the functions to where the data resides. Thus, for example, the remote procedure call is a mechanism for achieving control integration. The significant result of this technology push is to entice CASE vendors to provide interfaces for the remote execution of tool services. Thus, while IPSE architectures do not discourage the development of monolithic black-box tools, coalition architectures encourage the development of tools with programmatic interfaces.

The Frame Technology Live Links mechanism is an example of an innovative integration service which addresses data integration among multiple OMSs. Live Links combines data interchange standards with remote procedure execution to achieve the effect, from the user's perspective, of all tool data residing in a single OMS. That is, objects displayed by FrameMaker may in fact be managed in a design tool's private OMS. Concepts developed to support tool coalitions, such as Live Links, are beginning to be found in commercial integration frameworks in support of generalized control integration among CASE tools [5] [19] [21].

4.3 Localized, Implicit Fine-Grained Process Support

The trend for tools to provide programmatic interfaces for the non-interactive execution of traditionally interactive services is resulting in tool architectures that support a wide variety of fine-grained, function-level tool interactions. This, in turn, raises issues concerning process interactions among tools that occur at a much finer level of granularity than supported by first-generation IPSE. Two issues of particular concern are which fine-grained processes to support (and how to support them), and how to coordinate among multiple tools, each of which supports tool-idiosyncratic software processes.

For coalition integrators, determining which tool services to integrate often depends upon what processes the integrated toolset is intended to support, and how the tools should support these processes. For example, should module interface specifications generated by a design tool be automatically imported into a programming tool's database? Conversely, should changes to these specifications in the programming tool be automatically re-imported into the design tool? The answer to these questions will be reflected in the "hard-wired" integration strategy adopted by the coalition vendors. Hard-wired, proprietary coalition integrations result in software process support that is implicit and inflexible, and hence difficult to evolve.

The absence of centralized process support in coalitions results in the primacy of tool-supported software processes carried out in the local context of an executing tool. Localized processes become more significant as user requests for tool services cascade to other tools. In control-oriented integration this will result in the migration of the user's focus from tool to tool. The seamless migration of user focus through various tools has the potential for creating a conceptually cohesive environment, but it can also result in user disorientation if each tool provides a completely different set of process-related services, e.g., multi-user support. More fundamentally, the automatic propagation of actions through many tools in environments as a result of single user actions makes the software process supported by the CASE environment difficult to reason about. Further, since the mechanics of these control integrations among tools is achieved in a point-to-point fashion, and implemented in a hard-wired fashion, the supported processes are difficult or impossible to manage and evolve over time.

5 A Conceptual Model for Integration

From the discussion of IPSE and CASE limitations above, it is clear that significant improvements in technology must take place before integrated software development environments will be realized. However, perhaps more fundamentally, the discussion points to the need for a better understanding of the issues involved in designing, constructing, and using an integrated software development environment regardless of the available technology.

In the past few years attempts at providing a framework for a better understanding of integration have

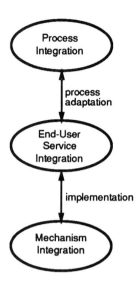

Figure 5: Three Levels of Integration.

and architectural aspects of the tools, such as process structure (e.g., client/server) and data management structure (e.g., derivers, data dictionary, database).

The middle level of integration, called "end-user services" integration, corresponds to the way in which environment services are perceived by the end-user. This refers to the high-level functions provided by tools, and integration at this level can be regarded as the specification of how services can be related in a coherent fashion. For example, the way in which a specification and a design service are seen as related through traceability of design components.

The top level of integration, called "process" integration, corresponds to the use of end-user services in the context of a particular software development process. Process integration can be regarded as a kind of process specification for how software will be developed. This specification can define a view of the process from many perspectives, spanning individual roles through larger organizational perspectives. For example, the way in which design documents gain approval before implementation is allowed to begin is a process constraint that affects the way in which end-user services are integrated.

Integration occurs within each of these 3 levels. Thus, mechanisms are integrated with mechanisms, end-user services with end-user services, and process elements with process elements. There are also relationships that span the levels. The relationship between the mechanism level and the end-user services level is an implementation relationship – end-user services may be implemented by different mechanism services, and conversely, a single mechanism may implement more than one end-user service. The relationship between the end-user services level and the process level is a process adaptation relationship – different end-user services may be combined, and tuned, to support different process requirements.

This three-level model provides a working context for understanding integration. We refer to this model of integration as the *federation paradigm*. For the moment, however, existing integration technology does not closely match this somewhat idealized model of integration. For example, many services provided by CASE tools embed process constraints that should logically be separate from the services (because these process constraints should reside in the process level). Similarly, tool services are often closely coupled to particular implementation techniques. However, we are able to speculate on the realization of such a model of integration in terms of existing CASE tools, drawing together current IPSE and CASE work.

been made, defining conceptual models for analyzing the issues that need to be addressed. Unfortunately, these models have been complex, and have focused on mechanistic aspects (i.e., a technology view) of integration with little regard for the semantic aspects (i.e., an end-user view) of an integrated environment. The European Computer Manufacturer Association (ECMA) CASE environments reference model [11] is typical in this regard. The model deals exclusively with the relationships between CASE mechanisms (e.g., the Object Management System services such as data modeling and their support for object versions) without then reflecting on the way in which those mechanisms are made available to environment end-users as services, or the way in which those services are tailored to support a particular software development process.

In this paper we propose a conceptual model for understanding integration in a software development environment based on a services view of an environment (i.e., an environment seen as a collection of services). We distinguish two levels of service – those that are available to environment end-users, and those that are mechanisms implementing the end-user services. In addition, a third level of interest is the process level at which end-user services are tailored to suit a particular development process. This is illustrated in Figure 5.

The bottom level of integration, called "mechanism" integration, corresponds to the infrastructure services discussed in the ECMA CASE reference model. Mechanism integration addresses the implementation aspects of software integration, including, but not limited to software interfaces provided by the environment infrastructure, e.g., operating system or environment framework interfaces; software interfaces provided by individual tools in the environment;

6   Realizing a Federated CASE Environment

While CASE coalitions represent the most mature technology on the integration product scale, the search for more generalized support for CASE integration is being pursued by computer manufacturers, software environment researchers, and CASE vendors and entrepreneurs. The most prominent approaches fall into two categories:

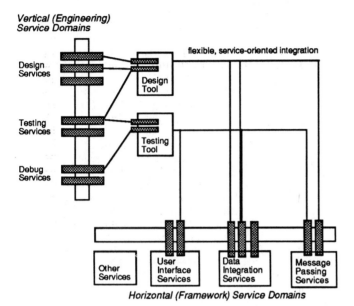

Vertical (Engineering) Service Domains

flexible, service-oriented integration

Design Services

Design Tool

Testing Services

Testing Tool

Debug Services

Other Services

User Interface Services

Data Integration Services

Message Passing Services

Horizontal (Framework) Service Domains

Federated environments are characterized by flexible, services-oriented integration. Federated environments evolve both horizontally through the introduction of new common services and vertically through the addition of new, specialized engineering services. Abstract service domains make the distinction between tool and intrinsic environment service moot, as tools integrate with services, not other tools. Service domains also encapsulate semantically related sets of services and define a virtual machine layer for describing executable software processes.

Figure 6: Federated CASE Environment.

1. Repository standards such as the CASE Interface Services proposal (CIS) [6], DEC's CDD/Plus [26], and the National Institute for Standards and Technology (NIST) Information Resources Dictionary Standard (IRDS) [15] and IRDS extensions [1].

2. Service broadcast models, such as in FIELD [19] and Hewlett-Packard's SoftBench Broadcast Message Server (BMS) [5].

While neither approach is itself sufficient for achieving CASE federation, both approaches are evolving towards each other and in unison will provide the foundations for CASE federation. Thus, while the description of CASE federation which follows is more of a vision than a reality, we believe this vision is useful for assessing the direction that integration technology is, and should, be moving.

The federated environment, depicted in Figure 6, extends the coalition view of partial access to tool functions and multiple OMSs into a generalized model of service domains. Federated environments also offer a more balanced view of data and control integration,

allowing tool integrators flexibility in making trade-off decisions concerning the cost/benefits of choosing one form over another. The service domains concept applies the IPSE concept of architectural support for software processes that can be made abstract, explicit and tailorable. Further, these processes promise to span course-grained IPSE processes through fine-grained coalition processes. These aspects of environment federation are discussed in the following sections.

6.1 Cooperating Service Domains

Both the message broadcast model and repository model encourage the abstraction of tool services into definitions of abstract service domains. In [5] and [19] protocols are defined in terms of discrete areas of tool functionality, such as editors and debuggers. The CIS specification defines service domains in terms of object types and operations associated with these types. Both models represent abstractions of tool functions into domains of semantically related services.

The process of services abstraction in both approaches has several beneficial implications:

- Modularizes tool services into more cohesive, complete service packages.

- Counters tool egocentrism by emphasizing what services are provided, not who provides them.

- Supports alternative service implementations, perhaps coexisting within an environment, by separating the service interface from the service itself.

- Facilitates recognition of commonly provided services and reorganization of these services into common framework services.

The cumulative result of these implications is the evolution towards environments providing cooperating sets of services. That is, framework services such as CM and documentation can be shared by many tools, while engineering services can be provided to the end user by domain-specific tools, such as structured design tools.

6.2 Flexible Control and Data Integration

CASE repository standards emphasize data integration while broadcast models emphasize control integration. Both models are evolving towards each other through the addition of control-integration services in repository standards [27], and the implementation of message broadcast services on current-generation IPSE frameworks. The resulting frameworks promise tool integrators flexibility in choosing among integration mechanisms.

CASE repository standards represent an architectural approach to tool integration very similar to that in IPSEs. The most significant variation from past realizations of IPSEs is the current exploration of object-orientation in some (but not all) repository data models. Object-orientation, by associating functional behavior with OMS object types, provides a data model basis for tool integration at the level of remotely-executable tool services, where tool services are accessed through references to repository objects. Note that object-orientation does not itself support remote service execution, nor does it imply a particular implementation. Instead, the data model provides uniform interfaces that can support a variety of remote execution implementations.

The service broadcast models represent a fundamentally different approach to tool federation. Rather than envisioning a centrally shared data modeling service, broadcast models envision a centrally shared message broadcast network and tool communication protocols. The conceptual model supported by this form of tool federation is one in which tools are thought of as nodes in a distributed network of CASE service nodes, with tool services accessed by requests broadcast in a well-defined protocol.

While object-oriented repository models associate tool services with data objects that appear to be centrally located, the message broadcast model separates the service from the data and treats all tool services as requests to a network of distributed services. We can view these approaches as complementary, with repository standards supporting data-oriented federation and message systems supporting control-oriented federation.

Flexibility in the choice of control or data integration is useful when considering the integration of tools within tool families (i.e., tools sharing significant functionality) versus the integration of tools in different families. For example, the coding/debugging/testing tool family will benefit from tight data sharing of an intermediate language and control integration to allow a rapid migration of user focus among the tools. A similarly "tight" integration may be cost-justifiable among the requirements/design tool family. However, it may not be necessary, or cost-effective, to require such extensive integration among tools that belong to different families.

6.3 Service Domains as Software Process Virtual Machines

Abstract service domains represent virtual interfaces to process abstractions in the same way that the implicit integration of tool services in coalition environments represents a kind of process encoding. For example, within a horizontal service domain such as configuration management, services can be provided that support various abstract models [12]. Such services can be viewed as a virtual machine layer for encoding those software process elements that depend upon configuration management and multi-user coordination. Similar examples can be drawn from vertical service domains.

Service domains will support a wide variety of mechanisms for process enaction. For example, a library of programmatic interfaces for configuration management could easily be made available to a process program interpreter [22]. Service domains provide a bridge between tool technology and IPSE technology, and herald a new generation of IPSEs, i.e., environments whose integration is driven by the particular software processes to be supported by the environment.

7 Conclusions

IPSEs represent an early vision of software environment architectures to support large-scale software development efforts. Despite a sophisticated array of environment framework technology, particularly with respect to object management and process support, IPSEs have failed to generate CASE vendor "buy-in." Instead, the CASE market has developed parallel to, and in relative isolation from, IPSE technology. As a result, CASE tools have evolved into remarkably functional systems, but are weak in terms of integrability and do not adequately support large-grained software processes. CASE vendors are forming coalitions in order to satisfy market demand for integrated, cohesive CASE support for software processes. However, CASE coalitions are only a stop-gap solution because the coalitions do not easily evolve to incorporate new tools and methods.

In an attempt to better understand the integration issues, we have proposed a model of integration that separates process, end-user service and mechanism concepts, relating them in a three-schema view of integration not unlike the ANSI/SPARC database model [24]. This model provides a vision for the future that we can consider the basis for integrated environment architectures. Such an implementation could combine the best features of available software environment technology, represented by the IPSE and coalition technologies, and merge them in the form of Federated CASE environments.

Federated CASE is based upon recent advances in integration technology, including repository standards and message broadcast systems, and the coalition-driven trend for open CASE tool architectures. The fundamental concept in the federated environment is the service domain. Service domains are abstractions of horizontal (typically framework-supplied) and vertical (typically tool-supplied) services. Service domains support flexible integration by rendering the implementation of a service, i.e., who provides the service, irrelevant. Service domains also provide a mechanism for migrating tool-originated services into common framework services, e.g., Live Links. Finally, service domains provide a virtual machine layer for process enaction. This virtual machine layer will provide the basis for exploration of process specification and enaction, and ultimately result in a new generation of IPSE technology in support of environment instantiation through flexible, process-driven tool integration.

References

1. Beyer, Hugh, R. Proposal For Extending Dictionary Standards to Support CASE:Proposed ANSI X3H4 ATIS Extensions. ANSI X3H4 Committee.

2. Boudier, G., Gallo, T., Minot, R., Thomas, I. An Overview of PCTE and PCTE+. Proceedings of ACM SIGSOFT/ SIGPLAN Software Engineering Symposium on Practical Software Engineering Environments, Boston, MA, 1988.

3. Bourguignon, J.P. Structuring for Managing Complexity. In Managing Complexity in Software

Engineering, Mitchell, R.J., Ed., Peter Peregrinus Ltd., 1990.

4. Buxton, J., Druffel, L. Requirements for an Ada Programming Support Environment: Rationale for Stoneman. Proceedings of IEEE Conference on Computer Software and Applications (COMPSAC80), Chicago, IL, October 1980.

5. Cagen, M.R. "The H.P. SoftBench Environment: An Architecture for a New Generation of Software Tools". HewlettPackard Journal 41, 3 (June 1990).

6. CASE Interface Services Base Document. Digital Equipment Corporation, Nashua, NH, 1990.

7. Clow, G., Ploedereder, E., Issues in Designing Object Management Systems. In Lecture Notes in Computer Science, volume 467, Fred Long, Ed., Springer-Verlag, 1990.

8. Dart, S., Ellison, R., Feiler, P., Habermann, N. "Software Development Environments". IEEE Computer Magazine (November 1987).

9. DoD-STD-1838A, Common Ada Programming Support Environment (APSE) Interface Set (CAIS), Revision A. U.S. Department of Defense, 1988.

10. Dowson, M. ISTAR An Integrated Project Support Environment. Proceedings of 2nd ACM SIGSOFT/SIGPLAN Software Engineering Symposium on Practical Software Engineering Environments, December 1986.

11. European Computer Manufacturer's Association (ECMA). A Reference Model for Computer Assisted Software Engineering Environment Frameworks. ECMA/TC33/TGRM, 1990.

12. Feiler, P. Configuration Management Models in Commercial Environments. Tech. Rept. CMU/SEI-91-TR-7, ADA235782, Software Engineering Institute, Carnegie Mellon University, March 1991.

13. Habermann, A.N. and Notkin, D. "Gandalf: Software Development Environments". IEEE Transactions on Software Engineering (December 1986), 1117-1127.

14. Huff, K. Plan-Based Intelligent Assistance: An Approach to Supporting the Development Process. Ph.D. Th., Computer and Information Science Dept., University of Massachusetts, September 1989. COINS 89-97.

15. ANSI X3H4, Draft Proposal American National Standard, IRDS, National Institute of Standards and Technology (NIST), Gathersburg, MD, 1986.

16. Katayama, T., Suzuki, M. Mechanisms for Software Process Dynamics. Proceedings of the IEEE/ACM 4th International Software Process Workshop, 1988.

17. Mercurio, V.J., Meyers, B.F., Nisbet, A.M., Radin, G. "AD/Cycle strategy and architecture". IBM Systems Journal 29, 2 (1990).

18. Penedo, M.H., Stuckle, E.D. PMBD A Project Master Database for Software Engineering Environments. Proceedings of 8th International IEEE Conference on Software Engineering, London, England, August, 1985.

19. Reiss, S. "Interacting with the FIELD Environment". Software Practice and Experience 20 (June 1990).

20. Strelich, T. The Software Life Cycle Support Environment (SLSCE) A Computer-Based Framework for Developing Software Systems. Proceedings of ACM SIGSOFT/SIGPLAN Software Engineering Symposium on Practical Software Engineering Environments, Boston, MA, 1988.

21. Swaine, M. "Applications are Talking Too". MacUser (May 1991).

22. Taylor, N., Belz, F., Clarke, L., Osterweil, L., Selby, R., Wileden, J., Wolf, A., Young, M. Foundations of the Arcadia Environment Architecture. Proceedings of ACM SIGSOFT/SIGPLAN Software Engineering Symposium on Practical Software Engineering Environments, Boston, MA, 1988.

23. Teitelman, W., Masinter, M. "The Interlisp Programming Environment". IEEE Computer 14, 4 (1981).

24. Tsichritzis, D., and Klug, A. (eds.). "The ANSI/X3/SPARC DBMS Framework: Report of the Study Group on Data Base Management Systems". Information Systems 3 (1978).

25. Version Management Common Services. G.I.E. Emeraude, 38 Bd Henri Selier, 92154 Suresnes, France, 1988.

26. Yourdon, E. "DEC's CASE Environment". American Programmer 3, 1 (January 1990).

27. Zarrella, P. CASE Tool Integration and Standardization. Tech. Rept. CMU/SEI-90-TR-14, ADA235640, Software Engineering Institute, Carnegie Mellon University, 1990.

Definitions of Tool Integration for Environments

IAN THOMAS, Hewlett-Packard
BRIAN A. NEJMEH
Innovative Software Engineering Practices

Reprinted from *IEEE Software*, Vol. 9, No. 2, March 1992, pp. 29-35. Copyright © 1992 by The Institute of Electrical and Electronics Engineers, Inc. All rights reserved.

◆ *What does "integration" mean? Integration is a property of tool interrelationships. Understanding it will help us design better tools and integration mechanisms.*

There has been considerable discussion in recent years about the integration of software-engineering environments, perhaps beginning with the use of "integrated" in the term IPSE (integrated project-support environment) and continuing with the coinage of the terms ICASE (integrated CASE) and ISEE (integrated software-engineering environment).

Although some have tried to define precisely what "integration" means in these terms, we believe these definitions are not as precise as they should be. We believe integration is not a property of a single tool, but of its relationships with other elements in the environment, chiefly other tools, a platform, and a process. Of these, we believe the key notion is the *relationships* between tools and the properties of these relationships.

Tool integration is about the extent to which tools agree. The subject of these agreements may include data format, user-interface conventions, use of common functions, or other aspects of tool construction. To determine how well tools agree — and how well they are integrated into an environment — we propose a framework that focuses on *defining* integration, independently of the mechanisms and approaches used to support integration.

Our purpose is to identify the goals of integration and propose some questions that establish what information is needed to know that these goals have been reached. In this respect, we are following Victor Basili and David Weiss's approach for metrics development, in which they advocate identifying goals, questions that refine the goals, and quantifiable metrics

that provide the information to answer the questions.[1] However, we do not propose quantifiable integration metrics here.

Anthony Wasserman identified five kinds of integration: *platform*, which is concerned with framework services; *presentation*, concerned with user interaction; *data*, concerned with the use of data by tools; *control*, concerned with tool communication and interoperation; and *process*, concerned with the role of tools in the software process.[2]

We extend Wasserman's analysis by building on his definitions of presentation, data, control, and process integration. Our elaborations are based on experience with framework services and integrated environments and an analysis of the issues. Because our focus is on the relationship among tools, we do not consider platform integration, which we regard as providing the basic elements on which the agreement policies and usage conventions for tools are built.

TWO POINTS OF VIEW

There are two points of view in the discussion of integration: the environment user's and the environment builder's. The environment user is concerned with perceived integration at the environment's interface. The user desires a seamless tool collection that facilitates the construction of systems on time and within budget. The environment builder, who assembles and integrates tools, is concerned with the feasibility and effort needed to achieve this perceived integration.

The user would like to see well-integrated tools; the builder would like to see easily integrable tools. Both perspectives are important, and many of the integration properties we describe are meaningful from both points of view.

Our more precise way of looking at integration has proved useful to four groups: users, tool evaluators, tool writers,

and framework-technology builders. It provides them with a definitional framework in which

♦ users can characterize areas in their environments in which tools should be better integrated;

♦ tool evaluators can identify criteria to evaluate tool sets they want to include in an integrated environment;

♦ tool writers can examine design and architectural issues as they develop the next generation of integrated environments and identify good practice for the use of emerging integration-support mechanisms; and

♦ framework-technology builders can explain how proposed and existing integration mechanisms contribute to improvements in integration in terms of the properties described here.

We have tried to separate integration properties so as to identify them as clearly and independently as possible. In practice, we know that tool writers can use a single integration-support mechanism to improve several integration properties.

TOOL INTEGRATION

The goal of a software-engineering environment is "to provide effective support for an effective software process."[3] We believe support is more effective if the environment is integrated — if all its components function as part of a single, consistent, coherent whole.

Integration means that things function as members of a coherent whole. When we say, "*A* is well integrated with *B*," we are really making many statements because *A* and *B* are composites with many characteristics. To understand how well *A* is integrated with *B* requires a careful examination and comparison of each characteristic.

We extend Wasserman's four kinds of integration by identifying several well-defined properties that characterize the various integration relationships between

> There are two viewpoints in the discussion of integration: the environment user's and the environment builder's.

tools. The software-engineering community generally agrees on the importance of these four tool relationships, but the definitions of integration properties are not as precise as they should be.

Figure 1 shows an entity-relationship diagram depicting a single tool, four relationships, and our elaborated properties for each relationship. The four well-known relationships are

♦ *Presentation*: The goal of presentation integration is to improve the efficiency and effectiveness of the user's interaction with the environment by reducing his cognitive load.

♦ *Data*: The goal of data integration is to ensure that all the information in the environment is managed as a consistent whole, regardless of how parts of it are operated on and transformed.

♦ *Control*: The goal of control integration is to allow the flexible combination of an environment's functions, according to project preferences and driven by the underlying processes the environment supports.

♦ *Process*: The goal of process integration is to ensure that tools interact effectively in support of a defined process.

Our approach uses binary relationships, which raises the issue of whether integration should be defined as how well *two* tools are integrated or if it should be defined as how well *many* tools are integrated. We believe that the second definition can be adequately captured as an aggregate property, derived from how well individual tool pairs are integrated. However, our focus on how well two tools are integrated does *not* mean that we support integration mechanisms that allow "private" tool agreements. It is important to distinguish a *definition* of integration from a good *mechanism* for integration support.

Presentation integration. The goal of reducing a user's cognitive load should apply to individual tools, tool sets, and the environment as a whole. It can be achieved by letting users reuse their experience in interacting with other tools by

♦ reducing the number of interaction and presentation paradigms in the environment,

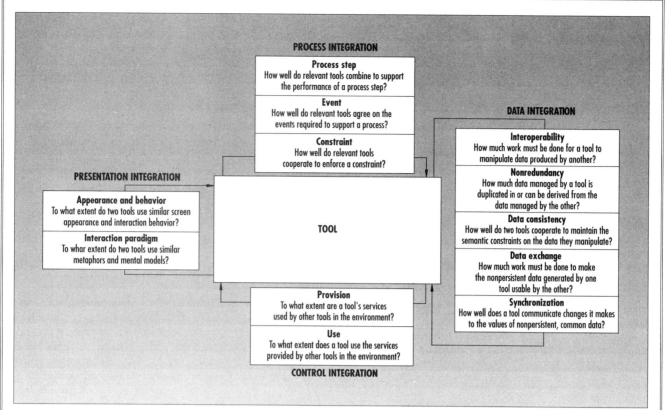

Figure 1. Entity-relationship diagram depicting a single tool, four relationships, and elaborated properties for each relationship.

♦ providing interaction and presentation paradigms that match the user's mental models,

♦ meeting the user's response-time expectations, and

♦ ensuring that correct, useful information is maintained at the disposition of the user.

We identify two properties in this class, which we base on the relationships between the user interfaces of two tools: appearance and behavior integration and interaction-paradigm integration.

Appearance and behavior. This property answers the question, How easy is it to interact with one tool, having already learned to interact with the other? In other words, how similar are the tools' screen appearance and interaction behavior?

Two tools are said to be well integrated with respect to appearance and behavior integration if a user's experience with and expectations of one can be applied to the other.

Appearance and behavior integration captures the similarities and differences between the *lexical* level of the two tools' user interfaces — how the mouse clicks, the format of the menu bars, and so on. It also covers some aspects of their *syntactic* level differences and similarities — the order of commands and parameters, uniformity of the presentation of choices in dialogue boxes, and so on.

Both Motif and OpenLook specify compliance levels that are relevant here. However, both leave aspects of appearance and behavior undefined, which may lead to unnecessary, confusing differences between the appearance and behavior of two tools.

A broader definition of appearance and behavior should also cover response-time aspects. Similar interactions with two tools should have similar response times for them to be well integrated with respect to this property. Appearance and behavior might also include using a common meaning for verbs and commands.

Interaction paradigm. This property answers the question, "How easy is it to interact with one tool having already learned the interaction paradigm of the other?" In other words, to what extent do two tools use similar metaphors and mental models to minimize learning and usage interference?

Two tools are said to be well integrated with respect to interaction-paradigm integration if they use the same metaphors and mental models.

Clearly, it is important to balance the use of one versus many metaphors. A sin-gle metaphor may be awkward or ill-adapted for some cases, while using many metaphors may provide one that is well-suited for each case but makes it difficult to transfer experience between tools.

For example, a tool to access and browse a database may use a filing-system metaphor, with filing cabinets, drawers, dossiers, and so on. This metaphor might impose a strict containment relationship between cabinets and drawers and between drawers and dossiers. Another tool for accessing the same information may present a different metaphor that involves navigating around a hypertext structure, with no emphasis on containment relationships.

A user who must use both tools may be confused by the different navigation metaphors, so we would say that these two tools are not well-integrated with respect to their interaction paradigms.

Data integration. The information manipulated by tools includes persistent and nonpersistent data (which does not survive the execution of the tools that are sharing or exchanging it). The goal is to maintain consistent information, regardless of how parts of it are operated on and transformed by tools.

Data integration between two tools is not

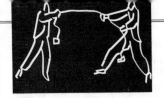

relevant when they deal with disjoint data. Also the data-integration properties should reflect the use of the "same" data by tools, even if that data is represented differently or can be deduced from other data.

We have identified five properties in this class, defined between the data management/representation aspects of two tools: interoperability, nonredundancy, data consistency, data exchange, and synchronization.

Interoperability. Suppose a tool using some data in the environment has a certain view of that data. Another tool may need to use some or all of the data used by the first tool but may have a different view of that data. How views differ can range from the peculiarities of character representations to differences in the information model each tool assumes and captures in schemas. Two tools may even assume different semantics for data stored using the same schema.

The interoperability-integration property answers the question, "How much work must be done to make the data used by one tool manipulable by the other?" In other words, what must be done for the two tools to see the data as a consistent whole?

This property illustrates the different viewpoints of the user and builder. The environment user may perceive that two tools are well integrated because they present a common schema at the user interface, even if each tool actually has a different data model. The environment builder will see that the tools are not well integrated, because they use different data models and require a lot of work to make the data of one tool manipulable by the other.

Two tools are said to be well integrated with respect to interoperability integration if they require little work for them to be able to use each other's data.

For example, suppose a design tool produces data in a certain format and that data must be manipulated by another tool that expects data in a different format. To make it available to the second tool, the data must be run through a conversion program. From the environment builder's point of view, these two design tools are not as well integrated with respect to interoperability integration as two tools that use the same format and model. If the user must initiate the conversion, the tools are also not well integrated from the user's point of view.

Tools are well integrated when they have a common view of data. Some environments achieve this common view by using common internal structures for the information they manipulate (such as programs and design artifacts). Examples include the Interlisp environment and Rational's Ada environment. Other environments use common schemas. Examples include Pact[4] and IBM's AD/Cycle Information Model.[5]

Nonredundancy. This property answers the question, "How much data managed by a tool is duplicated in or can be derived from the data managed by the other?" In other words, it identifies the redundancy in the data that the two tools independently store and manipulate.

Two tools are said to be well integrated with respect to nonredundancy integration if they have little duplicate data or data that can be automatically derived from other data.

Redundant information in a database, whether duplicate or derived, is undesirable because it is difficult to maintain consistency. Nonredundancy is relevant even if the tools store their data in the same database.

Well-integrated tools should minimize redundant data. For example, suppose two project-management tools, which operate on the same data, use the concept of a project task. One assumes that tasks have two attributes, start_date and end_date; the other assumes that tasks have two attributes, start_date and duration. Although both tools use the same start_date, they are not well integrated from the builder's

> ## Tools are well integrated when they have a common view of data.

point of view because duration can be derived from the start_date and end_date.

Designers of environments that must maintain consistent duplicate and derived data must choose strategies for timing the updates to the duplicate and derived data — the well-known "refresh-time" problem.

Avoiding duplicated data in a database still allows the use of *replicated* data, which a distributed database might provide to improve robustness or performance.

Data consistency. Maintaining the consistency of duplicate or derived data is a frequently observed special case of how to maintain some general semantic constraint on the data. For example, a designer may want to ensure that the sum of certain attributes in the database is less than some value: Tool 1 manipulates some data A, Tool 2 manipulates some data B, and there is a semantic constraint relating the permissible values of A and B.

The data-consistency property answers the question, "How well do the tools indicate the actions they perform on data that is subject to some semantic constraint so that other parts of the environment can act appropriately?" In other words, how well do two tools cooperate to maintain the semantic constraints on the data they manipulate?

Two tools are said to be well integrated with respect to data-consistency integration if each tool indicates its actions and the effects on its data that are the subject of semantic constraints that also refer to data managed by the other tool.

Data exchange. Two tools may want to exchange data. The data may be in the form of initial values communicated from the first tool to the second when it starts execution or it may be in the form of values passed to a tool while it is executing. To exchange data effectively, the tools must agree on data format and semantics.

This property answers the question, "How much work must be done to make the data generated by one tool usable by the other?" In other words, what must be done to make the data generated by one executing tool manipulable by the other?

Two tools are said to be well integrated

with respect to data-exchange integration if little work on format and semantics is required for them to be able to exchange data.

This definition is very similar to the interoperability definition, but data-exchange integration also applies to nonpersistent data.

Some environments may allow the environment builder, rather than the tool designer, to decide which data is persistent. We make the distinction between data-exchange and interoperability because the mechanisms that support data-exchange integration may be different from the mechanisms that support interoperability integration, although some environments may use the data-management system to implement interoperability integration. The definition of persistent data is independent of whether or not the data is stored in a database. Data-exchange integration is also relevant whether or not the two tools use the same database.

Suppose you have two project-management tools. The first is a scheduling tool that displays a network of project tasks, each represented as an icon. Each task icon has a user-defined name represented as a task-type attribute in the environment's database. The second tool is a time sheet that lets the user record time spent on project tasks. The user interface to the second tool is a spreadsheet, with each column headed by a task identifier that is used as an account number for charging. This task identifier is also stored as a task-type attribute in the environment's database.

Now suppose the user wants to copy a task icon from the scheduling tool and paste it into the task-identifier cell of the time-sheet tool, which would then display the task identifier of the task icon. Clearly, both tools must agree on the format and semantics of the data exchanged via the copy-and-paste mechanism.

Synchronization. In general, a single tool will manipulate some persistent data and will also need nonpersistent data for execution. This is also true of a set of cooperating tools, which typically will manipulate persistent data (and interoperability, nonredundancy, and data-consistency

properties determine how well integrated they are to do this). Cooperating tools may also need to maintain the consistency of the nonpersistent data that may be replicated in several tools in a set.

The synchronization property answers the question, "How well does a tool communicate changes it makes to the values of nonpersistent, common data so that other tools it is cooperating with may synchronize their values for the data?" Two tools are well integrated with respect to synchronization integration if all the changes to all shared nonpersistent data made by one tool are communicated to the other.

Suppose a set of development tools includes a debugger and a browser. The set might have been constructed with the idea that the debugger and browser would share a single current_source_code_line position. When the debugger stops at a breakpoint, it changes the current_source_code_line position, which the browser uses to display the lines above and below current_source_code_line. Both tools need a consistent view of this datum and must inform each other of changes they make to it.

This definition is very similar to data-consistency integration, except it applies to nonpersistent data. We make the distinction because the mechanisms used to support synchronization may be different from the mechanisms used to support data consistency. Both mechanisms must define a refresh time to communicate changes between tools.

Control integration. To support flexible function combinations, tools must share functionality. Ideally, all the functions offered by all the tools in an environment should be accessible (as appropriate) to all other tools, and the tools that provide functions need not know what tools will be constructed to use their functions.

For tools to share functionality, they must be able to communicate the operations to be performed. Because operations require data, the tools must also communicate data or data references. In this re-

gard, control integration complements data integration.

Data integration addresses data representation, conversion, and storage issues; control integration addresses control-transfer and service-sharing issues. We have identified two properties, defined on the control relationship between two tools: provision and use.

Provision. This property answers the question, "To what extent are a tool's services used by other tools in the environment?"

A tool is said to be well integrated with respect to provision integration if it offers services other tools in the environment require and use.

Suppose you are building a project-management tool that requires the user to enter a brief description of project tasks. Such a tool requires an editing service to enter textual task descriptions. In this case, provision integration refers to the extent to which the editing tool provides the services required by the project-management tool.

> Achieving high use
> integration requires
> modular tools.

Use. This property answers the question, "To what extent does a tool use the services provided by other tools in the environment?"

A tool is well integrated with respect to use integration if it appropriately uses the services offered by other tools in the environment.

Achieving high use integration requires modular tools. A tool written without regard for replacing services that it provides with similar services will not achieve good use integration. The same tool could be written so that it either expects certain services in its execution environment and provides a means of incorporating such services into the tool or provides a convenient way of replacing a tool-provided service with a comparable service offered by another tool in the environment.

The project-management tool in the earlier example would be highly inte-

grated with the editing tool with respect to use integration if it used the editing tool's services. The project-management tool would then have to provide a convenient way to replace its text-editing services with those offered by the editing tool.

Process integration. There are three dimensions to ensuring that tools interact well to support a defined process:[6]

♦ A *process step* is a unit of work that yields a result. Assessing design performance is a process step.

♦ A *process event* is a condition that arises during a process step that may result in the execution of an associated action. Conducting a successful compile may result in the scheduling of a unit test.

♦ A *process constraint* restricts some aspect of the process. A constraint might be that no person can have more than 10 process steps assigned to them concurrently.

A tool embodies a set of assumptions about the processes in which it may be used; two tools are well integrated with respect to process if their assumptions about the process are consistent. The degree of consistency between the process assumptions of tools strongly influences the degree of potential process integration for all the process-integration properties we identified.

Obviously, tools that make few process assumptions (like most text editors and compilers) are easier to integrate than tools that make many process assumptions (like those that support a specific design method prescriptively or generate test skeletons from a design notation).

Whether we need to consider how well two tools are integrated with respect to process integration depends on whether they are both relevant to the same process step. For example, the relevant tools in asessing design performance might be a graphical design tool and a performance-analysis tool. Other tools that may be irrelevant to this process step are the assembler and debugger. Whether a tool is relevant or irrelevant depends on the process property.

We identified three process-integration properties, defined on the process relationship between two tools: process step, event, and constraint.

Processs step. This property answers the question, "How well do relevant tools in the environment combine to support the performance of a process step?"

The performance of a process step will often be decomposed into executions of various tools. Tools often have preconditions that must be true before they can perform work to achieve their goals. A tool's preconditions are satisfied when other tools achieve their goals.

Tools are said to be well integrated with respect to process-step integration if the goals they achieve are part of a coherent decomposition of the process step and if accomplishing these goals lets other tools achieve their own goals.

Tools can be poorly integrated for several reasons. The goals achieved by two relevant tools can be incompatible in that one tool makes it harder for the other tool to achieve its goals. Similarly, the goals achieved by one relevant tool can be incompatible with the preconditions necessary for the other relevant tool to execute.

Suppose a compile-and-debug process step uses a C++ preprocessor, a C compiler, and a debugger. The C++ preprocessor accepts C++ and generates C, which is compiled. The debugger, which is intended to support source-level debugging, uses information generated by the C compiler. It does not know that the C program was generated by a C++ preprocessor.

In this case, the C++ compilation chain and the debugger are not well integrated with respect to process-step integration because the functions of the C++ compilation chain and the debugger do not form a coherent decomposition of the compile-and-debug step that would permit source-level debugging of the C++ program.

Event. This property answers the question, "How well do relevant tools in the environment agree on the events they need to support a particular process?"

There are two aspects to event agreement. First, a relevant tool's preconditions

> We should be designing and building tools to take advantage of the integration support mechanisms available.

should reflect events generated by other relevant tools. Second, a relevant tool should generate events that help satisfy other relevant tools' preconditions.

Tools are said to be well integrated with respect to event integration if they generate and handle event notifications consistently (when one tool indicates an event has occurred, another tool responds to that event).

Suppose you want to plan and schedule a module unit test. To do so, the process requires that

1. the module be completely developed (for example, it has run through the Unix lint tool cleanly),

2. the module be checked into the configuration-management system, and

3. test personnel be available.

In other words, the notification of all three events is a precondition to unit-test scheduling. In this case, the lint tool might generate an event indicating a module has passed through lint cleanly, the configuration-management tool might generate an event indicating a completed module has been checked into the system, and a resource-availability tool might generate an event indicating that test personnel are available. These tools would be well integrated with the unit-test scheduling tool because they generate the events necessary to satisfy its preconditions.

Events have some similarities with the data-trigger mechanisms that are part of some persistent object-management systems. One major difference is that events may be signaled without changes to persistent or nonpersistent common data; they indicate only that something of interest and relevance to the process has occurred.

Constraint. This property answers the question, "How well do relevant tools in the environment cooperate to enforce a constraint?"

There are two aspects to enforcing a constraint. First, one tool's permitted functions may be constrained by another's functions. Second, a tool's functions may constrain another tool's permitted functions.

Tools are said to be well integrated with respect to constraint integration if they make similar assumptions about the range of constraints they recognize and respect.

At first glance, constraint integration may appear to be the same as data-consistency integration. However, data-consistency integration is concerned with constraints on data values; whereas, constraint integration is concerned with constraints on process states and how such process constraints affect tool functioning. If process-state information, such as the status of various process steps, is modeled and managed in the environment's data-management system, then the mechanisms that support data-consistency integration can also support constraint integration.

Suppose a process constraint is that the same person cannot both code and test a module. In this case, if the resource-allocation tool that assigns a coding task to a person then prohibits the configuration-management tool from letting that person check out the same module for testing, the resource-allocation tool is well integrated with respect to constraint integration with the configuration-management tool.

In this article, we have emphasized definitions of integration properties on relationships between tools rather than the specific integration-support mechanisms.

The designs of integration-support mechanisms and tools do not proceed independently. Integration-support mechanisms are not developed assuming a constant model of how tools are written. Similarly, tools and tool architectures must evolve to take advantage of the new generation of integration-support mechanisms.

Instead of asking how the integration-support mechanisms support tools, we should be asking how to design and build tools so they can best take advantage of the mechanisms available. Brian Nejmeh offers advice on how to do this.[7]

This article describes a model of environment frameworks that identifies framework services, tools that offer other services, data-management services, and so on. Some proponents of object-orientation argue that these distinctions are false and unnecessary — that all services can be provided by operations associated with objects. However, it is still true that some object types are defined as important to the system and that these objects have predefined operations. Also, each object requires execution-engine services and persistent data management for its implementation, in addition to interobject communication. The integration properties we have identified are largely independent of an environment's technology base and are relevant to object-oriented environments.

We believe other environment elements — including the characterization of the software process — have relationships that could be analyzed using this technique. We look forward to extending and refining this set of relationships and properties as our understanding of tool integration grows. ◆

ACKNOWLEDGMENTS

A number of the initial ideas for this work evolved in working-group discussions involving Tim Collins, Kevin Ewert, Colin Gerety, and Jon Gustafson. We also received helpful comments from Frank Belz, Mark Dowson, Anthony Earl, John Favaro, Peter Feiler, Read Fleming, Steve Gaede, Mike Monegan, Dave Nettles, Huw Oliver, Lolo Penedo, Bill Riddle, Ev Shafrir, and Lyn Uzzle. The National Institute of Standards and Technology Working Group on ISEEs' subgroup on integration generated many test cases we used to refine these ideas.

REFERENCES

1. V.R. Basili and D.M. Weiss, "A Methodology for Collecting Valid Software Engineering Data," *IEEE Trans. Software Eng.*, Nov. 1984, pp. 728-738.
2. A.I. Wasserman, "Tool Integration in Software Engineering Environments," in *Software Engineering Environments: Proc. Int'l Workshop on Environments*, F. Long, ed., Springer-Verlag, Berlin, 1990, pp 137-149.
3. V. Stenning, "On the Role of an Environment," *Proc. Int'l Conf. Software Eng.*, IEEE CS Press, Los Alamitos, Calif., 1987, pp. 30-34.
4. M.I. Thomas, "Tool Integration in the Pact Environment," *Proc. Int'l Conf. Software Eng.*, IEEE CS Press, Los Alamitos, Calif., 1989, pp. 13-22.
5. V.J. Mercurio et al., "AD/Cycle Strategy and Architecture," *IBM Systems J.*, Vol. 29, No. 2, 1990, pp. 170-188.
6. M. Dowson, B. Nejmeh, and W. Riddle, "Fundamental Software Process Concepts," Ref. No. 7-7, Software Design and Analysis, Boulder, Colo., 1990.
7. B. Nejmeh, "Characteristics of Integrable Software Tools," Tech. Report 89036-N, Software Productivity Consortium, Herndon, Va., 1989.

Ian Thomas works on software-engineering environment infrastructure at Software Design and Analysis, a research and consulting company. While at Hewlett-Packard, he worked on next-generation object-oriented broadcast mechanisms to support control integration and the use of the Portable Common Tool Environment's Object-Management System to support data integration. His research interests include software-engineering environment frameworks, data management for software-engineering environments, environment-integration technology, and software process support.

Thomas received a BS in applied mathematics from the University of Wales, Aberystwyth and an MS in computer science from the University of London. He is a member of ACM and the IEEE Computer Society.

Brian Nejmeh is president of Innovative Software Engineering Practices (Instep), a firm specializing in software process improvement. Before founding Instep, Nejmeh led several groups at the Software Productivity Consortium. He has written widely on software-engineering topics and is the software-engineering editor for *Communications of the ACM*.

Nejmeh received a BS in computer science from Allegheny College and an MS in computer science from Purdue University. He is a member of Phi Beta Kappa, ACM, and the IEEE Computer Society.

Address questions about this article to Thomas at Software Design and Analysis, 444 Castro St., Ste. 400, Mountain View, CA 94041; Internet thomas@sda.com or to Nejmeh at Instep, 13526 Copper Bed Rd., Herndon, VA 22071; Internet nejmeh@instep.com.

Process Integration in CASE Environments

PEIWEI MI *and* WALT SCACCHI,
University of Southern California

R

Reprinted from *IEEE Software*, Vol. 9, No. 2, March 1992, pp. 45-53. Copyright © 1992 by The Institute of Electrical and Electronics Engineers, Inc. All rights reserved.

◆ *At a higher level than tool or object integration, process integration makes the implicit chain of development tasks explicit. This lets us develop process-driven software environments.*

esearch in CASE environments has focused on two kinds of integration: tool and object. Tool integration deals with the implicit invocation and control of development tools.[1-3] Object integration seeks to provide a consistent view of development artifacts and easy-to-use interfaces to generate, access, and control them.[4-5]

We propose a higher level of integration, *process integration*, which represents development activities explicitly in a *software process* model to guide and coordinate development and to integrate tools and objects. A CASE environment based on process integration is called a *process-driven* CASE environment. Our implementation strategy is to realize process integration using existing CASE environments or tools.

PROCESS INTEGRATION

Today's CASE environments generally support some form of tool or object integration. Tool integration provides a development tool set and an invocation mechanism that controls its use. In fact, the tools form a *conceptual tool-invocation chain* that facilitates related development activities. In Unix environments, for example, programming is supported by text editors, language compilers, object linkers, program debuggers, and shell programs.

The invocation chain is conceptual because it does not have an explicit representation in most CASE environments. Furthermore, every programmer has their own version of an invocation chain that has emerged through personal experience. However, for a small tool set, invocation chains vary only slightly.

Object integration is based on an object model of software artifacts and emphasizes artifact management. The production and consumption of these artifacts normally has a partial order — an artifact

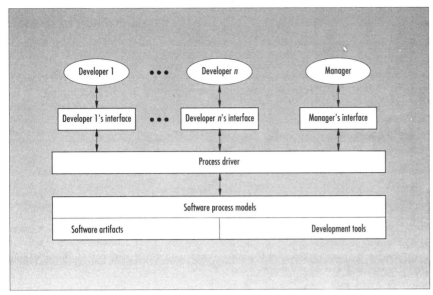

Figure 1. *Architecture of a process-driven CASE environment.*

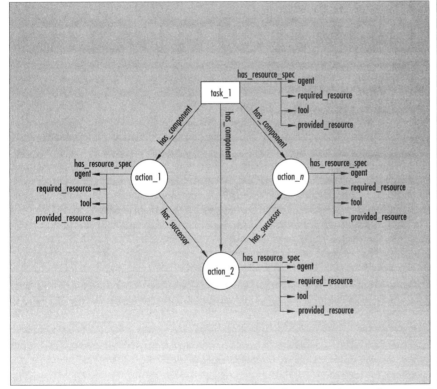

Figure 2. *A sample software process model, which is a repository of information on the status of processes and activities. An SPM is a hierarchy of tasks, subtasks, and actions. The top level is a task, depicted as a rectangle, that is recursively decomposed into subtasks. At the bottom of the hierarchy are actions, depicted as a circle, which are either single tool invocations or simple resource transformations. Each level specifies a partial order for subtask execution. An SPM also indicates four categories of resource requirements for a subtask, which are represented as independent object classes with relations that link them to the SPM.*

the final product. On the other hand, object integration does not address the activities that produce and consume artifacts.

A common feature of these two conceptual chains is that they describe *task execution*, albeit from different perspectives. The tool-invocation chain represents the use of tools in task execution, while the resource-transformation chain represents the task-execution I/O.

Process integration seeks to make the conceptual task-execution chain explicit, flexible, and reusable. We represent the task-execution chain as a software process model. By using an SPM representation, we can achieve more integrated CASE environments.

Process integration provides mechanisms to guide the software process and manage workspaces, tool invocations, and objects. Process integration also lets software managers monitor and control the progress of development. As Figure 1 shows, the key mechanisms for process integration are SPMs, a process driver, and interfaces for both the developer and manager. These are the key components of the architecture for a process-driven CASE environment.

SOFTWARE PROCESS MODEL

An SPM is a formal way to organize and describe how life-cycle models, development methods, software artifacts, CASE tools, and developers fit together — it is a collection of objects representing activities, artifacts, tools, and developers. Each SPM object has its own representation and describes a kind of information that is involved in software development. SPM objects are linked by many kinds of relations. Figure 2 shows the structure of a sample SPM.

An SPM, which we have described in detail elsewhere,[6] is a repository of information on the status of the processes and activities manipulated throughout a development project. It specifies an *activity hierarchy* and *resource requirements*.

An activity hierarchy decomposes an SPM into a hierarchy of smaller activities, *tasks* and *actions*. How many decomposition levels a project has is arbitrary and depends

produced early in the life cycle will be used later to create another artifact. For example, an early artifact in system development often is the informal requirements description. Intermediate artifacts are the requirements

specification and the architectural design. The final artifact is the system itself.

In this case there is a *conceptual resource-transformation chain* that progresses from initial artifacts to intermediate ones and then to

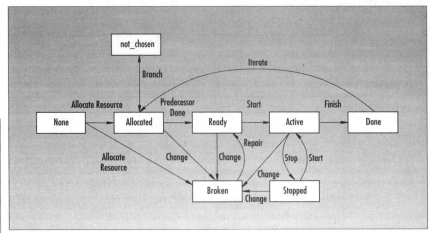

Figure 3. A status-transition graph, which is the internal representation of tasks, subtasks and actions. Boxes denote status values (defined in Table 1), arcs denote transitions that change those values and the result, and arc labels denote the transition type. The process driver implements the status-transition graph, and each status-transition graph is in turn represented as a node in the higher level SPM.

on the project's complexity. The top level of an SPM is a task that is recursively decomposed into a set of interrelated subtasks (which include tasks and actions). At the bottom of the hierarchy are actions, which are either single tool invocations or simple resource transformations.

Each level specifies a partial order for subtask execution. The execution order defines several types of precedence relationships among subtasks, including sequential, parallel, iterative, and conditional.

An SPM also indicates four categories of resource requirements for a subtask to be performed. As Figure 2 illustrates, an SPM models the

♦ various developer and organizational roles users take while performing a subtask,

♦ software artifacts that are needed (*required* resources*)* and created or enhanced (*provided* resources) during a subtask,

♦ tools used, and

♦ information about a subtask's schedule and its expected duration.

These resource requirements are represented as independent object classes with relations that link them to the SPM. For example, a system's product model might be defined to have a module-decomposition structure, with its modules linked to their producer and consumer subtasks.

PROCESS DRIVER

A process driver interprets and executes an SPM according to its activity hierarchy. It manages the order of subtasks and the constraints to be satisfied before they can be performed. It plays the role of an automated driver in that it initiates an SPM, enacts its subtasks, accepts developers' inputs, updates and propagates the status of these subtasks, and triggers other subtasks.

A key variable that represents the state of process enactment is *status*, which is attached to each task or action in an SPM. The value of an SPM's or subtask's status indicates its current development state. The status variable is updated by the process driver on the basis of interaction with

developers. Updates to a subtask's current status value represent the subtask's progress through enactment. To this end, process execution drives the status of an SPM from None to Done.

Table 1 lists process status values and their definitions for both actions and tasks. An action's status is primitive and is determined by operations on it; a task's status is recursively defined and is determined by the status of its component subtasks. The process driver updates these values according to input from an SPM and developers. Thus, while an SPM indicates a prescribed order of subtask enactment, the record of status transitions describes the order in which enactment actually occurred.

Figure 3 shows status transitions initiated by the process driver. In Figure 3, the

| | **TABLE 1** | |
| | **STATUS VALUES AND DEFINITIONS** | |
Value	Definition for actions	Definition for tasks
None	Initially set	Subtasks have status None
Allocated	Developers, tools, and required resources have been allocated	Subtasks have status Allocated
Ready	Allocated, either without predecessors or its precedecessors are done	Some subtasks are Ready, but none are Active
Active	Enactment is in progress; being performed by assigned developers.	Some subtasks are Active
Stopped	Not being performed; voluntarily stopped	Some subtasks are Stopped, but none are Active, Broken, or Ready
Broken	Either one or more required resources is unavailable or it is unable to continue for some reason	Some subtasks are Broken, but none are Active or Ready
Done	Execution has finished successfully	Subtasks have status Done
Not chosen	Not selected for execution	Not available

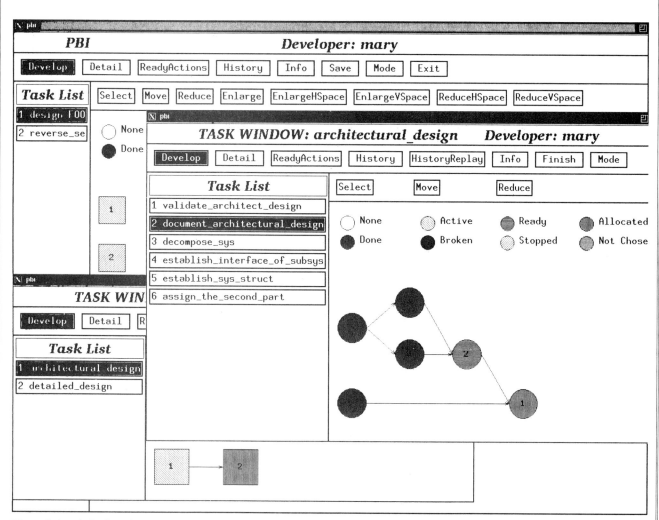

Figure 4. *A stack of task windows in the developer's interface. The graph in the top window is an SPM showing actions and their status.*

boxes denote status values and the arcs connecting them denote enactment transitions that change those values and the result. Arcs are labeled with transition types. For example, action Start changes an action's status from either Ready or Stopped to Active, signaling that the action is being executed. The process driver implements the status-transition graph. Each status-transition graph is in turn represented as a node in the higher level SPM.

Once managers have allocated resources to a project, developers start an SPM's enactment by informing the process driver, which issues a Start signal on initial Ready actions. The action's status is thereby changed to Active. As actions are performed, some of them may be Done, others may be Stopped, and still others will be Broken, which means they need repairing or rescheduling actions to recover.[7] When actions are Done, they trigger the process driver to update the SPM and assert more Ready actions. This enactment continues until the entire SPM is

Done. During enactment, managers monitor progress by observing the status change. Managers can elect to change the enacted SPM or its resource allocation at any time. Accordingly, developers enact and managers control SPMs through two separate user interfaces.

DEVELOPER'S INTERFACE

The developer's interface is a working environment that lets developers enact an SPM. Different developers execute SPMs concurrently and perform only their assigned subtasks through process guidance and workspaces.

Process guidance. Process guidance informs developers of the subtasks they can perform and when these subtasks are ready to start. The developer's interface supports process guidance through navigation within an SPM by the process driver.

A developer can start a subtask only if its status is Ready or Stopped. When a

subtask is finished, the developer's interface sends a Done signal to the process driver, which uses the signal to determine if successor Allocated subtasks are Ready. This lets developers start assigned tasks as soon as they become Ready.

The developer's interface provides process guidance through task windows, which show both explicit and implicit process representation. A task window presents a task's subtasks and their current status. Figure 4 shows a stack of task windows with an example of an SPM with explicit process representation.

Each task window displays the task's immediate subtasks as an SPM: Tasks are represented as squares, actions as circles, and precedence relationships as arrows from a subtask to its successor subtasks. The status of a subtask is indicated with different colors on a color display and with different icons on a monochrome display. Therefore, an SPM indicates both task-execution order and how enactment is progressing.

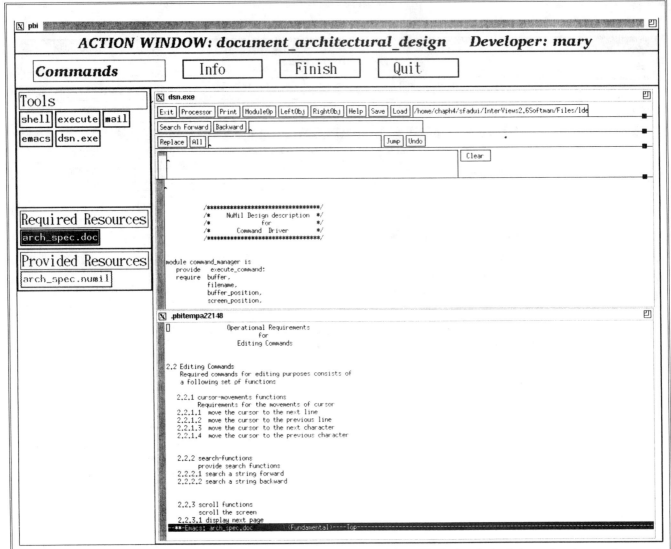

Figure 5. *An action window in the developer's interface. The action is document_architectural_design. The developer has invoked two tools — dsn.exe and emacs, each operating on one resource — arch_spec.numil and arch_spec.doc, respectively.*

A developer can start the execution of any Ready subtask by clicking on it, which opens another window. If the selected subtask is a task, the new window is a task window that shows a lower decomposition level. For example, Mary's developer interface in Figure 4 shows, in the task-list window in the upper left, the two SPMs assigned to her: design_FOO and reverse_se.

Mary has opened two levels of decomposition, one for design_FOO in the lower left window and one for architectural_design in the center window. In the center window, the architectural_design subtask is decomposed into a list of six actions, whose icons indicate that four are Done, one is Ready, and one is Allocated.

On the other hand, if the developer selects an action subtask, the new window is an action window, which provides a working environment.

A task window that shows an SPM with an implicit process representation would display a list of Ready actions, called a ready list, and an action window. The developer selects an action from the ready list and finishes it in the action window's workspace. The developer's interface updates the Ready list when an action is Done so the next Ready actions can be displayed. This implict process representation is a shortcut for developers who prefer not to be guided by an explicit process representation. The developer's interface nonetheless enforces the process description implicitly.

Workspaces. In the developer's interface, a workspace is used to perform an action and is accessed through an action window, as Figure 5 shows. Creating a workspace has two aspects: setting up a work area and invoking the necessary tools with re-

sources as parameters.

Selecting an action from an SPM causes its required resources, its provided resources, and its associated tools to be displayed in an action window. An action window also lets developers invoke the tools on specified resources. Furthermore, when an action specifies only one tool and one resource, tool invocation is automatic: The developer's interface invokes the tool when the action window opens.

Figure 5 shows the action window for the action document_architectural_design. In the window, two tools — dsn.exe and emacs — have been invoked. Each tool operates on one resource — arch_spec.numil and arch_spec.doc, respectively. When an action is finished, the action window gets its provided resources from the tools and puts them into the correct position according to the specification in the SPM so they can be used in successor subtasks.

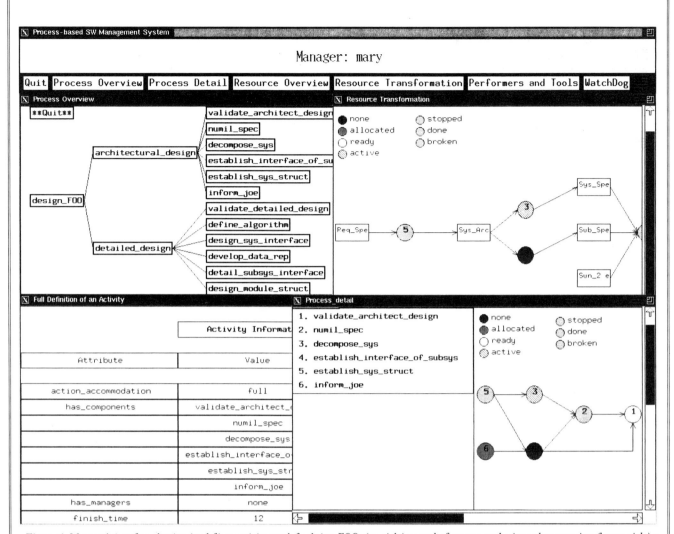

Figure 6. Manager's interface, showing (top left) an activity graph for design_FOO; (top right) a graph of resource production and consumption; (bottom right) a task-predecence graph for a group of subtasks and their current status; and (bottom left) the interface where the manager can modify the values of attributes in an SPM to assign tasks and allocate resources.

MANAGER'S INTERFACE

The manager's interface gives managers and analysts the tools to define, monitor, and control the SPMs that developers are working on concurrently.

From the process driver's point of view, a manager's interface does not change the status of an SPM. Instead, it initializes an SPM to ensure that the minimum required resources needed to start it are allocated and to monitor the progress of a process. Process managers use a different interface (not shown) to create, prototype, analyze, and simulate SPMs.[7]

The manager's interface simply retrieves information from the SPM and presents it in easy-to-understand graphs and tables, as Figure 6 shows. The process driver can update these graphs and tables in real time, as developers work.

Three windows in Figure 6 are concerned with monitoring the progress of things like subtask completion and resource creation. The upper left window shows an activity graph for design_FOO; the lower right window is a graph of the task-precedence relationships among a group of subtasks and their current status; the upper right window shows the resource production and consumption relationships among a task's subtasks.

The lower left window in Figure 6 is concerned with controlling the process, which involves changing the values of an SPM's attributes. This modification function lets a manager assign tasks and allocate resources.

SOFTMAN EXPERIMENT

An example of our strategy to implement process-driven CASE environments with existing CASE environments[8] is an experiment involving the Softman environment,[5] which was developed as part of the Univer-

sity of Southern California's System Factory project (although other CASE environments or tools could have served as well).

Softman is an integrated CASE environment for forward and reverse engineering large software systems. Its comprehensive set of support mechanisms and tools makes it a powerful environment for large-scale development. However, its development methodology and its tools can be difficult to learn. A process driven Softman environment can overcome, or mitigate, these difficulties.

We made Softman process driven by

1. Identifying its basic concepts, functions, component tools, and tool-invocation sequences.

2. Formally representing the information gathered in Step 1 in an SPM called the Softman process model.

3. Porting the Softman process model to a process-driven CASE environment

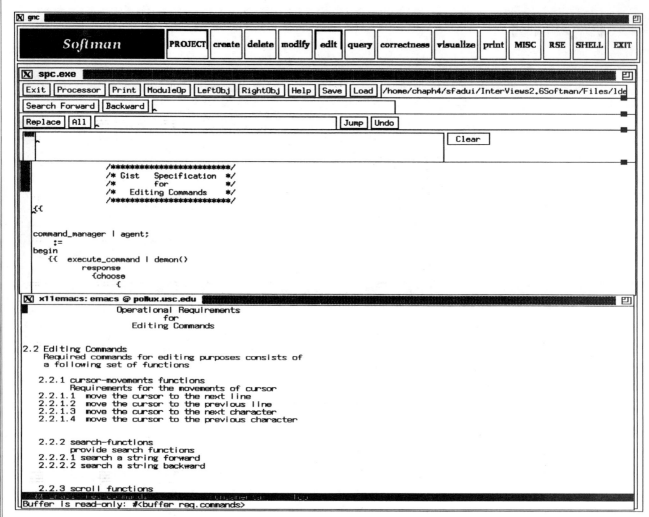

Figure 7. *Softman's user interface. The top window shows the editing of a design specification; the bottom window is a view of operational requirements.*

and integrating Softman's object model and tool set.

Identifying concepts. Figure 7 shows Softman's user interface. The top window shows the editing of a design specification; the bottom window is a view of operational requirements.

Through extensive studies, we identified these concepts as important to Softman:

♦ Softman supports an incremental, iterative tool-based methodology. It creates and manipulates a tree-structured collection of life-cycle documents such as requirements analyses, requirements specifications, designs, implementations, tests, and maintenance information. In Softman, development stages are decomposed until you identify the level of a single tool invocation.

♦ Softman's product model is a collection of life-cycle objects and their attributes and relationships.[9] It also provides more detailed information so that all objects have attributes that characterize their

interfaces and interconnections. Softman requires that you create an object's skeletal structure, called mod_struct, before you can create and maintain its content, called mod_cont, correctly. We call this a structure-first, content-second development method.

♦ For each development stage, Softman provides a set of structure-oriented, correctness-checking tools. You use these tools to create, modify, and maintain both an object's structure and content.[5] Softman's tools include language-directed editors to create object content and graphical editors to manipulate object structures. These tools communicate with an object-management repository that checks consistency, completeness, and traceability constraints on all objects so as to incrementally assure or track their (in)correctness.

This first step is the most critical. Here, the process analyst must understand the modeled process. The analyst must talk

with people who have extensive knowledge of the process that the environment will support. We worked with the original Softman developers.

Formal representation. We defined the Softman process model to include development activities, their prescribed execution order, their required tools (including multiple tool choices when necessary), and their associated required and provided objects. Overall, the Softman process model follows Softman's structure-first, content-second methodology.

Figure 8 gives the specification of an action, des_mod_cont, within the Softman process model. The action definition specifies its developer, execution order, required object, provided object, and two development tools.

This step is relatively easy, given the knowledge acquired in step 1. We are now building more tools to help automate this step.

```
{{ des_mod_cont
   INSTANCE: ACTION
   TASK_ASSIGNED_TO_AGENT_ROLE: software_engineer
   TASK_COMPONENT_OF: softman_model
   TASK_HAS_PREDECESSOR: des_mod_struct
   TASK_HAS_SUCCESSOR: imp_mod_cont
   TASK_REQUIRE_RESOURCE: arch_spec.doc
   TASK_PROVIDE_RESOURCE: arch_spec.numil
   TASK_REQUIRE_TOOL: vi dsn.exe}}
```

Figure 8. The specification of an action, des_mod_cont, within the Softman process model. The action definition specifies its developer, execution order, required object, provided object, and two development tools.

Porting the process model. Porting the Softman process model into a process-driven CASE environment is straightforward because the model is simply an instance of a defined SPM class.

In this step, we input the Softman process model into the process driver and made the Softman data model known to the driver. We then reused and integrated Softman's tool set by reattaching the Softman tool-invocation menu items to the Softman developer's interface and establishing links between the tools and the data model.

The problems that emerge in this step are how to invoke the tools and how to reconcile potential tool incompatibilities.

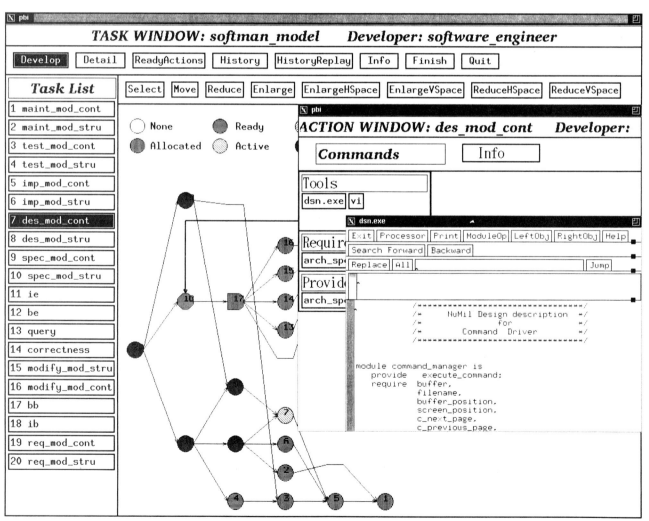

Figure 9. Developer's interface to the process-driven Softman environment. The bottom window shows the Softman process model; the action window at right executes des_mod_cont, defined in Figure 8.

We examine some of these tool-integration problems later.

Figure 9 shows the developer's interface to the new process-driven Softman environment. The bottom window shows the Softman process model; the action window at right executes des_mod_cont, defined in Figure 8.

The new Softman environment uses the interfaces and supports the Softman process model as well as reuses the original Softman data model and tool set. The process-driven Softman environment preserves the important Softman concepts and functions and adds support for process guidance and project management.

When they use the process-driven Softman environment, developers know what development stage they are performing, the tools available to them, the software documents they must produce, and the task they are to perform next.

We have delivered the new process-driven Softman environment to some industrial organizations and are now experimenting with it. We are also incorporating support for integrating distributed object repositories and heterogeneous data models.[10]

Observations. During our experiment, we observed that the process-driven Softman environment is flexible to change. In fact, we have defined variations of the Softman process model to support different development methodologies but use the same product model and tool set. This would not be possible with the original Softman CASE environment without a major reprogramming effort.

We also observed that this strategy for process integration should be applicable to other CASE environments that provide basic tool- and object-integration mechanisms.

Finally, we observed that the interfaces of existing development tools must be highly compatible for them to appear to be seamlessly integrated in a process-driven CASE environment. Our current strategy is to enable each CASE environment to define its own product and tool models and to have an open structure for process integration to incorporate them. The Softman experiment has shown promise in this regard, but more study is needed.

Process integration uses a few key components to form the backbone of a process-driven CASE environment. The key components are SPMs, a process driver, a tool set, and interfaces for both developers and managers.

Process integration supports an open system structure that we believe can be added to other CASE environments with reasonable effort.

Our successful migration of the Softman environment to a process-driven CASE environment proves the feasibility of our strategy. ◆

ACKNOWLEDGMENTS

This work was supported in part by contracts and grants from AT&T Bell Laboratories, Northrop, Pacific Bell, and the Office of Naval Technology through the Naval Ocean Systems Center. Anthony Karrer, Thomas Getzinger, Mary Li, Junhui Luo, and Yu-ling Young contributed to the implementation effort.

REFERENCES
1. G. Boudier et al., "An Overview of PCTE and PCTE+," *SIGPlan Notices*, Feb. 1989, pp. 226-227.
2. D. Garlan and E. Ilias, "Low-Cost, Adaptable Tool Integration Policies for Integrated Environments," *Proc. SIGSoft Symp. Software Development Environments*, ACM Press, New York, 1990, pp. 1-10.
3. I. Thomas, "Tool Integration in the PACT Environment," *Proc. Int'l Conf. Software Eng.*, IEEE CS Press, Los Alamitos, Calif., 1989, pp. 13-22.
4. E.W. Adams, M. Honda, and T.C. Miller, "Object Management in a CASE Environment," *Proc. Int'l Conf. Software Eng.*, IEEE CS Press, Los Alamitos, Calif., 1989, pp. 154-165.
5. S.C. Choi and W. Scacchi, "Softman: An Environment for Forward and Reverse CASE," *Information and Software Technology*, Nov. 1991, pp. 664-674.
6. P. Mi and W. Scacchi, "A Knowledge-Based Environment for Modeling and Simulating Software Engineering Processes," *IEEE Trans. Knowledge and Data Eng.*, Sept. 1990, pp. 283-294.
7. P. Mi and W. Scacchi, "Modeling Articulation Work in Software Engineering Processes," *Proc. Int'l Conf. Software Process*, IEEE CS Press, Los Alamitos, Calif., 1991, pp. 188-201.
8. C. Fernstrom and L. Ohlsson, "Integration Needs in Process-Enacted Environments," *Proc. Int'l Conf. Software Process*, IEEE CS Press, Los Alamitos, Calif., 1991, pp. 142-158.
9. S.C. Choi and W. Scacchi, "Assuring the Correctness of Configured Software Descriptions," *ACM Software Eng. Notes*, Oct. 1989, pp. 67-76.
10. J. Noll and W. Scacchi, "Integrating Diverse Information Repositories: A Distributed Hypertext Approach," *Computer*, Dec. 1991, pp. 38-45.

Peiwei Mi is a PhD candidate in the computer science department at the University of Southern California. His research interests include knowledge-based systems to support the software process, process-driven software-engineering environments, organizational analysis of systems-development projects, and distributed problem-solving.

Mi received a BS and an MS in computer science from the University of Science and Technology of China.

Walt Scacchi is an associate research professor in the decision systems department at USC. He created and directs the USC System Factory Project. His research interests include very large scale software production, knowledge-based systems for modeling and simulating organizational processes and operations, CASE technologies for developing large heterogeneous information systems, and organizational analysis of systems-development projects.

Scacchi received a PhD in information and computer science from the University of California at Irvine. He is a member of the ACM, IEEE, the American Association for Artificial Intelligence, Computing Professionals for Social Responsibility, and Society for the History of Technology.

Address questions about this article to Scacchi at Decision Systems Dept., USC, Los Angeles, CA 90089; Internet scacchi@pollux.usc.edu.

PART III: THE ROLE OF DATA-BROWSING TECHNOLOGY IN CASE

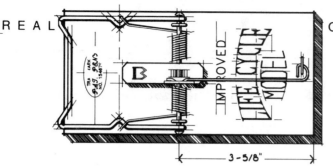

Hypertext and CASE

James Bigelow, *Tektronix*

CASE systems must tie text and code into coherent documentation and keep a complete version history of everything. A hypertext database fits the bill.

The heart of any CASE system is its database, which must, at least, let designers

• logically associate documentation and source code,

• make annotations to record explanations and assumptions, and

• manage different versions of the software.[1-3]

A CASE environment places other demands on a database, due to the nature of large-scale, team projects. The database must support simultaneous access by team members, editing, and authorship in a computer network. Also, it must let team members work independently and then merge their work back into the main project — a taxing demand on a configuration management system.

The database must let programmers build specific configurations and version trees, and subsequently merge version branches back into the primary version. Meeting this requirement provides the fundamentals for good version management as well as the functionality for a configuration manager.

In search of such a system, researchers at Tektronix built Neptune, which demonstrates that hypertext provides an appropriate data model for CASE systems. Hypertext is a medium-grained, entity-relationship-like data model that lets information be structured arbitrarily and keeps a complete version history of both information and structure.

Hypertext and Neptune

Hypertext was first conceived in 1945 as a way to store all kinds of information, both for ready access and cross referencing.[4,5] There are now several commercial and research packages that have hypertext capabilities.[6]

However, the key to the future success of hypertext is an efficient, application-independent data-storage method. Neptune, introduced in 1986, achieves application independence by using a layered system architecture: At the bottom is a transaction-based server, the Hypertext Abstract Machine, and layered above it are applications and the user interface.

The HAM provides distributed access

Reprinted from *IEEE Software,* Vol. 5, No. 2, March 1988, pp. 23-27. Copyright © 1988 by The Institute of Electrical and Electronics Engineers, Inc. All rights reserved.

over a computer network, and is synchronized for multiuser access with recovery and rollback of interrupted or incomplete transactions (where a transaction is a group of one or more HAM operations that are treated as a single unit). The HAM also presents a generic hypertext model because it defines operations for creating, modifying, and accessing hypertext components. It provides quick access to a complete history of all versions of the information stored in the database.

The basic ingredients of a hypertext system are nodes and links. Nodes store data, and links provide the relationship between data in different nodes. Links and nodes are the essence of hypertext — they store and link information in a way that allows nonlinear organization of information. The HAM identifies nodes and links by associating an attribute/value pair with them. For example, a node's Name attribute is given a value such as "module 1" to identify the contents as the source code in module 1. Information is grouped into configurations by using contexts, which are collections of nodes and links. Since nodes and links may be thought of as directed graphs, a collection of nodes, links, and contexts is called a graph.

Dynamic Design

A C-based CASE environment developed at Tektronix, Dynamic Design, has all of its project components in the HAM:

- requirements and specifications,
- design notes and documents,
- implementation notes,
- source and object code,
- test specifications and results, and
- user documentation.

Nodes contain the project components and links depict the relationships among components. Attributes label the types of nodes and links, and attributes have values assigned to them. Table 1 shows the possible values of two node and link attributes.

In Dynamic Design, nodes have an attribute, projectComponent, that identifies which project component they contain. Links have an attribute, relatesTo, that shows the type of relation the link provides. For example, sequential information may be associated by connecting two nodes with a link whose attribute, relatesTo, has a value of leadsTo. In Figure 1, module 1 calls module 2, so their nodes are connected by a link with the attribute value callsProcedure.

The relationship between a specification and the code that implements it is shown with links. The node containing the part of the specification (projectComponent = spec) and the node containing the code (projectComponent = source) are related with a link that has the attribute/value pair relatesTo = implements. Also, a link can show which module contains the definition of a variable by relating the module with the variable to the module with the defini-

tion using a link having the attribute/value pair refersTo = isDefinedBy.

Nodes. Nodes, similar to nodes in directed graphs, hold any object in the CASE system (text, graphics, object code, and so on). Hypertext does not place any constraint on node format, which makes it particularly useful for holding the wide variety of information found in a CASE environment in one database.

Nodes are atomic data units, so the issue of node content is important. If a piece of data is referenced in more than one place (for example, if a section of text is found in both the requirements and in the comments for a section of code), it should be stored in a node by itself. However, in a hypertext system it is the application that is the final arbiter of how much information should be placed in a node because it determines the unit of incrementality when it processes the information. For example, a compiler that can recompile a changed procedure individually without recompiling an entire module[7,8] will use the procedure as the unit of incrementality. Other compilers may enforce a larger increment, such as a module.

In the HAM, version history is kept at the node and link level. While lookup time is proportional to the age of the version, all versions of a node's content may be archived and retrieved on demand. When combined with the concept of contexts, this creates the fundamentals of a configuration manager.

Links. Links are similar to arcs in directed graphs. In Figure 1, the link that connects nodes paragraph 1 and module 1 provides the logical association that paragraph 1 comments on module 1. In addition to association, the HAM lets you traverse a link in either direction. For example, Figure 1 shows that, while reading paragraph 2, you can traverse the link to module 2, read the module, traverse the link to paragraph 3, and read that paragraph.

In the HAM, a link is not restricted to pointing to the entire node; it can be attached to any object or place in a node. For example, a link can be attached to a character in text, an extent of text (a sen-

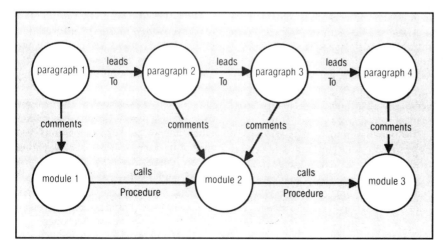

Figure 1. Commenting source code with nodes and links.

tence or paragraph), an x,y coordinate in graphical information, and a graphics object (such as a process bubble in a dataflow diagram).

The history of a link is the history of its attribute/value pairs and its attachment object in a node. By looking at a link's history, you can tell if its name or attachment location ever changed and what the changes were.

Attribute/value pairs. Attribute/value pairs extend the power of hypertext by allowing the organization of nodes and links into subgraphs in a single context. Attribute/value pairs make it easy to access all needed information and yet restrict access to only that which is needed. Attributes identify and categorize nodes, links, and contexts. The HAM provides an unlimited number of attribute/value pairs, so numerous attribute categories can be applied to nodes, links, and contexts.

Table 1 shows how attribute values identify the content of nodes and the meaning of links. Attributes values can also identify contexts. In Dynamic Design, for example, contexts have an attribute, projectCategory, that has values such as Specifications, Design documentation, Program documentation, User documentation, Implementation notes, Source code, Object code, Symbol tables, and Product. This context attribute is used in query operations to locate or filter information. A thorough example of attribute usage in CASE environments has been described for the Project Master Database.[1]

Query operations. The HAM provides a sophisticated set of query operations to traverse and retrieve nodes, links, and contexts. The query operations use predicates based on attribute/value pairs to determine which nodes, links, and contexts satisfy the queries. For example, Dynamic Design nodes containing source code are placed in the context projectCategory = source code and have an attribute System attached to them. The System attribute can assume any of the following values: All, Amiga, Bsd, Eunice, Osk, Sysv, and Vms. When you use the node predicate System = All in a retrieval query, the database

shows only those nodes that contain source code applicable to all systems. On the other hand, the node predicate of System = Vms returns only those nodes with source code applicable only to Digital Equipment Corp.'s VAX/VMS operating system. A traversal query using the predicate System = All Or System = Vms returns the version of the product source code tailored for the VAX/VMS environment.

Code and comments. The documentation of a program usually is either squeezed into the margins of the program (where it is generally too terse to be useful) or interspersed throughout the program text (breaking up the flow of both the program and the documentation).[9] Dynamic Design lets the documentation and source code exist in separate, linked nodes.

Figure 1 illustrates two node types: program code and program documentation. The nodes labeled module 1, module 2, and module 3 contain source code and the nodes labeled paragraph 1, paragraph 2, paragraph 3, and paragraph 4 contain documentation. Figure 1 also shows three uses of links: sequential (leadsTo), annotative (comments), and nonlinear (callsProcedure). With this arrangement, either the documentation or source code may be viewed by following leadsTo or callsProcedure links without interruption. However, if the source code requires an explanation, the comments link connects the source to the documentation. Also, while reading the documentation, you can view the source code at any time by traversing the comments link. This method frees the documentation from space restrictions found in conventional, in-code documentation methods.

Contexts

The concept of a context — the collection and partitioning of nodes and links into a set — was missing from hypertext until 1987.[10] Contexts group common nodes and links, but they do more than that. Contexts indirectly support cooperative, multiperson design and documentation of large-scale software systems by directly supporting partitioning, version trees, and configuration management.

Table 1.
Two node and link attributes
and their values.

Attribute name	Possible values
projectComponent	requirement, spec, designNote, design assumption, comment, source, object, symbolTable, documentation, report
relatesTo	leadsTo, comments, refersTo, callsProcedure, followsFrom, implements, isDefinedBy

The HAM has operations to create and populate contexts with nodes, links, and subcontexts. A merge operation lets you copy a subset of nodes and links from one context into another context, an operation that has several uses and ramifications.

Configuration management. A context lets you designate a configuration of nodes and links. Once a group of source nodes are in a baseline configuration, they can be moved with the merge operation into another context that holds released products. Figure 2 depicts the state transitions of two contexts, Project and Release. The states are labeled V0, V1, V2, and so on, and show differences in the nodes and links that comprise the content of both contexts. Figure 2 illustrates the merging of the content of the context Project, at state V0, into context Release, at state V0. Development continues in Project, as shown by the intermediate states V1, V2, and V3. At state V3, the content of Project is again merged into Release, yielding release state V1.

One of the properties of the merge operation is that node and link histories are not moved from one context to another. Therefore, while complete node and link histories are preserved in Project, the version history in Release is that of the versions of the nodes and links in Project when they were merged into Release. This means that the nodes and links in Release do not have a record of the states V1 and V2 in Project, only of states V0 and V3.

Local workspaces. Contexts can also be used to define a workspace and partition a project into a project workspace and local workspaces.[11] A local workspace

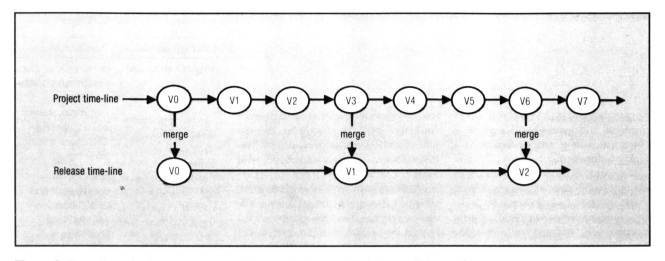

Figure 2. Time-lines for two contexts, project and release, with intermediate versions.

lets a developer abstract a subset of nodes and links from the project workspace and place them in a workspace where he can make local modifications and test them against the rest of the project. When satisfied, the developer merges the changes into the system.

Ideally, the partitioning of workspaces between developers is disjoint. In practice, however, project or requirement constraints may mean that two or more developers are working on nodes concurrently. The chance of concurrent development means that some method of detecting and resolving concurrent updates must be used when local workspaces are merged into the project workspace. Detection of changes is mandatory to avoid overwriting work done by one or more developers. Therefore, the HAM provides operations for detecting differences between both nodes and contexts. These two operations detect the differences that may have been made in the project workspace after the developer created the local workspace.

Interconnections

A project component is any piece of information or data associated with a project. Broad categories are

- management reports,
- specification and requirements,
- design, program, and user documentation,
- implementation notes,
- source code,
- test specifications and results,
- object code, and
- products.

In each of these categories are the actual documents, memos, papers, binary codes, and so on that make up the project. By placing all the components in hypertext, they are archived, recoverable, and available for use in other parts of the project.

Interconnections between project components exist even in a project that uses paper documents. However, there is also much duplication of effort and documentation when you use paper. Furthermore, many opportunities to point out the relationships between components are missed because the effort involved is too great for the time permitted.

Dynamic Design has all the information about a project in its hypertext database. Contexts group the data into the categories shown in Figure 3. The lines that connect the ellipses in Figure 3 represent contexts and show the direct interconnections and interrelationships between the data in the contexts. Because the database uses links, one piece of data can be present in several contexts. A paragraph about a design may do triple duty: as a comment in the program documentation and as a paragraph in both the user and design documentation.

Links also trace functional requirements. A link from a Specifications requirement leads to a dataflow diagram

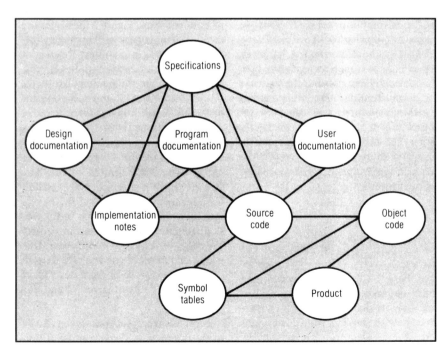

Figure 3. The interconnections of project categories in Dynamic Design.

in the Design documentation. From there, a link leads to a structure chart or some other design document and then back to the requirement. This provides a check on the one-to-one relationship between requirements and designs.

Links also connect nodes in design documents to nodes in program documents and then to nodes in source code. Implementation notes provide a repository for documenting assumptions and decisions based on the actual implementation of the design. There are links between the nodes in implementation notes and those in design documentation and source code to record the associates between them.

One real benefit of this system is that it is easy to demonstrate that all requirements have been fulfilled. Starting at specifications, links radiate through the project through design documentation, implementation notes, source code, user documentation, and back to specifications, forming a graph cycle. Every path from specifications that is not a cycle indicates an unfulfilled requirement.

Dynamic Design also aids program maintenance. Maintenance personnel can read the designer's design documents, assumptions, and implementation notes and link them directly to the relevant code sections. So the job of gauging the effect of a program modification is aided by easy access to documentation linked to specific portions of the code.

Figure 3 shows that the object code and symbol tables are directly related only to the source code, even though they are still part of the project. A compiler integrated with hypertext makes good use of its storage abilities. Module symbol tables need not be reconstructed for every compile, merely updated. A symbolic debugger can make excellent use of the module symbol tables left in hypertext and, since they are in hypertext and not in the object code, the symbol table and debugging information can be quite extensive. When a compiler is used with a facility similar to the Unix Make facility to generate recompilation commands, Dynamic Design becomes a programming environment.

H ypertext provides an appropriate data model for CASE, but it is only a part — albeit a powerful part — of a CASE environment. With the other parts (editors, compilers, linkers, electronic-mail systems, and so on) integrated with hypertext, there is the possibility of a powerful and productive programming environment. Much work remains to fully explore and devise ways to exploit the capabilities of hypertext.

Work on building systems using hypertext can focus on how to automate the creation of sequential and relational links. Sequential links show that one node logically follows another ("leadsTo" in Figure1) and relational links show that two node are logically related, but not sequentially ("comments" in Figure 1). Automating the linking process, based on how a node is used, would spare users the chore of repetitive linking. However, there will always be the need for a way to create a link at the user's command, to point out a relationship the system has missed and only a person can see.

A weakness that has not been addressed is how to represent fine-grained information. One solution is to create a partnership between hypertext and relational databases. A relational database can hold fine-grained information such as definition-use links in an incremental compiler's symbol tables. A relationally complete query language could extend the functionality of hypertext to provide even more capabilities.   -ₒ-

Acknowledgments
I thank Norm Delisle and May Schwartz of Tektronix for their work and the inspirations I derived from it. Also, I'm proud to acknowledge my wife, Sheila Ames, who first suggested I write a paper.

References
1. M.H. Penedo and E.D. Stukle, "PMDB: A Project Master Database for Software-Engineering Environments," *Proc. Int'l Conf. Software Engineering*, CS Press, Los Alamitos, Calif., 1985, pp. 150-157.
2. *Software-Engineering Environments*, H. Hünke, ed., North-Holland, Amsterdam, 1981.
3. N. Delisle and M.D. Schwartz, "Neptune: A Hypertext System for CAD Applications," *Proc. ACM SIGMOD*, ACM, New York, 1986, pp. 132-143.
4. T.H. Nelson, *Literary Machines*, T.H. Nelson, Swarthmore, Penn., 1981.
5. V. Bush, "As We May Think," *Atlantic Monthly*, July 1945, pp. 101-108.
6. D. Goodman, *The Complete Hypercard Handbook*, Bantam Books, New York, 1987.
7. N.M. Delisle and V.S. Begwani, "Incremental Compilation in Magpie," *Proc. SIGPlan Symp. Compiler Construction*, ACM, New York, 1984, pp. 122-131.
8. R. Medina-Mora and P.H. Feiler, "An Incremental Programming Environment," *IEEE Trans. Software Eng.*, Sept. 1981, pp. 472-482.
9. J. Conklin, "A Survey of Hypertext," Tech. Report STP-356-86, MCC, Austin, Texas, Oct. 1986.
10. N. Delisle and M.D. Schwartz, "Contexts: A Partitioning Concept for Hypertext," *ACM Trans. Office Information Systems*, April 1987, pp. 168-186.
11. V.B. Erickson and J.F. Pellegrin, "Build: A Software Construction Tool," *AT&T Bell Laboratory Tech. J.*, July-Aug. 1984, pp. 1049-1059.

James H. Bigelow is a software engineer on the hypertext project in the CASE Division of Tektronix.

His research interests include hypertext applications for the support of software engineering and programming-in-the-large and programming-in-the-small. He is a member of IEEE and ACM.

Questions about this article should be addressed to the author at Tektronix, PO Box 4600, Beaverton, OR 97075.

A Hypertext Based Sofware-Engineering Environment

JACOB L. CYBULSKI and KARL REED

Amdahl Australian Intellegent Tools Program

Reprinted from *IEEE Software*, Vol. 9, No. 2, March 1992, pp. 62-68. Copyright © 1992 by The Institute of Electrical and Electronics Engineers, Inc. All rights reserved.

◆ *Tools from information management and software development combine to provide document developers with maximum flexibility plus a guarantee of correctness and consistency.*

The recent explosion in computer use has put pressure on software developers to use software-engineering methods that adhere to approved life-cycle models, specific types of deliverable documents, and detailed project organization and control techniques.[1] Many believe that these methods can effectively deal with the explosion, but if development costs are to decrease, they must also be automated.

As early as the 1970s, software researchers attempted to improve development efficiency by automating and integrating aspects of software development.[2] Initial efforts in CASE focused on source-code formatting, structured-programming support, and test-case generation. The emphasis has since shifted to creating development environments that support flexible or customizable process models. These environments comprise tools for interactively constructing system descriptions that rely on standard diagraming techniques and allow code generation. Integrating such tools into a uniform CASE environment is not possible, however, unless certain conditions are met:

◆ You can use different document classes at various development phases.

◆ Documents produced by one tool can be used by other tools farther along development.

◆ You can efficiently and conveniently traverse (navigate) among diverse documents that describe the system and its components. Figure 1 shows how software engineers might navigate through these documents.

◆ All documents can be guaranteed to be coherent and consistent throughout the software's life cycle.

For example, when viewing a process symbol in a dataflow diagram, you may wish to display the code associated with the process, display its representation in a state-transition diagram, and inspect the relevant section of a (standard) system requirements specification or a corresponding paragraph in the feasibility description. To do this, you would have to be able to access a variety of documents simultaneously.

These conditions suggest that a CASE system should have mechanisms for constructing software documents, for creating navigable links among them, and for navigating through the repository's components. A straightforward way to give a CASE system these features is to integrate it with a system that already has them.

CASE AND HYPERTEXT

We decided to integrate our CASE tools under an extended hypertext system, an information-management concept that evolved quite independently of CASE. Table 1 shows how we relate the features of hypertext to CASE components. In hypertext, information fragments in various forms are grouped and linked in a way that lets you search and browse through them nonsequentially.[3] By extending this environment to accommodate an integrated CASE tool set, we could guarantee correctness and consistency and provide maximum flexibility. This approach has been adopted by only a few significant CASE projects like Tektronix's Neptune project[4] and the University of Southern California's System Factory Project. (For more details on this project, see Peiwei Mi and Walt Scacchi's article on pp. 45-53.)[5,6]

The resulting environment, called HyperCASE, is an architectural framework for integrating the collection of tools. It is being produced as part of the Amdahl Australian Intelligent Tools Program, which is a joint project between Amdahl Australia, La Trobe University, and Prometheus Software Developments. The system provides a visual, integrated and customizable software-engineering environment consisting of loosely coupled tools for presentations involving both text and diagrams. HyperCASE's objective —

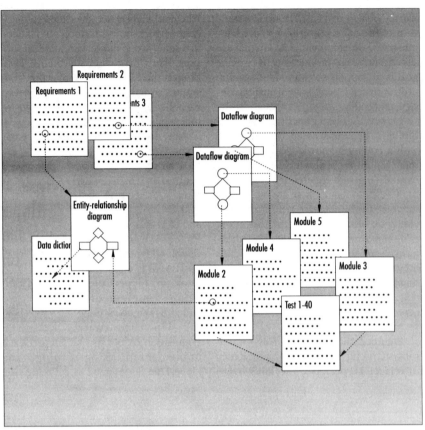

Figure 1. Navigating among software documents.

TABLE 1 HYPERTEXT APPLICATIONS TO CASE	
Hypertext	**CASE**
Document authoring	Diagram editors Text-oriented tools
Browsing and navigation	Traversing through program slices and refinement levels and across semantic terms
Document aggregation	Module libraries Data-structure groups
Virtual structures	Code generation
Dynamic computation	Runtime results
Revision management	Software-configuration management
Group work	Project-team development
Extensibility/tailorability	Multiple methodologies
Concept annotation	Design-decision recording
Consistency checking	Validation Verification
Completeness assessment	Project-plan tracking

like the objective of CASE tools in general — is to provide a powerful, user-friendly, integrated development platform that can significantly raise productivity. Its specific goal is to support software developers in project management, system analysis, design, and coding.

HyperCASE integrates tools by combining a hypertext-based user interface with a common knowledge-based document repository. It also includes extensive natural-language capabilities tailored to the CASE domain. These are used in the interface to the software repository, providing an alternative to hypertext information management and interdocument navigation. You can also analyze English input during informal system-requirements specification, allowing a significant degree of automation for design and concept reuse at the earliest development stages.

Figure 2 shows HyperCASE's three subsystems: HyperEdit, the graphical user interface; HyperBase, the knowledge base; and HyperDict, the data dictionary. As the figure shows, the tools can function in a stand-alone mode with minimal support from proprietary systems, even though the HyperCASE collection constitutes an integrated system. In this way, we hoped to maximize the opportunity for independent tool development.

We developed a number of early HyperCASE prototypes on a variety of platforms, including Sun with Unix/X, Macintosh with HyperCard, and Macs and IBM ATs with C and Prolog. We are now developing HyperCASE on an IBM AT with Open Desktop. HyperEdit is being implemented under X Windows using the Open Software Foundation's Motif tool kit, HyperBase is implemented using Prolog, and HyperDict is designed as a Prolog data store in Ingres. We expect the final system to be implemented on Amdahl's UTS system (Amdahl's version of Unix based on System V).

HYPEREDIT

HyperEdit integrates many of the window-based, customizable graphics or text editors/browsers that a software engineer is likely to use in creating, modifying, and presenting software documents. More important, it can also generate such tools. HyperEdit — which comprises the interface manager, authoring system, and event manager — lets you construct, edit, and display a variety of documents, including requirements statements, dataflow diagrams, entity-relationship diagrams, structure charts, state-transition diagrams, Petri nets, flowcharts or Nassi-Shneiderman diagrams, source code, and test cases.

The main responsibility of HyperEdit's interface manager is to manage HyperCASE's graphical user interface under a native windowing system. The authoring system lets you construct software documents of hypertext buttons, which you activate while interacting with the document by typing or clicking or dragging the mouse. The event manager captures the button events and translates them into database updates, which it then sends to HyperBase or any other program via a special communication protocol, called EventTalk. In this way, HyperBase can interpret your actions in terms of the software design elements and interdocument relationships stored in its database.

Interface manager. The core of HyperEdit's presentation system consists of text and graphics primitives. These primitives let you easily express functions and flexibly create windows, dialogue boxes, menus, palettes, buttons, text, and graphics by using the mouse or keyboard.

> HyperCASE combines a hypertext-based user interface with a common knowledge-based document repository.

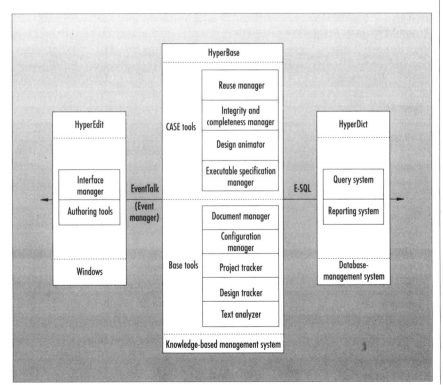

Figure 2. HyperCASE architecture.

Authoring system. HyperCASE offers several standard text and diagram editors that support major software-development methods. Each editor is simply an instantiation of HyperEdit's graphical environment. The instantiation is tailored to manipulate specific classes of objects with a range of attributes and behaviors. Authorized users can visually interact with HyperEdit's metaeditor to describe new object types and their subcomponents' shapes, sizes, colors, fonts, and styles; specify object behavior and the constraints governing the objects; and define the new editor's appearance and functions.

To construct a diagram or text, you
♦ compose software documents, of the editor-specific objects (like dataflow-diagram processes, stores, and entities);
♦ link them into object sets (with dataflows or into domains); and
♦ specify their logical attributes (like names) and visual attributes (like color, size, and position).

Authoring can be restricted according to the type of user. For example, analysts may be permitted to modify design documents without any restraints, while technical writers can be limited to altering the documents' visual attributes only, without affecting content. Programmers can be confined to *viewing* existing software design documents, with no ability to alter any document aspects.

The authoring system's browsing and navigational mechanisms include an extended button facility in which all diagram objects, regardless of shape and form, may act as hypertext buttons, thus becoming active document components. Button events are invoked not only when you click or drag a mouse, but also whenever a document's state changes as a result of modification, verification, or completion.

Other mechanisms include
♦ document retrieval by classification, content, or relationship with other documents in the system;
♦ document browsing with panning and zooming over individual documents or collections; and
♦ navigation among documents with history lists, route maps, bookmarks, and the like.

These capabilities give you rapid access to all relevant software documentation, which increases the chances of its reuse.

Event manager. All through the user's graphical interaction, Hyper-CASE maintains the data needed to describe developed diagram structures. Presentation records are kept in the HyperEdit repository. Conceptual information is kept in HyperBase or any other software that supports EventTalk.

Although the presentation records and conceptual information (contents) are distinctly different representations, they have certain overlapping aspects. For example, a graphics field denoting an entity-relationship entity name will contain a string that will also be stored in the contents database. Consequently, information is replicated across the repositories of all currently opened HyperEdit sessions and HyperBase. For this reason we devised EventTalk, a special communication protocol that maintains the conceptual integrity and completeness of HyperEdit's multiple diagram images.

The main objective of EventTalk is to advise HyperBase of all user-instigated changes (as opposed to tool-instigated changes) to the document's content. Such changes may arise when a user creates, deletes, or edits a document's components (for example, creates or deletes entities, relationships, or attributes in entity-relationship diagrams). HyperBase can then validate these actions.

After HyperBase is updated (for example, when an entity has been deleted), the knowledge-base rules may be triggered to make additional changes to the database to ensure document consistency (deleting all relationships connected to the deleted entity, for example). In this case, HyperBase will also send appropriate EventTalk commands back to HyperEdit to correct the displayed document. Changes in document presentation that do not affect document content (like repositioning or resizing graphical objects) are not immediately communicated to HyperBase.

EventTalk also advises HyperBase of all user actions that cannot be interpreted within the context of the displayed document. Such events may include browsing and navigating by clicking on a diagram component like a dataflow diagram process. These events require access to HyperBase's interdocument linking information and the details of the destination documents. For example, you may need information about all the links leading from the selected dataflow diagram process to the set of its refinement diagrams.

EventTalk gives HyperEdit an object-oriented view of HyperBase even though a relational schema may be in use. It provides mechanisms for transaction rollbacks in the long transaction model, which organizes the undo facility but which also aids document versioning. The EventTalk transaction logs are useful in implementing a project-tracking system to assist in project and configuration management.

HYPERBASE

HyperBase is a knowledge-based hypermedia repository of software documents. All user actions performed within HyperEdit are reflected in and possibly extended by HyperBase. As Figure 2 shows, HyperBase comprises Base tools and CASE tools. Base tools accommodate the mechanisms and structures to organize a generic hypertext system, while CASE tools help ensure that a document is consistent and complete and that design components are reusable.

Base tools. Base tools evolved from our initial experiments with HyperCASE. At first, we planned to use hypertext principles in the implementation of only one CASE tool, a design tracker. But we real-

> The authoring system gives you rapid access to all relevant software documentation, which increases the chances of its reuse.

ized as development progressed that hypertext systems could satisfy many CASE requirements — particularly the need for multimedia document presentation; interdocument analysis, browsing, and navigation; version change and delivery control; planning and tracking; and capturing reflections about the product and its development.

We discovered that commercial tools could not deliver all the required features affordably. Hence, we decided to develop a whole suite of CASE programs that could provide the basis of a hypertext framework. This suite, which we call Base tools, includes a document manager, configuration manager, project planner and activity tracker, design tracker, and text analyzer.

Document manager. Software documents produced by HyperEdit become an integral part of HyperCASE. The document manager analyzes, indexes, aggregates, and stores graphics and text attributes to enable interdocument linking and navigation over program slices and refinement levels or across semantic terms.

Configuration manager. The configuration manager controls the current state of the knowledge base and determines semantic and temporal dependencies in the project's structure. Its role is to apply heuristics to ensure that system descriptions, their versions, and the products they define are consistent.

With a few notable exceptions (namely, Neptune[4] and DIF[5]), most commercial hypertext systems seriously neglect the need for elaborate version management.[6] The simple revision models applied to ordinary documents are inadequate to maintain complex software documentation. Software documents involve a number of additional constraints:

♦ compositional and referential dependencies (that result from make files, for example);

♦ document generation through executable programs;

♦ document verification through parsing and compilation;

♦ delivery sets (baselines);

♦ development distribution from collaborative development;

♦ the need for private workspace; and

♦ prototyping.

We believe that incorporating elements of software configuration management into the traditional hypertext model will benefit the hypertext mechanisms themselves. This belief led us to develop HyperCASE as a comprehensive set of customizable revision-control hypertext tools.

Project tracker. Hypertext's ability to organize software into a complex structure of internal and external documentation opens new opportunities for planning software-development and tracking-development activities. HyperCASE's project tracker provides a suite of project-management diagram editors in which a project manager defines the tasks, required resources, milestones, adopted standards, and project deliverables. The project team can then use the relationships and dependencies from such a project plan to determine the structure of deliverable documentation.

The project tracker also helps project development by tracking system activities like tool use, monitoring resources allocated to a given task, and checking the status of individual documents and their components.

Design tracker. A major reason for the high cost of software maintenance is that development and delivery systems don't record or preserve the history of design activities. Completed software-engineering systems, in particular, often omit intermediate design documentation. HyperCASE's

> ## HyperCASE's design tracker forces designers to document their decisions and the reasons for them. Managers can then trace the evolution of system concepts.

design tracker forces designers to document their decisions and the reasons for them. An integral part of HyperCASE's navigation system, the design tracker lets maintainers and managers retrace the evolution of system concepts, follow the reasons used to implement them in either chronological or logical order, and identify previous problem-solving attempts — thus avoiding potentially dangerous and expensive code and documentation modifications.

Like the configuration manager and project tracker, the design tracker provides a way for developers to precisely record their reasoning patterns. This feature makes HyperCASE a suitable environment for researching software processes because it identifies discrepancies between a developer's explicit design reasoning and the development plan implied by tool use.

Text analyzer. HyperCASE's text analyzer lets users access HyperBase through a restricted form of English. Unconstrained user queries are an alternative way to access software documents across the HyperBase data structures that support hypertext navigation. This alternative is attractive because although HyperBase is intelligent and comprehensive, it is highly structured and thus inflexible.

The text analyzer also makes it easier to recognize references to reusable concepts in requirements statements and to provide mechanisms for automatically classifying requirements and indexing and linking text for hypertext navigation.

CASE tools. Because HyperCASE's tools vary considerably in form and function, documents must be continually monitored to ensure consistency, integrity, and completeness. Software-development tools for assessing a project's state and condition must deal with volumes of incomplete and, in some cases, incorrect information. Typical problems include partial specifications, unfinished designs, error-ridden code, patchy documentation, and dated schedules and plans.

To remedy these problems, the HyperBase subsystem uses recent advances in artificial-intelligence applications to software systems.[7-9] The subsystem organizes a sophisticated knowledge base of reusable software documents and their components, provides heuristic rules to check their integrity, and aids their execution and testing.

CASE tools include a reuse manager, an integrity and completeness manager, a design animator, and executable diagram descriptions.

Reuse manager. Important to reusability — the fundamental aspect of software development — is having a uniform declarative representation of all document components that lets you see multiple views of the same component.

HyperBase provides such a uniform representation, which it uses to devise a set of knowledge-base rules about software and design reusability. The reuse manager offers a way to index and classify analyzed texts of requirements statements, design diagrams, plans, and schedules that lets you retrieve software documents relevant to the problem at hand with only a partially completed design or requirements statement. It also gives suggestions on how to incorporate the reusable components into the system being developed.

Integrity and completeness manager. Throughout the evolution of a project, each software entity is necessarily described from several vantage points. Relationships in entity-relationship diagrams, for example, may be defined as files or records in a data dictionary but appear as dataflows or stores in dataflow diagrams. Processes initially shown in HIPO (hierarchical input-process-output) charts may be refined with decision tables or state-transition diagrams, used in dataflow diagrams, and finally laid down as activity charts or program code.

When handling multiple software descriptions, you must analyze document se-

mantics, correlate document content, check design integrity, and define completeness. Such tasks are usually laborious and difficult, frequently requiring the use of complex logic and heuristics. The integrity manager provides the inference framework for devising rules that ensure semantic integrity and document completeness. It analyzes the syntactic and semantic contents of documents produced over the life cycle, including the highest design levels.

Design animator. As system development progresses, the design animator monitors the sequence of systematic refinements to modules and data structures. In this way, HyperCASE provides complete functional and structural mappings from the requirements specification; through the design of program logic, flow, and control; through the definition of the data structure; to the construction of source and binary program modules. Once the programs are compiled and linked, you can exercise the code using a standard Unix symbolic debugger and visually trace the execution progress across all the system's diagrammatical and textual descriptions.

Executable diagram descriptions. We are also working on ways to create a software-diagram specification that is constructed in much the same way a circuit diagram is built —made from standard module families, and requiring no further logical or functional elaboration for implementation. We expect the systems described by tools supporting this diagraming formalism to be truly executable from early specifications.

HYPERDICT

All HyperCASE documents are stored in HyperDict, a common data dictionary.

> HyperCASE provides complete functional and structural mappings from the requirements specification to the construction of source and binary modules.

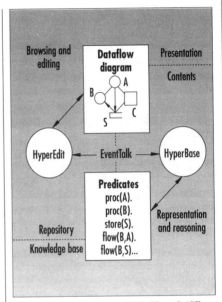

Figure 3. *Document processing in HyperCASE.*

Figure 3 shows how data dictionary updates are triggered by EventTalk transactions, channeled through the HyperBase knowledge base, and finally translated into the statements of embedded primitives in a high-level query language like Embedded SQL. This approach guarantees that HyperBase rules will check database integrity constraints or invoke them when necessary, thus keeping the database logically consistent. Several types of database operations — like reporting, querying, backing up, or recovering — do not alter the database contents and may be performed freely without any fear of constraint violation.

HyperCASE is our attempt to integrate a collection of disparate applications — namely, a CASE tool set — under a more general information-management and presentation paradigm, hypertext. We believe that this integration can improve concept reuse, simplifying the implementation of the CASE system and increasing its users' power and productivity.

The choice of tools has, in our view, been vindicated by exercises such as that conducted at CASE '90, the Fourth International Workshop on Software Engineering. During the workshop, users and implementers catalogued the desired features of CASE systems. We believe that the HyperCASE project addressed a considerable number of the issues users considered of immediate importance to any future CASE research.

Our initial goals were to focus on front-end issues that we believe to be critically important yet lacking in sufficient attention from existing research teams. We have not, therefore, proposed the development of code generators or support for specific methods. The project team anticipates a number of opportunities for future development, providing direct support for the software tools being marketed by both Amdahl and Prometheus. This will take the form of tailored diagramming and design-capture capabilities that reflect the needs of individual development systems.

We expect HyperCASE to significantly decrease maintenance efforts as well as make it easier to cope with the large document collections typical of software development. We also expect the combination of natural-language processing, a design-reasoning record, and project tracking to substantially improve the economy of software development because it promotes design reuse and enhances project control. ♦

ACKNOWLEDGMENTS

We acknowledge the direct financial support of Amdahl Australia and of both La Trobe University and Prometheus Software Developments, as well as the assistance from the Victorian State Government. We also gratefully acknowledge the moral support and encouragement of Tharam S. Dillon and the members of the Amdahl Australian Intelligent Tools Program team: Kevin Alldritt, David Cleary, Mel Hatzis, Daniel Jitnah, Austin McClaughlin, Jane Philcox, Arthur Proestakis, Bev Teague, and Chris Wignall.

REFERENCES

1. R. Rock-Evans and B. Engelien, *Analysis Techniques for CASE: A Detailed Evaluation*, Ovum Ltd., London, 1989.
2. R. Rock-Evans, *CASE Analyst Workbenches: A Detailed Product Evaluation*, Ovum Ltd., London, 1989.
3. J. Conklin, "Hypertext: An Introduction and Survey," *Computer*, Sept. 1987, pp. 17-40.
4. J. Bigelow, "Hypertext and CASE," *IEEE Software*, March 1988, pp. 23-27.
5. P. Garg, "Abstraction Mechanisms in Hypertext," *Comm. ACM*, July 1988, pp. 862-870.
6. W. Scacchi, "The USC System Factory Project," *Proc. Software Symp.*, Software Engineers Assoc., ACM Press, New York, Jan. 1989, pp. 9-41.
7. P. Carando, "Shadow Fusing Hypertext with AI," *IEEE Expert*, Winter 1989, pp. 65-78.
8. P. Garg and W. Scacchi, "Ishys: Designing an Intelligent Software Hypertext System," *IEEE Expert*, Fall 1989, pp. 52-63.
9. P. Puncello et al., "ASPIS : A Knowledge-Based CASE Environment," *IEEE Software*, March 1988, pp. 58-65.

Jacob L. Cybulski is deputy director of the Amdahl Australian Intelligent Tools Program and a lecturer in software engineering for the computer science and engineering department at La Trobe University. He is also a consultant and independent software developer. Cybulski's interests include artificial intelligence applications in software engineering, specifically interfaces and knowledge-based systems.

Cybulski received a BAppSci and MAppSci in computer science from the Royal Melbourne Institute of Technology. He is a member of the IEEE Computer Society, ACM, and American Association of Artificial Intelligence.

Karl Reed is director of the Amdahl Australian Intelligent Tools Program and a senior lecturer in software engineering for the computer science and engineering department at La Trobe University. He is also a senior visiting fellow in information technology, industry structure, and industry policy at the Royal Melbourne Institute of Technology. His research interests include general software-engineering issues, computer architecture, and industry policy.

Reed received an Associate Diploma from the RMIT in communications engineering and an MS in computer science from Monash University at Clayton. He is a fellow and honorary life member of the Australian Computer Society and director of its technical board.

Address questions about this article to Cybulski at Dept. of Computer Science and Computer Engineering, La Trobe University, Bundoora Victoria, Australia 3083; Internet jacob@latcs1.lat.oz.au.

SODOS: A Software Documentation Support Environment—Its Use

ELLIS HOROWITZ AND RONALD C. WILLIAMSON

Abstract—This paper describes a computerized environment, SODOS (Software Documentation Support), which supports the definition and manipulation of documents used in developing software. An object oriented environment is used as a basis for the SODOS interface. SODOS is built around a Software Life Cycle (SLC) Model that structures all access to the documents stored in the environment. One advantage of this model is that it supports software documentation *independent* of any fixed methodology that the developers may be using. The main advantage of the system is that it permits *traceability* through each phase of the Life Cycle, thus facilitating the test and maintenance phases. Finally the effort involved in learning and using SODOS is simplified due to a sophisticated "user-friendly" interface.

Index Terms—Objects, requirements traceability, software development environment, software documentation, software life cycle.

I. INTRODUCTION

THE objective of this research has been to develop a computerized environment, SODOS (Software Documentation Support), which supports the definition and manipulation of documents used in developing software. The principal use of documents in many projects is for reporting purposes. The documents invariably lack adequate correspondence with the "real" application problem definition and the specification and implementation of the solution. The documentation is viewed as a burden and becomes a separate process lagging behind the development of the software. Consequently, the evolution or maintenance of software becomes one of the major costs in the Software Life Cycle (SLC) since SLC documents of the system being maintained are of little assistance [19]. The basic thesis of this paper is twofold: 1) to have all information generated at the specifications and development phases available to the maintenance personnel in a complete, uniform, structured, and fully accessible form and 2) to generate the necessary information without significantly adding to the documentation burden or deteriorating the productivity of the system developers.

The SODOS environment differs from others in that it is based on a database management system (DBMS) and an object-based model of the Software Life Cycle. All of the documents used during the life-cycle of a software project are stored in a project database. The documents are developed using a predefined document structure and set of document relationships. The document structure consists of the chapter, section, paragraph, and figure hierarchy and the document relationships consist of mappings between components of a single document or several documents.

The SLC definition used is based on the classical one [24], [9], [12]. However, by emphasizing an object oriented view, the information generated at each phase (including documents, data definitions, and code) is interrelated based on a set of predefined and user-defined relationships, which are then stored in the project database. It is the representation of these relationships that distinguishes the SLC definition used in this reseach from the classical SLC definition. Within an SLC phase, the relationships among the objects are structured according to the methodology selected at the phase. The methodology chosen varies from problem definition and specification to the problem solution's implementation and test. In addition, the relationships between information at different phases are structured to allow the system developer to trace the development of an implementation from a set of requirements. The requirement made by SODOS in using methodologies and in relating each phase is that the project database be used for storage of all objects and relationships.

Viewing the development of software as an information management problem, the solution used here is to define all information entering the environment to be part of a structured database. To formally describe the information and how it is used, a model was developed which identified the information in the SLC, the relationships among the information, and how the information is used at each phase of the SLC. To develop an information model consistent with the SLC, the approach was to initially study some actual software development systems.

From this study and after reviewing current research and literature [16], [8], [3], [1], [2], [5], [6], [15], we were able to identify the objects produced during the SLC and the relationships among those objects. The principal objects identified in this study were the documents produced during each phase of the SLC. We then used document generation as a central concept in structuring and accessing the objects at each phase.

Fig. 1 shows the components of the object-based model.

Manuscript received November 30, 1984; revised November 29, 1985. This work was supported in part by the Hughes Aircraft Company Fellowship Program.

E. Horowitz is with the Department of Computer Science, University of Southern California, Los Angeles, CA 90089.

R. C. Williamson was with the Department of Computer Science, University of Southern California, Los Angeles, CA 90089. He is now with Hughes Aircraft Company, Software Engineering Division, AI Technology Department, El Segundo, CA 90245.

IEEE Log Number 8610241.

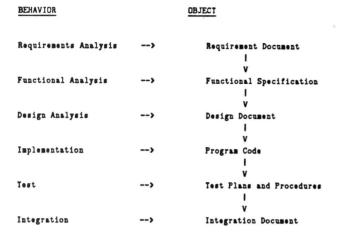

BEHAVIOR		OBJECT
Requirements Analysis	-->	Requirement Document
		↓
Functional Analysis	-->	Functional Specification
		↓
Design Analysis	-->	Design Document
		↓
Implementation	-->	Program Code
		↓
Test	-->	Test Plans and Procedures
		↓
Integration	-->	Integration Document

Fig. 1. An integrated environment: behavior + objects + relationship.

The information model describes the behavior during the SLC, the principal objects in the environment and the relationships among the objects. As the figure illustrates, the behavior describes the context in which the information is used in the SLC (i.e., each phase). The objects themselves consist of the documents and the components of the documents including individual requirements, design modules, code segments, test plans, and test procedures. The relationships, as illustrated by the (left-right and up-down) arrows in the figure, relate the documents with the phase of the SLC that produces the document and with the next document in sequence.

Using this model, the descriptions from each SLC phase are organized and managed as structured documents. The document is represented within the database not as a sequential file but as a complex object with an internal structure and well-defined relationships with other objects in the SLC model. The document representation as an object is defined in a companion paper [20].

The approach in this research was to use an object oriented model that would provide a uniform and productive method of developing and evolving the software and documentation. Thus, Smalltalk-80 [10], [11] was chosen for the prototype implementation because of its rigorous definition of objects and the availability of an existing system, the Xerox 1100 workstation. The classification of objects and the inheritance rules followed in the Class hierarchy of Smalltalk-80 are ideal for defining the structure and the operations on the objects defined in the model of the SLC environment. However, this work is not dependent upon Smalltalk or the Xerox 1100 and may be implemented in a more conventional computer environment.

In Section II we briefly describe how SODOS is used in every phase of the SLC, then in Section III we show more detail concerning how the software developer actually creates documents and relationships. Two companion papers, [20] and [21], describe the internal representation and the implementation of SODOS. In [21] the details of the prototype implementation of the document window interface, the extended relational data model, and the query interface are discussed.

II. USING SODOS ON A SOFTWARE DEVELOPMENT PROJECT

The uniform framework provided by SODOS is available from project inception through the specification and implementation and finally to the maintenance and evolution of the completed software product. A discussion of how to incorporate SODOS at each phase of the SLC is presented in the next section.

A. Using SODOS Throughout the SLC

At the beginning of a software project a document administrator would be responsible for defining a set of software document standards and software development methodologies. These guidelines are either predefined based on previous standards or defined by other requirements (such as from a customer or another company). If the project is to follow the general guidelines, with standard documentation and methodologies, the existing document definitions may be used with no modification. Otherwise, the document administrator is responsible for creating new document definitions. This process is described in [20]. Each document type is subsequently defined by him, in SODOS, using a database schema that describes the document structure, internal relationships, keywords, and related documents. After the document types have been defined, the project database model is then created and loaded based on the set of document types and methodologies chosen for the project. The requirements, design, and implementation documents are entered by the software developer within SODOS. SODOS supports this entry by acting as both an editor and by reflecting the form of each document type. Moreover, it supports the developer as he highlights keywords and relationships within the documents. As each document is updated the document components and the relationships among components are defined and entered into the database by the software developer/analyst. Each component consists of text for either requirements, design modules, code elements, or test procedures. Each relationship consists of a link between the component being defined and another component either in the same document or in another document. If no methodology is defined, the user has the option of using pure natural language text for specifying the Requirements or Design Documents. Otherwise, the text may correspond to the formal language of a predefined methodology (such as PSL/PSA, SREM, PDL or the implementation language [18], [17], [1], [2], [4]).

The final product of the software development project is a database containing the Requirements Documents, the Design Documents, the Implementation Notebook, and the testing specifications, plans, and procedure documents. The relationships among the components in each document are also stored in the database, based on the SLC information model representation of the documents. The database can then be used during testing, maintenance, and evolution of the software system to more easily test the application or change the requirements, the design specification or the implementation.

During the requirements phase of the project, as the requirement components are defined and included as part of the Requirements Document, the system engineer or project manager can query the component content and relationships defined within the document. The structural consistency and completeness of the document can also be verified or checked as the document is written. At this point in the SLC, no design modules have yet been defined. Therefore, no interrelationships can yet be specified. However, relationships among the requirements can be specified as the individual requirements are defined. These intradocument relationships include, for example, data input or output dependencies among the requirements. As portions of the Requirements Document are completed and approved, the Design Document can then be written. Design modules, code components, and testing specifications are structured and defined based on the content of the corresponding requirements. As each design module is defined, the detailed description of the module is entered along with the relationships to the related requirement. Individual design modules are also related to each other based on relationships such as structure, control flow, or data flow. These relationships are entered into the SODOS database as the modules are defined. Next, the implementation of each design module is defined and documented in the Implementation Notebook. Each function or procedure is entered in the required programming language and tested for proper syntax. The relationship of the function or procedure to the design module is entered into the database as the procedure is defined. The testing documents associated with the implementation are completed next and the relationships of individual tests with requirements, design modules, and the code itself are entered into the database.

The final phase of software development is integration and test, where each subfunction in the software project is merged together to form an integrated system which is then thoroughly tested. During this phase, integration and test plans and procedures are used to coordinate the effort. The content of these documents are also related to the corresponding requirements, design, and code by storing the relationships in the database.

During the maintenance or evolution phase, all of the requirements, design, implementation, and testing documents are available to the maintenance personnel. Changes in requirements and the corresponding changes in design and implementation can be traced using the relationships stored in the database. Queries may be issued against the database to determine design modules, code, or tests associated with the requirement which has changed. The maintenance personnel then use the SODOS interface to update the Requirement Document, the Design Documents, the Implementation Notebooks, and the testing documents. These changes create new versions of the database which are then used for subsequent changes.

B. Using Development Methodologies in SODOS

When updating a document and adding text to each component within a section, a number of methodologies may be applied. During the requirements phase a formal description of each requirement may be used, such as in PSL/PSA, or SREM [9]. During the design phase a formal description of the design may be given in a language such as PDL [9], and a definition of the structure of the design modules may be given in a module interconnection language [14]. During the implementation phase several languages may be used to code the design.

Within each of the SLC phases, the methodology chosen for each software development project phase is finalized before the phase begins. The document administrator, in addition to defining the structure and initial content of each of the documents, also defines the required methodology to be associated with each document. When a document is created, the fact that a specific methodology is to be used when updating the document, is also represented within the document instance. The formal methodology is assumed to have a formal syntax definition, as in [7], [13], [5], [17], [22], [23], [24], and [25], which can be used to correct the syntax of the specification before entry of the component into the database. When the user updates the text of a component in a document the editor is either in the simplest case of a pure text editor, or a syntax directed editor. The formal syntax is based on the language definition used within the methodology.

The editor and syntax verification method is selected by the document administrator and is automatically associated with each type of document. Document instances are associated with a syntax directed editor for the particular language, e.g., Ada, Pascal, Modula, Lisp, etc. The code is stored in the database in source format.

The database structure associated with each methodology can vary. The document adminstrator defines the schema associated with each document definition and each methodology. The schema definition need only be done once for a project and can then be used on future projects. If a BNF description of the formal language is available, the task of developing the database schema and text editors structure can be automated using a table-driven approach.

C. Document Relationships

Documentation of the software development process using current methodologies involves specifying solutions to a problem in several levels of abstraction. These levels of abstraction are not necessarily easily transformed from one to another. Inconsistencies and incompleteness in the specifications may arise and are usually not discovered until well into the implementation and test phases, when more rigorous and detailed analyses are required. The approach taken in SODOS to resolve some of the consistency and completeness issues is to relate each component of a document to the components of other documents and components within the document itself. This approach addresses the issue of structural and syntactic completeness and consistency and not the consistency or completeness of the semantic content of the document or documents.

Consistency and completeness constraints apply within a document and across documents. Within a requirement specification, a requirement description may define inputs and outputs which relate to other requirements in the specification. Inconsistent references and incomplete specifications may arise and can be checked, if a predefined generic structure is available during the update of the specification. For example, there must exist a design module description and code for every requirement specified in the Requirements specification. Alternatively every design module must be derived from a requirement, unless the designer is adding more functionality than is actually required.

To address these issues, each document is SODOS contains information describing the kinds of interdocument and intradocument relationships expected. In the current prototype design, these relationships are predefined within the document definition as a relational schema for interdocument relationships. More flexibility might be desirable in a production system, where the author of a document could dynamically add or modify inter- and intradocument constraints.

III. The SODOS Document Interface

The SODOS document interface enables the system and software engineer to 1) create documents of a specific type, 2) modify a document based on the document's predefined structure, 3) relate selected components of one document with those of another, and 4) query the document structure and content. The following set of documents are predefined in SODOS:

Requirement Phase
   1) Requirement Documents
      (B-5 Specification)
   2) User Manual

Design Phase
   3) Designer Document
      (CPC Notebook)
   4) Structure Chart
   5) Requirements Matrix
   6) Test Plan

Implementation Phase
   7) Implementation Notebook
   8) Test procedures

In subsequent sections, we will use the User Manual as an example to show how specific documents are created and modified.

A document administrator would define and control these documents in the software development project. The definition of the documents consists of a representation of the structural hierarchy, the content, the internal relationships, and the interrelationships among the documents. The user creates and updates the documents through the

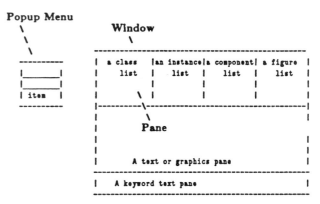

Fig. 2. Windows, panes, and popup menus.

SODOS document browser window. In this way the user creates an arbitrarily complex set of associations (between the documents and the document components) that may be queried, examined, and tested. In the rest of this paper when we mention the STRUCTURE, CONTENT, KEYWORD, INTER-DOCUMENT, or INTRA-DOCUMENT relations we are referring to the underlying SODOS representation of the objects and the associations among the objects that are input for each document. The template of relations, or schema, for each document is predefined by the document administrator.

A. The Window Interface

The SODOS document interface consists of a specialized Smalltalk-80 window containing several panes or subwindows that represent the class, instance, structure, content, and keywords of each document, as shown in Fig. 2. Interaction with the window involves command selection from pop-up menus using screen cursor, which is controlled by the display pointing device (a "mouse"). The pop-up menu is a list of commands which are displayed on the screen when a "mouse" button is pressed inside one of the panes. Text and graphics are entered via text and graphics editor windows. The text is input from the keyboard and the graphics are entered by selecting graphics primitives (such as line, curve, and box drawing functions) and specifying points using the pointing device.

In the following sections the use of SODOS will be explained in terms of window selections and pop-up menu selections within each subview of the main SODOS window. The top-level window in SODOS is a variation of the "System Browser" used in Smalltalk-80 to browse through and edit code. More detail about the SODOS implementation in Smalltalk-80 can be found in [21].

The document interface consists of the document browser window and eight subviews or panes. Figs. 3 and 4 show the window format and the pop-up menus associated with each plane. Each pane maintains a list of document types, document instances (after the type has been selected), document section names (after a document instance has been selected), document paragraph and figure names, keywords, text, and graphics. A query window is also defined and allows the user to issue queries against

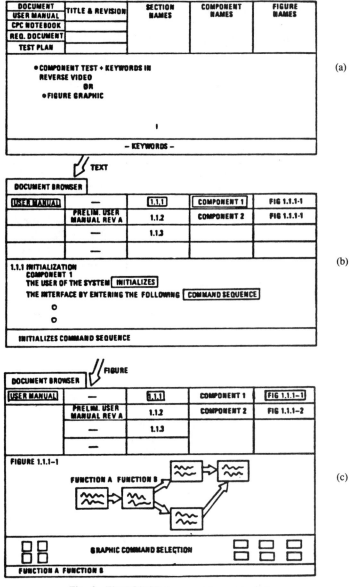

Fig. 3. The SODOS document browser window.

the document database. The following sections will describe the role of each of the panes in creating, updating, and querying the documents.

B. Creating a Document

The first pane in the upper left corner of the document browser window [see Fig. 3(a)] contains an item list of document types including:

DOCUMENT
USER MANUAL
CPC NOTEBOOK
REQUIREMENT DOCUMENT
TEST PLAN

The system designer creates documents from each document type and follows the default structure when entering the text and associations. To access an instance of a document, for example the Preliminary User Manual, the following actions are performed within the document browser window. The system designer selects the USER MANUAL class using the "mouse" (pointing device) by pressing and then releasing the leftmost button. After selecting this class, all user manual instance titles and revision identification are displayed in the adjacent pane, as shown in Fig. 3(b). To create a new document instance the user slects "NewDocument" in the instance pane's menu (shown as box B in Fig. 4) and then enters the document's date, author(s) name, identification, title, and revision, in this case "HAC00123 : Preliminary User Manual—REV-A" [shown in Fig. 3(b), (c)] The pop-up menu defined in the first document browser pane (shown as box A in Fig. 4) allows printing of all instances of the selected class, general querying over all documents, and deletion of a document class and all of its document instances. The pop-up menu associated with the second pane allows creation, deletion, copying, and querying of each document.

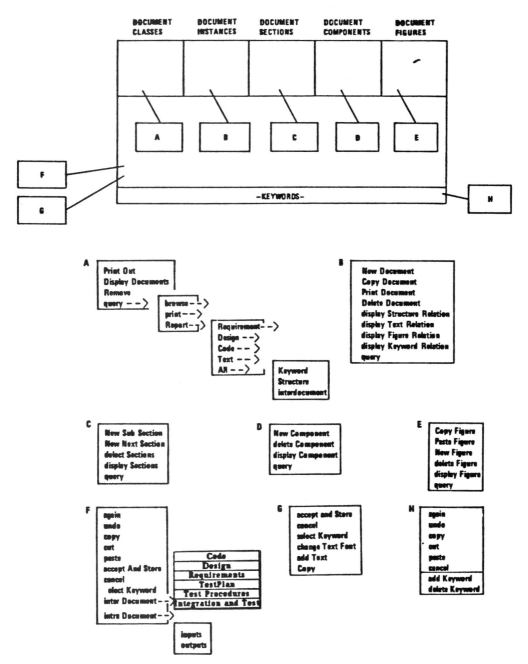

Fig. 4. The document browser pop-up menus.

In addition, the underlying relations which represent the document structure and content can be selected and displayed on the screen.

The new document instance is added to the DOCUMENT relation with all the data values initialized and internal STRUCTURE and CONTENT relations defined based on the document definition. All of the STRUCTURE and CONTENT relations are initially empty and are updated as sections, paragraphs, figures, text, and keywords are added. Deleting a document removes all of the content and structure information. All references to the document within other documents are updated and checked for consistency. Copying a document instance creates a new document instance with the same structure and content as the original document but with a new identification, title, and revision.

C. Updating a Document

To build or modify a document after creating a new document or selecting an existing one from the document instance pane, the user selects ''new Sub-Section'' or ''new Next-Section'' (shown in box C in Fig. 4) from the structure pane pop-up menu and enters the section name. If the document already has sections defined, the existing section names will appear in the structure pane. The new section can be added as a subsection of a selected section or a section at the same level, but next in sequence to a selected section (that is, the new section is inserted between existing sections). To see the section hierarchy as related to the section names, selected ''Section Hierarchy'' in the structure pane. If no existing section has been selected then the new section will be added to the

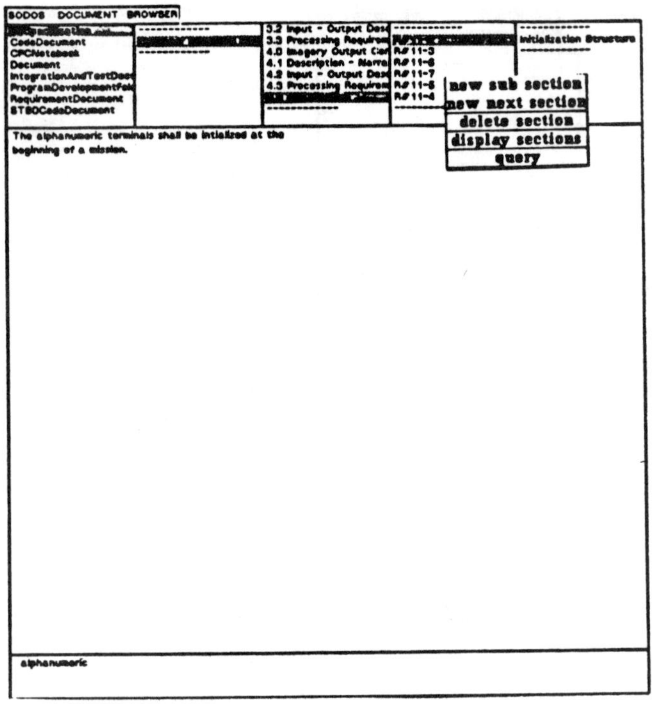

BEHAVIOR:
    Enter a new sub-section or a new next-section after
    an existing section (Sec 1.0).

ACTIONS:
    Select the (Sec 1.0) section entry by clicking
    the mouse button

    Select 'newSubSection' or 'newNextSection'
    from the pop-up menu

    Type in the new section name when prompted

Fig. 5. Adding a new section to the subsection, next-section hierarchy.

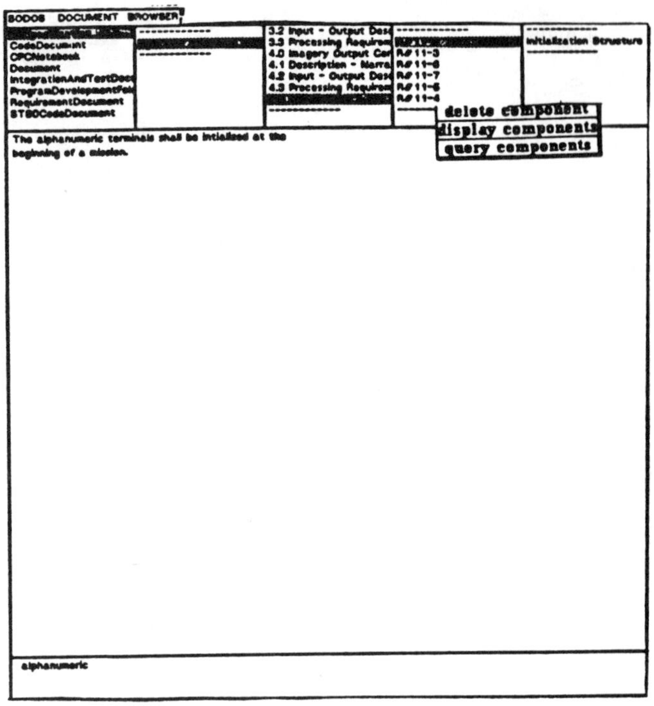

BEHAVIOR:
    Updating the contents of a text component.

ACTIONS:
    Select an existing component from the fourth pane
  or
    Select 'newComponent' and fill in the prompts
    (if no other component is
    preselected, the new component
    will be added to the beginning of
    the section)

    When the text window contents appear the
    text can be modified.

    Select 'acceptAndStore' to add the new component
    to the database

Fig. 6. Creating a paragraph and text.

beginning of the document. Fig. 5 shows the display associated with adding a new section.

The STRUCTURE relations are updated as a result of defining a new section. The actions necessary to create new paragraphs, text, figures, and keywords are shown in Figs. 6, 7, and 8. To add text or graphics to the document, select a section and then select or add either a component name or a figure name. The pop-up menus in the two top right panes allow addition, deletion, or querying of paragraph or figures as shown in boxes D and E in Fig. 4.

Selecting or adding a paragraph causes the text pane to be initialized with the previous or blank text and the keyword pane to be initialized with the keywords associated with the paragraph. The text pane allows full edit functions such as undo, copy, cut, and paste. When editing is completed, the "acceptAndStore" selection, shown in box F in Fig. 4, stores the text in the content relations.

Selecting or adding a figure causes the graphics pane to be initialized with the previous or a blank figure graphic. The graphics pane allows the full graphics editing capability of the Smalltalk-80 form editor extended with additional functions for defining and adding internal text to the graphic. When graphics editing is completed the

"acceptAndStore" (shown in box G in Fig. 4) selection stores the graphic into the CONTENT relations.

The keywords are selected either directly from the text by moving the cursor across the keyword with the leftmost button depressed and then selecting the "selected Keyword" option (shown in boxes F, G in Fig. 4) or adding the keyword directly into the keyword pane and selecting the "add Keyword" option (shown in box H in Fig. 4).

D. Relating Documents

Fig. 9 shows how the Document Browser is used to specify both inter- and intradocument Relationships. The process involves relating a selected component in the document being updated with one or more components of another document or documents. The document identification, title, revisions, and the component name are used to related the components. The type of the relationship is selected from a list defined for each document type.

To add these relationships in the SODOS document browser involves selecting the component associated with

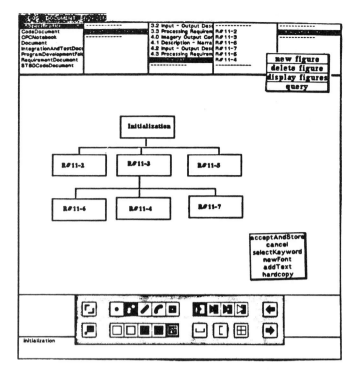

BEHAVIOR:
Updating the contents of a graphic component.

ACTIONS:
Select an existing component from the fifth pane.
or
Select 'newFigure' and fill in the prompts.
(if no other figure is
preselected, the new figure
will be added to the beginning of
the list of figures in the section)

When the figure window contents appear the
graphics can be modified.

Select 'acceptAndStore' to add the new component
to the database.

Fig. 7. Creating a figure.

BEHAVIOR:
Selecting keywords for text and figure components

ACTIONS:
Select the keyword text with the cursor

Select the 'selectKeyword' item from the pop-up menu
or
Type in a select a keyword from the keyword pane

Select the 'addKeyword' item from the pop-up menu

SODOS adds the keyword text to the database and
updates the keyword pane

Fig. 8. Selecting keywords.

a requirement. Within the text pane select, "inter-Document" or "intraDocument," then select the relationship type and the document and component name for each related component. The related components would be the design module description, the procedure, and the test procedure. The relationship types include "derived from," "derives," "generates," "implemented by," "tests," "inputs," "outputs," etc. The set of relationships are predefined for each document. Similar steps are taken when completing the module, procedure, and test descriptions.

Selecting the "check consistency" item in the document instance pane's pop-up menu initiates a check for the structural inconsistencies that can develop within documents. All inconsistencies that can be corrected are and others are brought to the user's attention by displaying a separate window of inconsistent components.

Structural completeness is checked by selecting the "check completeness" item in the document instance pane's pop-up menu. Internal document completeness determines whether every section, component, and figure has a content, either text or graphics. Interdocument completeness, or document traceability, checks that every component in one document has a related component in a requirements, design, code, or test document. Document traceability determines the existence of relationships between two document components. Selecting the "check traceability" item and a related document type initiates a trace of all components between the two related documents. All document components which have a content must also have a relationship with a component in the related document and vice versa. If such is not the case, the document is characterized as not being traceable and the nontraceable components are listed in a separate window on the display. Each document instance, corresponding to the individual document types, related to the document being updated is specified during the update of the interrelationships.

IV. QUERYING THE DOCUMENTS

One of the benefits in representing the documents as part of a database in SODOS is the ability to query the information and relationships associated with the docu-

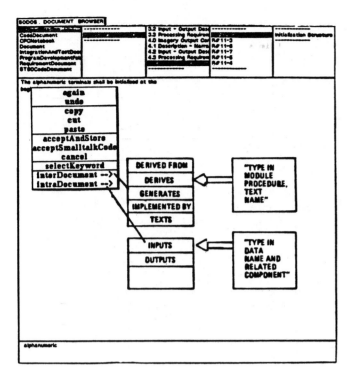

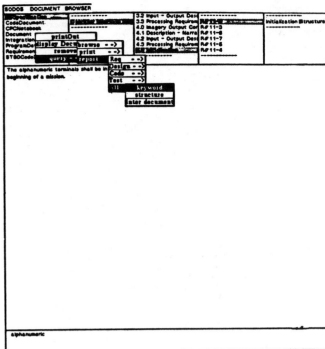

BEHAVIOR:
 Specifying document relationships

ACTIONS:
 Select the relationship type from the pop-up menu:
   either 'interDocument'
    or 'intraDocument'

 Select the type of component to be related from
 the pop-up menu
   either document types
    or internal relationships

 Select the related component from the pop-up menu
  or type in the component name

Fig. 9. Specifying inter- and intradocument relationships.

BEHAVIOR:
 Querying the document components

ACTIONS:
 Select the query option from each pane's pop-up menu

 Enter query selections as shown in Figure 4-2

Fig. 10. Querying the documents—initiating the query.

ments. The query language interface is initiated from within the Document Browser window and is basically a simplified Query by Example (QBE) [26] approach.

The query interface supports general database queries. Each query relates to a preselected aspect of the document such as structure, keywords, or intra/interdocument relationships. Each aspect is inspected by selecting the "Query" menu selection in the appropriate pane. Fig. 10 shows the actions necessary to initiate a specific query. Queries are issued by selecting the "Query" menu selection in the document class pane. Each query is formed by making selections in a hierarchy of query windows, as shown in Fig. 11(a)–(d), are displayed after making the menu selection above. Fig. 11 shows the actions necessary to complete a general query. First the query command, document types and document characteristics are selected from pop-up window represented in Fig. 11(a). Next each table template window associated with each document characteristic [i.e., KEYWORD in (b), STRUCTURE in (c), and INTER-DOCUMENT in (d)] appears on the display. The table template windows allow

the formulation of queries specific to the document characteristic. Subsequent query examples show how complex queries can be defined by combining selections from each of the document characteristic windows.

A general query supports multiple levels of queries, that is, an entry may either be a simple piece of text or the results of a subsequent query. The subsequent query is issued by selecting the "Query" menu selection again in the value pane instead of typing in a text value. Menu selections such as "Backup," "Reset," "Exit," and "Accept" are available to correct mistakes when composing the query or to accept and issue the query. Boolean operators "and," "or," "not," "(" and ")" are also available to form more complicated queries.

A. Example SODOS Queries

Several examples of the kinds of questions that a system or software engineer may want to ask regarding requirements, design, and code are now presented. First we state the queries in a pseudo-English style and then in Figs. 12–15 the equivalent SODOS query interface formats are shown. The internal representation and processing of the queries are defined in two companion documents [20] and [21].

The following queries involve several types of information:

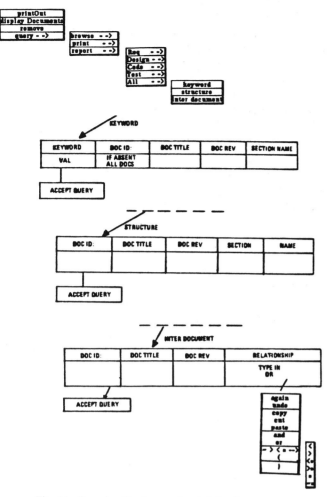

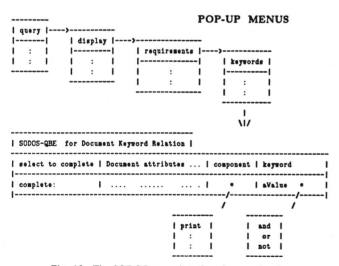

Fig. 11. Querying the documents—defining the query.

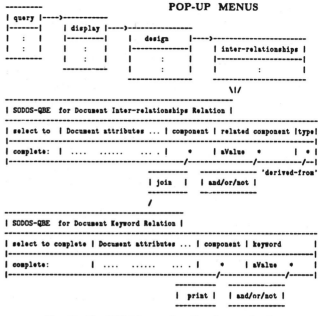

Fig. 13. The SODOS query interface for question 2.

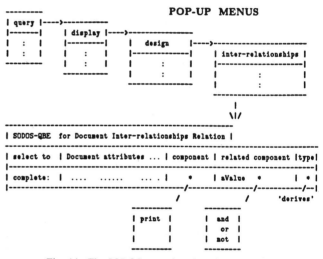

Fig. 14. The SODOS query interface for question 3.

Fig. 12. The SODOS query interface for question 1.

1) document components such as specific requirements, design modules, code segments;

2) the relationship among requirements, design modules, and code (such as a design module is "derived from" a requirement);

3) the attributes of each of the document components (such as, author, date, completion status, component type, keywords).

Four types of queries are characterized below. The { .. } denotes a choice of zero or more items and the [..] denote a choice of exactly one item.

1) Display all REQUIREMENTS with
   { keyword [= or #] aValue {and, or} }.

2) Display all DESIGN MODULES 'derived from'
   { a set of REQUIREMENTS }
        where
   { keyword [= or #] a Value {and, or} }.

3) Display all REQUIREMENTS which 'generate'
   a set of DESIGN MODULES.

4) Display all CODE 'generated by'
   { a set of REQUIREMENTS }
   where
   {keyword [= or #] aValue { and, or } }
   and
   { state-of-code [= or #] 'complete'
                        'tested'
                        'in-progress' }

The steps necessary to ask the four questions above using the SODOS query interface are shown in Figs. 12,

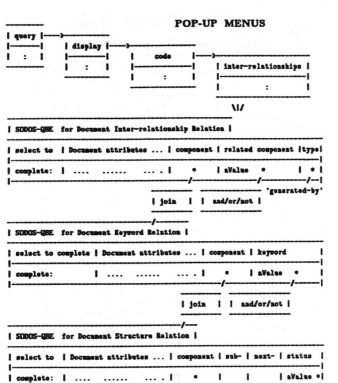

Fig. 15. The SODOS query interface for question 4.

13, 14, and 15. The set of actions for each of the four questions include first selecting the "display" option of the query command in the document class pane's pop-up menu. Then either REQUIREMENTS, DESIGN, CODE, TEST or all of the documents may be searched by the query, as well as either the structure, the keywords or the interrelationships among the components. Boolean operators are available for each column entry to form Boolean expressions using the selected values. Selecting an entry from each column and typing a value forms a **select** operation to be performed on the selected columns. Within a column entry, selecting **print** causes a **project** operation to be performed on the column and selecting **join** causes the selected relation to be "joined" with the original relation over the selected column.

The query in Fig. 12 involves a projection over the Requirement Document's component column and a selection of keyword values. The query in Fig. 13 involves a projection over the Design Document's component column, a join of the Interrelationship Relation and the Keyword relation and finally a selection of the related component, the relationship type and the keyword values. The query in Fig. 14 involves a projection over the Design Document's component column and a selection of both the related component and the relationship type. The query in Fig. 15 involves a projection over the Implementation Notebook's component column; a join of the INTER-RELATIONSHIP Relation, the KEYWORD Relation, and the STRUCTURE Relation; and a selection of the related component, relationship type, keyword, and component status.

V. Conclusions

The objective of our research was to combine object oriented representation and database technology with a "user-friendly" interface to produce an integrated software development environment that would significantly decrease software life-cycle costs. The purpose of this paper has been to describe the resulting system, SODOS, as it is seen by a potential user. Two companion papers, [20] and [21], describe the internal representation and the implementation of SODOS.

SODOS is an attempt to support SLC document production through the application of database technology. SODOS is methodology independent, meaning it supports document written using either natural language or a formal system (e.g., PLS/PSA, SREM and even code). SODOS requires the system/software engineer to identify keywords or key elements as he creates his documents. Making these identifications requires only marginal extra effort due to user-friendly interface consisting of multiple windows and a mouse for selecting menu items. The resulting database contains all documents, code, test data, and relationships both within and between documents. These relationships may be used to determine consistency within a document, structural completeness of a document, and traceability across documents.

References

[1] M. W. Alford, "A requirements engineering methodology for real time processing requirements," *IEEE Trans. Software Eng.*, vol. SE-3, no. 1, pp. 60–68, 1977.

[2] T. E. Bell, "An extendable approach to computer-aided software requirements engineering," *IEEE Trans. Software Eng.*, vol. SE-3, no. 1, pp. 49–59, 1977.

[3] B. W. Boehm, "Software engineering—As it is," in *Proc. 4th Int. Conf. Software Eng.*, 1979, pp. 11–21.

[4] S. H. Caine and E. K. Gordon, "PDL: A tool for software design," *AFIPS Comput. Surveys*, vol. 44, pp. 272–276, 1975.

[5] X. Oeters, "A language for describing software system architecture," Technische Universitat Berlin, Tech. Document, pp. 1–23, 1980.

[6] M. Bayer *et al.*, "Software development in the CDL2 laboratory," Technische Universitat Berlin, Tech. Document, 1981.

[7] A. M. Davis, "The design of a family of application oriented requirements languages," *Computer*, pp. 21–28, May 1982.

[8] Data Systems Division, *EDSG—Software Engineering Standards and Procedures*, 1982.

[9] P. Freeman and A. I. Wasserman, *Tutorial on Software Design Techniques*, 3rd ed. Washington, DC: IEEE Computer Society, Cat. No. EHO 161-0, 1980.

[10] A. Goldberg, "Smalltalk-80: The interactive programming environment," Xerox Corp., 1982.

[11] ——, *Smalltalk-80: The Language and its Implementation*. Reading, MA: Addison-Wesley, 1983.

[12] H. L. Hausen and M. Mullerburg, "Conspectus of software engineering environments," in *Software Development Environments: A Tutorial*. 1981, pp. 462–476.

[13] K. L. Heninger, "Specifying software requirements for complex systems: New techniques and their application," *IEEE Trans. Software Eng.*, vol. SE-6, no. 1, pp. 2–13, 1980.

[14] R. Prieto-Diaz and J. Neighbors, "Module interconnection languages: Survey," Univ. California, Irvine, Tech. Rep. 189, pp. 1–90, 1982.

[15] X. Oeters, "A language for describing software system architecture," Technische Universitat Berlin, Tech. Document, pp. 1–23, 1980.

[16] M. Powell and M. Linton, "Visual abstraction in an interaction programming environment," *Proc. SIGPLAN*, vol. 18, no. 6, pp. 14–21, 1982.

[17] W. E. Rzepka, "Using SREM to specify command and control software requirements," RADC In House Rep., pp. 1–21, 1982.

[18] D. Teichroew and E. A. Hershey, III, "PSL/PSA: A computer-aided technique for structured documentation and analysis of information processing systems," *IEEE Trans. Software Eng.*, vol. SE-3, no. 1, pp. 41–48, 1977.

[19] A. I. Wasserman, "Toward integrated software development environments," in *Proc. Int. Seminar Software Eng. Applications*, 1980, pp. 1–21.

[20] E. Horowitz and R. Williamson, "SODOS—Its definition," Dep. Comput. Sci., Univ. Southern California, Tech. Paper, pp. 1–35, 1984.

[21] ——, "SODOS—Its implementation," Dep. Comput. Sci., Univ. Southern California, Tech. Paper, pp. 1–40, 1984.

[22] M. L. Wilson, "A semantics-based method for requirements analysis and system design," *Proc. IEEE*, pp. 107–112, 1979.

[23] E. W. Winters, "An analysis of the capabilities of problem statement language: A language for system requirements and specifications," in *Proc. Compsac 1979*, pp. 283–288.

[24] Y. Yamamoto, R. V. Morris, *et al.*, "The role of requirements analysis in the system life cycle," in *Proc. NCC*, 1982, pp. 381–387.

[25] R. T. Yeh and P. Zave, "Specifying software requirements," *Proc. IEEE*, vol. 68, no. 9, pp. 1077–1984, 1980.

[26] M. Zloof, "Query by example," in *Proc. NCC*, vol. 44, 1975.

and in addition has published over forty research articles on computer science subjects ranging from data structures, algorithms, and software design to computer science education. His current research is on software development environments that support the definition of software requirements and design by pictures.

Dr. Horowitz has been an Editor for the journals *Communications of the ACM* and *Transactions on Mathematical Software*.

Ellis Horowitz received the B.S. degree from Brooklyn College, Brooklyn, NY, and the Ph.D. degree in computer science from the University of Wisconsin.

He was on the faculty at the University of Wisconsin and at Cornell University before assuming his present post as Professor of Computer Science and Electrical Engineering at the University of Southern California, Los Angeles. He is Past Chairman of the Department of Computer Science at USC. He is the author/coauthor of five books

Ronald C. Williamson received the M.A. degree in applied mathematics from the University of California, Los Angeles, in 1976, and the Ph.D. degree in computer science from the University of Southern California, Los Angeles, in 1984.

He joined Hughes Aircraft Company in 1978, where he is a Program Manager for Information Processing projects within the AI Technology Department. The areas of technology he has pursued are artificial intelligence applied to database environments, user interfaces, object oriented design and programming, image understanding, and expert system development within a situation assessment domain.

Dr. Williamson is a member of the Association for Computing Machinery, the American Association for Artificial Intelligence, and the IEEE Computer Society.

PART IV: THE ROLE OF ASSISTANTS AND EXPERT-SYSTEM TECHNOLOGY IN CASE

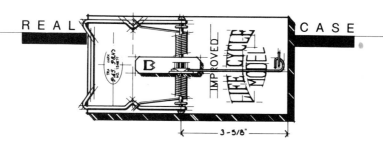

ASPIS: A Knowledge-Based CASE Environment

P. Paolo Puncello, **Piero Torrigiani**, **Francesco Pietri**, **Riccardo Burlon**, **Bruno Cardile**, and **Mirella Conti**, *Tecsiel*

This project seeks to improve the quality and productivity of the first phases of the life cycle by combining artificial intelligence with software engineering techniques.

This article reports on ESPRIT Project 401, building the Application Software Prototype Implementation System. ASPIS exploits artificial intelligence techniques in a software-development environment. Our goal is to encourage a more flexible and effective software-development life cycle, smoothing the transition between user needs, analysis, and design.

The ASPIS environment includes a set of tools that specifically address tasks in the early phases of the software life cycle: requirements analysis and design. These phases are very knowledge-intensive, requiring the expertise of skilled practitioners. The processes that convert requirements into a specification and then into a detailed design are often informal, labor-intensive, and undocumented. It is impractical with current techniques to automate them fully.[1]

However, AI techniques can contribute to improving quality and productivity in these early phases by providing a basis for defining new formal languages and a suitable way to represent the large amount of knowledge they involve. Logic programming is a suitable specification language,[2] and knowledge-based tools can support the specification and design of a software system.[3]

We adopted an evolutionary life-cycle model in ASPIS, to bridge the gap between the analysis and design phases. We have established suitable languages and methods for analysis and design and have investigated some application areas, including access-control systems and banking systems. The novel aspects of our project are the knowledge-based tools called assistants and the definition of a logic-based formalism for specifications.

ASPIS has four assistants. Two knowledge-based assistants — an Analysis Assistant and a Design Assistant — are used directly by the developers of a particular application adhering to a particular methodology. They embody knowledge about both the method and the application domain. Once defined, the specifications can be executed by the Prototype Assistant, which verifies the system's properties. A fourth assistant, the Reuse Assistant, helps developers reuse specifications and designs. Figure 1 shows the four assistants and their logical connections.

This article focuses on the Analysis Assistant, Tecsiel's main project task.

Reprinted from *IEEE Software*, Vol. 5, No. 2, March 1988, pp. 58-65. Copyright © 1988 by The Institute of Electrical and Electronics Engineers, Inc. All rights reserved.

Evolutionary life cycle

Traditional software-development support includes defining different phases in a life-cycle model, defining the methodology for each phase, and supplying supporting tools, which are sometimes integrated in a sophisticated environment.

During development, different representations of a system are produced in the various phases from particular viewpoints and with different purposes. Each representation must be complete and consistent with the others. Research in the last few years has focused on accomplishing this consistency checking with formal specification languages.[4,5]

Today's life-cycle models differ on the granularity of the phases, but most include requirements analysis, design, implementation, test, and maintenance. In all models, the major bottleneck is between analysis and design. Moreover, analysis and design are now recognized universally as the most crucial phases because the errors made in those phases have major consequences on the successive phases.

Our efforts have concentrated on smoothing the transition between these two phases. We have chosen two methods (one for analysis and one for design), modified them, and defined a way to move from one phase to the other. The ASPIS development cycle is shown in Figure 2.

Analysis. The analysis method we chose comprises several phases and uses the Structural Analysis language[6-8] to analyze functions and entity-relationship schemas to represent data.[9] Developed by Italsiel in the late 1970s, this analysis method is now used by thousands of application developers in the IRI-Finsiel group. *

---

* The Instituto per la Ricostruzione Industriale is Italy's largest state-owned holding company and is a leader in several industries. The IRI owns 83 percent of the Finsiel Group, Italy's largest and Europe's second-largest software group. It includes 10 software companies and employs 4000 software professionals.

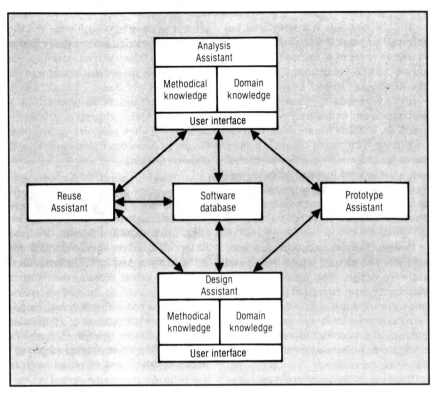

Figure 1. The four assistants in ASPIS.

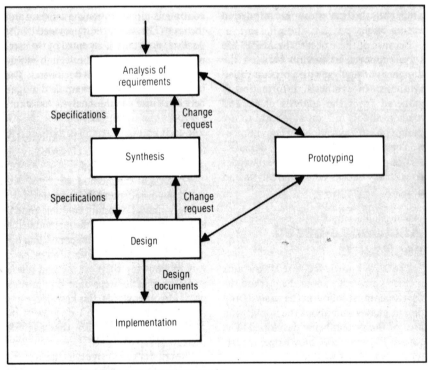

Figure 2. The ASPIS development cycle.

The SA language is a structured but informal language that lets you describe a system in terms of functions (boxes) and data (arrows). We defined a formalism, the Reasoning Support Logic,[10] to augment SA diagrams so we could check the correctness and consistency of our specifications. RSL lets you specify properties of a system with a set of axioms in a logic-based language. Using RSL, an analyst can write axioms in terms of functions, predicates, and positions in an SA diagram. These axioms are transformed into Prolog code to be executed.

Design. The design process has been split into two phases: system design and software design. The former seeks to describe a system in terms of the hardware and software global architecture. The latter seeks to describe the software functions in terms of processes and transitions. In both phases, we have adopted a top-down approach for now.

Typically, a designer must retrieve the specifications to read them or to ask the analyst to modify them if they are inconsistent. Futhermore, the customer's needs (and thus the specification) may change, and the design must be modified accordingly.

Because of these needs, the ASPIS life cycle supports interaction between the designer and analyst with a process called synthesis. In synthesis, information is gathered from the analysis phase and made available in a suitable form to the design phase, thus allowing communication between the analyst and the designer. It is a continuous process that also includes consistency checks between analysis and design.

Knowledge-based assistants

The two knowledge-based assistants include knowledge about the method the developer must follow in the analysis and design phases and about the application area of the system being developed. The former is *methodical* knowledge; the latter is *domain* knowledge.

Including both types of knowledge lets the assistants provide general suggestions and checks on the steps in the method, the

criteria to observe in each step, and the heuristics needed to observe such criteria. In addition, the assistants can provide more specific suggestions and checks on the analysis and design of systems in a given application area. Assistance consists of advice, checks, some automatic transformation (when possible), support for document development and retrieval, and decision tracking.

Analysis Assistant

Within the two major subsets of knowledge, methodical and domain, we have further classified the knowledge contained in the Analysis Assistant. The methodical knowledge subset contains the rigorous laws of our analysis method and some good criteria and well-established, empirical expertise independent of a particular application that lets us satisfy the method's laws. The domain-knowledge subset contains well-established, empirical expertise that helps us adhere to the method in a particular application.

The Analysis Assistant makes substantive suggestions and checks through analysis documents, which are the basis of the communication between the assistant and the user. The suggestions provided by the Analysis Assistant, if accepted by the user, are transformed automatically into editing operations on the analysis documents. The box on pp. 62-63 is an example dialogue between a user and the Analysis Assistant.

Methodical knowledge. The knowledge in the methodical base is classified as
- syntax of the method,
- criteria of the method, or
- domain-independent heuristics.

The Analysis Assistant contains knowledge about the syntax of the method so the user can ask about the links connecting the method's phases. The user always has a way of knowing the next method phase and the specific steps that comprise a phase. In other words, this knowledge lets the user ask "What do I do now?" or "How do I accomplish this analysis phase?"

The criteria knowledge is included to tell the user what must be done to accomplish each step in a phase. These criteria are part of the method and describe the required

contents of analysis documents. Specifically, they tell the user what must be described in each phase, from which viewpoint, and at what level of detail, to create optimal (as complete and consistent as possible) specifications. Besides providing explicit criteria to the user, the Analysis Assistant applies the criteria to verify the methodical consistency among the analysis documents.

The set of domain-independent heuristics is expertise gained from following the analysis method. They let a nonexpert analyst act like an expert when developing analysis documents.

Domain knowledge. The most useful heuristics, however, are those that relate to the application domain. For example, it is surely more useful to have alternative functional decompositions of the system at hand instead of just general domain-independent heuristics. Even more useful are alternative decompositions based on parameters such as data and results. The domain knowledge, then, is an enhancement and a specialization of the methodical knowledge.

By exploiting the domain knowledge, the Analysis Assistant can verify, in some cases, the adequacy of the current analysis documents against some general concepts of the domain. The checks on domain adequacy are designed to advise the analyst when the requirements specified are not in accord with the domain criteria in its knowledge base.

Another function that exploits domain knowledge is support for synonyms. When the user creates the analysis documents representing the system requirements, he may want — or be forced — to use names different from those known to the assistant. Letting the analyst associate synonyms between his own labels and the assistant's lets the user connect these labels with the right domain concepts. The analyst can thus access domain information through his own labels.

Editor. Because our analysis methodology includes the development of various kinds of documents by using different formalisms, the Analysis Assistant has a set of syntax-oriented tools that lets the user and the system itself manage analysis documents.

The editor component, which is composed of these tools, operates on the basis of syntactical rules that are represented internally either as integrity constraints associated with the classes of the syntactical objects of the various languages or as production rules.

The editor can be invoked while carrying out a method phase whose purpose is the create an analysis document. In this way the editor, on the basis of the method phase at hand, supplies the possibility of developing the proper analysis documents.

Knowledge organization

The Analysis Assistant's main goal is to provide the user with domain-dependent suggestions and advice during a particular method phase. Methodical and domain knowledge are used and organized at two levels of abstraction so that domain knowledge is seen through methodical knowledge. The Analysis Assistant exploits a domain rule or fact only when it relates to a specific method step.

We use semantic networks with production systems attached as node attributes to represent this knowledge. The knowledge in the Analysis Assistant is organized in three subnetworks that contain representation of documents, domain concepts, and procedural knowledge.

Representing documents. An SA model is a tree of diagrams containing boxes and arrows. Using semantic networks, the representation of a model is straightforward. Each component of the model (diagrams) and each component of diagrams (boxes and arrows) are represented as separate objects. Such objects are linked to reflect the SA model's structure. Figure 3 shows the classes that define the shape of the objects and the names of the links.

Diagrams are organized into a tree structure with refinement and boxlist links, which let you state that a box is both a component of a diagram (a boxlist link) and the parent of another diagram (a refinement link).

Representing domain concepts. Facts and assertions typical of the domain at hand are represented as a separate semantic network. This network represents possible combinations of the basic

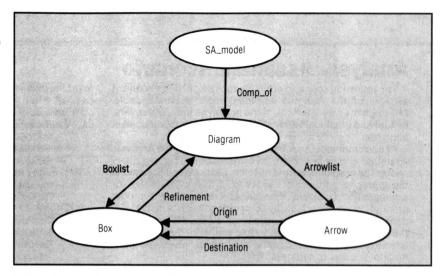

Figure 3. ASPIS represents a Structured Analysis model as a tree of diagrams that contain boxes and arrows. Each component of the model (diagrams) and each component of diagrams (boxes and arrows) are represented as separate objects, which are linked to reflect the SA model's structure. A box can be both a component of a diagram (a boxlist link) and the parent of another diagram (a refinement link).

functionalities of the system, or possible alternative refinements of a given functionality or given data. Figure 4 shows the organization of this network. This network is investigated by procedural knowledge to obtain the proper suggestions.

Representing procedural knowledge. To represent methodical and domain knowledge, each phase of the analysis method and each domain heuristic is represented by a class in another sematic network. Each class can have production systems as attributes. Such production systems represent the chunks of procedural knowledge

concerning both the method and the domain.

The classes representing method phases are linked according to the method sequence. Because domain knowledge can be considered specialized methodical knowledge, the classes representing domain knowledge are connected with is_a links to their related methodical knowledge classes. Figure 5 shows a network representing a subset of the method phase with an example of a domain class that is a specialization of the model-of-the-environment class.

To exploit the knowledge contained in

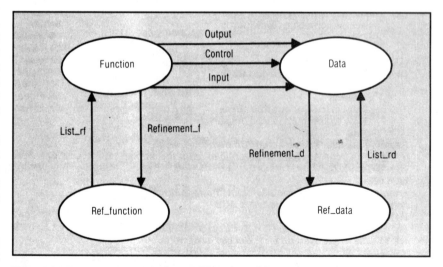

Figure 4. The organization of the ASPIS network that represents domain concepts. The network represents the possible combinations of basic system functions or the possible alternative refinements of a functions and data.

Analysis Assistant scenario

The following scenario attempts to make the most relevant aspects of the Analysis Assistant more understandable. Although the real interface of the prototype includes several textual and graphical windows, this dialogue is reproduced in plain text.

At each moment in each phase of the method, the Analysis Assistant shows in a menu all the items the user can query about. The assistant, according to the user's selection, exploits the appropriate chunks of knowledge. If a check is involved or a suggestion is asked, the assistant activates the proper production system which, by compairing the documents with domain and methodical knowledge, provides the user with all the inferenced information. In this scenario, the help key is used to refresh the menu, while in the actual prototype a permanent window is dedicated to it.

The sample session uses the following notation to represent SA diagrams.

For boxes,

$bn . label (n = 1, ..., 6)$

where bn is the box identifier and *label* is the box label.

For arrows,

$an [biT -> biT] . label (i = 1, ..., 6) (T = I,C,O,M)$

where an is the arrow identifier, T is the box side (input, control, output, or mechanism), and *label* is the arrow label. One value of biT can be $b0$, which is the external environment.

In the following sample session, Analysis Assistant text is in typewriter font, user text is in bold typewriter font, and comments are in italics. Invocation of the help key is reverse video.

⟨A⟩: What would you like to do?
⟨U⟩: **help**
⟨A⟩: – analysis of a new system
      – analysis of an old system
⟨U⟩: **analysis of a new system**
The Analysis Assistant focuses on the related methodological phase: the analysis of a new system.
⟨A⟩: OK
⟨U⟩: **help**
⟨A⟩: – Domain knowledge information
      – Information about this phase
      – How to accomplish this phase
      – Edit
⟨U⟩: **Domain knowledge information**
⟨A⟩: The domains in which I am expert are:
      – Access control systems (ACS)
      – Domain X
      – . . .
⟨U⟩: **help**
⟨A⟩: – Domain knowledge information
        – More about . . .
        – Select . . .
      – Information about this phase
      – How to accomplish this phase
      – Edit
Because the user has selected "Domain knowledge information," the Analysis Assistant can tailor the menu.
⟨U⟩: **Select ACS**
⟨A⟩: OK
From now on, the Analysis Assistant knows that the domain the user is interested in is ACS.
⟨U⟩: **Edit**
⟨A⟩: Name of the analyst: ⟨U⟩: **Francesco Pietri**
⟨A⟩: Name of the system: ⟨U⟩: **Access control to TECSIEL**
⟨A⟩: Date of the analysis: ⟨U⟩: **1 March 1988**
The Analyst Assistant knows the kind of information to be edited at this phase. It also knows what editing environment

to let the user enter, based on the analysis phase.
⟨A⟩: OK
⟨U⟩: **How to accomplish this range**
⟨A⟩: To accomplish this phase you have to carry out:
      – the model of the environment (in the analysis of needs phase)
      – the model of the organization (in the analysis of needs phase)
      – the analysis of system requirements
      – the definition of software requirements
⟨U⟩: **help**
⟨A⟩: – Domain knowledge information
     – Information about this phase
     – How to accomplish this phase
       – Select . . .
     – Edit
⟨U⟩: **Select model of the environment**
⟨A⟩: OK
The Analysis Assistant now focuses on the model-of-the-environment development phase.
⟨U⟩: **help**
⟨A⟩: – Domain knowledge information
     – Domain knowledge adequacy check
     – Criteria of this phase
     – Methodical check
     – How to accomplish this phase
     – Edit
     – Leave the development of this phase (for the time being)
⟨U⟩: **Criteria of this phase**
⟨A⟩: Criteria:
      – the purpose of this phase is the functional subsystem decomposition
      – the viewpoint is external with respect to the overall system
      – the halt criteria are . . .
⟨U⟩: **help**
⟨A⟩: – Domain knowledge information
     – Domain knowledge adequacy check
     – Criteria of this phase
       – More about
         – functional decomposition
         – external viewpoint
         – halt criteria
     – Methodical check
     – How to accomplish this phase
     – Edit
     – Leave the development of this phase (for the time being)
⟨U⟩: **More about functional decomposition**
⟨A⟩: The best thing to do first is establish the external interfaces of the system
⟨U⟩: **Edit**
The Analysis Assistant knows the user must edit a SA model.
⟨A⟩: [edit operations:
      for frame:
        – change user
        – . . .
      for diagrams:
        – add/delete box
        – add/delete arrow
        – add/delete label to box/arrow
        – . . .]
The current document is:
    FRAME (A–0):
        USED AT: Model of the environment
        AUTHOR: Francesco Pietri
        PROJECT: Access control to TECSIEL
        . . .
    DIAGRAM (A–0):

BOX: b1 . Access control to TECSIEL
The Analysis Assistant shows the current
values, some of which it automatically creates.
⟨U⟩: **Change author: Pier Paolo Puncello**
⟨A⟩: OK
⟨U⟩: **Domain knowledge information**
The user now asks the assistant for domain
suggestions about carrying on the development
of the current diagram.
⟨A⟩: The external interfaces of an access
control system (at least as far as I know) are:
– person details
– place details
– access permission
– . . .
– alarm
⟨U⟩: help
⟨A⟩: –Domain knowledge information
– functional decomposition information
– select . . .
– synonym
– more about . . .
– Domain knowledge adequacy check
– Criteria of this phase
– Methodical check
– How to accomplish this phase
– Edit
– Leave the development of this phase (for the time being)
The user can select the external interfaces
suggested by the Analysis Assistant. If the user
does, the Analysis Assistant will perform some
implicit editing.
⟨U⟩: **select: person details, access permission**
⟨A⟩: OK
⟨U⟩: **Edit**
The current document is:
FRAME (A–O):
USED AT: Model of the environment
AUTHOR: Pier Paolo Puncello
PROJECT: Access control to TECSIEL
. . .
DIAGRAM (A–O):
BOX: b1 . Access control to TECSIEL
ARROW:
a1 [b0 –> b1I] . Person details
a2 [b1O –> b0] . Access permission
⟨U⟩: **add ARROW: a3 [b1O –> b0] . Red light**
⟨A⟩: OK
⟨U⟩: **Domain knowledge adequacy check**
The assistant activates a production system that
applies domain heuristics to find inadequacies.
⟨A⟩: I find some inconsistencies between knowledge
about ACSs and your edited diagrams: Every ACS
should have:
– an alarm signal
– an access request
– . . .
⟨U⟩: **synonym alarm signal, red light**
The user tells the Analysis Assistant to bind the concept
represented by the alarm arrow with the label "red light."
⟨A⟩: OK
⟨U⟩: **select access request**
⟨A⟩: OK
⟨U⟩: **Edit**
The current document is:
FRAME (A–O):
USED AT: Model of the environment
AUTHOR: Pier Paolo Puncello
PROJECT: Access control to TECSIEL
. . .

DIAGRAM (A–O):
BOX: b1 . Access control to TECSIEL
ARROW:
a1 [b0 –> b1I] . Person details
a2 [b1O –> b0] . Access permission
a3 [b1O –> b0] . Red light
a4 [b0 –> b1I] . Access request
⟨U⟩: help
⟨A⟩: Domain knowledge information
– functional decomposition information
– select . . .
– synonym
– more about . . .
– Domain knowledge adequacy check
– Criteria of this phase
– Methodical check
– How to accomplish this phase
– Edit
– Leave the development phase (for the time being)
⟨U⟩: **More about Red light**
The Analysis Assistant can now exploit the synonym
introduced by the user.
⟨A⟩: Message output to security guards to inform
them that some unauthorized event has occurred;
this must occur very soon after such an event.
⟨U⟩: **Leave the development of this phase**
⟨A⟩: OK
⟨U⟩: **Select model of the organization**
⟨A⟩: OK
The Analysis Assistant now focuses on the model-of-
the-organization development phase.
⟨U⟩: help
⟨A⟩: – Domain knowledge information
– Domain knowledge adequacy check
– Criteria of this phase
– Methodical check
– How to accomplish this phase
– Edit
– Leave the development of this phase (for the
time being)
⟨U⟩: **Edit**
The current document is:
FRAME (A–O):
USED AT: Model of the organization
AUTHOR: Francesco Pietri
PROJECT: Access control to TECSIEL
. . .
DIAGRAM (A–O):
BOX: b1 . Access control to TECSIEL
⟨U⟩: **add BOX b2 . error**
⟨A⟩: OK
⟨U⟩: **Methodical check**
⟨A⟩: Syntactic error: A–O cannot contain more than one
box
⟨U⟩: **delete b2**
⟨A⟩: OK
⟨U⟩: **add ARROW a1 [b0 –> b1O] . Person details**
⟨A⟩: OK
⟨U⟩: **add ARROW a2 [b1O –> b0] . Access permission**
⟨A⟩: OK
⟨U⟩: **add ARROW a3 [b0 –> b1I] . Access request**
⟨A⟩: OK
⟨U⟩: **add ARROW a4 [b0 –> b1M] . Security
controller**
⟨A⟩: OK
⟨U⟩: **Methodical check**
⟨A⟩: I find an inconsistency between A–O of model of the
environment and A–O of the model of the organization:
Both of them should have the same external interfaces.
A–O of the model of the environment has "Red light" arrow
while A–O of the model of the organization has not.

these classes, the Analysis Assistant navigates the method classes according to their links, focusing at each moment on one specific class representing a method step. At each method class, the Analysis Assistant gives the user a list of predefined operations associated with that class. This list generally includes an opportunity to obtain suggestions, consistency checks, and the knowledge contained in a related domain class. Domain knowledge is exploited by focusing on the domain classes that are the specializations of the current method step.

The inheritance mechanism and movement of focus is transparent to the user, who sees only a greater set of feasible operations and requests when he exploits the domain knowledge in addition to the method knowledge. Thus, there are two levels of abstraction in the user interaction; the analyst can decide the proper level of interaction and the kind of help the analyst needs.

Support assistants

The Prototype Assistant and the Reuse Assistant depend on the possibility of specifying formal properties of the analysis and design documents. The Prototype Assistant uses information about the formal properties to animate the specifications. The Reuse Assistant uses it to retrieve the proper analysis document.

We have built a subset of the Prototype Assistant on top of Prolog. This subset environment includes a translator, an executor, and an interface module. The translator gets the RSL axioms as input and produces a set of Prolog clauses that are then interpreted by the executor. Because the RSL axioms define semantic properties of the components of an SA model, their execution time shows the actual behavior of the system being analyzed. Thus, the user can tell if the written specifications match the customer's needs.

Development of the Reuse Assistant is still in a preliminary phase. We are trying to increase the power of the basic structural approach to reuse by categorizing software components in terms of standard concepts. Formal specifications can play a significant role in classifying the reusable components. We are investigating how to evaluate the components in terms of the amount of effort required to tailor them to the target application. Our approach is based largely on the work of Freeman and Prieto-Diaz.[11]

The project

Our project has two phases, a one-year research phase (1985-1986) and a three-year development phase (1986-1989). We have put our efforts into defining the ASPIS life cycle and the formal specification language, investigating the assistants' features and capabilities, and designing the knowledge-based assistants. We have developed a prototype that includes the Analysis and Design Assistants and very simple facilities for transforming the results of the former into the input of the latter.

Also, we have implemented a tool that transforms RSL axioms into Prolog code and have integrated it with the Analysis Assistant.

To build the assistants, we developed a knowledge representation system on top of Prolog, which offers the possibility of defining semantic networks and production systems. The development environment for this prototype is a Sun Microsystems workstation running under Unix 4.2 BSD.

The ASPIS project tackles several problems whose solutions are crucial to improving the software life cycle: defining a formal specifications language, rapid prototyping, software reuse, and developing knowledge-based tools that embody knowledge both about the methodology and the application domain.

Our investigative work on applying AI techniques to software engineering is complete, and we have reached an important milestone — delivery of the first prototype. In 1987, we presented our prototype at the International Joint Conference on Artificial Intelligence in Milan and at the ESPRIT conference in Brussels. We have received positive and useful feedback that has encouraged us to pursue the approach we had chosen.

Our goal now is to build a new prototype that includes more domain knowledge and some functional enhancements designed to ease the modification and creation of the knowledge base. In fact, the cost of knowledge acquisition is one of the most important features to measure the impact of such tools on real developments.

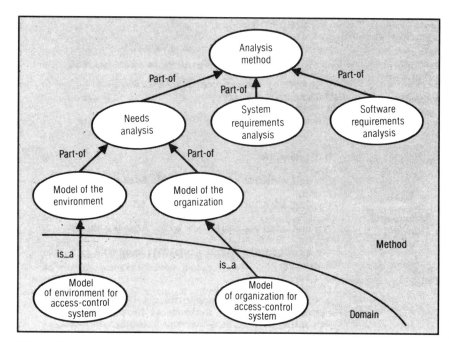

Figure 5. An example of a domain class that is a specialization of the model-of-the-environment class.

Acknowledgments

The partners in Project 401, sponsored by the European Strategic Program for Research in Information Technology, are CAP Sogeti Innovation, France; GEC Research, United Kingdom; Olivetti, Italy; and Tecsiel, Italy. Olivetti is the prime contractor; the universities of Pisa, Italy, and Grenoble, France, are subcontractors.

We are especially grateful to G. Ferrari who was working at Tecsiel when we began this project and to G. Pacini and F. Turini of the University of Pisa for their contributions.

References

1. R. Balzer, C. Green, and T. Cheatham, "Software Technology in the 1990s Using a New Paradigm," *Computer*, Nov. 1983, pp. 39-45.

2. R. Kowalski, "Logic Programming," *Proc. IFIP Conf.*, R.E.A. Mason, ed., Elsevier Science, North-Holland, Amsterdam, 1983.

3. Special issue on artificial intelligence and software engineering, *IEEE Trans. Software Eng.*, Nov. 1985.

4. R. Balzer et al., "Operational Specification as a Basis for Specification Validation," *Theory and Practice of Software Technology*, D. Ferrari, M. Bologani, and J. Goguen, eds., North-Holland, Amsterdam, 1983.

5. P.P. Chen et al., "Formal Specification and Verification of Distributed Systems," in *Theory and Practice of Software Technology*, D. Ferrari, M. Bologani, and J. Goguen, eds., North-Holland, Amsterdam, 1983.

6. D.T. Ross, "Structured Analysis: A Language for Communicating Ideas," *IEEE Trans. Software Eng.*, Jan. 1977, pp. 16-34.

7. D.T. Ross and K.E. Schoman, "Structured Analysis for Requirements Definition," *IEEE Trans. Software Eng.*, Jan. 1977, pp. 6-15.

8. D.T. Ross, "Applications and Extensions of SADT," *Computer*, April 1985, pp. 25-33.

9. P.P. Chen, "The Entity-Relationship Model: Toward a Unified View of Data," *ACM Trans. Database Systems*, March 1976, pp. 9-36.

10. G. Pacini and F. Turini, "Animation of Software Requirements," in *Industrial Software Technology*, R.J. Mitchell, ed., P. Peregrinus Ltd., London, 1987.

11. P. Freeman and R. Prieto-Diaz, "Classifying Software for Reusability," *IEEE Software*, Jan. 1987, pp. 6-16.

P. Paolo Puncello is project leader of ESPRIT's ASPIS project at the Tecsiel laboratory in Pisa, Italy. He worked at the University of Pisa before joining Tecsiel. His research interests include programming languages, software engineering, and artificial intelligence.

Puncello received a degree in computer science from the University of Pisa.

Piero Torrigiani is research manager for software engineering and artificial intelligence at the Tecsiel laboratory. He has worked for GMD in Bonn, West Germany, and has taught at the University of Milan. His research interests include advanced programming environments, expert system shells, and software engineering.

Torrigiani received a degree in computer science from the University of Pisa.

Francesco Pietri is principal research staff member of the ASPIS project at Tecsiel. His research interests include software engineering, artificial intelligence, and object-oriented user interfaces.

Pietri received a degree in computer science from the University of Pisa.

Riccardo Burlon is a research staff member at Tecsiel. His research interests include expert systems, planning systems, and user interfaces.

Burlon received a degree in computer science from the University of Pisa.

Bruno Cardile is a research staff member at Tecsiel. His research interests include expert systems, knowledge representation, and logic programming.

Cardile received a degree in computer science from the University of Pisa.

Mirella Conti is a research staff member at Tecsiel. She has worked on knowledge-representation paradigms for the Italian National Research Council. Her research interests include expert systems and knowledge representation.

Conti received a computer science degree from the University of Pisa.

Questions about this article can be addressed to the authors at Tecsiel S.p.A., via S. Maria, 19, 56100 Pisa, Italy.

An Automated Software Design Assistant

JAHANGIR KARIMI AND BENN R. KONSYNSKI

Abstract—An automated software design assistant was implemented as part of long term project, with the objective of applying the computed-aided technique to the tools in a software engineering environment. A set of quantitive measures are derived based on the degree to which a particular design satisfied the attributes associated with a structured software design. The measures are then used as a decision rules for a computer-aided methodology for structured design. The feasibility of the approach is also demonstrated by a case study using a small application system design problem.

Index Terms—Cohesion, coupling, modularization, structured design.

INTRODUCTION

THE software design process is difficult to describe formally, since much depends on the individual designer and on the specific design problem to be solved. Although each software design effort is unique, there are striking similarities between many of them. A carefully laid out set of these similarities may form a systematic framework to design process.

Software design is a continual process of making decisions. From a set of requirement specifications, decisions are made to decompose the requirement specification into certain basic elements and partitioning the set of decomposed elements into modules.

A number of manual design methodologies are explained below. These techniques fall short in providing a systematic approach to the design process. In applying these techniques, the design process is viewed as a problem solving process, in which the designer proceeds from some perceived problem through a series of transformations to the model of a solution for that perceived problem. Many unstructured activities and information gathering take place at the outset, then, the numerous design views and the abundance of information are reduced through judgment, and finally, a single design is identified and refined. Successful design using these methodologies rely upon the designer's self-discipline and professional judgment to ensure that design decisions are not based on speculation or premature selection of alternatives.

This paper deals with the development of a computer-aided tool for providing intelligent assistance in one portion of software life cycle, namely the determination of program modules in the design of software.

In the following section, we illustrate the scope of our approach and present a brief overview of the different approaches taken for the development of automated tools to evaluate the quality of large scale software products. In the second section, we briefly discuss the features of the system that relate to the design process and the design decisions that must be made in order to derive a system with the desired properties. The third section contains the mechanism used to derive a set of quantifiable measures for the desired system properties in order to provide a "scientific" basis for an automated software design assistant. The section also contains a detailed explanation of the methodology to use the derived measures as the decision rules for a computer-aided approach to design. Finally, the applicability of the approach is illustrated using a small system design problem.

NEED FOR AN AUTOMATED SOFTWARE MODULE DESIGN

The need for a systematic approach to software design was recognized in the mid-1970s as a result of continual problems with software development. A number of automated tools are now available for software requirement specification, for example, two automated tools are IS-DOS [1], and SREM [2]. Some work has been done recently with respect to building an automated tool to evaluate the quality of a design given the design specifications. Henry [3] defined and validated set of software metrics which were based on the measurement of information flow between system components. Specific metrics were defined for procedure complexity, module complexity and module coupling. The metrics were demonstrated to be useful in finding structural flaws in the design and implementation of the UNIX® operating system.

Similar recent studies have focused attention on the development of a design evaluator based on a set of metrics which quantifies the relationships between the components within a system [4]–[10]. In Giddings and Colburn [10], rules were developed to quantify notions of good design based on the connectivity and the complexity of the components. In the process a set of arbitrary thresholds were set for some design attributes, including number of interconnections per part and the ratio of data to active parts. The design rules that were implemented consider the intercorrectivity of individual software parts, the

Manuscript received August 30, 1985.

J. Karimi is with the College of Business and Administration, University of Colorado at Denver, 1475 Lawrence Street, Denver, CO 80202.

B. R. Konsynski is with Harvard Business School, Cambridge, MA 02138, on leave from the Department of Management Information Systems, College of Business and Public Administration, University of Arizona, Tucson, AZ 85721.

IEEE Log Number 8718387.

®UNIX is a registered trademark of AT&T Bell Laboratories.

Reprinted from *IEEE Transactions on Software Engineering*, Vol. 14, No. 2, February 1988, pp. 194-210. Copyright © 1988 by The Institute of Electrical and Electronics Engineers, Inc. All rights reserved.

complexity of the design as a whole, and the relationships among software design iterations.

The work of Karimi [11] described here is an attempt to apply metrics to a design phase that is earlier in the life cycle. Specifically, it deals with building an automated software design assistant which will derive a structured design from the logical model of a system. The process is associated with the development of nonprocedural specifications of modules within the system. The specifications are related to all module interconnections and module function(s).

Given a system specification, there are a number of steps that should take place before one can derive a structured design from the logical model of the system. These steps include [12] deriving a complete data flow diagram, identifying error conditions within the system, identifying alternative physical implementations by recognizing different automation boundaries that might exist, building a data dictionary, and defining the logic of the processes and the content of the data stores (files).

Once the decisions have been made about different subsystems, the processes and physical files and the data flows among the files can fall into these physical subsystems. These subsystems may be implemented as one program or several. Before this implementation is made, each subsystem needs to be structured as a hierarchy of modules in which each module surfaces as a clearly defined function.

Several problems need immediate consideration when building automated tools for the software design process. Among them are the lack of unique standard attribute of design quality, the lack of quantifiable measure of quality [based on the attribute], and the fact that design process is not merely a search of a solution space, because an infinite number of "correct" solutions might exist. These points are discussed in more detail in the following sections.

Design Criteria

Many of the design heuristics are devoted to the attainment of modules that have three specific properties, expressed by White and Booth [13] as properties they "would like to see a design possess": 1) components are relatively independent, 2) existing dependencies can be easily understood, and 3) there are no hidden or unforeseen interactions between modules.

Myers [14] and Yourdon and Constantine [15] have proposed a series of qualitative rules and guidelines for obtaining software modules with these properties. In particular, they introduce the terms of "internal module strength" (or cohesion), which refers to level of association between component elements of a module, and "module coupling," which refers to a measure of the strength of interconnection between modules.

A high level of cohesion and a low level of coupling within a system of modules in turn results in a number of overlapping system properties [14]-[17]. These are explained briefly in the following:

1) improving module independence as a result of low coupling and high cohesion,

2) reducing complexity of design and implementation as a result of reducing dependence of the modules on one another,

3) improving understandability of the logical organization of the system by reducing the complexity,

4) improving reliability by increasing the independence of the modules and its effect on the way the system is constructed and tested,

5) improving maintainability and flexibility by reducing the number of connections between modules. While maintaining a module there is a reduced risk that a change in one module causes a change in another one (ripple effect),

6) improving reusability (of design and implementation) and shareability of the modules. Increasing the cohesiveness of a module results in the improved operational unity of that module. This increases the chance of creating a generally useful module that can be shared by other modules within the system and can be reused in different systems.

Stevens among others [16] has recognized seven levels of cohesion. They state that "these levels have been distinguished over the years through experience of many designers." The seven levels are, in order of decreasing strength or cohesion, functional, sequential, communicational, procedural, temporal, logical, coincidental. A brief description of each level of cohesion is given below. For more detail see [14]-[17].

A functionally cohesive module contain elements that all contribute to the execution of one, and only one, problem oriented task. This is the strongest type of cohesion.

The order of processing in sequentially cohesion module is determined by data. The data that result from one processing function are the input for the next processing function. Sequentially cohesive modules are almost as maintainable as the functionally cohesive ones; they are not easily reusable because they usually contain activities that will not in general be useful together.

Communicational cohesion occurs when the activities are procedural but are performed on a unique data stream. The functions reference the same data and pass data among themselves. In contrast to sequentially cohesive modules, the order of processing is unimportant.

In procedurally cohesive modules, activities are performed together because they can be accomplished in the same procedure, not because they should be. The elements are involved in different and possibly unrelated activities in which control (not necessarily data) flows from each activity to the next one.

Crossing from easily maintainable modules with higher level of cohesion to the less easily maintainable modules with low level of cohesion we reach to temporal cohesion module. Elements within a temporally cohesive module are related in time. They are similar to the procedurally cohesive ones, in that they tend to be composed of partial functions whose only relationship to one another is that they all happen to be carried out at a certain time.

A module is considered to be logically cohesive that consist of groups of activities which in some way belong logically to the same class. Because a generalized class of problems is performed, some specific piece of data is usually required to tell the function what specific actions to take. This type of cohesion results in tricky program code and the passing of unnecessary parameters which make support difficult.

Coincidentally cohesive modules occur where there is no meaningful relationship among activities in a module. Like logical modules they have no well-defined function. However, the activities in logically cohesive module are at least in the same category; in a coincidentally cohesive module, even that is not true.

Others have reported studies in support of the above findings [18], [19]. While principles of cohesion and coupling can be useful guides in evaluating the structure of a program, they do not provide a methodology for attaining programs with a high level of cohesion or a low level of coupling.

In addition to the properties of the individual module, the collective structure assumed by those modules must also be considered. Structured design guidelines [15] imply that a good structure is one in which modules are structured in a hierarchy, where the modules on a given lower level may or may not be shared by the modules on the higher level. In addition to the extent of sharing, there are restrictions on the number of levels relative to the total size of the system, and the number of intermediate subordinates for a given module at each level. Although these are considered to be the characteristics of a good design, there is no clear methodology for the designer to follow during the design process.

As Yourdon and others [15] state, ". . . these heuristics can be extremely valuable if properly used, but actually can lead to poor design if interpreted too literally . . . results often have been catastrophic . . ."

The concept of modularity also leads to a fundamental problem of finding the appropriate decomposition criteria. The principle of information hiding [20] suggests that modules should be specified and designed so that information (procedure and data) contained within a module is inaccessible to other modules that have no need for such information. Deriving a set of independent modules that communicate with one another only that information necessary to achieve the software function would, by and large, satisfy the information hiding principle.

The volume of data transported between modules within the software structure also has a significant influence on the quality of the design. The higher the volume of data transported between modules, the higher the processing time of executing software. The total transport volume is a useful measure of comparison between candidate designs. The procedure for computing the transport volume and its usage is presented below.

Several software design methodologies have been derived from consideration of information structure and information flow. Both the Jackson Methodology [21] and Warnier's Logical Construction of Programs [22] rely on the hierarchical organization of input and output data, circumvent direct design derivation of modular structure, move directly toward a processing hierarchy followed by detailed procedural constructs, and provide supplementary techniques for more complex problems. The ultimate objective of these methods is to produce a procedural description of the software. The concept of software structure is not explicitly considered. Modules are considered as a by-product of procedure, and a philosophy of module independence is given little emphasis. For small problems with well-defined problem specifications, this approach would result in consistent designs even when applied by different people. The limits of the utility of this approach in design of large-scale systems are not clear.

The data flow design method was first prepared by Yourdon and Constantine [15] and has since been extended by Myers [24]. The technique is applicable to a broad range of application areas since it makes use of data flow diagrams, a popular representation tool used by analysts.

Design begins with an evaluation of the data flow diagram. The information flow category (i.e., transform or transaction flow) is established, and flow boundaries that delineate the transform or transaction center are defined. Based on the location of boundaries, processes are mapped into software structure as modules. The resulting structure is next optimized in order to develop a representation that will meet all functional and performance requirements and merit acceptance based on design measures and heuristics. A data flow-oriented design approach is easy to apply, even when no formal data structure exists.

For a large system, the data flow diagram may represent the flow characteristics of both the transaction and transformation analysis. In these situations it is not always clear how to select overriding flow characteristics. Many unnecessary control modules will be specified if transform and transaction mapping are followed explicitly.

There is a growing need for a design tool that can be applied to the detailed design process regardless of the scope of the design effort. The tool would not replace the designer, but rather would support the design activities and provide a unified approach to the design process. The tool should also provide a quantitative measure of design quality in order to facilitate the design evaluation by the analyst. The measure of the goodness should be derived from the degree to which a particular design satisfied the design heuristics.

COMPUTER AIDED PROCESS ORGANIZATION (CAPO)

In order to systematize the design process, a process structuring workbench has been developed to organize the activities in the detailed design state of software life cycle.

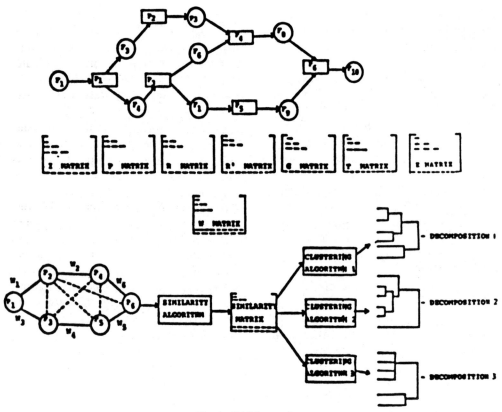

Fig. 1. CAPO overview.

The objective is to derive a nonprocedural specification of modules, given the logical model of a system.

From the analysis of the system under study, a flowgraph is generated. For the purpose of this discussion the term flowgraph is defined as a generic term that refers to the data flow diagrams, finite state machines, and Petri nets. The flowgraph represents a logical model of the system. It also represents the network of processes within the system. Processes and their relationships are represented as the graph nodes and the links joining the nodes, respectively. Processes must be performed and data supplied in a certain sequence. The logical view of the system may be expanded by functional decomposition of processes. Essentially, one process on the diagram is selected and broken down into its subprocesses. These lower-level processes then become processes on a new flowgraph. However, the scope of a process is determined by the scope of the design. Different levels of process interactions can be represented based on different design objectives.

The level of cohesion of each module depends on the processes which constitute that module. A module consisting of several logically related complete processes would be more cohesive than a module that consists of fragments of several processes. Depending on the size of the module and the size of the processes that constitute the module, different process groupings will result in different levels of cohesiveness.

To automate the process organization phase of design, a framework is needed for computer-aided methodology that would incorporate all the properties of a good design at the design time. The objective of our approach is a system of modules with the following properties:

a) High level of cohesion.
b) Low level of coupling.
c) Low level of reference distribution.
d) Low level of information distribution.
e) Low level of transport volume.

Fig. 1 depicts the overall structure of the computer-aided process organization (CAPO) for grouping processes to form software modules. The system provides interactive design, related to other analysers (i.e., PSA) and fits within PLEXSYS-84 methodology [25].

The information represented by the flowgraph is used by the CAPO analysis package. The system reads an input file (which is created interactively) with the information about each process as is shown in Fig. 2.

The methodology starts with converting the flowgraph into a series of six matrices. The objective is to capture all the control, data, logical, and timing interdependencies between the processes. The purpose of each matrix and the procedure for deriving it are explained below. These definitions are extensions of the work of [26].

1) Incidence Matrix (E): The matrix shows the relationships of the processes and files.

Let

$e_{ij} = 1$ if f_j is an input to P_i, $i = 1, 2, \cdots, n$,
$e_{ij} = -1$ if f_j is an output of P_i, $j = 1, 2, \cdots, k$,
$e_{ij} = 0$ if there is no incidence between f_j and P_i.

```
PROCESS-NAME
PROCESS-MAJOR-KEY
PROCESS-MINOR-KEY
NUM-OF-PRECEDENT-PROCESSES
    PRECEDENT-PROCESS-MAJOR-KEY
    PRECEDENT-PROCESS-MINOR-KEY
NUM-OF-PROCESSES-ACTIVATED-BY-THE-PROCESS
    NAME-OF-ACTIVATED-PROCESS
    PROB-OF-BEING-ACTIVATED
NUM-OF-INPUT-FILE-USED-BY-THE-PROCESS
    INPUT-FILE-NAME
    MAJOR-KEY
    RECORD-SIZE
    NUMBER-OF-RECORDS
    FREQUENCY-OF-ACCESS-TO-FILE
NUM-OF-OUTPUT-FILE-CREATED-BY-THE-PROCESS
    OUTPUT-FILE-NAME
    MAJOR-KEY
    RECORD-SIZE
    NUMBER-OF-RECORDS
```

Fig. 2. Cobol record description for the input file.

The incidence matrix (E) is useful in the process of finding the total transport volume of data between processes and files within the system.

Let

V_j = volume of file f_j,
L_i = the number of logical inputs and output of P_i,
MP_j = multiplicity of file transport for f_j or the number of times f_j is an input or output of a set of processes;

then

$$L_i = \sum_{j=1}^{k} |e_{ij}|, \quad i = 1, 2, \cdots, n$$

$$MP_j = \sum_{i=1}^{n} |e_{ij}|, \quad j = 1, 2, \cdots, k.$$

The transport volume for f_j is

$$TV_j = MP_j * V_j.$$

The transport volume for the set of data files is

$$TV = \sum_{j=1}^{k} TV_j.$$

2) Precedence Matrix (P): The matrix shows if a particular process is a direct precedent to any other process. Namely:

$P_{ij} = 1$ if P_i is a direct precedent to P_j,
$P_{ij} = 0$ otherwise.

3) Reachability Matrix (R): The matrix shows if a process has any precedence relation with any other process. In other words, is there any logical path between any two processes?

$R_{ij} = 1$ if P_i has any precedence relationship with P_j,
$R_{ij} = 0$ otherwise.

4) Partial Reachability Matrix (R*): The matrix is used to check the precedence violations which are necessary in order to compute the matrix of feasible grouping (G).

$R_{ij}^* = 1$ if P_i has a higher (two or more) order precedence with P_j,

$R_{ij}^* = 0$ otherwise.

Higher order precedence between two processes is an indication that the two may not be executed in parallel and/or in sequence. There is at least one step of processing that needs to take place between the two.

5) Matrix of Feasible Process Pair Grouping (G): The G matrix is derived using the precedence matrix and the partial reachability matrix. The element of the G matrix shows the feasible and/or profitable process pairs grouping.

If $G_{ij} = -1$, there exists a higher order relationship between P_i and P_j, and P_i cannot be combined with P_j. If $G_{ij} = 0$, there is no precedence ordering (direct link), and P_i can be grouped with P_j. This indicates a feasible, but not necessarily profitable, grouping (saving on I/O time). If $G_{ij} = 1$, there is a direct precedent relationship and P_i can be grouped with P_j because this indicates a feasible and a profitable grouping. If $G_{ij} = 2$, there is an immediate reduction in logical input/output requirements when P_i and P_j are grouped. Therefore,

$$G_{ij} = -1 \quad \text{if} \quad R_{ij}^* \quad \text{or} \quad R_{ji}^* = 1 \quad \text{or} \quad i = j$$

$$G_{ij} = 0 \quad \text{if} \left[(R_{ij}^* = 0 \quad \text{and} \quad R_{ji}^* = 0) \right.$$
$$\left. \text{and} \quad (P_{ij} = 0 \quad \text{and} \quad P_{ji} = 0) \right]$$

except when

$(P_{i1} = 1 \quad \text{and} \quad P_{j1} = 1)$ or $(P_{1i} = 1 \quad \text{and} \quad P_{1j} = 1)$.

Grouping is feasible but not necessarily profitable.

$$G_{ij} = 1 \quad \text{if} \quad (R_{ij}^* = 0 \quad \text{and} \quad R_{ji}^* = 0) \quad \text{and} \quad [(P_{ij} = 1)$$
$$\text{or} \quad (P_{ji} = 1) \quad \text{or} \quad (Pi1 = 1) \quad \text{and} \quad (P_{ji} = 1)$$
$$\text{or} \quad (P_{1j} = 1 \quad \text{and} \quad P_{1i} = 1)]$$

$$G_{ij} = 2 \quad \text{if} \quad (R_{ij}^* = 0 \quad \text{and} \quad R_{ji}^* = 0) \quad \text{and} \quad [(P_{i1} = 1$$
$$\text{and} \quad P_{j1} = 1) \quad \text{or} \quad (R_{1i}^* = 1 \quad \text{and} \quad R_{1j}^* = 1)].$$

6) Matrix of timing relationship (T): The Marimont procedure [27] is used to find the earliest time and the latest time of execution of each process. Using the procedure, the matrix T is defined in the following manner:

$T_{ij} = 1$ if P_i is invoked in the same time interval as P_j,
$T_{ij} = 0$ otherwise.

Using these six matrices, the relationship between each pair of processes is examined in order to determine the extent of their interdependencies with respect to implementation alternatives in the target system. This would generate an interdependency weight that would be assigned to the link joining each pair of processes.

In order to assign an interdependency weight (W_{ij}) to the links joining each pair of processes, first a weighting scheme is developed. Second, appropriate weights should be assigned to the appropriate link in the [0, 1] range. The objective of assigning weight to links joining any two processes is to discourage or encourage their grouping in a single module. Modules should be designed with the objective of a high level of cohesion and a low level of coupling. A high level of cohesion results when the processing elements within a module have a strong data or functional relationship.

There are seven levels of cohesion which might result from grouping different processing elements in a module. These are shown, in order, in Table I.

The order indicates the degree of association or closeness with respect to data or the functional or logical relationship of the processes within a module. Different attempts have been made in the literature to assign a relative weight or "cohesion factor" to each level [14], [15]. The objective has been to show the extent of the difference between levels by the cohesion factor rather than to show just simple ranking. The same principle is used here to assign interdependency weights. However, the weights are chosen in the [0, 1] range for normalization and, later, decomposition purposes.

A close look at each level of cohesion and the above six matrices, which identify the process relationships, suggests the following weighting scheme to be used when automating the design.

When processing elements have no logical or data relationships and they are grouped in a poor design just to avoid repeating a segment of code, the resulting module will have coincidental cohesion. Therefore:

if $G_{ij} = -1$ and, for all time periods ($T_{ij} = 0$), then $W_{ij} = 0$.

In other words, if two processes have no direct precedence relationships and they are not required to be invoked at the same time, then a zero weight would be assigned to the link joining the two processes, indicating the coincidental cohesion as a result of their grouping.

When two processes do not have a data relationship but they are invoked at the same time interval, grouping of them would result in a module with temporal cohesion. A weight of (0.3) is assigned to the link joining them, i.e.,

if $G_{ij} = 0$ and at time t ($T_{ij} = 1$) then $W_{ij} = 0.3$.

Two processes have procedural relationships if they are activated by the same process, but they do not therefore necessarily use the same data set (files) as input:

if $G_{ij} = 2$ and not ($e_{i1} = 1$ and $e_{j1} = 1$) then $W_{ij} = 0.5$.

Communicational cohesion results when the processing elements within the module use the same input data sets or they produce the same output data sets. Therefore,

if $G_{ij} = 2$ and ($e_{i1} = 1$ and $e_{j1} = 1$) then $W_{ij} = 0.7$.

A higher weight indicates a high level of cohesion.

Sequential cohesion between processes is easily recognizable from the flowgraph and related matrices. In terms of a data flow graph, sequential association results from a linear chain of successive transformation of data.

TABLE I
COMPARISONS OF LEVELS OF COHESION

Level of Cohesion	Cohesion factor
Coincidental	0
Logical	1
Temporal	3
Procedural	5
Communicational	7
Sequential	9
Functional	10

Since sequential cohesion produces fewer intermodule communications, therefore,

if $G_{ij} = 1$ then $W_{ij} = 0.9$.

Two processes may have a logical relationship by being part of a single operation. For example, processing elements that perform all the edit function within a module are logically related. In such cases, the designer would be asked to identify the processes. A weight of (0.1) is assigned to the link joining them.

It should be noted that these are not the only conditions for the various levels of cohesion. These are merely representative indicators and serve our identification purpose. These measures are representative of the factors that indicate the levels of cohesion. A more exhaustive profile is being developed by the authors, but the current list is quite adequate for our purposes.

As a result of the preceding analysis, the flowgraph is transformed into a weighted directed graph. The weighted graph must be decomposed into a set of non overlapping subgraphs. There are a number of different methods available in current practice. These techniques are divided into two main categories: the graph theoretic approach, and the heuristic approach.

Cluster analysis has been defined [28] as "grouping similar objects." One major assumption made in using any clustering method deals with the characteristics of the information employed to define similarities among objects. The procedure used to define similarity depends on the characteristics of the objects and their attributes. The extend of the similarity of two objects in a graph is measured by the extend to which the objective function of the clustering improves as a result of the grouping of the two objects in a single cluster.

One major difficulty in performing a cluster analysis is deciding on the number of clusters of the objects. One class of clustering techniques, hierarchical, gives a configuration of every number of clusters from one (the entire set of objects) to the number of objects (each cluster has only one member). Depending on the size of the cluster, the level of coherence would also change (i.e., clusters with only one member have a maximum level of coherence). On the other hand, some algorithms begin with a selected number of clusters and alter this number as indicated by certain criteria, with the objective of determining simultaneously both the number of clusters and their configurations. Several parameters can be used in order to limit the range of the solution.

The method used to generate the similarity matrix for the flowgraph was first suggested by Gottleib [29] in the context of clustering index terms in library management. The approach is based on the concept of core set, which is used in heuristic graph decomposition techniques to find high strength subgraphs.

The core set concept is defined below.

Assuming

0: $[0_i; i = 1, \cdots n]$ set of (n) nodes in a graph.

Then

$A = a_{ij}$ is the graph adjancy matrix

such that

$$a_{ij} = \begin{matrix} 0 & \text{if no link connects node } i \text{ and } j \\ w_{ij} & \text{if there is a link with a weight of} \end{matrix}$$

(wij) between node i and j.

Then

$Q(i) = \{ j: a_{ij} > 0 \}$ is set of nodes connected to i in the graph including i itself, namely the core set.

The core set concept has been used by Huff and Madnick [30] to define similarity measure between a pair of nodes in a weighted directed graph in the following manner.

Let

U_{ij} = average (mean) weight on links joining node i and j to nodes within $Q(I) \cap Q(J)$.
V_{ij} = average (mean) weight on all links from node i and j to other nodes in $Q(I) \cup Q(J)$.

Then, define the similarity measure as:

$$P_{ij} = \frac{|Q(i) \cap Q(j)|}{|Q(i) \cup Q(j)|} * \frac{U_{ij}^2}{V_{ij}}.$$

The definition may be viewed from a "gravitational" point of view: the larger a given node's core set, the stronger is the "force" pulling that node into the core set and respectively away from nodes not in the core set. Also the larger the intersection of pairs of core sets, relative to the size of the two core sets, the stronger the force pulling the two core nodes together. The more the similarity of two objects (with higher similarity weights on the link joining the two objects), the more will be the level of the cohesiveness of the module that results after their grouping. The notion of core set intersection size to core set union size captures the essential notion of the internode similarity central to the strength/coupling criterion which underlines the entire graph decomposition problem.

For a given pair of nodes (x, y) and corresponding core

sets $Q(x)$ and $Q(y)$ (where it is assumed $|Q(x) \cap Q(y)| > 0$), the higher the weights on the links connecting nodes x and y to nodes in $Q(x) \cap Q(y)$, relative to the weights on the links within $Q(x)$ and $Q(y)$, the stronger the similarity between nodes x and y.

The reason for raising U_{ij} to the second power is the possibility in which the core set union and the core set intersection differ only by the nodes x and y themselves. In this special case, the similarity measure insures that the link weights on the x–y path to have an impact, as desired. That is, it produces higher value for a case which the two nodes are linked with higher weights as opposed to lower weights.

A goodness measure is needed for assessment of partition subgraph strength and subgraph coupling. The procedure for deriving the goodness measure for a given partition is explained below.

Let

L_i = number of links within a subgraph (i).
N_i = number of nodes within a subgraph (i).
S_i = subgraph strength.
L_{ij} = number of links connecting nodes in subgraph (i) to nodes in subgraph (j).
K = number of nonoverlapping subgraphs.
W_i = sum of the weights on the links in subgraph (i).
W_{ij} = sum of the weights on the links connecting nodes in subgraph (i) to nodes subgraph (j).
C_{ij} = coupling between subgraph (i) and subgraph (j).
M = goodness measure for a partition.

Therefore:

$$S_i = \frac{L_i - (N_i - 1)}{(N_i * (N_i - 1)/2) - (N_i - 1)} * \frac{W_i}{L_i}$$

$$C_{ij} = \frac{L_i}{N_i * N_j} * \frac{W_{ij}}{L_{ij}} = \frac{W_{ij}}{N_i * N_j}$$

$$M = \sum_{i=1}^{K} S_i - \sum_{i=1}^{K-1} \sum_{j=K+1}^{K} C_{ij}.$$

The rationale behind the development of the strength and the coupling measures are as follows. Given a subgraph of N nodes, $N - 1$ is the minimum number of links which can form a subgraph without disjoint components. Any number of links greater than this minimum is an indication of subgraph internal coherence beyond the minimum required for it to be coherent at all. This number is normalized by the maximum number of links that may exist in a subgraph $(N * (N - 1)/2)$.

The above strength measure, however, is not very well-defined for a graph with only two nodes since the denominator becomes zero in such a case. The difficulty is resolved by special calculations. Considering the general application of the methodology and the fact that subgraphs of such a small size is of little interest, the approach that is taken is to assign strength value of 1.0 (modified by the link weight factor) to the subgraph of this size.

There are nice properties to the strength and coupling measures. They both carry equal weights in the determination of the M index. Both fall in the range $[0, 1]$. The measures are also normalized in terms of the size of the subgraphs (i.e., for a given number of links, larger subgraphs have lower strengths). The measures are invariant in terms of "proportional connectness" regardless of n, a tree—connected subgraph always has strength of 0, a fully connected subgraph always has strength of 1.00 (assuming all links have unity weight).

Goodness measures for a partition have been used in other similar graph model application in the literature, see for example [30]-[34]. Choices such as this, in the present research effort, are perhaps guided more by intuition and "what makes sense" then by provable theorems. The strong intuitive appeal of the above properties lend credence to the appropriateness of the definitions of subgraph strength and coupling.

In order to select a good design then, a sequential search by the analyst among the generated M values, for finding the maximum, is considered to be sufficient at the current stage of the CAPO development. The associated design is the one with modules that possess high strength and which simultaneously are weakly interconnected.

Based on the procedure for the hierarchical clustering methods originally each node is viewed as a separate cluster. Then, each method proceeds to join together the most "similar pair of" clusters. Subsequently, the similarity matrix is searched to find the most similar pair (cluster). Different clustering methods are implemented by varying the procedure, used for defining the most similar pair. The cluster pair with the largest similarity value is then merged to form a single cluster, producing the next level up in clustering tree. The joining of similar pair is continued until the number of clusters is reduced to 1 (the entire set of objects). The order in which the objects are assigned to clusters is then used to select reasonable set of clusters.

At each stage of clustering, the identity of clusters merged are recorded. Also the goodness measure or the objective function of the clustering after each cluster merger is calculated and the information is recorded in order to find a particular decomposition exhibiting the highest objective function.

The above procedure once again emphasizes the importance of the weighting scheme to the decomposition procedure and the methodology as a whole. A higher weight on the link joining any two process is an indication of a higher level of cohesion that would result from their grouping in a single module. For the same reason a higher interdependency weight also produces a higher similarity weight which in effect put the two process in some sort of "priority" list as being the (next) most appropriate candidates to be selected to form a cluster.

Using the CAPO analysis package, the analyst can ask the system to compute the goodness measure for each stage of clustering and for any of the different clustering methods which are available. The value of the objective function changes as the number of processes in the clus-

ters increases. It starts with a low value (low cohesion, high coupling) and reaches to a maximum level (high cohesion, low coupling) and then continues to decrease (low cohesion, low coupling).

Success in producing designs that result in reliable software, even using structured design techniques, is dependent on the experience level of the designer. CAPO provides a quantitative measure of quality necessary in order to ease the dependence on the rare availability of expert designers.

As mentioned earlier, one property of a "good" design is lower data transport volume in the system. Lower transport volume results in lower processing time and lower data organization complexity. Using the CAPO analysis package, the analyst can ask the system to provide volume of data transported between processes and determine total transport volume within the system. This would indicate the necessity of grouping of any pair of processes and/or the effect of grouping of any number of processes on the total transport volume of data within the system.

A CASE STUDY USING A SMALL APPLICATION SYSTEM

To illustrate the application of the approach discussed in this paper, including the use of the CAPO analysis package, a small design problem [11] is presented below. The problem addressed is the design of an order-entry subsystem. The narrative statement of requirements for the order entry subsystem is taken from systems specifications and is presented below.

Orders will be received by mail, or taken over the phone by the inward WATS line. Each order will be scanned to see that all important information is present. Where payment is included, the amount is to be checked for correctness. Where payment is not with the order, the customer file must be checked to see if the order comes from a person or organization in good credit standing; if not, the person must be sent a confirmation of the order and a request for a prepayment. For orders with payment or good credit, inventory is then to be checked to see if the order can be filled. If it can, a shipping note with an invoice (marked "paid" for prepaid orders) is prepared and sent out with the books. If the order can only be part-filled, a shipping note and invoice is prepared for the part shipment, with a confirmation of the unfilled part (and paid invoice where payment was sent with the order), and a back-order record is created.

Fig. 3 depicts the graphical representation of the DFD for this design problem.

Each process on the graph by itself is an independent functional entity that might best be performed as a separate module. Combining the functions into a single module can reduce the degree of cohesiveness within the system. However, since the objective function is to maximize cohesion and to minimize coupling, maximizing the cohe-

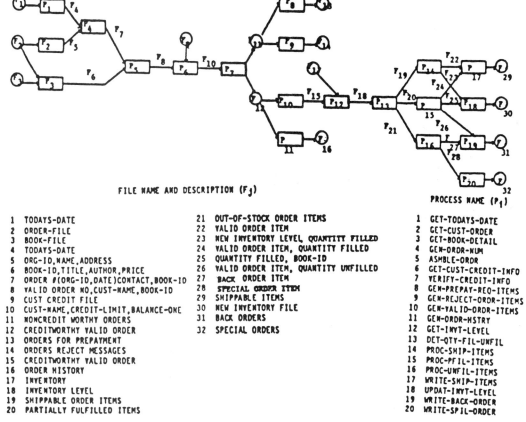

FILE NAME AND DESCRIPTION (F_j)

1	TODAYS-DATE	21	OUT-OF-STOCK ORDER ITEMS
2	ORDER-FILE	22	VALID ORDER ITEM
3	BOOK-FILE	23	NEW INVENTORY LEVEL, QUANTITY FILLED
4	TODAYS-DATE	24	VALID ORDER ITEM, QUANTITY FILLED
5	ORG-ID,NAME,ADDRESS	25	QUANTITY FILLED, BOOK-ID
6	BOOK-ID,TITLE,AUTHOR,PRICE	26	VALID ORDER ITEM, QUANTITY UNFILLED
7	ORDER #(ORG-ID,DATE)CONTACT,BOOK-ID	27	BACK ORDER ITEM
8	VALID ORDER NO,CUST-NAME,BOOK-ID	28	SPECIAL ORDER ITEM
9	CUST CREDIT FILE	29	SHIPPABLE ITEMS
10	CUST-NAME,CREDIT-LIMIT,BALANCE-ONE	30	NEW INVENTORY FILE
11	NONCREDIT WORTHY ORDERS	31	BACK ORDERS
12	CREDITWORTHY VALID ORDER	32	SPECIAL ORDERS
13	ORDERS FOR PREPAYMENT		
14	ORDERS REJECT MESSAGES		
15	CREDITWORTHY VALID ORDER		
16	ORDER HISTORY		
17	INVENTORY		
18	INVENTORY LEVEL		
19	SHIPPABLE ORDER ITEMS		
20	PARTIALLY FULFILLED ITEMS		

PROCESS NAME (P_i)

1	GET-TODAYS-DATE
2	GET-CUST-ORDER
3	GET-BOOK-DETAIL
4	GEN-ORDR-NUM
5	ASMBLE-ORDR
6	GET-CUST-CREDIT-INFO
7	VERIFY-CREDIT-INFO
8	GEN-PREPAY-REQ-ITEMS
9	GEN-REJECT-ORDR-ITEMS
10	GEN-VALID-ORDR-ITEMS
11	GEN-ORDR-HSTRY
12	GET-INVT-LEVEL
13	DET-QTY-FIL-UNFIL
14	PROC-SHIP-ITEMS
15	PROC-PFIL-ITEMS
16	PROC-UNFIL-ITEMS
17	WRITE-SHIP-ITEMS
18	UPDAT-INVT-LEVEL
19	WRITE-BACK-ORDER
20	WRITE-SPIL-ORDER

Fig. 3. Data flow diagram for an order-entry subsystem design problem.

sion within the system by itself would not create a satisfactory design. What we hope to create is a set of functionally cohesive modules that are also data coupled. Simply designating each process in data flow diagrams as a separate module would create a system with an excessive number of calls (one per each module) with a high degree of data transport.

Relatively high levels of coupling would also occur when modules are tied to an environment external to software. For example, I/O couples a module to specific devices, formats, and communication protocals. External coupling is essential but should be limited to a small number of modules within a structure. Achieving these objectives would require a balance level between cohesion, coupling (both internal and external) and volume of data transported within the system. Such a balance would be accomplished by proper grouping of the processes within modules.

In the graph above, for example, grouping two processes GET-BOOK-DETAIL (P3) and GEN-PREPAY-REQ-ITEMS (P8) would result in a coincidental cohesion module. In contrast sequential cohesion would result if two processes, GET-INVT-LEVEL (P12) and DET-QTY-FIL-UNVIL (P13) were grouped as a separate module.

In a procedural cohesion module, the processing elements are part of the same procedure, (they are driven by a unique process); however, they are not necessarily using the same data set(s). For example grouping processes

PROC-SHIP-ITEMS (P14), PROC-PFIL-ITEMS (P15), PROC-UNFIL-ITEMS (P16) would create a procedural cohesion module since all of them are controlled by the process DET-QTY-FIL-UNFIL (P13).

Communicational cohesion would result if two processes GEN-PREPAY-REQ-ITEMS (P8) and GEN-RE-JECT-ORDR-ITEMS (P9) are grouped in single modules since both are controlled by the process VERIFY-CREDIT-INFO (P7) and they both use information related to NONCREDIT-WORTHYORDERS (F11). However, grouping two processes GEN-PREPAY-REQ-ITEMS (P8) and GEN-ORDR-HISTORY (P11) would result in a procedural cohesion module.

Several preliminary reports are produced using the input. These are shown in Figs. 4 and 5. Fig. 4 shows the name of each process, the number of processes preceding it, the number of input and output data sets and their identification number (generated by the system). Fig. 5 shows similar information for each data set. The identification numbers generated for the processes and data sets are required for the subsequent analysis.

CAPO next generates the incidence matrix (E), and the total volume of data transported between processes given the logical model of the system (see Fig. 6). A separate report shows the level of data transported between each two processes (see Fig. 7). This information is necessary in the process of evaluating alternative designs. The system asks the user for alternative grouping, and for each

	NAME	NUM OF PRECEDING PROCESSES	PRECEDING PROCESS ID	NUM OF INPUTS FILES	INPUT FILES ID	NUM OF OUTPUT FILES	OUTPUT FILES ID
1	GET-TODAYS-DATE	00	0000000000	01	0100000000	01	0200000000
2	GET-CUST-ORDR	00	0000000000	01	0300000000	01	0400000000
3	GET-BOOK-DETAIL	00	0000000000	02	0305000000	01	0600000000
4	GEN-ORDR-NUM	02	0102000000	02	0204000000	01	0700000000
5	ASMBLE-ORDR	02	0403000000	02	0607000000	01	0800000000
6	GET-CUST-CREDIT-INFO	01	0500000000	02	0809000000	01	1000000000
7	VERIFY-CREDIT-INFO	01	0600000000	01	1000000000	02	1112000000
8	GEN-PREPAY-REQ-ITEMS	01	0700000000	01	1100000000	01	1300000000
9	GEN-REJECT-ORDR-ITEMS	01	0700000000	01	1100000000	01	1400000000
10	GEN-VALID-ORDR-ITEMS	01	0700000000	01	1200000000	01	1500000000
11	GEN-ORDR-HSTRY	01	0700000000	01	1200000000	01	1600000000
12	GET-INVT-LEVEL	01	1000000000	02	1517000000	01	1800000000
13	DET-QTY-FIL-UNFIL	01	1200000000	01	1800000000	03	1920210000
14	PROC-SHIP-ITEMS	01	1300000000	01	1900000000	02	2223000000
15	PROC-PFIL-ITEMS	01	1300000000	01	2000000000	03	2425260000
16	PROC-UNFIL-ITEMS	01	1300000000	01	2100000000	02	2728000000
17	WRITE-SHIP-ITEMS	02	1415000000	02	2224000000	01	2900000000
18	UPDAT-INVT-LEVEL	02	1415000000	02	2325000000	01	3000000000
19	WRITE-BACK-ORDR	02	1516000000	02	2627000000	01	3100000000
20	WRITE-SPCL-ORDR	01	1600000000	01	2800000000	01	3200000000

Fig. 4. Processes and their input output files.

	FILE NAME	RECORD KEY	RECORD SIZE	NUM OF RECORDS	FREQ. OF ACCESS
1	F1	DATE	000006	0000000001	01
2	F4	DATE	000006	0000000001	00
3	F2	CUST-NAME	000080	0000001000	01
4	F5	CUST-NAME	000080	0000001000	00
5	F3	BOOK-ID	000080	0000002000	01
6	F6	BOOK-ID	000080	0000002000	00
7	F7	CUST-NAME	000080	0000001000	00
8	F8	CUST-NAME	000080	0000001000	00
9	F9	CUST-NAME	000080	0000003000	01
10	F10	CUST-NAME	000080	0000001000	00
11	F11	CUST-NAME	000080	0000000300	00
12	F12	CUST-NAME	000080	0000000700	00
13	F13	CUST-NAME	000080	0000000200	00
14	F14	CUST-NAME	000080	0000000100	00
15	F15	CUST-NAME	000080	0000000700	00
16	F16	CUST-NAME	000080	0000000700	00
17	F17	BOOK-ID	000080	0000002000	01
18	F18	BOOK-ID	000080	0000000700	00
19	F19	BOOK-ID	000080	0000000400	00
20	F20	BOOK-ID	000080	0000000200	00
21	F21	BOOK-ID	000080	0000000100	00
22	F22	BOOK-ID	000080	0000000400	00
23	F23	BOOK-ID	000080	0000000400	00
24	F24	BOOK-ID	000080	0000000200	00
25	F25	BOOK-ID	000080	0000000200	00
26	F26	BOOK-ID	000080	0000000200	00
27	F27	BOOK-ID	000080	0000000100	00
28	F28	BOOK-ID	000080	0000000100	00
29	F29	BOOK-ID	000080	0000000400	00
30	F30	BOOK-ID	000080	0000000200	00
31	F31	BOOK-ID	000080	0000000100	00
32	F32	BOOK-ID	000080	0000000100	00

Fig. 5. Files and their characteristics.

configuration given, the system generates the new incidence matrix and the total transport volume figure.

The precedence matrix (P), the reachability matrix (R), matrix of partial reachability (R^*), matrix of feasible grouping (G), and matrix of timing relationships of the processes (T) for the example problem are shown in Figs. 8–12. Using the above matrixes and the weighting scheme, the interdependency weight matrix is computed (see Fig. 13).

As was mentioned above, the weights that are given to links within the graph are the measures for the evaluating the different forms of cohesion that might result if the processes connected by those links are grouped. The interdependency weight between process 8 (GEN-PREPAY-REQ-ITEMS) and process 9 (GEN-REJECT-ORDER-ITEMS), for example, is 0.7 which is the indication that

if these two processes are grouped, the module would be communicationally cohesive.

Fig. 14 shows the similarity matrix. The weights represent the degree to which groupings of any two process would satisfy the objective function. One of the nice features of the CAPO analysis package is the natural presentations of the results to the user. The previous matrices (Figs. 8–14) are generated automatically for the purposes of the decomposition only. The analyst has the option to look at them if he or she chooses to do so.

The similarity matrix is used as input to six different hierarchical clustering methods [28], [35]. There is no obvious way of determining which method would produce the best partition with respect to the objective function. All of the algorithms are included in the CAPO analysis package. Fig. 15 shows how the (partial) result of one

PROCESS TO FILES RELATIONSHIP

```
      1  2  3  4  5  6  7  8  9 10 11 12 13 14 15 16 17 18 19 20 21 22 23 24 25 26 27 28 29 30 31 32
 1    1 -1  0  0  0  0  0  0  0  0  0  0  0  0  0  0  0  0  0  0  0  0  0  0  0  0  0  0  0  0  0  0
 2    0  0  1 -1  0  0  0  0  0  0  0  0  0  0  0  0  0  0  0  0  0  0  0  0  0  0  0  0  0  0  0  0
 3    0  0  1  0  1 -1  0  0  0  0  0  0  0  0  0  0  0  0  0  0  0  0  0  0  0  0  0  0  0  0  0  0
 4    0  1  0  1  0  0 -1  0  0  0  0  0  0  0  0  0  0  0  0  0  0  0  0  0  0  0  0  0  0  0  0  0
 5    0  0  0  0  0  1  1 -1  0  0  0  0  0  0  0  0  0  0  0  0  0  0  0  0  0  0  0  0  0  0  0  0
 6    0  0  0  0  0  0  0  1  1 -1  0  0  0  0  0  0  0  0  0  0  0  0  0  0  0  0  0  0  0  0  0  0
 7    0  0  0  0  0  0  0  0  0  1 -1 -1  0  0  0  0  0  0  0  0  0  0  0  0  0  0  0  0  0  0  0  0
 8    0  0  0  0  0  0  0  0  0  0  1  0 -1  0  0  0  0  0  0  0  0  0  0  0  0  0  0  0  0  0  0  0
 9    0  0  0  0  0  0  0  0  0  0  1  0  0 -1  0  0  0  0  0  0  0  0  0  0  0  0  0  0  0  0  0  0
10    0  0  0  0  0  0  0  0  0  0  0  1  0  0 -1  0  0  0  0  0  0  0  0  0  0  0  0  0  0  0  0  0
11    0  0  0  0  0  0  0  0  0  0  0  1  0  0  0 -1  0  0  0  0  0  0  0  0  0  0  0  0  0  0  0  0
12    0  0  0  0  0  0  0  0  0  0  0  0  1  0  1 -1  0  0  0  0  0  0  0  0  0  0  0  0  0  0  0  0
13    0  0  0  0  0  0  0  0  0  0  0  0  0  1 -1 -1 -1  0  0  0  0  0  0  0  0  0  0  0  0  0  0  0
14    0  0  0  0  0  0  0  0  0  0  0  0  0  0  1  0  0 -1 -1  0  0  0  0  0  0  0  0  0  0  0  0  0
15    0  0  0  0  0  0  0  0  0  0  0  0  0  0  0  1  0  0 -1 -1 -1  0  0  0  0  0  0  0  0  0  0  0
16    0  0  0  0  0  0  0  0  0  0  0  0  0  0  0  0  1  0  0  0  0 -1 -1  0  0  0  0  0  0  0  0  0
17    0  0  0  0  0  0  0  0  0  0  0  0  0  0  0  0  0  1  0  1  0  0  0 -1  0  0  0  0  0  0  0  0
18    0  0  0  0  0  0  0  0  0  0  0  0  0  0  0  0  0  0  1  0  1  0  0  0 -1  0  0  0  0  0  0  0
19    0  0  0  0  0  0  0  0  0  0  0  0  0  0  0  0  0  0  0  1  1  0  0  0  0 -1  0  0  0  0  0  0
20    0  0  0  0  0  0  0  0  0  0  0  0  0  0  0  0  0  0  0  0  1  0  0  0  0  0 -1  0  0  0  0  0
```

FILE NO.	1	2	3	4	5	6	7	8	9	10
NUM ACCES	1	2	2	2	1	2	2	2	1	2
FLSIZE/1000	.006	.006	80.000	80.000	160.000	160.000	80.000	80.000	240.000	80.000
VOL/1000	.006	.012	160.000	160.000	160.000	320.000	160.000	160.000	240.000	160.000

FILE NO.	11	12	13	14	15	16	17	18	19	20
NUM ACCES	3	3	1	1	2	1	1	2	2	2
FLSIZE/1000	24.000	56.000	16.000	8.000	56.000	56.000	160.000	56.000	32.000	16.000
VOL/1000	72.030	168.000	16.000	8.000	112.000	56.000	160.000	112.000	64.000	32.000

FILE NO.	21	22	23	24	25	26	27	28	29	30
NUM ACCES	2	2	2	2	2	2	2	2	1	1
FLSIZE/1000	8.000	32.000	32.000	16.000	16.000	16.000	8.000	8.000	32.000	16.000
VOL/1000	16.000	64.030	64.030	32.000	32.000	32.000	16.000	16.000	32.000	16.000

FILE NO.	31	32
NUM ACCES	1	1
FLSIZE/1000	8.000	8.000
VOL/1000	8.000	8.000

TOTAL TRANS. VOLUME   2656.010

Fig. 6. Incidence graph of processes (E).

THIS IS THE VOLUME BETWEEN PROCESSES /1000 CHAR

1	TO	4	.006
2	TO	4	80.000
3	TO	5	160.000
4	TO	5	80.000
5	TO	6	80.000
6	TO	7	80.000
7	TO	8	26.000
7	TO	9	24.000
7	TO	10	56.000
7	TO	11	56.000
10	TO	12	56.000
12	TO	13	56.000
13	TO	14	32.000
13	TO	15	16.000
13	TO	16	8.000
14	TO	17	32.000
15	TO	17	16.000
14	TO	18	32.000
15	TO	18	16.000
15	TO	19	16.000
16	TO	19	8.000
16	TO	20	8.000

Fig. 7. Volume of data transported between processes.

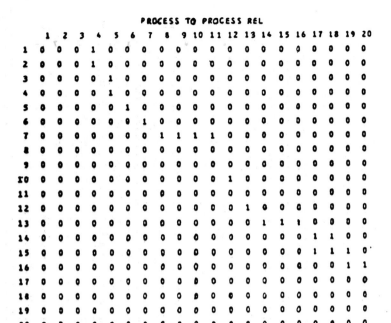

Fig. 8. Precedence matrix of processes (P).

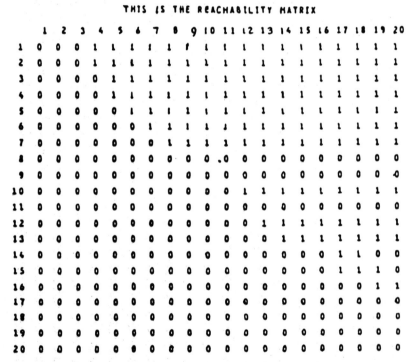

Fig. 9. Reachability matrix (R).

clustering algorithm and the associated goodness measure for each step of clustering is presented to the analyst. Table II shows the clustering results for the example.

Analyzing the Result of the Best Groupings

In analyzing the best partition produce in the table above, one comes to the conclusion that the system has provided an effective partitioning of the data flow diagram. There are four functionally cohesive modules, (1), (2), (6), (12); one sequentially cohesive module, (13, 15); one communicationally cohesive module, (8, 9) and four procedurally cohesive modules, (3, 4, 5) (7, 10, 11), (14, 17, 18), (16, 19, 20). Coupling within the system is low; apart from a few instances, modules are coupled largely by the passage of data, with a few control variables "reporting back" what has happened. As a result of the partitioning, the system is more adaptable to change and the

THIS IS THE PARTIAL REACHABILITY MATRIX

	1	2	3	4	5	6	7	8	9	10	11	12	13	14	15	16	17	18	19	20
1	0	0	0	0	1	1	1	1	1	1	1	1	1	1	1	1	1	1	1	1
2	0	0	0	0	1	1	1	1	1	1	1	1	1	1	1	1	1	1	1	1
3	0	0	0	0	0	1	1	1	1	1	1	1	1	1	1	1	1	1	1	1
4	0	0	0	0	0	1	1	1	1	1	1	1	1	1	1	1	1	1	1	1
5	0	0	0	0	0	0	1	1	1	1	1	1	1	1	1	1	1	1	1	1
6	0	0	0	0	0	0	0	1	1	1	1	1	1	1	1	1	1	1	1	1
7	0	0	0	0	0	0	0	0	0	0	0	0	1	1	1	1	1	1	1	1
8	0	0	0	0	0	0	0	0	0	0	0	0	0	0	0	0	0	0	0	0
9	0	0	0	0	0	0	0	0	0	0	0	0	0	0	0	0	0	0	0	0
10	0	0	0	0	0	0	0	0	0	0	0	0	1	1	1	1	1	1	1	1
11	0	0	0	0	0	0	0	0	0	0	0	0	0	0	0	0	0	0	0	0
12	0	0	0	0	0	0	0	0	0	0	0	0	0	1	1	1	1	1	1	1
13	0	0	0	0	0	0	0	0	0	0	0	0	0	0	0	0	1	1	1	1
14	0	0	0	0	0	0	0	0	0	0	0	0	0	0	0	0	0	0	0	0
15	0	0	0	0	0	0	0	0	0	0	0	0	0	0	0	0	0	0	0	0
16	0	0	0	0	0	0	0	0	0	0	0	0	0	0	0	0	0	0	0	0
17	0	0	0	0	0	0	0	0	0	0	0	0	0	0	0	0	0	0	0	0
18	0	0	0	0	0	0	0	0	0	0	0	0	0	0	0	0	0	0	0	0
19	0	0	0	0	0	0	0	0	0	0	0	0	0	0	0	0	0	0	0	0
20	0	0	0	0	0	0	0	0	0	0	0	0	0	0	0	0	0	0	0	0

Fig. 10. Partial reachability matrix (R^*).

THIS IS MATRIX OF FEASIBLE GROUPING

	1	2	3	4	5	6	7	8	9	10	11	12	13	14	15	16	17	18	19	20
1	-1	2	0	1	-1	-1	-1	-1	-1	-1	-1	-1	-1	-1	-1	-1	-1	-1	-1	-1
2	2	-1	0	1	-1	-1	-1	-1	-1	-1	-1	-1	-1	-1	-1	-1	-1	-1	-1	-1
3	0	0	-1	2	1	-1	-1	-1	-1	-1	-1	-1	-1	-1	-1	-1	-1	-1	-1	-1
4	1	1	2	-1	1	-1	-1	-1	-1	-1	-1	-1	-1	-1	-1	-1	-1	-1	-1	-1
5	-1	-1	1	1	-1	1	-1	-1	-1	-1	-1	-1	-1	-1	-1	-1	-1	-1	-1	-1
6	-1	-1	-1	-1	1	-1	1	-1	-1	-1	-1	-1	-1	-1	-1	-1	-1	-1	-1	-1
7	-1	-1	-1	-1	-1	1	-1	1	1	1	1	-1	-1	-1	-1	-1	-1	-1	-1	-1
8	-1	-1	-1	-1	-1	-1	1	-1	1	1	2	0	0	0	0	0	0	0	0	0
9	-1	-1	-1	-1	-1	-1	1	1	-1	1	2	0	0	0	0	0	0	0	0	0
10	-1	-1	-1	-1	-1	-1	1	1	1	-1	2	1	-1	-1	-1	-1	-1	-1	-1	-1
11	-1	-1	-1	-1	-1	-1	1	2	2	2	-1	0	0	0	0	0	0	0	0	0
12	-1	-1	-1	-1	-1	-1	-1	0	0	1	0	-1	1	-1	-1	-1	-1	-1	-1	-1
13	-1	-1	-1	-1	-1	-1	-1	0	0	-1	0	1	-1	1	1	1	-1	-1	-1	-1
14	-1	-1	-1	-1	-1	-1	-1	0	0	-1	0	-1	1	-1	2	1	1	1	0	0
15	-1	-1	-1	-1	-1	-1	-1	0	0	-1	0	-1	1	2	-1	2	1	1	1	0
16	-1	-1	-1	-1	-1	-1	-1	0	0	-1	0	-1	1	1	2	-1	0	0	1	1
17	-1	-1	-1	-1	-1	-1	-1	0	0	-1	0	-1	-1	1	1	0	-1	2	2	0
18	-1	-1	-1	-1	-1	-1	-1	0	0	-1	0	-1	-1	1	1	0	2	-1	2	0
19	-1	-1	-1	-1	-1	-1	-1	0	0	-1	0	-1	-1	0	1	1	2	2	-1	2
20	-1	-1	-1	-1	-1	-1	-1	0	0	-1	0	-1	-1	0	0	1	0	0	2	-1

Fig. 11. Matrix of feasible grouping of processes (G).

EXECUTION TIME OF EACH PROCESS

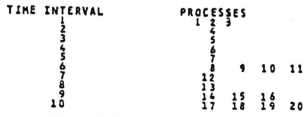

Fig. 12. Timing relationships of the processes.

THIS IS THE INTERDEPENDENCY WEIGHT MATRIX

```
      1   2   3   4   5   6   7   8   9  10  11  12  13  14  15  16  17  18  19  20
 1  0.0 0.5 0.3 0.9 0.0 0.0 0.0 0.0 0.0 0.0 0.0 0.0 0.0 0.0 0.0 0.0 0.0 0.0 0.0 0.0
 2  0.5 0.0 0.3 0.9 0.0 0.0 0.0 0.0 0.0 0.0 0.0 0.0 0.0 0.0 0.0 0.0 0.0 0.0 0.0 0.0
 3  0.3 0.3 0.0 0.5 0.9 0.0 0.0 0.0 0.0 0.0 0.0 0.0 0.0 0.0 0.0 0.0 0.0 0.0 0.0 0.0
 4  0.9 0.9 0.5 0.0 0.9 0.0 0.0 0.0 0.0 0.0 0.0 0.0 0.0 0.0 0.0 0.0 0.0 0.0 0.0 0.0
 5  0.0 0.0 0.9 0.9 0.0 0.9 0.0 0.0 0.0 0.0 0.0 0.0 0.0 0.0 0.0 0.0 0.0 0.0 0.0 0.0
 6  0.0 0.0 0.0 0.0 0.9 0.0 0.9 0.0 0.0 0.0 0.0 0.0 0.0 0.0 0.0 0.0 0.0 0.0 0.0 0.0
 7  0.0 0.0 0.0 0.0 0.0 0.9 0.0 0.9 0.9 0.9 0.9 0.0 0.0 0.0 0.0 0.0 0.0 0.0 0.0 0.0
 8  0.0 0.0 0.0 0.0 0.0 0.0 0.9 0.0 0.7 0.5 0.5 0.0 0.0 0.0 0.0 0.0 0.0 0.0 0.0 0.0
 9  0.0 0.0 0.0 0.0 0.0 0.0 0.9 0.7 0.0 0.5 0.5 0.0 0.0 0.0 0.0 0.0 0.0 0.0 0.0 0.0
10  0.0 0.0 0.0 0.0 0.0 0.0 0.9 0.5 0.5 0.0 0.7 0.9 0.0 0.0 0.0 0.0 0.0 0.0 0.0 0.0
11  0.0 0.0 0.0 0.0 0.0 0.0 0.9 0.5 0.5 0.7 0.0 0.0 0.0 0.0 0.0 0.0 0.0 0.0 0.0 0.0
12  0.0 0.0 0.0 0.0 0.0 0.0 0.0 0.0 0.0 0.9 0.0 0.0 0.9 0.0 0.0 0.0 0.0 0.0 0.0 0.0
13  0.0 0.0 0.0 0.0 0.0 0.0 0.0 0.0 0.0 0.0 0.0 0.9 0.0 0.9 0.9 0.9 0.0 0.0 0.0 0.0
14  0.0 0.0 0.0 0.0 0.0 0.0 0.0 0.0 0.0 0.0 0.0 0.0 0.9 0.0 0.5 0.5 0.9 0.9 0.0 0.0
15  0.0 0.0 0.0 0.0 0.0 0.0 0.0 0.0 0.0 0.0 0.0 0.0 0.9 0.5 0.0 0.5 0.9 0.9 0.9 0.0
16  0.0 0.0 0.0 0.0 0.0 0.0 0.0 0.0 0.0 0.0 0.0 0.0 0.9 0.5 0.5 0.0 0.0 0.0 0.9 0.9
17  0.0 0.0 0.0 0.0 0.0 0.0 0.0 0.0 0.0 0.0 0.0 0.0 0.0 0.9 0.9 0.0 0.0 0.5 0.5 0.3
18  0.0 0.0 0.0 0.0 0.0 0.0 0.0 0.0 0.0 0.0 0.0 0.0 0.0 0.9 0.0 0.5 0.0 0.5 0.3
19  0.0 0.0 0.0 0.0 0.0 0.0 0.0 0.0 0.0 0.0 0.0 0.0 0.9 0.9 0.5 0.5 0.0 0.5
20  0.0 0.0 0.0 0.0 0.0 0.0 0.0 0.0 0.0 0.0 0.0 0.0 0.9 0.3 0.3 0.5 0.0
```

Fig. 13. The interdependency weight matrix.

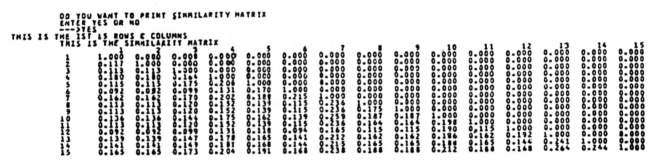

DO YOU WANT TO PRINT SIMMILARITY MATRIX
ENTER YES OR NO
--->YES
THIS IS THE 1ST 15 ROWS & COLUMNS
THIS IS THE SIMMILARITY MATRIX

Fig. 14. The similarity matrix.

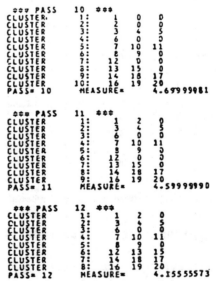

```
*** PASS  10  ***
CLUSTER   1:   1    0    0
CLUSTER   2:   2    0    0
CLUSTER   3:   3    4    5
CLUSTER   4:   6    0    0
CLUSTER   5:   7   10   11
CLUSTER   6:   8    9    0
CLUSTER   7:  12    0    0
CLUSTER   8:  13   15    0
CLUSTER   9:  14   18   17
CLUSTER  10:  16   19   20
PASS= 10    MEASURE=   4.69999981

*** PASS  11  ***
CLUSTER   1:   1    2    0
CLUSTER   2:   3    4    5
CLUSTER   3:   6    0    0
CLUSTER   4:   7   10   11
CLUSTER   5:   8    9    0
CLUSTER   6:  12   13    0
CLUSTER   7:  13   15    0
CLUSTER   8:  14   18   17
CLUSTER   9:  16   19   20
PASS= 11    MEASURE=   4.59999990

*** PASS  12  ***
CLUSTER   1:   1    2    0
CLUSTER   2:   3    4    5
CLUSTER   3:   6   10    0
CLUSTER   4:   7   10   11
CLUSTER   5:   8    9    0
CLUSTER   6:  12   13   15
CLUSTER   7:  14   18   17
CLUSTER   8:  16   19   20
PASS= 12    MEASURE=   4.15555573
```

Fig. 15. Clustering result and the associated goodness measure for three
levels of aggregation.

"ripple effects" of possible user changes are limited in scope. This would relieve the analyst from using design techniques such as transform analysis and transaction analysis to find the boundaries that delineate the transform and/or transaction centers. Further, the system has identified the mapping of the processes into software structure as modules with the consideration of optimizing the coupling and cohesion principals. The utility of the approach

TABLE II
COMPARISON OF CLUSTERING RESULTS OF THREE "BEST" DECOMPOSITION
ALGORITHMS

METHOD	BEST M	NUMBER OF CLUSTERS	BEST PARTITION GROUPINGS
* Complete linkage clustering	3.90	7	(1),(2),(3,4,5,),(6),(7,8,9,10,11) (12), (13,14,15,16,17,18,19,20)
* Average linkage within new group <u>and</u> * centroid clustering	4.70	10	(1),(2),(3,4,5),(6), (7,10,11),(8,9),(12), (13,15),(14,17,18),(16,19,20)

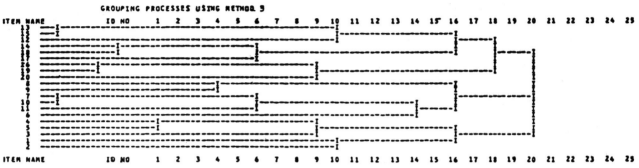

Fig. 16. Hierarchical clustering using median method of power.

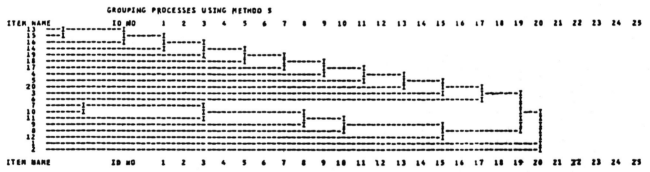

Fig. 17. Hierarchical clustering using centroid clustering method.

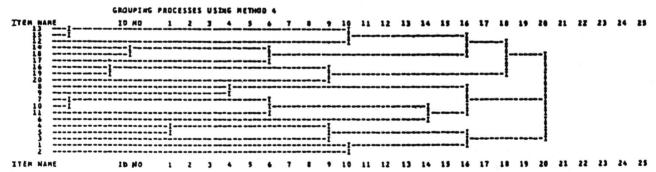

Fig. 18. Hierarchical clustering using average linkage within the new group method.

for designing systems with a complex data flow diagram is more obvious.

In order to compare the different partitions and investigate closely the sequence in which the clusters are formed, the information generated by the clustering algorithms are used to draw a hierarchical tree. Trees pro-vide an effective visual aid of the clustering results which permit the analyst to grasp rapidly the hierarchical relationships and visualize the membership of each cluster at any level of aggregation. Figs. 16–18 show trees for the three best candidate partitions. The associated goodness measure for each level of aggregation (maximum 25 levels are presented on the tree) can also be read from the output of each clustering algorithm (see Fig. 15).

The tasks that remain, then, are to study the decomposition and to formulate a set of specifications for structuring the modules required to implement the design. At the same time, effort should be concentrated on identification of anomalies, counterintuitive results, etc., that might indicate errors in assessments of interdependency weights.

In order to highlight the restrictions and to appreciate the flexibility of the CAPO analysis framework, an overview of the design process in a nonsequential environment is given in [11]. In [36], the interprocess communications in such an environment are summarized as follows:

1) A set of processes may be required to be executed in sequence. Namely, given a set of processes $P1$, $P2$, $\cdots Pn$, the execution of $P2$ requires the successful completion of $P1$ and so forth.

2) A certain process may be selected to be executed according to a test condition. This implies that the processes are mutually exclusive and the selection depends on the probability associated with the occurrence of the individual input data. The control structure is similar to the case statement in programming languages.

3) A set of processes may be selected to be executed repeatedly.

4) A set of processes may be executed, regardless of whether or not they involve communicating or accessing shared data.

5) A set of processes may be required to be coordinated for termination, although they may not be required to be executed concurrently.

A number of approaches have been proposed in literature [36]–[39] for analyzing the complex interactions among processes in parallel processing environment. Similar to the approach in [36], a "new" type of node ("control node") is added to the flowgraph. A control node is represented as triangle in order to distinguish itself from the process node, and it is represented explicitly in the graph by its type (i.e., CON for concurrent, ONE-OF for exclusive processes, REPEAT for repeated execution, and TERM for coordinated termination).

As in the case of sequential environment, the interactions among processes are captured in terms of series of matrices. However, because of the possibility of cycles in the graph (REPEAT control node) more research is needed to determine the proper effect of the control nodes on the subsequent analysis (the generation of the interdependency weight matrix). This is the subject of the future research and will not be further addressed here.

One might wonder for a large system and a "real world" application how many processes, of roughly the equivalent level of complexity as in the above example, must be dealt with. In a large system development effort that was done for the Navy in [40], 647 processes and 791 unique files were defined and 62 program modules specifications were generated through analysis of interprocess relationships. The software designs were generated as a result of partitioning the application areas. This was done in an iterative fashion consistent with the generation of more than 50 alternative hardware configurations.

We expect some minor modifications to be necessary in the form of the user interface and report generations facilities of the CAPO analysis package in order to handle a system of such a size. However, no further changes will be required in any of the computations regarding the generations of the similarity matrix, decomposition algorithms and the determination of the goodness measure for a design.

The CAPO system is operational on VAX/VMS and DECSYSTEM-10. It operates on interactive mode and performs in seconds. A set of test cases has been developed and the experience with the system has been quite favorable. The package may slightly be modified in the areas of user interface. Further modifications are planned to make the system operational in microenvironment under UNIX operating system.

SUMMARY

This paper has demonstrated the feasibility of the automated software assistant (CAPO). The result of the analysis is an effective modularization of the system of processes and a specification of program modules. Better (more) cohesion leads to better (less) coupling, which leads to better (more maintainable) systems. The analysis reveals inherent organization among the set of processes and imposes organization on borderline cases. This eliminates the problem that often arise from prior knowledge or bias on the part of the analyst. Thus, the analyst is aided in objectivity of design and design for maintainability.

REFERENCES

[1] D. Teichroew and E. Hershey, "PSL/PSA: A computer aided technique for structured documentation and analysis of information processing systems," *IEEE Trans. Software Eng.*, vol. SE-3, no. 1, pp. 41–48, Jan. 1977.

[2] M. W. Alford, "Software requirements engineering methodology (SREM) at the age of two," in *Proc. COMPSAC 1978, IEEE*, Nov. 1978, pp. 332–339.

[3] S. M. Henry, "Information flow metrics for the evaluation of operating systems' structure," Ph.D. dissertation, Iowa State Univ., 1979.

[4] J. E. Kottemann and B. R. Konsynski, "Complexity assessment: A design and management tool for information system development," *Inform. Syst.*, vol. 8, no. 3, pp. 195–206, Mar. 1983.

[5] L. Belady and C. Evangelisti, "System partitioning and its measure," T. J. Watson Research Center, IBM, Yorktown Heights, NY, Tech. Rep. RC 7560, Mar. 1979.

[6] J. Silverman, N. Giddings, and J. Bean, "An approach to design-for-maintenance," in *Proc. Software Maintenance Workshop*, Monterey, CA, Dec. 1983.

[7] J. Silverman, J. Bean, and N. Giddings, "A component interconnection language for evaluating software design quality," Honeywell Rep., Mar. 1983.

[8] J. Bean, N. Giddings, and J. Silverman, "A software engineering experiment," Honeywell Rep., Apr. 1983.

[9] ——, "Quantifying software designs," in *Proc. 7th Int. Conf. Software Engineering*, Orlando, FL, Mar. 1984.

[10] N. Giddings and T. Colburn, "An automated software design evaluator," in *Proc. Annu. Conf.—ACM 84* San Francisco, CA, Oct. 1984.

[11] J. Karimi, "Computer-aided process organization," Ph.D. dissertation, Univ. Arizona, May 1983.

[12] C. Gans and T. Sarson, *Structured Systems Analysis, Tools and Techniques*. Englewood Cliffs, NJ: Prentice-Hall, 1979.

[13] J. R. White and T. L. Booth, "Towards an engineering approach to software design," in *Proc. Second Int. Conf. Software Engineering*, IEEE Catalog No. 76Ch1125-4C, 1976.

[14] G. J. Myers, *Reliable Software Through Composite Design*. New York: Petro-Cell Charter, 1975.

[15] E. Yourdon and L. L. Constantine, *Structured Design Fundamentals of a Discipline of Computer Program and Systems Design*. Englewood Cliffs, NJ: Prentice-Hall, 1979.

[16] W. P. Stevens, G. I. Myers, and L. L. Constantine, "Structured design," *IBM Syst. J.*, vol. 13, no. 2, pp. 115–139, May 1974.

[17] M. Page-Jones, *The Practical Guide to Structured Systems Design*. New York; Yourdon, 1980.

[18] D. Gelperin, "Testing maintainability," *Software Eng. Notes* (ACM—SIGSOFT), vol. 4, pp. 7–12, Apr. 1979.

[19] R. R. Willis and E. P. Jensen, "Computer aided design of software systems," in *Proc. 4th Int. Conf. Software Engineering*, Munich, West Germany, Sept. 1979, IEEE Catalog No. 79CH1479-SC, 1979.

[20] D. L. Parnas, "On the criteria to be used in decomposing systems into modules," *Commun. ACM*, vol. 15, no. 12, pp. 1053–1058, Dec. 1972.

[21] M. A. Jackson, *Principles of Program Design*. New York: Academic, 1975.

[22] J. D. Warnier, *The Logical Construction of Programs*, 3rd ed., translated by B. M. Flanagan. New York: Van Nostrand Reinhold, 1975.

[23] E. Yourdon and L. L. Constantine, *Structured Design*. New York; Yourdon, 1975.

[24] G. J. Myers, "The need for software engineering," *Computer*, Feb. 1978.

[25] B. Konsynski, J. Kottemann, J. Nunamaker, and J. Scott, "PLEXSYS-84: An Integrated Development Environment for Information Systems," *J. Management Inform. Syst.*, vol. 1, no. 3, pp. 62–104, Winter 1984–1985.

[26] J. F. Nunamaker, Jr., W. C. Nylin, Jr., and B. Konsynski, Jr., "Processing systems optimization through automatic design and reorganization of program modules," in *Information Systems*, J. Tou, Ed. New York: Plenum, 1974, pp. 311–336.

[27] R. B. Marimont, "A new method of checking the consistency of precedence matrices," *J. ACM*, vol. 6, no. 2, Apr. 1959.

[28] J. Hartigan, *Clustering Algorithms*. New York: Wiley, 1975.

[29] C. Gottlieb and S. Kumar, "Semantic clustering of index terms," *J. ACM*, vol. 15, no. 4, Oct. 1968.

[30] S. I. Huff, "Decomposition of weighted graph using the interchange partitioning algorithm," Center for Inform. Syst. Res., Sloan School of Management, M.I.T., Tech. Rep. 8, Mar. 1979.

[31] G. F. Estabrook, "A mathematical model in graph theory for biological classification," *J. Theor. Biol.*, vol. 12, 1966.

[32] L. Hubert, "Some applications of graph theory to clustering," *Psychometrika*, vol. 39, no. 3, Sept. 1974.

[33] R. Andreu, "A systematic approach to the design and structuring of complex software systems," Ph.D. dissertation, Sloan School of Management, M.I.T., Feb. 1978.

[34] S. L. Huff and S. E. Madnick, "Analysis techniques for use with the extended SDM model," Sloan School of Management, M.I.T., Tech. Rep. 9, Feb. 1979.

[35] M. R. Anderberg, *Cluster analysis for applications*. New York: Academic, 1973.

[36] S. Yan, S. Yang, and S. Shatz, "An approach to distributed computing system software design," *IEEE Trans. Software Eng.*, vol. SE-7, no. 4, July 1981.

[37] E. Dijkstra, "Co-Operating sequential problems," in *Programming Languages*, F. Genuys, Ed. New York: Academic, 1972.

[38] C. Hoare, "Monitors: An operating system structuring concept," *Commun. ACM*, vol. 17, pp. 549–559, Oct. 1974.

[39] J. Keedy, "On structuring operating systems with monitors," *ACM Operat. Syst. Rev.*, vol. 13, pp. 5–9, Jan. 1979.

[40] J. F. Nunamaker, B. Konsynski, and C. Singer, "Computer-aided analysis and design of information systems," *Commun. ACM*, vol. 19, no. 12, pp. 674–687, Dec. 1976.

Jahangir Karimi received the B.S. degree in managerial economics from the University of Tehran, Iran, in 1974, and the M.S. and Ph.D. degrees in management information systems from the University of Arizona, Tucson, in 1978 and 1983, respectively.

Since 1983, he has been with the Department of Information Systems, University of Cincinnati, Cincinnati, OH, for a year, and the University of Colorado at Denver where he is currently an Assistant Professor. His research interests include computer aids in the systems development process, user interface design, and information systems modeling techniques.

Dr. Karimi is a member of the Association for Computing Machinery, the Computing Society, and the Society for Information Management.

Benn R. Konsynski received the Ph.D. degree in computer science from Purdue University, West Lafayette, IN.

He is a Professor of Management Information Systems at the School of Business and Public Administration at the University of Arizona. His major research focus is computer-aided approaches to information system design and implementation. His current research interests include model management, learning paradigms in decision support systems, business dialogs in distributed office environments, and interorganizational systems.

PART V: THE ROLE OF PROTOTYPING IN CASE

This radical approach to software switches the noncreative aspects of maintenance and modification from man to machine. It could profoundly change computing.

Software Technology in the 1990's: Using a New Paradigm

Robert Balzer, Information Sciences Institute
Thomas E. Cheatham, Jr., Harvard University
Cordell Green, Kestrel Institute

One possible direction for Department of Defense software initiatives is toward incremental improvement in each portion of the existing software cycle. This is a conservative, evolutionary approach with a high probability of short-term payoff. It definitely deserves a major role in the DoD's initiatives.

But because it is based on the existing software paradigm, the evolutionary approach is ultimately limited by any weakness of that paradigm. Since this paradigm arose in an era of little or no computer support of the software life cycle, it is important to examine how appropriate this paradigm will be in the future.

In the past, computers were more expensive than people; now, people are more expensive. The gap will continue to widen as hardware costs plummet. Not only are people the expensive commodity, there is a shortage of those who are adequately trained. Furthermore, society's major sectors—commercial, governmental, and military—are becoming increasingly reliant on software. The speed with which this software can be produced, the functional complexity it can embody, and the reliability it can attain could become major factors in these sectors.

Two flaws and the maintenance problem

Thus, there is a clear need to investigate a software paradigm based on automation, which augments the effectiveness of the costly and limited supply of people producing and maintaining software. Unfortunately, the existing software paradigm is not a good candidate, because of fundamental flaws that exacerbate the maintenance problem.

First, there is no technology for managing the knowledge-intensive activities that constitute software development processes. These processes, which convert requirements into a specification and then into an implementation, are informal, labor intensive, and largely undocumented. Information about these processes and the rationale behind each of their steps is crucial for maintenance, but unavailable.

This flaw causes problems for other life-cycle phases, but is particularly acute for maintenance. The time lag and personnel changeover normally involved in maintenance preclude reliance on informal mechanisms, such as "walking down the hall," that are typically used in the other phases.

Second, maintenance is performed on source code, that is, the implementation. All of the programmer's skill and knowledge have already been applied in optimizing this form (the source code). These optimizations spread information. That is, they take advantage of what is known elsewhere and substitute complex, but efficient, realizations for (simple) abstractions. Both of these effects exacerbate the maintenance problem by making the software harder to understand, by increasing the dependencies among the parts (especially since these dependencies are implicit), and by scattering related information.

With these fundamental flaws—and the fact that our most junior people are assigned this onerous task—it is no wonder that maintenance is such a major problem in the existing software paradigm.

We must look elsewhere for an appropriate, automation-based software paradigm if we are to achieve orders-of-magnitude improvement. This search and the technology needed to support it represent a viable and important additional direction for the DoD's software initiative. As will be explained below, the technology needed to support an automation-based software paradigm does not yet exist. This is the reason the current paradigm persists and incremental improvements to it are an essential short-term component of the DoD's software initiative.

The rest of this article is devoted to the longer term, higher payoff, and higher risk task of shifting from the current informal, person-based software paradigm to a formalized, computer-assisted software paradigm.

Reprinted from *Computer,* Vol. 16, No. 11, November 1983, pp. 39-45. Copyright © 1983 by The Institute of Electrical and Electronics Engineers, Inc. All rights reserved.

Characteristics of the automation-based software paradigm

The nature and structure of this new software paradigm become evident as we examine the objectives it must meet.

Maintainability. Foremost among these objectives is maintainability, meaning not only activity to correct bugs, but also the much more important activity of enhancing the released system. As important as maintenance is today—and it is 80 to 90 percent of total effort—its importance will increase in direct proportion to our ability to handle it. The tremendous backlog of pent-

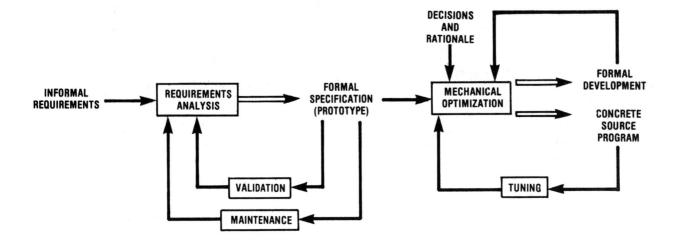

AUTOMATION-BASED PARADIGM

FORMAL SPECIFICATION
PROTOTYPING STANDARD
SPECIFICATION IS THE PROTOTYPE
PROTOTYPE VALIDATED AGAINST INTENT
PROTOTYPE BECOMES IMPLEMENTATION
IMPLEMENTATION MACHINE AIDED
TESTING ELIMINATED
FORMAL SPECIFICATION MAINTAINED
DEVELOPMENT AUTOMATICALLY DOCUMENTED
(a)   MAINTENANCE BY REPLAY

CURRENT PARADIGM

INFORMAL SPECIFICATION
PROTOTYPING UNCOMMON
PROTOTYPE CREATED MANUALLY
CODE VALIDATED AGAINST INTENT
PROTOTYPE DISCARDED
IMPLEMENTATION MANUAL
CODE TESTED
CONCRETE SOURCE CODE MAINTAINED
DESIGN DECISIONS LOST
MAINTENANCE BY PATCHING

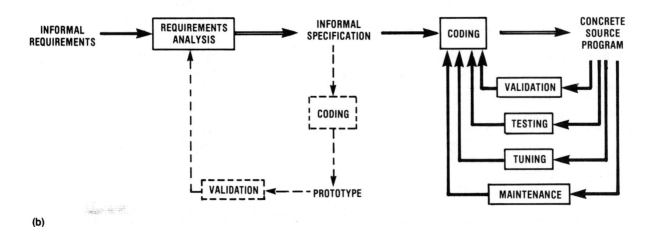

(b)

Figure 1. Paradigm comparison: (a) automation-based paradigm and (b) current paradigm.

up user demand for changes in existing systems is unanswered because of the delay and expense resulting from limited human resources.

Maintaining the specification. The two fundamental flaws in the existing paradigm—the spread of optimization information and the undocumented development processes, decisions, and rationales—that impede maintenance could be avoided with a new paradigm. In this new paradigm, maintenance is performed on the specification rather than the implementation (source program), and the revised specification is then reimplemented with computer assistance. Maintenance becomes a simple continuation of the processes by which the system was initially developed. Figure 1 compares this automation-based paradigm with the current paradigm.

By performing maintenance on the specification, we modify the form that is closest to the user's conceptual model, least complex, and most localized. This level comes before optimization decisions have been integrated, so modifications are almost always simple, if not trival. We are constantly reminded of this insight by end users and managers who understand systems only at this (unoptimized) specification level; they have no trouble integrating new or revised capabilities in their mental models. It is only at the implementation level that those "simple" changes can have massive effects, both structural and textual.

Thus, by maintaining the specification directly, we drastically simplify the maintenance problem. In fact, because end users understand this specification level and generate the new or revised capability requirements, they should be able, with suitable specification languages, to perform this specification maintenance themselves. This would fundamentally improve the software paradigm by employing a user-created and user-maintained specification as the interface between users and implementers.

The user as systems analyst. For this to become a reality, the end users must be given a means of ensuring that the specified system matches their intent, a means that avoids the delay and expense of producing an implementation. This feedback is the second objective of the automation-based software paradigm.

Today, systems analysts handle this task informally. Because of their experience, they are expected to predict the behavior of the unimplemented system and determine whether it matches the user's needs. This awesome responsibility grows more unrealistic with the increasing complexity and specialization of systems.

Suppose, though, that the specification is "operational." That is, it has a formal semantics and can be executed as a program, albeit slowly. Then its behavior, except for speed, would be identical to that of a valid implementation. Hence, the specification itself could serve as a prototype of the system. Users could experiment with this prototype to determine whether or not it matches their requirements. Experience shows that such prototypes normally lead users to improved perceptions of their needs. Thus, the resulting systems are more responsive to those needs.

Three objectives. Thus far, we've characterized the new, automation-based software paradigm as having formal specifications created and maintained by end users. These revised specifications become prototypes of the desired system and ensure that the system will be responsive to user needs.

But where is the automation in the automation-based software paradigm?

Its most obvious manifestation occurs in the implementation process. In this paradigm, the specification is reimplemented after each revision, which brings us to the final three objectives for our paradigm: The implementation process must be fast, reliable, and inexpensive.

If it is to be repeated after each modification, it must obviously be fast and inexpensive. More important it must be reliable to the point that the entire testing process need not be reperformed on each iteration.

Fully automatic implementation via a compiler clearly fulfills these objectives. Unfortunately, such a solution is not feasible because of the wide gap between high-level specification languages and implementations. The next section describes an alternative to full automation.

Automated implementation support

There are two main reasons for the difficulty in creating a fully automatic compiler to translate high-level specifications into efficient implementations. First, very little is known about how local optimizations influence global optimizations; second, the space of possible implementations is too large to search.

Existing compilers avoid these problems because their input is at a low enough level that purely local optimizations are sufficient. The systems analyst has already answered strategic questions about algorithm choice, control structure, representation selection, caching intermediate results, buffering, etc. In our new software paradigm, such implementation issues are specifically excluded from the specification; they must be addressed as part of the implementation process. Although some of these decisions can be automated through heuristic methods, a person must address those remaining.

After these decisions have been made, either by computer or by a person, they can be carried out automatically. This defines a new division of labor for the implementation process. Systems analysts and programmers still make decisions about which optimizations to employ, but the formal manipulations needed to realize these optimizations have been automated.

Four benefits. Such a division would yield four important benefits.

No clerical errors. First, because the system performs all the manipulations that convert the specification into an efficient implementation, they would be performed without clerical error and would be checked for any special applicability criteria. Thus, the validity of the resulting implementation is guaranteed by the *process* from which it is derived rather than by testing or correctness proofs.

Increased optimization. Second, by automating the manipulation of the program, developers are freed of this duty and the corresponding need to maintain consistency, which occupies the vast majority of current effort. They could spend more time considering optimization issues and, hence, do a better job. In fact, implementation could become cheap enough that developers would experiment with alternative implementations, thereby gaining experience and insight leading to better designs.

Better documentation. Third, since the developer's optimization decisions are explicitly communicated, both they and any automated optimization decisions can be recorded and used as documentation of the implementation process in any later maintenance. When maintenance is performed (by modifying the specification), the revised specification must be reimplemented.

Some modifications do not affect the set of optimizations to be employed. For these, the previously recorded optimization decisions (called the *development*) can be "replayed" to produce a new implementation.

Usually, however, modifications to the specification make some previous optimization decisions inappropriate and/or cause the set of decisions to be augmented. After the development has been suitably modified, it can be replayed to produce a new implementation and then used as documentation of the implementation during the next round of modification.

Reusable software. Finally, since maintenance has been simplified (by maintaining the specification and then reimplementing it) and the implementation process

has been recorded (as the development) and is modifiable, the elusive goal of reusable software can be attained.

Software libraries—with the exception of mathematical subroutine libraries—have failed because the wrong things are in those libraries. They are filled with implementations, which necessarily contain many arbitrary decisions. The chance that such an implementation is precisely right for some later application is exceedingly small.

Instead, we should be placing specifications and their recorded development in libraries. Then, when a module is to be reused, the specification can be modified appropriately—that is, maintained—and its development changed accordingly. Thus, maintenance of both the specification and its development becomes the basis of reuse, rather than a fortuitous exact match with a previously stored implementation.

An automated assistant

Automated implementation support is a particular instance of the general role of automation in the automation-based software paradigm. This general role is to assist people in developing and maintaining software. This assistance involves recording the development activities, carrying out decisions made by people, and producing, accessing, and formatting the information needed to make those decisions.

These capabilities must be integrated into a single entity, an assistant that mediates and supports all software life-cycle development activities, as directed by the developers.

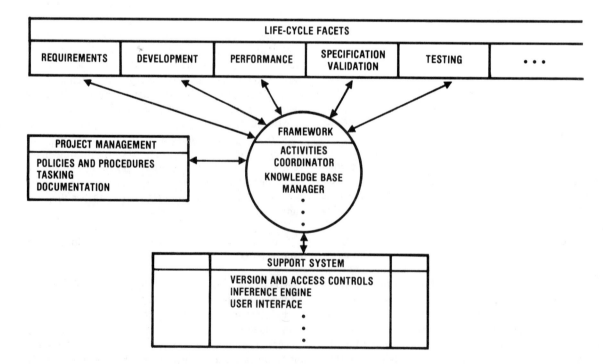

Figure 2. Generalized knowledge-based software assistant structure. (Adapted from Green et al., "Report on a Knowledge-Based Software Assistant," Technical Report KES. U.83.2, Kestrel Institute, Palo Alto, Calif., July 1983.)

A development history. These activities are recorded to provide the corporate memory of the system evolution. The assistant uses this record to determine how the parts interact, the assumptions they make about one another, the rationale behind each evolutionary step (including implementation steps), how the system satisfies its requirements, and how to explain each of these to the developers of the system.

This knowledge base is dynamically acquired as a byproduct of the development of each system. Again, it includes not only the individual manipulation steps, which ultimately lead to an implementation, but also the rationale behind those steps; the developers might have to explicitly state both. Explicit statement of the rationale by the developer might enable the automated assistant to select and perform a set of manipulations that achieves that objective for the developer.

A participating assistant. For the assistant to participate in the activities described above and not merely record them, the acitivities must be at least partially formalized; the most fundamental basis for automated support is formalization. Formalization allows the assistant to undertake responsibility for performing the activity, analyzing its effects, and, eventually, deciding which activities are appropriate. Individual development activities will become increasingly formalized, and so will coordinated sets of activities—thus accomplishing even larger development steps. In fact, the development process itself will be increasingly formalized into coordinated activities of multiple developers.

The automation-based software paradigm both facilitates and requires the existence of such an assistant. This is a consequence of having all the development processes—requirements analysis, specification, implementation, and maintenance—machine mediated and supported. The development processes must be broken into individual activities so that the individual activities can be mediated and supported, and the decisions and rationales behind them recorded.

This assistant aids the developer by participating in all the coordinated development activities, including the coordination itself. The existence of such an assistant, in turn, fundamentally alters the software life-cycle activities, since its capabilities alter the feasibility and cost of the various development activities.

How the assistant supports the new paradigm. This assistant supports the new software paradigm by recording the development activities, performing some of them, analyzing their effects, and aiding their selection. Because of the sophistication of the capabilities involved and because several different sources of knowledge are involved (knowledge of requirements, specification, implementation, evolution, validation, analysis, etc.), this assistant is knowledge based. It consists of a set of agents, or facets, each expert in one particular life-cycle activity. Portions of the corporate memory flow among these agents to initiate and coordinate their activity. Its general structure is shown in Figure 2.

Because the assistant mediates all development activities, it can support overall development as well as individual activities. It can coordinate one activity with another to maintain consistency; it can alert management if resources are, or are about to be, exceeded; it can help prevent maintainers from reexploring unfruitful implementations.

In short, by mediating all development activity and by being knowledgeable about that development, the assistant can help people apply whatever knowledge is relevant for their particular task. This is especially important on large projects in which it is currently difficult, if not impossible, for people to comprehend and assimilate all relevant information because it is fragmented, incomplete, or inconsistent.

Thus, the assistant is more than just the sum of its parts. It is an intelligent assistant that interfaces people to the computerized corporate memory, helps them perform their tasks, and coordinates their activities with each other.

The evolving assistant. The evolution of the software assistant and the incremental formalization of the development activities upon which it is based are the means of realization for the automation-based software.

As we learn how to formalize the various life-cycle activities, the assistant can incorporate them. Over time, this will allow developers to concentrate more and more on the higher level aspects of the development process, as the assistant takes over more of the low-level details. That is, as the development process is incrementally formalized, it can be increasingly automated. But since both the developer and the machine will be in the loop for the foreseeable future, suitable interfaces are necessary to allow the developers and the assistant to work together effectively.

One such evolving knowledge base is general-purpose and domain-specific implementation knowledge. Examples include data structure choices, algorithm design principles, and other optimizations. Such a knowledge base forms an abstract library in its most reusable form.

The assistant's role. To summarize the role of the automated assistant, we begin with a commitment to having the machine in the loop. This commitment will cause the development processes of requirements, specifications, design, implementation, and maintenance to be divided into smaller, more formal steps. This finer granularity and increased formality will lead to an assistant that aids developers in coordinating and performing all activities and in recording them as the documentation of the system's development.

This incremental approach is the foundation of the shift from the current informal, person-based software paradigm to the new formalized, computer-assisted paradigm.

Capabilities of the assistant. The following list of user requests illustrates the range and comprehensiveness of computer support in the new paradigm; we expect the assistant to fulfill such requests.

- Give the history of changes made to some module, along with the rationales for those changes.
- Find all methods for solving some domain-specific task (e.g., clustering methods).
- Find certain programs or rules, such as all rules that select data structures to implement ordered sets.
- Produce explanations of requirements, specifications, code, program derivations, etc.
- Provide help in debugging. For example, locate an inconsistency in a large rule base or in a large program specification that has been modified.
- Find some part of a program specification or requirement that a proposed change could affect.
- Find all relevant test programs that might be affected by a change in a specification so that a re-implementation can be retested.
- Monitor a program execution. For example, monitor a derivation to find all uses of an optimization rule that combines loops.
- Analyze alternative implementation paths to predict their likely cost.
- Analyze the execution of some program to see which operations are using large amounts of space or time.
- Analyze two nonintegrated programs to help to interface them.

The next list contains examples of some of the kinds of tools or capabilities that could carry out the above tasks, as well as many others.

- A monitor that measures performance, frequency of execution of program statements, data set sizes, etc. This information could be useful in deciding when pieces of a program should be recompiled. It could also help guide a smart, knowledge-based compiler in selecting appropriate implementations.
- An efficiency estimator that predicts which proposed implementation will be best, where the bottlenecks will be, or which pieces of the program should be made into modules.
- A help system that includes summarization and natural-language explanation capabilities for specifications and behavior tracers, etc.
- A tutor system to help maintenance personnel become familiar with existing specifications. Newcomers to the system could use the help, explanation, and program analysis tools to learn to modify specifications and requirements as needed.
- A deductive inference and simplification system to help optimize and analyze programs.
- A project management and communications system that sends out notices or reminders of bugs, changes, tasks, schedules, etc. It would have sets of procedures for handling common management situations.
- A requirements definition assistant that helps with requirements consistency, simplification, explanations, walk-throughs, trade-offs, etc., during requirements acquisition and modification.
- A verification tool to help verify the correctness or consistency of a new program optimization rule (since only transformations need to be verified).

Sociological effects of the automation-based software paradigm

Beyond the clear and dramatic benefits on the reliability and cost of producing software, the new paradigm might cause other less obvious, but equally profound, benefits.

Greater enhancements. First, systems will be enhanced after release to a much greater degree than they are at present. Today, maintenance tends to destroy structure, thus increasing the difficulty of further maintenance. Maintaining the specification should eliminate this problem. The pace of maintenance will be limited by the user's ability to generate and assimilate change rather than by technological constraints. Software will finally reach its potential; it will stay "soft" and modifiable rather than become ossified and brittle with age.

Because these systems will be able to evolve more, they will have longer lives. They will become larger and will integrate more capabilities. Evolution, rather than creation, will be the dominant programming mode.

No more standard packages. Because systems will be easier to modify, the standard packages that dominate today's market (due to cost and personnel limitations) will disappear. Users might start from a "standard" application, but they will personalize and augment it for their own purposes.

No more portability problem. Portability will disappear as a problem because the machine on which software runs will be just one of the decisions made during the implementation process. Like any other decision, it will be subject to change.

Personnel savings. Because the programmer's responsibility will be limited to decision-making, even very large systems will be implemented and maintained by a single programmer.

Increased user involvement. The most profound sociological effect will be the vastly increased involvement of end users in the specification process. Prototyping will be the means for debugging specifications before implementation; that is, evolution will also be the means for deriving an "initial specification." This will open up programming to a much wider population—many systems will be created and successfully used without proceeding beyond the prototype stage because the performance of the prototype itself will be adequate. ∎

For further reading

Balzer, Robert, "Transformational Implementation: An Example," *IEEE Trans. Software Engineering,* Vol. SE-7, No. 1, Jan. 1981, pp. 3-14. Demonstrates feasibility of automation-based approach to building software.

Balzer, Robert, Neil Goldman, and David Wile, "Operational Specification as the Basis for Rapid Prototyping," *ACM Sigsoft Software Engineering Notes,* Vol. 7, No. 5, Dec. 1982, pp. 3-16. Describes role of prototyping in automation-based approach and presents an operational specification language for such prototyping.

Barr, Avron, and Edward Feigenbaum, *The Handbook of Artificial Intelligence,* Vol. 2, William Kaufman, Inc., Los Altos, Calif., 1982. This book covers the theory of the knowledge-based approach to software tools. In particular, Chapter 10, on automatic programming, surveys current and past research.

Cheatham, Thomas E., "Reusability Through Program Transformation," *Proc. IT&T Workshop Program Reusability,* Sept. 1983, pp. 122-129. Study on automated assistance in implementation via program refinement.

Cheatham, Thomas E., "An Overview of the Harvard Program Development System," in *Software Engineering Environments,* H. Hunke, ed., North Holland, New York, 1981. Demonstrates feasibility of automation-based approach to building software tools.

Hunke, Horst, ed., *Software Engineering Environments,* North Holland, New York, 1981. The traditional software engineering view of programming environments.

Green, Cordell, Jorge Phillips, Stephen Westfold, Tom Pressburger, Susan Angebranndt, Beverly Kedzierski, Bernard Mont-Reynaud, and Daniel Chapiro, "Towards a Knowledge-Based Programming System," tech. report KES.U.81.1, Kestrel Institute, Palo Alto, Calif., 1981. Demonstrates feasibility of automation-based approach to building software tools.

Green, Cordell, David Luckham, Robert Balzer, Thomas Cheatham, and Charles Rich, "Report on a Knowledge-Based Software Assistant," tech. report KES.U.83.2, Kestrel Institute, Palo Alto, Calif. July, 1983. An approach to defining an integrated, knowledge-based software assistant. The report formulates a technical plan for developing knowledge-based assistance for selected facets of the life cycle, including project management, requirements, specifications, implementation, testing, and documentation. Goals for the near, mid- and far terms are suggested for each facet.

Green, Cordell, and Steve Westfold, "Knowledge-Based Programming Self Applied," in *Machine Intelligence,* Vol. 10, Jean E. Hayes, Donald Michie, and YH. Pao, eds., John Wiley & Sons, New York, 1982, pp. 339-359. Prototype with an emphasis on self-description.

Kant, Elaine, and David R. Barstow, "The Refinement Paradigm: The Interaction of Coding and Efficiency Knowledge in Program Synthesis," *IEEE Trans. Software Engineering,* Vol. SE-7, No. 5, Sept. 1981, pp. 458-471. Study of automated assistance in implementation via program refinement.

Kedzierski, Beverly I., *Knowledge-Based Communication and Management Support in a System Development Environment,* PhD dissertation, tech. report KES.U.83.3, Kestrel Institute, Palo Alto, Calif., Aug. 1983. A knowledge-based system for project communication and management support.

Rich, Charles, and Richard C. Waters, "Abstraction, Inspection and Debugging in Programming," MIT AI Lab memo 634, MIT, Cambridge, Mass., June 1981. A prototype with an emphasis on program analysis.

Swartout, William, "The Gist Behavior Explainer," *Proc. American Association Artificial Intelligence Conf.,* Aug. 1983, pp. 402-407. A knowledge-based system for natural-language explanation of specifications.

Waters, Richard C, "The Programmer's Apprentice: Knowledge Based Program Editing," *IEEE Trans. Software Engineering,* Vol. SE-8, No. 1, Jan. 1982. Demonstration of feasibility of the automation-based approach to building software tools.

Robert Balzer, who helped form the University of Southern California Information Sciences Institute, is currently an associate professor of computer science and director of ISI's Software Sciences and Systems Division. The division combines artificial intelligence, database, and software engineering techniques to automate the software development process.

Before joining USC, Balzer spent several years with the Rand Corporation. He is a past president of ACM's Special Interest Group on Artificial Intelligence and was program chairman for the First National Conference of the American Association for Artificial Intelligence.

Balzer recieved his BS, MS, and PhD degrees in electrical engineering from the Carnegie Institute of Technology, Pittsburgh, Pennsylvania, in 1964, 1965, and 1966, respectively.

Thomas E. Cheatham, Jr., has been the Gordon McKay professor of computer science and director of the Center for Research in Computing Technology at Harvard University since 1969. For the past two years, he has also been chairman of Software Options, Inc., a Cambridge, Massachusetts, firm specializing in research in software technology. His current research interests include symbolic evaluation of programs, mechanical theorem proving for program verification, and the construction of systems for program development and maintenance.

Cheatham is a fellow of the American Academy of Arts and Sciences and a member of Sigma Xi and ACM. He received BS and MS degrees in mathematics from Purdue University, Lafayette, Indiana, in 1951 and 1953, respectively.

Cordell Green is director and chief scientist of the Kestrel Institute, where he leads the Chi knowledge-based software project. He previously directed the Psi program synthesis project at Stanford University. His early work at SRI in 1967 demonstrated how theorem proving formed a basis for logic programming, program synthesis, and problem solving. He has served as R&D program manager at DARPA, as area editor for *JACM*, and on the editorial board of *Cognitive Science.* He is a consulting professor of computer science at Stanford University, a consultant to Systems Control Technology, and member of the IEEE, ACM, and Tau Beta Pi.

Green received a BA and BS from Rice University, and an MS and PhD in electrical engineering from Stanford University.

Questions about this article can be directed to Robert Balzer, USC Information Sciences Institute, 4676 Admiralty Way, Suite 1001, Marina del Rey, CA 90291.

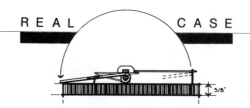

A Computer-Aided Prototyping System

Luqi, *Naval Postgraduate School*
Mohammad Ketabchi, *Santa Clara University*

Computer-aided prototyping shows promise. One system under development frees designers from implementation details by executing specifications via reusable components.

Asignificant improvement in software technology is needed to improve programming productivity and software reliability.[1] Computer-aided, rapid prototyping via specification and reusable components is a promising approach that makes this improvement possible. In this approach, the traditional software life cycle is replaced by a life cycle with two phases: rapid prototyping and automatic program generation.[2]

Completely automatic generation of programs from very high-level specifications is not practical today, but automatic generation of prototypes is feasible. Current manual prototyping methods require too much time and effort, but a computer-aided prototyping system would reduce the cost of prototyping and improve the efficiency of the process. However, before such a system can be developed, methods for specifying, selecting, retrieving, and composing reusable components into a prototype that meets a set of requirements must be addressed.

Our approach to rapid prototyping uses a specification language (the prototype-system description language PSDL) integrated with a set of software tools, including an execution support system, a rewrite system, a syntax-directed editor with graphics capabilities, a software base, a design database, and a design-management system. The prototyping language lets the designer use dataflow diagrams with nonprocedural control constraints as part of the specification of a hierarchically structured prototype. The resulting description is free from programming-level details, in contrast to prototypes constructed with a programming language.

The underlying computational model unifies dataflow and control flow, providing a vehicle for developing top-down decompositions. Such decompositions let large prototypes be executed with practical computation times, in contrast to prototyping by simulating specifications via logic programming without providing a system architecture.

The prototype is executed with the aid of reusable components drawn from a software base. The prototyping language is an integral part of the design-management system because specifications are used to organize and retrieve reusable components in the software base.

Reprinted from *IEEE Software*, Vol. 5, No. 2, March 1988, pp. 66-72. Copyright © 1988 by The Institute of Electrical and Electronics Engineers, Inc. All rights reserved.

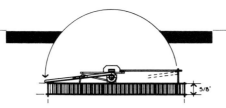

A rewrite system makes retrievals more effective by reducing syntactic variations in equivalent retrieval requests.

The retrieval mechanism does limited bottom-up design to compose requested components without requiring the designer to be aware of all the modules in a large software base. Retrievals based on formal specifications can be made more selective than those based on keywords, reducing the number of inappropriately retrieved components examined by the designer.

Specifications are better for retrieval than implementations because the properties of implementations are too difficult to recognize mechanically. It is not feasible to automatically choose routines from a conventional program library without special annotations.

Figure 1 illustrates the major steps in computer-aided prototyping. The designer begins the process by entering the specifications of the intended software component. A rewrite subsystem maps the specification into an internal abstract form that is used by a design-management system to search for the software component. If it finds a unique software component that meets the specification, it retrieves the component; if it finds several software components that meet the specification, the designer must choose one. Otherwise, the specification cannot be met by an existing component and the designer should decompose the specification into simpler specifications by using the system's prototyping language.

When a specification is decomposed into a network of simpler components, the required interconnections are recorded in the design database with a dataflow diagram, which is part of the syntax of the prototyping language and serves as design documentation. After the designer decomposes the specification into simpler specifications, the entire process is applied to those specifications.

Information about how the system can compose components that meet the simpler specifications into a component that meets the requested specification is preserved in the design database when the designer decomposes the specification. The designer uses that information to compose the missing implementation of the requested specification after the implementations of simpler components become available. If the designer cannot decompose the specification, a new component must be hand-coded and stored in the component base.

The computer-aided prototyping system reduces the designer's efforts by automating time-consuming tasks in conventional prototyping, such as turning specifications into prototypes, modifying prototypes,

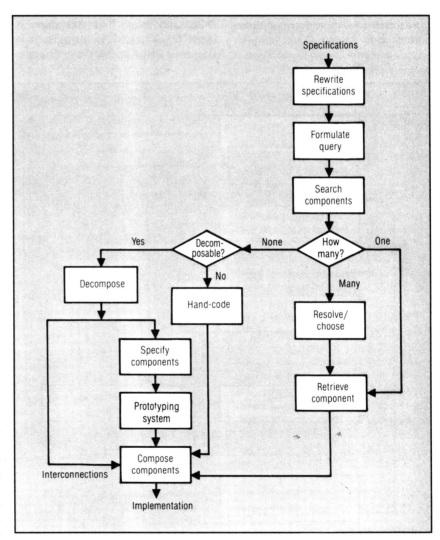

Figure 1. Prototype development using the computer-aided prototyping system.

and searching for available reusable components.

Software tools are needed to support this automated prototyping method. The major parts of such a system are

- the Prototype System Description Language,[3]
- user interfaces to speed up design entry and prevent syntax errors,
- an execution-support system to demonstrate and measure prototype behavior and to perform static analyses of the prototype design,
- a design-management system to manage reusable software components and design data,
- a software base to store reusable components, and

- a design database to store the prototype design.

Yeh and colleagues[2] have proposed an initial framework for a rapid-prototyping environment based on reusability. We further developed a prototyping method, an executable prototyping language, its execution-support system, and better automated methods for component organization and retrieval using normalized specifications. Figure 2 shows the architecture of a prototyping system that supports the process shown in Figure 1.

Language and method

A good language for expressing design thoughts in terms of a precise model is important for rapid prototyping. It is impossible to do a good design without a language designed especially for this purpose. A powerful, easy-to-use, and portable prototype-description language is a critical part of a computer-aided prototyping system. Such a language is needed before the tools in the system can be built.

PSDL was designed together with the prototyping method[4] to ensure the most efficient use of the language. It serves as an executable prototyping language at a specification or design level and has special features for real-time system design.

PSDL provides two kinds of basic building blocks for prototypes: data types and operators. These constructs are sufficient to specify a prototype's design and structure. Software systems are modeled as networks of operators communicating via data streams. The networks are represented as dataflow diagrams with a bubble for each operator and an arrow for each data stream. The data streams can carry data values of an abstract data type as well as tokens representing exception conditions. PSDL provides graphical notation for dataflow diagrams enhanced with nonprocedural control and timing constraints. A formal syntax describes these constraints and other attributes for specifying a prototype.

Each operator is atomic or composite. Atomic operators are realized by retrieving an implementation from a software base.[5,6] Composite operators are realized by decomposing them into networks of more primitive operators represented as enhanced dataflow diagrams. Both atomic and composite operators are used as components of prototypes.

Good modularity is important for increasing productivity because it significantly reduces the debugging effort for producing a correct, executable system. It also influences the system's understandability, reliability, and maintainability, which are especially important in rapid prototyping.

The PSDL computational model is based on dataflow under semantically unified control and timing constraints. It prevents hidden interactions between system components to encourage designs with good module independence since dataflow provides simple and clear interfaces

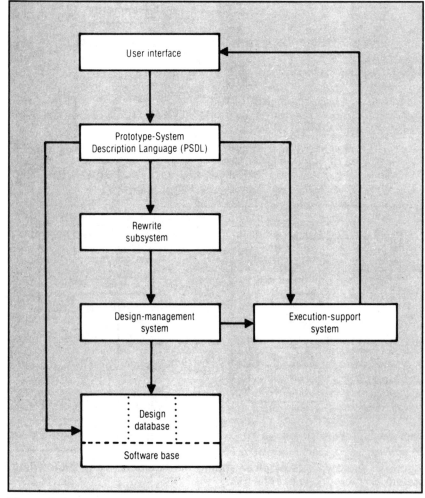

Figure 2. Prototyping system architecture.

between operators, since all data inside operators is local, and since operators with internal states cannot be implicitly shared. The worst coupling problems caused by external references in common control-flow structures are eliminated completely.

The nonprocedural control constraints are easy to use because their meaning does not depend on the order in which they appear. Control constraints make execution more efficient and provide more flexible input and output facilities for triggering operators and selectively generating data values than conventional dataflow. We use a clear and powerful modularization model for building and describing the prototype.

Figure 3 shows an enhanced dataflow diagram with operators A, B, and C and data streams a, b, c, d, e, and f. The maximum execution times of the operators are 10 ms for A, 20 ms for B, and 10 ms for C. The control constraint on A says the output d is produced if a equals c and is suppressed otherwise. The control constraint on B says the operator is triggered whenever new data arrives on b or d. If a new data value arrives on stream b, the operator fires using the new value of b and the most recent data value it has read from d.

We combine control constraints with the dataflow model to achieve the best modularity with sufficient control information, and use dataflow to simplify the interactions among modules, eliminating direct external references and communication caused by side effects.

The language and its associated prototyping method[7] lead to PSDL prototypes with a highly cohesive structure and few coupling problems because they support the model and combine it with a powerful set of data and control abstractions to make it easy to describe systems at a high level. This structure is suitable for multiple modifications at a specification level during the prototyping iterations of the new life cycle.

The PSDL prototyping method provides a hierarchical decomposition strategy for filling in more design details at any level of the prototype design. It helps the designer concentrate on the critical subsystems that must be refined. The prototyping method uses stepwise refine-

ment to selectively refine and decompose critical components. These refinements and decompositions are kept in the design database. Each higher level component is described in terms of lower level components and the relations among them. The decomposition of each composite component is a realization of the system at a lower level of detail.

The prototype design is based on abstract functions, abstract data, and abstract control. This high-level view emphasizes the overall configuration at each level without bogging down in programming-level details. The designer refines the design by decomposing abstract functions and data types into lower level ones. Functional, data, and control abstractions can be used to hide lower level details.

Rewrite subsystem

We based our approach to component specifications on term rewriting, which reduces the variations in the representation of software specifications. We call this approach normalizing, which is mapping semantically equivalent specifications to a common form that is used by the design-management system to search for components. Normalized components are easier to retrieve because there are fewer keys to search for in the software base and because the information is stored in a standard form. The designers can choose from several specifications, but the information-retrieval system is not burdened with handling all these variations because the designers' specifications are automatically normalized before storage.

Because there can be many syntactic forms for the same semantic description, reduction to a normal form is a more practical approach than trying to generate all variations of a description and searching the software base for each variation. Table 1 shows an example of an informal term-rewriting system.

The rewrite rule defined by such a table simply replaces all occurrences of the aliases by the associated basic terms. The sentence "Fetch the order from the transaction file and modify the inventory" would be rewritten to "Read the order from the transaction file and update the

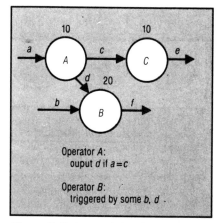

Figure 3. Enhanced dataflow diagram with control constraints.

inventory."

The rewrite subsystem translates equivalent specifications into normalized specifications (see Figure 4) that will be used by the design-management system to find and retrieve the required components from the software base. Two kinds of normalization techniques, for formal and informal specifications,[8] store the normalized specifications with the components in the software base.

Design manager

The design-management system is responsible for organizing, retrieving, and instantiating reusable components from the software base and for managing the versions, refinements, and alternatives of prototypes. A design-management system must efficiently select and retrieve the relevant components from a software base because, for computer-aided prototyping to be practical, the retrieval must take less effort than constructing the components.

A design-management system is essentially a database-management system that can efficiently manage long transactions, data describing complex objects (such as software components), the iterative and tentative nature of the design process that leads to versions, refinements, and alternatives of the design objects, and concurrent design operations in a distributed computing environment. It also provides special-purpose operations to compose components, browse the software base, and manipulate the normalized specifi-

Table 1.
Sample rewrite-subsystem rule table.

Term	Aliases
update	change, modify, refresh, replace, substitute
read	fetch, obtain, input, get, retrieve

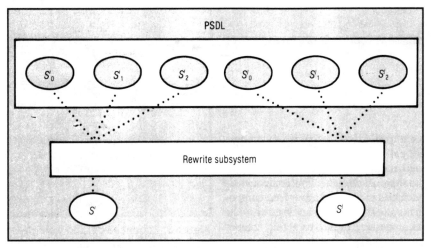

Figure 4. Normalizing specifications

cations.

We have compared conventional database-management systems with the requirements of computer-aided design applications. Because conventional database-management systems do not meet the data-management requirements of CAD applications, we are developing an object-oriented database-management system based on our object-oriented data model[9] for the design-management systems. Our data model meets the requirements of CAD applications with considerable simplicity and economy of concepts. We will tailor the model to meet the requirements of prototyping systems, but we do not exclude the use of a commercial database-management systems to experiment with and study the features of a prototyping system.

Software base

Reusable components must be self-contained and portable. The software base must be easily extensible to allow the evolutionary growth of the available components. You must be able to browse, select, and retrieve components from the software base efficiently. To achieve these goals, we are developing a highly structured software base. Three major structural foundations of the software base are generalization by category, specification approximation, and component composition.

Components have certain properties, called categorical properties, that are used to categorize them. Figure 5 shows categorical properties "implementation languages" and "system environments" with some of their subcategories. Generalizing components according to their properties imposes a lattice structure on the set of components.[10] Figure 6 shows the generalization lattice of components based on the categorical properties "implementation languages" and "system environments."

The lattice structure of components allows efficient browsing of the software base and supports efficient selection and retrieval of the components by partitioning the set of components into meaningful subsets. For example, if an Ada component for the Digital Equipment Corp. VAX/VMS environment is needed, only those components that belong to VMS_Ada node of the lattice are of interest. If an Ada component is needed and the system environment is irrelevant, only those components that belong to Ada node of the lattice must be examined.

In general, there is more than one component in each subset generated by generalization per category. The specification of the desired component is used to select a unique component in a subset.

The software base contains a large set of normalized specifications corresponding to unique implementations. These specifications are called singleton specifications (from the card-playing term for a card that is the only one of its suit held in a hand). A pair containing a singleton specification and its implementation is a singleton component. A normalized specification requested by the designer may not be singleton but an approximation of some singleton specifications. A specification S_i is an approximation of a specification S_j if S_j implies S_i. In this case, S_j is a refinement of S_i.

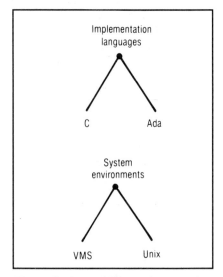

Figure 5. Categorical subproperties with subcategories.

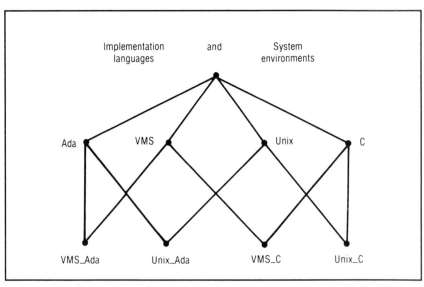

Figure 6. Generalization lattice of categorical properties.

The design-management system lets you derive the best approximation of a set of singleton specifications. The set of singleton specifications and their approximations has a lattice structure, and the explicitly stored specifications are the basis of this lattice. Other specifications can be derived from singleton specifications. Figure 7 illustrates a software base with four singleton specifications (S_s) and three approximate specifications (S_a). If the specification of a requested component matches a singleton specification, the system retrieves the implementation. If it matches one of the approximate specifications, the designer can select any refinement of that specification. Otherwise, a new singleton component is hand-coded and inserted into the base.

The design-management system controls the insertion of components into the base and updates the approximation lattice after each insertion. Creating a new singleton component becomes necessary only if the specification cannot be decomposed into simpler specifications. When a specification is decomposed, the design-management system builds a composition template. A composition template contains the specifications of the components that are needed to construct the requested component.

Components that meet the composite specifications are called composite components. (Singleton components, by contrast, are atomic.) Composite components are virtual because only the recipe for their construction is stored. However, the design-management system may cache the implementations of composite templates that are used frequently.

Execution support

The PSDL execution-support system contains a translator, static scheduler, and dynamic scheduler. The translator generates code binding together the reusable components extracted from the software base. Its main functions are to implement data streams and control constraints. The static scheduler allocates time slots for operators with real-time constraints. If the allocation succeeds, all operators are guaranteed to meet their deadlines even with worst-case execution times. The dynamic scheduler invokes operators without real-time constraints in the time slots not used by the operators with real-time constraints. The dynamic scheduler also lets the designer control and examine the execution of the prototype.

Our research addresses several key problems in automated prototyping with reusable software. These problems include conceptual design of an integrated prototyping system, prototyping language and methodology, normal-form specification for reusable components, a design-database-management system, and a software base that supports efficient retrieval of components by their specifications.

The computer-aided prototyping system combines a high-level prototyping language, a systematic design method to rapidly construct prototypes, a large software base, and a design-database-management system. We believe the system will sharply reduce the need for requirements changes after implementation has begun, as well as for many requirements changes during the design of a new feature in an evolving system.

Demonstrating the prototypes constructed with the prototyping system will give users feedback early enough in the development cycle so they can extensively adapt the design without wasting a lot of effort. This should lead to products that closely match users' needs.

Our approach uses specifications as an intimate part of the computer-aided implementation, making documentation a natural by-product of development rather than a costly extra task and helping to ensure that the documentation corresponds to what the system actually does. The specification of a prototype written in PSDL provides formal documentation for the system, which is a hierarchically structured design with specifications of all components and the interconnections among them. The language syntax includes dataflow diagrams. Informal English explanations of the decomposition represented in the dataflow diagram can be generated by a paraphraser.

The prototyping system is extensible because it provides facilities for adding new components to its software base. The integrated approach to the maintenance and the management of prototype design data simplifies the adaptation of new tools and techniques. It also provides a knowledge base for expert design and analysis tools.　　　-ф-

Acknowledgments
This work was supported in part by the National Science Foundation under grant CCR-8710737. We thank the editors for their extensive comments, which significantly improved this article.

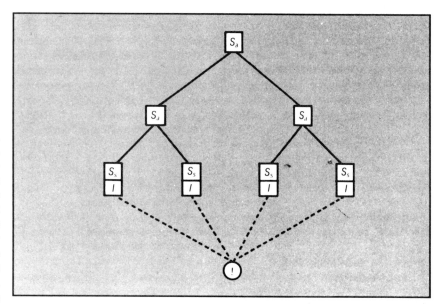

Figure 7. A component base with four singleton components.

References

1. V. Berzins, M. Gray, and D. Naumann, "Abstraction-Based Software Development," *Comm. ACM*, May 1986, pp. 402-415.

2. R.T. Yeh et al., "A Programming Environment Framework Based on Reusability," *Proc. Int'l Conf. Data Engineering*, CS Press, Los Alamitos, Calif., 1984, pp. 277-280.

3. Luqi, V. Berzins, and R. Yeh, "A Prototyping Language for Real-Time Software," Tech. Report 86-4, Computer Science Dept., University of Minnesota, Minneapolis, Minn., 1986; to appear in *IEEE Trans. Software Eng.*, 1988.

4. Luqi, *Rapid Prototyping for Large Software-System Design*, doctoral dissertation, Computer Science Dept., Univ. of Minnesota, Minneapolis, Minn., June 1986.

5. N. Roussopoulos, "Architectural Design of the SBMS," tech. report, Computer Science Dept., Univ. of Maryland, College Park, Md., April 1985.

6. R.T. Yeh, N. Roussopoulos, and B. Chu, "Management of Reusable Software," *Proc. Compcon*, CS Press, Los Alamitos, Calif., 1984, pp. 311-320.

7. Luqi and V. Berzins, "Rapid Prototyping of Real-Time Systems," Tech. Report 87-5, Computer Science Dept., Naval Postgraduate School, Monterey, Calif., 1987; to appear in *IEEE Software*, 1988.

8. Luqi, "Normalized Specifications for Identifying Reusable Software," *Proc. Fall Joint Computer Conf.*, CS Press, Los Alamitos, Calif., 1987, pp. 46-49.

9. M. Ketabchi and V. Berzins, "Modeling and Managing CAD Databases," *Computer*, Feb. 1987, pp. 93-102.

10. M. Ketabchi, V. Berzins, and K. Maly, "Generalization Per Category: Theory and Application," *Proc. Int'l Conf. Information Systems*, ACM, New York, Dec. 1985, pp. 227-237.

Luqi is an assistant professor at the Naval Postgraduate School. She has also worked on software research and development and taught at University of Minnesota. Her interests include software development tools, rapid prototyping, and languages.

Luqi received a BS in computational mathematics from Jilin University, China, and an MS and PhD in computer science from the University of Minnesota.

Mohammad A. Ketabchi is an assistant professor of electrical engineering and computer science at Santa Clara University. His research interests include database support for computer-aided design and software engineering and design and implementation of object-oriented systems.

Ketabchi received a BS in electrical engineering and an MS and PhD in computer science, all from the University of Minnesota.

Address questions to Luqi at Computer Science Dept., Naval Postgraduate School, Monterey, CA 93943.

IEEE Software

PART VI: TAILORING ENVIRONMENTS: EXTENSION, METASPECIFICATION, AND GENERATION

Extending Teamwork for Architecture Diagrams

TOM NICINSKI, *Fermi National Accelerator Laboratory*

◆ *The methodology
behind a tool
extension to associate
dataflow and
architecture
diagrams was sound,
but practical
considerations
limited its
effectiveness.*

o specify requirements for the data-acquisition system for the Sloan Digital Sky Survey, Fermilab needed a way to supplement dataflow diagrams with an architectural view so that its designers could work around hardware and performance constraints. While dataflow diagrams capture *what* the system's requirements are, architecture diagrams capture *how* the system will physically fulfill the requirements. We wanted the architecture view to map to and interact with the dataflow diagrams so that each could prompt refinements in the other.

Derek Hatley and Imtiaz Pirbhai's architecture-diagram methodology was the answer,[1] but the DSS project (described in the box on the facing page) was too large to draw architecture diagrams using only

This article also appears in the Proceedings of the Symposium on Assesment of Quality Software Development Tools, IEEE CS Press, Los Alamitos, Calif., 1992.

Reprinted from *IEEE Software*, Vol. 9, No. 3, May 1992, pp. 54-60. Copyright © 1992 by The Institute of Electrical and Electronics Engineers, Inc. All rights reserved.

a stand-alone drawing package. Controlling access to the large number of diagrams and maintaining information about which dataflow diagrams were associated with which architecture diagrams became tedious and error-prone.

We needed help from a CASE tool, but none was available that merged Cadre Technology's Teamwork, which we used for dataflow diagramming, and support for Hatley and Pirbhai's architecture diagrams. We decided to extend Teamwork to accommodate architecture models.

The extension I developed lets designers associate architecture-flow diagrams with dataflow diagrams. It also supports the creation of architecture-interconnect diagrams and the maintenance of an architecture-module specification. (The box on pp. 58-59 is a brief tutorial on architecture diagrams.)

Designers can access these modeling

methodologies from the graphical editors they use to draw dataflow diagrams in Teamwork: Using my extension, they can open an architecture-flow or -interconnect diagram for an entire dataflow diagram or a selected process within a dataflow diagram.

One important reason to perform this modeling exercise is that the architecture model may suggest or even necessitate process repartitioning in the dataflow diagram. As Hatley and Pirbhai point out, transforming a process model into an architecture model is an iterative exercise that resolves all process interfaces and allocations, exposing design tradeoffs and decisions. The result is a fully integrated specification that models both function and physical design.[1]

TWKAFD

The Teamwork Architecture-Flow Diagram extension manages FIG format files representing architecture-flow and -interconnect diagrams and invokes XFIG (the X Window version of FIG) to let designers graphically edit them. Designers edit the diagrams using simple drawing primitives instead of object primitives. For example, you draw an optical link (-o-o-o-) with a line (———) and circles (o o o) to get o o o .

Although TWKAFD is built using Teamwork facilities, because of weaknesses in these facilities, it is not tightly integrated with Teamwork. Thus, it does not do all the designer's work, especially not bookkeeping:

♦ It does not automatically reflect changes to dataflow diagrams, especially deletions and renumberings, in the corresponding architecture models and specification. For example, deleting a process does not remove its allocation from the architecture-module specification; the designer must do that.

♦ It does not automatically reflect changes made to an architecture-flow diagram in the corresponding architecture-interconnect diagram and vice-versa.

TWKAFD uses Teamwork's approach to handling the relationships between dataflow and architecture-flow diagrams,

so the designer does not have to learn two sets of behaviors. For example, reallocating a dataflow diagram to another architecture-flow diagram does not update the allocations of descendent dataflow diagrams to the new descendent architecture-flow diagrams for use outside TWKAFD.

Diagram library. TWKAFD maintains generations of architecture-flow and -interconnect diagrams with a source-code control-system library, in a manner similar to Teamwork's maintenance of dataflow diagrams. The library also maintains the architecture-module specification, although it keeps only one version. A stand-alone utility, twkafd_fetch, retrieves the architecture diagrams.

User interface. When a designer opens a dataflow diagram, the editor displays the menu in Figure 1a, which I have extended to allow access to architecture diagrams. The pull-down architecture menu works just like any Teamwork menu.

When the designer selects an architecture menu item, TWKAFD tries to determine as much about what must be done as possible without querying the user. However, this is not always possible because TWKAFD cannot be tightly coupled to the dataflow-diagram editor. For example,

Teamwork's dataflow-diagram editor will automatically assign diagram names (it uses numbers, actually) to new processes. However, TWKAFD can't associate a dataflow diagram with an architecture-flow module without asking the user for the module's name (which is also a number, because I followed Teamwork's style).

Open and create. The designer can open an architecture-flow diagram for the entire dataflow diagram being edited or a selected bubble. (Because every bubble in a dataflow diagram can expand to a dataflow diagram, TWKAFD treats each bubble as a dataflow diagram.) If the selected diagram or bubble is not already allocated to an architecture-flow diagram, TWKAFD will create a new architecture-flow diagram; otherwise it opens the latest generation of the associated architecture-flow diagram.

When an architecture-flow diagram has as yet no ancestor or descendent dataflow diagrams allocated to it when it is being created, the designer must enter a complete name for the architecture-flow diagram, as shown in Figure 1b. The architecture-flow diagram name must have the same number of levels as the dataflow diagram being allocated to it.

A selected dataflow diagram could

MAPPING THE UNIVERSE: SLOAN DIGITAL SKY SURVEY

The Sloan Digital Sky Survey project will map a quarter of the sky (away from the Milky Way) and the structures within it. A dedicated 2.5-meter telescope and data-acquisiton system are being constructed and will be commissioned in November 1994 at Apache Point Observatory, New Mexico. Formal observations will begin in November 1995 and will take five years to complete.

Some 10^8 galaxies and 10^5 quasars will be imaged photometrically with 30 charge-coupled devices, each measuring 2048^2 pixels. From this pool of objects, using the same 2.5-meter telescope, 10^6 spectra will be obtained in a redshift survey of galaxies and color-selected quasars. This survey will provide an unprecedented map of the universe, boosting the number of galaxy redshift measures from the current 30,000 to 1,000,000 and the number of known quasars from the current 5,000 to 100,000.

During photometric imaging, data will be acquired at a rate of 5 Mbytes per second. Overall, 12 Tbytes (10^{12} bytes) of raw data will be collected. The acquisition rate and the enormous amount of data require close cooperation between hardware components being designed and software being developed. The coupling of dataflow diagrams and architecture diagrams is perfectly suited to this task.

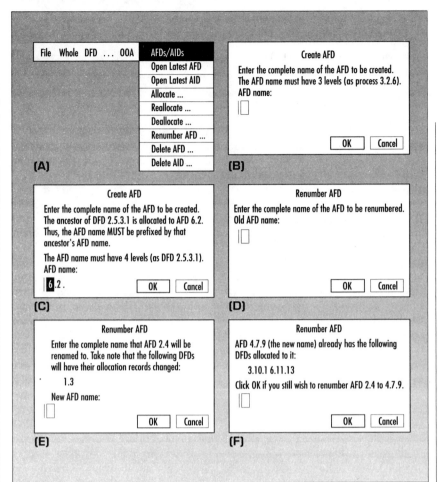

Figure 1. *TWKAFD's user interface. (A) The pull-down editor menu works just like any Teamwork menu; (B) when creating an architecture-flow diagram, the designer must enter a complete name for the architecture-flow diagram; (C) the name of the new diagram must begin with the number of its nearest ancestor diagram; (D) renaming a diagram is a two-step process (E); the system will flag duplicate names (F).*

have an ancestor dataflow diagram that is already allocated to an architecture-flow diagram. In this case, the name of the new architecture-flow diagram must begin with the number of its nearest ancestor diagram, as Figure 1c shows.

The selected dataflow diagram could also have a descendent dataflow diagram that is already allocated to an architecture-flow diagram. In this case, TWKAFD automatically assigns the name to the new architecture-flow diagram. It begins with the first numbers of the nearest descendent's ancestor. For example, if you select dataflow diagram 6.1 and it has a descendent dataflow diagram, 6.1.4.7, which is already allocated to architecture-flow diagram 2.10.7.1, the new architecture-flow diagram's name will be 2.10.

In TWKAFD, you cannot open an architecture-interconnect diagram unless its corresponding architecture-flow diagram exists, both in the architecture-module specification (as an allocation of a dataflow diagram) and in the library (a dataflow diagram can be allocated to a nonexistent architecture diagram).

When an architecture-interconnect diagram is created, the latest generation of the architecture-flow diagram is copied and becomes its first generation. The architecture-interconnect diagram takes the same name as the architecture-flow diagram. This creation procedure is followed because an architecture-interconnect diagram's modules must match those of the architecture-flow diagram.

However, the designer must still convert the duplicated architecture-flow diagram into an architecture-interconnect diagram by

♦ converting all data and control flows to the appropriate module interconnections, which do not have to match routing or count in the architecture-flow diagram, and

♦ labeling the interconnections with

the media type instead of the communication content.

Renaming. Figures 1d and 1e show how the designer can rename an architecture-flow diagram and its corresponding interconnect diagram. You cannot use a name that already exists; Figure 1f shows the message you get if you try to use an existing name.

When a diagram is renamed, TWKAFD will automatically update the architecture-module specification and reallocate all the dataflow diagrams that were allocated to the old name. The designer must be very careful, because there are no restrictions or checks on the number of levels when the name is changed. And, in keeping with Teamwork's behavior, children of the diagram will not be renamed.

Error messages. When it encounters an error, TWKAFD displays a message. The message title indicates if the error occurred in an architecture-flow or architecture-interconnect diagram. The title also has a condition name, which narrows the error location. The message text gives a fuller explanation.

In most instances, the error message indicates that the requested operation was not completed. TWKAFD makes every effort to return the state of the architecture model to what it was just before the operation. If it can't, the message briefly describes what you should try to do to resolve the problem.

Restrictions. Although there are no hard and fast rules (at least according to Hatley and Pirbhai) as to how an architecture hierarchy relates to a corresponding dataflow hierarchy, TWKAFD does place some restrictions on architecture modeling:

♦ An architecture-flow diagram can have more than one dataflow diagram allocated to it, but a dataflow diagram cannot be allocated to more than one architecture-flow diagram. A dataflow process cannot be split among architecture modules.

♦ Dataflow diagrams at one level of the hierarchy can be allocated only to architecture-flow diagrams at the same depth in the corresponding architecture-flow hierarchy.

♦ If a parent dataflow diagram is allocated to an architecture-flow diagram, its children can be allocated only to modules of the same architecture-flow diagram.

These restrictions resolve ambiguities and lead to clearer model interpretations. Other tools can help refine this method. For example, although Teamwork does not restrict how stores are interpreted (for example, are "reads" destructive?), Cadre's Teamwork/SIM uses rules to resolve this ambiguity to improve dataflow simulations.

Merging Teamwork. TWKAFD is implemented with the Teamwork Extensibility Language and a group of Unix C shell scripts. The Teamwork Extensibility Language lets you add pull-down menus to Teamwork editors, but it is not intuitive.

In the Teamwork Extensibility Language, menu definitions are of the form

```
(Menu
    (Name "string")
    (Variable variable_definition)
    (MenuItem
        (Name "string")
        (Variable variable_definition)
        (Action(SysCall "interpreted_string")
) ) )
```

where Menu, Name, Variable, MenuItem, Action, and SysCall are keywords, and variable_definition, string, and interpreted_string are user-defined. A string is any set of ASCII characters between double quotes. An interpreted_string is a string parsed for variables. Definitions are nested and scoping rules apply to variables.

Interpreted strings. Interpreted strings are the key to working with the Teamwork Extensibility Language. When interpreted strings are parsed, the code references variables, whose return value is substituted into the interpreted string. To reference a variable, you prefix it with a percent sign. You can pass arguments to variables and you can enclose them in parentheses if the character following the variable is not a variable terminator:

```
% variable        or  %(variable)
% variable(arg1, ...) or  %(variable(arg1, ...))
```

```
(MenuItem
    (Name "Open Latest AFD")
    (Variable (Id afd$afd_open)                                 (Value "
    # Initialize and determine what object we'll be working with (this DFD or one of its
    #   processes).
    %afd$init
    %afd$check_objtyp
    %.IF(%.EQ(%afd_objtyp,%.NULL),%afd$return(
        %.STRING(%AFDBADCHOICE),
        %.STRING(An AFD cannot be opened for a
    %(t.SELECTED_OBJECT_TYPE). Select a process to open an AFD for it, or
    select nothing to open a AFD for DFD
    %(t.OBJECT).)),
        %.NULL)
    # Check whether the chosen object is already allocated to AFD. If it is, there's no
    # need to query the user for an AFD number. Otherwise, afd$afd_afdnam_get will
    # query the user for an AFD name and do legality checking. If all is fine,
    # afd_afdnam will have the AFD name.
    %.SYS_CALL(%.STRING(ams_get %afd_stdarg 'AFD' 'EXACT' > %afd_stsf))
    %.ASSIGN(%afd_afdnam,%.REMOVE_WS(%.STRING(%afd$status)))
    %.IF(%.EQ(%afd_afdnam,%.NULL),
        %afd$afd_afdnam_get(%.QUOTE(Create AFD})),
        %.NULL)
    # Open AFD. aXd_open obtains exclusive access to the chosen object, invokes
    # XFIG, and updates the AMS.
    %.SYS_CALL(%.STRING(
        aXd_open%afd_stdarg 'AFD' '%afd_afdnam' > %afd_stsf))
    %afd$return_on_error (%.STRING(%AFDOPENERR))
    "
    )
    (Action(SysCall "afd$afd_open"))
)
```

Figure 2. The Teamwork Extensibility Language code that implements the "Open Latest" architecture diagram menu item.

Subroutine calls. The Teamwork Extensibility Language does not provide subroutines. Instead, it references variables. Almost everything done with Teamwork Extensibility Language involves variable references, even performing conditional tests:

```
%.IF(%.EQ(%var1, %var2),
    %then_action, %else_action)
```

where .IF and .EQ are Teamwork control variables.

Two important control variables are

```
.SYS_CALL(command)
.RETRIEVE(file)
```

where .Sys_Call passes the interpreted string, command, to the native shell for execution and the variable .Retrieve reads the result from a file. For example:

```
%.SYS_CALL(%.STRING(echo 'Hello!'
    %tmpfile))
%.IF(%.EQ(%.RETRIEVE(%tmpfile),
    %.QUOTE(Hello)),...,...
```

tests the output of the .Sys_Call. In this case, the condition is true and then_action would be performed.

Implementation. I did as much work as pos-

sible with the Teamwork Extensibility Language, to reduce TWKAFD's dependence on its native system. TWKAFD now runs only under SunOS, but it's X-based, so it does not restrict designers to Sun platforms.

Even so, the C shell scripts do a considerable amount of work. All the scripts have a standard set of arguments passed to them (via the variable afd_stdarg), mainly to indicate which Teamwork object the user has selected. Each script returns a status by echoing to stdout. Usually, an output of "Success" indicates successful completion by the script. Any other output is the actual error message to be displayed by code written in the Teamwork Extensibility Language.

Figure 2 is the code that implements the "Open Latest" architecture diagram menu item. The Action(SysCall "...")) line is invoked when the designer selects the menu item. Few extensions to Teamwork are simple enough to let Action do all the work. Instead, I had to define a variable under MenuItem to do the work; Action simply references that variable.

In this example, Teamwork variables are prefixed by t., so t.Object is the name of the selected Teamwork object (dataflow diagram, bubble, store, and so on), and t.Selected_Object_Type specifies that object's type (process, store, dataflow, and so on). This example also uses additional control variables: .Remove_WS removes white space, including carriage returns, from its argument; .Assign assigns its argument's value to a variable; and .Null, as an action, does nothing for .If conditionals.

As this example shows, user-defined variables behave like subroutines:

♦ afd$init: Initializes variables to known values.

♦ afd$check_objtyp: Determines which object the user selected and its type.

♦ afd$return: Returns a message to

Teamwork, aborting the current menu operation.

♦ afd$status: Retrieves the status text from the file described by the variable afd_stsf.

♦ afd$afd_afd_get: Gets an architecture-flow diagram name from the user (through a menu like the one in Figure 1b) and checks its legality.

♦ afd$return_on_error: Returns to

SPECIFYING PHYSICAL REQUIREMENTS WITH ARCHITECTURE DIAGRAMS

System designers model a system's functional requirements — its processes — with dataflow diagrams. They use architecture-flow diagrams to allocate processes to the physical entities in the system where they will be carried out. Architecture-flow diagrams are composed of modules (where the processes occur) and interconnections (data and control connections between modules).

The architecture model uses diagrams, text, and a module specification to fulfill three main purposes

♦ Show the system's physical entities (its modules).

♦ Define the information flow among those entities (its vectors).

♦ Specify the channels on which this information flows (in a corresponding interconnect diagram).

Diagram elements. A module in an architecture diagram corresponds to one or more bubbles, or processes, in a dataflow diagram. You should name them appropriately, but their names need not correspond directly to dataflow bubbles. Allocating a process to an architecture module implicitly allocates the process's children to that module.

Information-flow vectors represent information flow among architecture modules. They include both dataflow (represented by solid arrows) and control flow (represented by dashed arrows). As in dataflow diagrams, you should label vectors with the type of information that goes through them. Again, vector labels do not have to be the same as they are in the corresponding dataflow diagram.

An architecture-interconnect diagram shows the same

modules as its corresponding architecture-flow diagram, but focuses on the physical connections among modules. These physical information-flow channels do not necessarily match the vectors, but there is a mapping between channels and vectors, since data and control must flow across some medium.

The interconnect diagram models different channel types. For example, ——— represents an electrical bus; +++ represents a mechanical link; and -O-O-O- represents an optical link. In addition, you can label channels with the type of media they use. An optical link can be labeled "fiber optic cable," or "infrared beam," for example. If two modules are linked with several channels, they are represented with more than one symbol. A channel's characteristics (timing needs, interconnection bandwidths, burst rates, and so on) are described in text.

Functionality views. Both architecture-flow and -interconnect diagrams display four major perspectives on a system's functionality. (Designers can omit any view their architecture diagrams don't use.)

♦ I/O processing shows the data and control flows that the

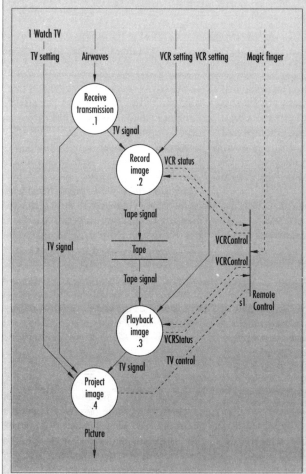

Figure A. A dataflow diagram of home entertainment — by either recording or playing a movie on a videocassette recorder.

Teamwork when there is an error and displays the error text returned by afd$status.

IMPRESSIONS AND RESULTS

Our experiment to extend Teamwork to accommodate architecture models succeeded only in part. The methodology of using architecture diagrams to supplement and enhance our use of dataflow diagrams was quite fruitful. On the other hand, using Teamwork, with its limited extension capability, was not completely successful.

Methodology. The architecture diagrams did provide us with a useful alternate view of the Sloan Digital Sky Survey data-acquisition system. At first we thought that software designers would use the dataflow diagrams and hardware designers would use the architecture diagrams.

However, in practice we found that each view showed flaws in the other. For example, the data-acquisition system had hardware constraints placed on it before specification. While these constraints were easily incorporated into the architecture-flow and -interconnect diagrams, they did not surface in the initial dataflow

---

control or process model will use and produce. The processing performed here is not necessarily required by the dataflow diagram. Instead, it represents the additional processing necessary to let architecture modules communicate. It may also transform data to an internally usable form.

♦ *User-interface processing* shows the user interface to the architecture-flow and -interconnect diagrams. We do not include it under I/O processing because it has unique considerations, such as ergonomics, that affect its implementation.

♦ *Control/process model* contains the bulk of the requirements specified in the dataflow diagram.

♦ *Maintenance, self-test, and redundancy-management processing* shows what must be done to maintain the control/process model, such as monitoring or data-collection modules used for system maintenance.

Example. Figure A shows a dataflow diagram of something many people do every day: entertain themselves while sitting on a couch — in this case, by either recording or playing a movie on a videocassette recorder. This sample dataflow diagram, which is neither complete nor rigorous, is one level down from the operation of a complete entertainment system.

Figure B shows the corresponding architecture-flow diagram, which has only three modules instead of four process bubbles. Although many names, especially of data and control flows, match the names in the dataflow diagram, they do not have to.

Which bubbles are allocated to which modules is maintained in an architecture-module specification. In this case, the specification is

♦ AFD 1 is allocated to DFD *Watch TV* (1).

♦ AFD module *Remote Control* (1.1), has no DFD processes allocated to it. It does correspond to the control specification s1 of the DFD, but the architecture model does not reflect this.

♦ AFD module *VCR* (1.2), has DFD processes *Receive Transmission* (1.1), *Record Image* (1.2), and *Playback Image* (1.3) allocated to it.

♦ AFD module *TV* (1.3) has DFD process *Project Image* (1.4) allocated to it.

Figure C shows the corresponding architecture-interconnect diagram. This diagram has the same modules as the architecture-flow diagram, but shows the different media used to transport data and control among the modules. In this example, the channels do not correspond directly to the vectors, which is allowable. However, at least one physical channel must be depicted to show the information flow on a vector or group of vectors.

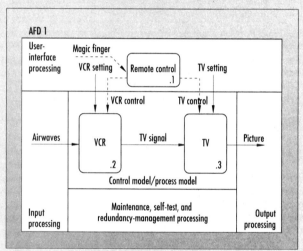

Figure B. *The architecture-flow diagram that corresponds to Figure A. It has only three modules instead of four process bubbles.*

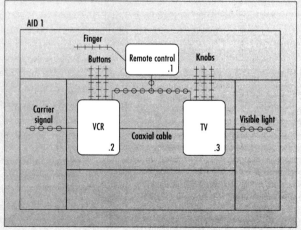

Figure C. *The architecture-interconnect diagram that corresponds to Figures A and B. It has the same modules as Figure B, but shows the different media used to transport data and control among the modules.*

diagrams. In addition, the hierarchical decomposition went down further in the architecture-flow diagrams than in the dataflow diagrams allocated to them.

It's important that the dataflow diagram reflect these real-world constraints. The iterative feedback between dataflow diagrams and architecture-flow diagrams helped us converge on two views that specified the same system.

Tools. The tools to facilitate our methodology did not work as smoothly. Both Teamwork and TWKAFD provide exclusive access to objects being edited and both enforce some formalism, so they do let multiple users work concurrently on the same project. Still, we encountered some problems:

♦ The XFIG Utility is inadequate for drawing and manipulating architecture-flow and -interconnect diagrams. Its greatest deficiency is that it provides no architecture-diagram constructs, so designers must use simple drawing primitives to build symbols. Moving or modifying these constructed symbols is cumbersome and sloppy.

♦ XFIG has no means to correlate vectors and channels, so this must still be maintained by hand. To read an architecture-interconnect diagram, you may need to refer to the architecture-flow diagram because my tool does not correlate vectors with channels.

♦ We had no automatic bookkeeping operations to reflect changes in a dataflow

diagram in its corresponding architecture-flow diagrams and architecture-module specification, or vice versa. This prevented us from making full use of either tool. Especially in the initial stages of specification, when many changes were necessary, we were reluctant to make edits because it meant manually updating all the affected structures.

I could have automated TWKAFD if the Teamwork Extensibility Language let me do more than just add menu items. For example, I could have had the dataflow-diagram editor call a TWKAFD-supplied routine when a bubble was deleted, and TWKAFD could have reflected that change in its architecture diagrams.

Language. Developing with the Teamwork Extensibility Language is inefficient. The language is not very readable and the need to devise communication techniques between it and the host-system scripts impedes productivity. In addition, it has no debugging facilities! (The beta release did dump somewhat useful information when it encountered an error in the Teamwork Extensibility Language code. But, this "feature" disappeared with the standard release.)

Nevertheless, it took only one man-month to design, implement, and test TWKAFD, including the time it took to learn the Teamwork Extensibility Language. I could have saved considerable time if Teamwork's documentation was clearer and provided extended examples (more than one line).

Given these problems, it is imperative that designers work closely and consistently with each other. Extending a commercial tool to incorporate a new methodology is a powerful capability that can enhance a designer's performance. However, in this case, there is considerable room for improvement in the Teamwork product.

Because of its deficiencies, we use TWKAFD only when architectural constraints are placed on a system and only in the initial stages of specifying requirements with a dataflow model.

If the Teamwork Extensibility Language is greatly improved, we will consider upgrading TWKAFD. The interaction between dataflow and architecture diagrams should not be impeded by a tool. ♦

ACKNOWLEDGMENTS
This work was sponsored by the US Dept. of Energy under contract DE-AC02-76CH03000.

REFERENCES
1. D.J. Hatley and I.A. Pirbhai, *Strategies for Real-Time System Specification*, Dorset House, 1988.

Tom Nicinski is a senior software developer at Fermi National Accelerator Laboratory, where he specializes in the development of data-acquisition and control systems for high-energy physics experiments and astronomical instruments.

He received a BS in computer science from Northwestern University and is a member of the IEEE Computer Society.

Address questions about this article to Nicinski at Fermi National Accelerator Laboratory, MS 120, PO Box 500, Batavia, IL 60510; Internet nicinski@fnal.fnal.gov.

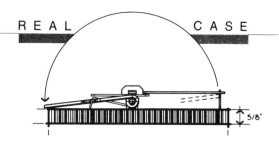

The Metaview System for Many Specification Environments

Paul G. Sorenson and **Jean-Paul Tremblay**, *University of Saskatchewan*
Andrew J. McAllister, *University of New Brunswick*

Metasystems can automatically generate the major parts of a software-development environment. Although such systems are still in their infancy, they hold significant promise for CASE.

Providing adequate support environments for the development of software has been a recognized problem for several years. Unfortunately, support environments have emerged only recently that seriously aid the development of large software systems. Perhaps the most well-known support of these efforts is the Ada programming-support environment. However, it focuses on the life cycle's implementation stage, with facilities to improve program reliability and to promote the development of portable software and software-development tools.

Several support environments have been developed to aid the requirements-analysis and design stages.[1,2] Recently, commercial CASE environments have been introduced that apply these concepts to the entire life cycle. In addition, some support systems, such as the User Software-Engineering methodology,[3] extend system analysis and design support with prototyping facilities.

McAllister worked on this research while at the University of Saskatchewan.

The effort to develop such support environments is considerable, as are enhancements or changes to a support environment to address an application's special requirements. To significantly reduce the implementation effort of producing a support environment, some researchers have proposed metasystems.[4]

A metasystem's primary purpose is to generate automatically the major parts of a particular software-development environment. Metasystems are systems used to develop system-development environments just as compiler-writing systems are systems used to develop compilers.

Figure 1 shows a metasystem's architectural overview. Figure 1a shows the components of an environment that could be used to specify some aspects of a system description. Many specification-environment support facilities (commonly called tool support) are included, such as graphics interfaces, graphics layout, and query languages. Figure 1b shows the generalized metasystem approach to developing an environment-support facility that includes an environment-model

Reprinted from *IEEE Software*, Vol. 5, No. 2, March 1988, pp. 30-38. Copyright © 1988 by The Institute of Electrical and Electronics Engineers, Inc. All rights reserved.

analyzer and an environment-model processor.

An environment, such as a dataflow-specification environment, can be generated at environment-generation time by first defining that environment in a special language called the Environment-Model Definition Language. The specific environment-model description is compiled by the environment-model processor to create a set of tables that are used by the environment-model analyzer to help compile a specification database for the environment.

With the specification database complete, you can then undertake the generalized tool-set definition process, using a common environment-model definition. The subsequent completeness and consistency checking and reporting functions for a specification are also handled by the generalized environment-model analyzer, which works with the environment-definition tables and tool-set definitions.

Metasystems

Figure 2 presents a high-level architectural overview of Metaview. There are three levels of specification: the metalevel, environment level, and requirements level.

At the metalevel, the metadefiner defines the specification data model for the system, called the metamodel. The metadefiner should also oversee software development to support the definition of specification environments (the activities of creating the database engine, the environment generator, and the tool-set facilities).

At the environment level, the software engineer defining the environment uses the environment-model-processor software provided at the metalevel to process an environment definition. The environment definition includes an environment-model definition and definitions for one or more support tools generated as part of the

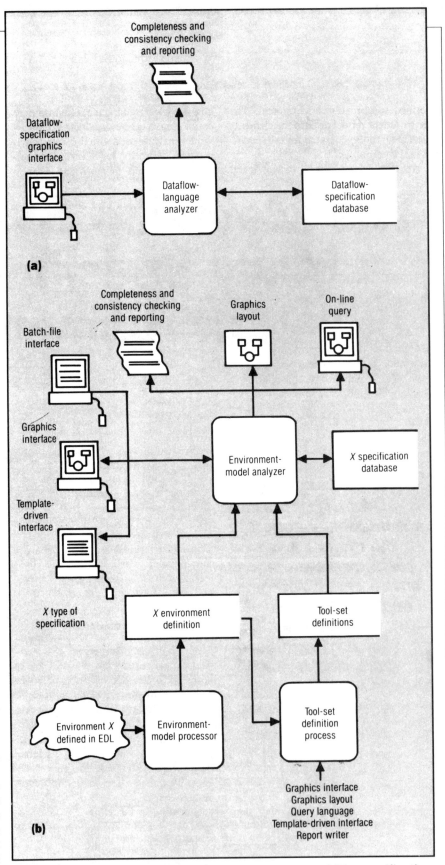

Figure 1. (a) Typical specification support environment and **(b)** a specification environment produced with a metasystem approach.

defined specification environment. The environment model defines the elements used in all tools generated for the specification environment.

At the requirements (user) level, analysts use a requirements environment containing a generalized environment-model analyzer used with the stored environment definition (or library) and tool-support routines to store and analyze requirement specifications for any information-processing system they want to define. Each requirement specification is stored in a requirements-specification database using a set of common database-

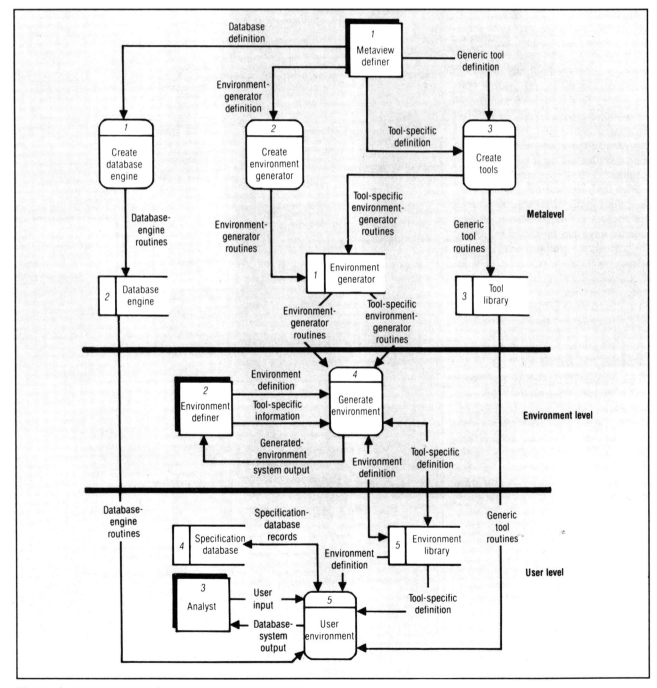

Figure 2. High-level dataflow diagram for Metaview.

access routines that form the database engine.

Formulating a comprehensive and robust metamodel is critical to creating a metasystem. (The box on p. 37 summarizes some previous efforts in metasystem research.)

Metamodel development requires that several factors be taken into account:

- The metasystem is intended to be used by both environment definers and lead analysts, yet neither group can be assumed to be database experts. Thus, the simplicity of the metasystem architecture and associated metamodel in terms of learning and use is important.
- The expressive power of the metamodel should be maximized (keeping in mind simplicity) so it places as few restrictions as possible on how you can represent information. As an example, it is not always desirable to restrict relationships among elements to binary form.
- Automatic checking for consistency and completeness is a major advantage of computer-aided support for specifications, so the metasystem should support stating constraint conditions that specify the type of information considered valid.
- Specifications tend to be created incrementally, so the metasystem should be able to represent partially complete information simply.
- Requirements and design specifications are created and maintained for a long time. Many small revisions are made as the specification evolves toward a desired state, so the metamodel should let small parts of the specification be identified uniquely so revisions can be made conveniently.
- The ability to represent complex design objects is a problem in current CAD database-management research. The relational model, for example, forces the user to represent a design object as several tuples in relations. A command to delete a design object cannot typically be issued as a single operation but must be considered as several delete-tuple operations. The ability to represent and manipulate design objects conveniently is important for a Metaview metamodel.

$SS = (ET, RT, RN, r, A, a)$

where

ET: is a finite set of entity types;

RT: is a finite set of relationship types where a relationship type contains a finite set of entity-type participants ($ET1, \ldots, ETn$);

RN: is a finite set of roles;

r: is a mapping [RT -> Powerset* $ET \times RN$)] where Powerset* ($ET \times RN$) is the set of all subsets of the Cartesian product of ET and RN that includes two or more members of RN;

A: is a finite set of attributes;

a: is a mapping from an element of the set of entity types, ET, or the set of relationship types, RT, to an element of the set of attributes A.

Figure 3. Metamodel definition for specification schema *SS*.

Environment definition

Before you can create an environment-definition language, you must first model the information required to support a general specification-environment definition as well as special-purpose specification databases conforming to this definition.

Basic model. There are many ways to describe information-systems specifications. Therefore, a metasystem model must be general enough to let multiple environments be defined. To be this general, the metasystem model must behave like a metamodel.

The types of information contained in a specification are defined by a schema called the specification schema. For example, the specification schema for the entity-relationship model defines the notions of entity set, relationship set, attributes, and

ET = {Process, Data_Flow, Data_Store, Interface}

RT = {Sends = {Process, Data_Flow, Interface, Data_Store}
    Receives = {Interface, Data_Flow, Process, Data_Store}}

RN = {Message, Sender, Receiver}

r = {Sends ->
    (Process:Sender, Data_Flow:Message, Data_Store:Receiver),
    (Process:Sender, Data_Flow:Message, Process:Receiver),
    (Process:Sender, Data_Flow:Message, Interface:Receiver);

  Receives ->
    (Process:Receiver, Data_Flow:Message, Data_Store:Sender),
    (Process:Receiver, Data_Flow:Message, Interface:Sender)}

A = {problem_definer, defn_date, frequency, description, size}

a = {Process -> problem_definer, defn_date, description;
    Data_Flow -> problem_definer, defn_date;
    Data_Store -> problem_definer, defn_date, size;
    Interface -> problem_definer, defn_date;
    Sends -> problem_definer, defn_date, frequency;
    Receives -> problem_definer, defn_date, frequency}

Figure 4. Dataflow-specification schema *SS(DF)*.

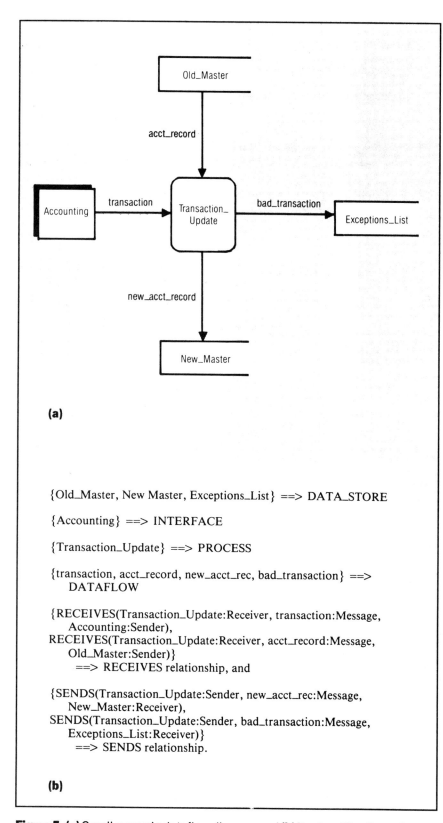

(a)

{Old_Master, New Master, Exceptions_List} ==> DATA_STORE

{Accounting} ==> INTERFACE

{Transaction_Update} ==> PROCESS

{transaction, acct_record, new_acct_rec, bad_transaction} ==>
    DATAFLOW

{RECEIVES(Transaction_Update:Receiver, transaction:Message,
    Accounting:Sender),
RECEIVES(Transaction_Update:Receiver, acct_record:Message,
    Old_Master:Sender)}
    ==> RECEIVES relationship, and

{SENDS(Transaction_Update:Sender, new_acct_rec:Message,
    New_Master:Receiver),
SENDS(Transaction_Update:Sender, bad_transaction:Message,
    Exceptions_List:Receiver)}
    ==> SENDS relationship.

(b)

Figure 5. (a) Small example dataflow diagram and **(b)** its classification schema.

how these concepts are related.

The metamodel must support a specification scheme, *SS*, that contains a set of descriptive elements. Figure 3 shows a minimum set of elements. Although based on Chen's entity-relationship model,[5] the model shown here has several major changes to the definitions in the original entity-relationship model.

As a simple example, consider the definition of a specification scheme for a dataflow model based on the concepts used in dataflow diagrams as proposed in Gane and Sarson's structured systems-analysis methodology.[6] The dataflow specification schema, *SS(DF)*, would have the elements shown in Figure 4. A complete specification schema should also include the notion of value set and a mapping of attributes to value sets.

Advanced modeling. This metamodel is deficient in several more advanced, semantic-based data-modeling features that are found in semantic data models today and that should be present in a metasystem for specification environments. Some features that should be considered are the abstraction mechanisms of aggregation, generalization, and classification. These advanced features are needed to properly model the hierarchical nature of the relationships among software components in a complex system.

Aggregation combines a set of entities and their relationships to form a simple, higher level aggregate object. Of course, the notion of aggregation applies recursively — an aggregate object can be used as part of the definition of a still-higher level object. Aggregation is a fundamental abstraction mechanism in developing an extended component-based metamodel.

Generalization forms a higher level generic entity from its categories. It establishes the is-a relationship between entity types. Generalization can be used to develop specification environments. For example, it is helpful to generalize (or, inversely, categorize) the notion of Interface from the subcategories Human_Interface and Mechanical_Interface — a Human_Interface is an Interface and a Mechanical_Interface is an Interface.

The third abstraction technique, classification, is a simple form of abstraction in which an object type (in this case, entity or relationship type) is defined as a set of instances. It establishes an instance-of relationship between a type and its instances. As an example, consider the small dataflow diagram in Figure 5a; the classifications are in Figure 5b (==> reads "are instances of"). Although not shown in the example, "McAllister" and "Nov. 12, 1987" are examples of instances of values for the attributes problem_definer and defn_date value sets, respectively.

Components, versions, and configuration. The final major aspects that should be included in a metamodel for specification environments are the notions of components, versions, and configurations. Basic to the component-modeling approach is the notion of a component-based design object (also called a molecular object). A design object is a modeling

> **Basic to the component-modeling approach is the notion of a component-based design object, which is also known as a molecular object.**

construct that has a interface definition and an implementation description.

The interface definition specifies the inputs to, outputs from, and high-level functional description of the design object. The implementation is defined by lower level design objects and their interconnections.

Each component object may, in turn, be assigned its own interface and implementation. The concept of abstracting a set of design objects and their relationships into a single, higher level entity is called component aggregation, and the set of design objects in the aggregation is called an aggregate component. Figure 6 presents the expansion of the Transaction_Update

process to a more detailed dataflow-diagram description.

In this example, the boundary definition for the aggregate component corresponding to Transaction_Update is defined by four relationships (the role names of the relationship participants have been left out of these abbreviated definitions):

• Receives(Transaction_Update, transaction, Accounting),

• Receives(Transaction_Update, acct_record, Old_Master),

• Sends(Transaction_Update, new_acct_rec, New_Master), and

• Sends(Transaction_Update, bad_transaction, Exceptions_List).

The implementation of the aggregate

component for the Transaction_Update process can be defined formally in terms of the sets and mappings (*ET, RT, RN, r, A, a*) as was done for the dataflow diagram in Figure 5a.

If many analysts may work on essentially the same specification at the same time, version support becomes an important consideration.

To address version support, we have defined a component/version graph that is very similar to an And/Or graph.[7] Grouping components to form a higher level aggregate object is Anding the components, while selecting one of many versions to represent a particular object is Oring sets of components. A configura-

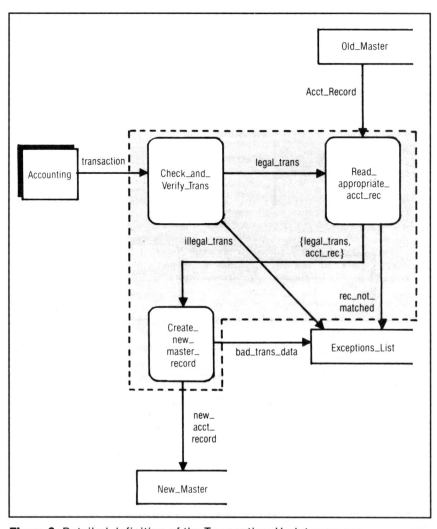

Figure 6. Detailed definition of the Transaction_Update process.

tion (also called a system version) is simply a selected set of versions from the Or part of the component/version graph.

In the component/version graph, every component except the ultimate ancestor must belong to at least one version. A system version is formed by traversing the Or part of the graph beginning at the ultimate ancestor component and proceeding, using Or selection, to a leaf version node (a version node with no versions of its own).[8]

Tool development

Once an environment has been established, its users need tools to fully exploit it. Our Deview project[9] has developed several specification-environment tools that support the SPSL problem-statement language and its associated analyzer.[10] SPSL/SPSA lets a user formally define the logical structure and requirements of an information system, store this description in a database, and later produce various reports about system structure, requirements, and completeness and consistency constraint violations. The tool set that accompanies SPSL/SPSA includes:

• Mondrian, a subsystem that accesses an SPSA database to produce automatically dataflow diagrams on a plotter or laser printer. This tool can produce a series of hierarchically related diagrams corresponding to the growth of process descriptions in a system-requirements definition.

• Cubus, a tool that draws structure charts on a graphics plotter or printer, using a special input file with information about system structure.

• Depict, an interactive graphics environment for the development of requirements using dataflow diagrams and SPSL/SPSA, Depict has an object-oriented user interface, advanced graphics, and multiwindowing approach to expressing specifications. Requirements are specified by creating or modifying a dataflow diagram on the screen.

• Tempro (a Depict subsystem), an interactive template-driven editor. With Tempro, you can specify other requirements such as system dynamics, system properties, system size, data derivation, and data structure.

Based on the experience of developing SPSA and the associated tools, we have designed a set of generalized database-access routines that let a variety of tools interact efficiently with a common specification database. We implemented these routines in Prolog.

We are developing a set of generalized tools for Metaview, as Figure 1b shows. Figure 7 shows the architecture of a template-based editor[11] that is a generalized version of Tempro. A software engineer specifies the environment model using an environment-definition language program for the specification environment, which is stored in environment-definition tables. A tool definer specifies additional syntax and semantics that dictate the general form and actions of the template-based editor generator. The generator uses the information in the environment-definition tables to interact with an analyst when storing and updating a specification in a requirements database.

The semantic checking to be performed by a generated template-based editor is specified by action routines of an attributed translation grammar.[12] The advantages of using such grammars are similar to those realized in compiler-compiler systems: Semantic checking can be incorporated in the grammar and be syntax-directed.

While the requirements for defining and storing diagrams for a variety of diagrammatical specification methodologies have been identified elsewhere,[8] we have proposed how the types of diagrams associated with a particular methodology can be defined as part of an environment definition. We have extended the environment-definition language to allow definitions of diagram types (such as dataflow

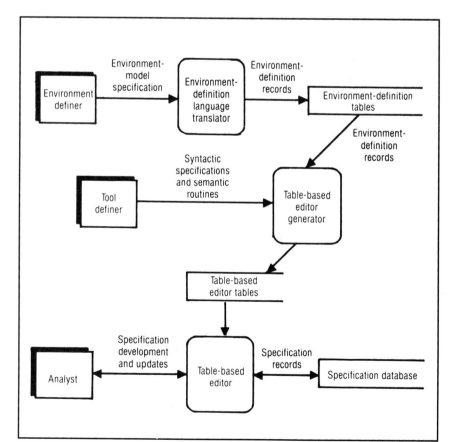

Figure 7. Overview of the templated-based editor generator.

diagrams and entity-relationship diagrams), icon types, geometric procedures, and graphical constraints.

You can view a diagram for a specification as a collection of icons. These icons are associated with the existence of entities or relationships of a particular type. The complete definition of a diagram type has two parts:

• First, you must specify the form of the diagram type, including the types of icons needed, the type of entity or relationship (if any) with which each icon type is associated, and the graphical attributes of each icon type.

• Second, the validity of a diagram type must be specified by defining constraints on the graphical information. These constraints describe which combinations of

---

You can view a diagram for a specification as a collection of icons. These icons are associated with entities or relationships of a particular type. The diagram type's definition must include the form of the type and the constraints on that type.

---

icons represent a member of the class of diagrams for the particular diagram type.

Each icon description contains a list of graphic attributes, any entity or relationship with which it is associated, and the name of a subprogram that creates a graphical image of the icon. We use a procedural language with data-abstraction capabilities (similar to Modula-2 and Ada) to define a set of icon primitives. From this set, more complicated icon types can be constructed modularly.

With the extension of the Metaview metamodel to include icons, the Metaview database is made up of instances of aggregates, entities, relationships, and icons.

Other metasystems

One of the earliest systems that provided some generalization in the development of specification environments was RSL/REVS.[1] RSL, the Requirements Specification Language, is a language for stating requirements specifications based on SREM, the Software Requirements-Engineering Methodology, and REVS, the Requirements-Engineering Validation System, includes a translator for RSL, a specification-database manager, and a collection of analysis tools. Although RSL/REVS has a built-in language and methodology, it shares some of the properties of a metasystem by providing a facility for extending RSL to include new concepts associated with an updated or modified specification methodology.

ISDOS, the Information-Systems Design and Optimization System metasystems project at the University of Michigan, included two major projects, Meta/GA[2] and MDS/MSS,[3] that were pioneer efforts in metasystem research. The metamodel used in both systems was based on the entity-relationship data model. Differences from the original entity-relationship model and the one used in the Meta/GA system included the introduction of intrinsic attributes (attributes such as basic name and synonym that apply to all entities), the restriction that relationships could not have attributes, and the introduction of constants in roles of a relationship.

Meta/GA supported two types of environment-definition-level constraints: combination and connectivity. The combination constraint ensured the correctness of the types of entities and constants that were allowed to occupy the various roles of a relationship. The connectivity constraint defined the maximum number (either "one" or "many") of relationship instances that could exist in the database with a particular entity in a given role.

MDS/MSS extended the Meta/GA system by extending the concept of relationship so relationships could occupy roles in other relationships (tiered relationships were supported) and by letting roles in relationships be occupied by sets of entities or constants and not just single entities or constants. The connectivity constraint was extended to include an integer occurrence value rather than just "one" or "many." A major constraint specification subsystem was also added to MDS/MSS to let the software engineer supply additional environment constraints in predicate notation.

The SDLA metasystem and associate concept metamodel[4] were developed at the Hungarian Academy of Sciences in collaboration with the ISDOS project. Information in a concept database is organized as a set of reference relations. These relations differ from those of the relational model by letting the domain for an attribute be defined as abstract types that refer to entries in other relations. Both entity types (such as process) and relationship types (such as accesses) are treated as concepts, and entities and attributes (such as frequency) are mixed in roles in concept definitions. One of the more powerful features available in the concept model is the use of subtypes (or generalization) to form is-a concept hierarchies.

The Plexsys metasystem[5] developed at the University of Arizona is also based on the entity-relationship model. However, some concepts of the metamodel and all of the environment-definition and -specification information are stored in the same database. The main reason for this dynamism is the desire to modify an environment definition over time with minimum interference with on-going specification activities. Therefore, changes to an environment definition should cause immediate changes to the specification information consistent with the updated environment definition.

References

1. M. Alford, "SREM at the Age of Eight: The Distributed Computing Design System," *Computer*, April 1985, pp. 36-46.

2. Y. Yamamoto, *An Approach to the Generation of Software Life-Cycle Support Systems*, doctoral dissertation, Industrial Engineering Dept., Univ. of Michigan, Ann Arbor, Mich., 1981.

3. K.C. Kang, *An Approach for Supporting System-Development Methodologies for Developing a Complete and Consistent System Specification*, doctoral dissertation, Industrial Engineering Dept., Univ. of Michigan, Ann Arbor, Mich., 1982.

4. J. Demetrovics, E. Knuth, and P. Rado, "Specification Metasystems," *Computer*, April 1982, pp. 20-35.

5. J.E. Kotteman and B.R. Konsynski, "Dynamic Metasystems for Information Systems Development," *Proc. Fifth Int'l Conf. Information Systems*, ACM, New York, 1984, pp. 187-204.

Metaview is intended to let a software engineer define the environment model and associated tool support for the specification methodology desired. Once defined, a meta-system-developed environment should ensure that analysts adhere to the chosen methodology strictly. This adherence to a methodology could be specified as a set of rules that operate on an environment definition to diagnose deviations from the standards dictated by the methodology.

But much work remains to be done to allow further efforts in this area, including the development of a rule-based specification language and rule checker and the development of a language to define specification transformations between life-cycle phases.

We intend to fully develop the aggregate-component model and integrate it with our existing database engine. We must also define a constraint processor and more completely specify our approach to a generalized graphical interface before implementation — an interface that fully integrates graphical and nongraphical information in a common metamodel. We must develop a generalized, template-based editor, which we can use to verify the current implementation of our database-support facility. Finally, and perhaps most importantly, we must test the metasystem by defining a wide class of specification environments and have analysts use the different environments. ⊙

Acknowledgments

The authors completed this research with the support of Canada's National Science and Engineering Research Council through strategic grant G1153.

References

1. Special issue on requirements-engineering environments, *Computer*, April 1985, pp. 9-91.

2. *Information Systems Design Methodologies: A Comparative Review*, E.W. Olle, H.G. Sol, and A.A. Verrijn-Stuart, eds., North-Holland, Amsterdam, 1982.

3. A.I. Wasserman, "The User Software-Engineering Methodology: An Overview," *Proc. IFIP Working Group 8.1 Conf. Comparative Reviews of Information Systems Design Methodologies*, IFIP, Geneva, 1982, pp. 591-628.

4. J. Demetrovics, E. Knuth, and P. Rado, "Specification Metasystems," *Computer*, April 1982, pp. 20-35.

5. P. Chen, "The Entity-Relationship Model: Towards a Unified View of Data," *ACM Trans. Database Systems*, Jan. 1976, pp. 9-36.

6. C. Gane and T. Sarson, *Structured Systems Analysis: Tools and Techniques*, Prentice-Hall, Englewood Cliffs, N.J., 1979.

7. W.F. Tichy, "A Data Model for Programming-Support Environments and Its Application," in *Automated Tools for Information Systems Design*, B. Schneider and A. Wasserman, eds., North-Holland, Amsterdam. 1982, pp. 31-48.

8. A.J. McAllister, "Metasystem Support for Specification Environments," Tech. Report 88-1, Computational Science Dept., Univ. of Saskatchewan, Saskatoon, Sask., Canada, Jan. 1988.

9. P.G. Sorenson and J.-P. Tremblay, "The Deview Project Update," Tech. Report 86-3, Computational Science Dept., Univ. of Saskatchewan, Saskatoon, Sask., Canada, March 1986.

10. P.G. Sorenson, J.-P. Tremblay, and A.W. Friesen, "SPSL/SPSA: A Minicomputer Database System for Structured Systems Analysis and Design," *Proc. ACM SIG-Small and SIGMOD Workshop Small Database Systems*, ACM, New York, 1981, pp. 109-118.

11. T.H. Chew, *Automated Template Generation for Requirements-Specification Languages*, masters thesis, Computational Science Dept., Univ. of Saskatchewan, Saskatoon, Sask., Canada, 1987.

12. J.-P. Tremblay and P.G. Sorenson, *The Theory and Practice of Compiler Writing*, McGraw-Hill, New York, 1985.

Jean-Paul Tremblay is a professor in the Computational Sciences Dept. at the University of Saskatchewan. His research interests include compilers and software engineering.

Tremblay received a BS and MS in electrical engineering from the University of New Brunswick and a PhD in computer science from the Case Institute of Technology. He is a member of ACM.

Paul G. Sorenson is a professor in the Computational Sciences Dept. at the University of Saskatchewan. His research interests include database-management systems, software engineering, and compiler construction.

Sorenson received a BS in mathematics and an MS in computing science from the University of Alberta and a PhD in computer science from the University of Toronto. He is a member of ACM, Computer Society of the IEEE, and Canadian Information-Processing Society.

Andrew J. McAllister is an assistant professor in the Computer Science Dept. at the University of New Brunswick. His research interests include CASE and programming languages.

McAllister received a BA in psychology and an MS in computer science from the University of New Brunswick and a PhD in computer science from the University of Saskatchewan.

Address questions about this article to the authors at Computational Science Dept., University of Saskatchewan, Saskatoon, Sask. S7N 0W0 Canada.

PART VII: EVALUATING TOOLS AND MANAGING CASE

WHAT PRODUCTIVITY INCREASES TO EXPECT FROM A CASE ENVIRONMENT:
RESULTS OF A USER SURVEY

Peter Lempp
SPS Software Products
& Services, Inc.
New York, New York

Rudolf Lauber
University of Stuttgart
Stuttgart, West Germany

ABSTRACT

Computer Aided Software Engineering (CASE) tools and environments are gradually becoming a reality in industry. Nevertheless, they have not reached a utilization level equal to that of tools in other related engineering disciplines.

In part, some managers are reluctant to start using such tools because they anticipate introduction problems, like the need to train engineers in the use of a disciplined method. And since most CASE tools have been introduced only recently, solid quantitative data is rarely available to show that a CASE environment will generate overall productivity increases which justify the costs, and confirm the necessity, of a transition.

To obtain insights into what productivity gains and overall lifecycle cost reductions can be achieved, and to learn whether the CASE technology indeed justifies its costs, we conducted a survey of 22 major projects supported by the CASE environment EPOS in the last 5 years.

Based on estimates of project managers, the survey showed moderate productivity increases (considering the development phases only), and underlined the enormous potentials for savings in maintenance. This paper summarizes and discusses the survey results, and draws conclusions as to which support features can be expected to improve productivity further.

CR Categories: D.2, D.2.2, D.2.9, J.7, K.6.3

1. Background

To increase productivity and to produce better quality software at lower cost: these are the key issues in applying CASE (Computer Aided Software Engineering) technology. Although most people monitoring the state of the art of CASE tools intuitively agree that these tools can contribute to increased productivity, little quantitative data is available to support these expectations. Given this lack of data, it is not surprising that potential users are skeptical about the transferability of results from a single "success story," or about reports of enormous productivity increases produced by a tool in one phase of the system life cycle. Most of these reports neglect to describe the problems in transferring the data to another tool and representation to support the next life cycle phase.

To obtain solid user information, a major survey was conducted for projects developed in the last 5 years with the support of the CASE environment EPOS. Although the restriction to only one CASE environment has limitations in the applicability of detailed results to other situations, it has the advantages that one can request very specific information, and that the chances of misunderstandings caused by different terminology, etc. are minimized. Therefore, the confidence in the validity of the survey results increases. Another reason for evaluating experiences with one CASE environment only was the underlying objective to measure the effects of a CASE environment particularly on actual medium-size to large-scale projects. These projects naturally take years to complete, and since only very few of the software engineering environments have been commercially available for some years [1], [2], [3], [4], [5], [6], actual long-range experiences with various CASE environments cannot be reported. To the knowledge of the author, no evaluation based on long-term industrial experiences with CASE environments has yet been published.[1] The underlying support environment for the survey, the EPOS System, has been used in industry, government agencies, universities and research institutes since the end of 1980, first in Europe, and since 1985 in growing numbers in the USA as well. By October 1987, about 340 installations were in use worldwide.

The conducted survey focused on obtaining data from two areas: the impact of CASE environments on productivity, project costs and software quality (economic aspect of the CASE environment) and the impact on people working with CASE tools (human aspects). The survey was based on mailed questionnaires which were completed during on-site interviews. The survey form consisted of about 80 questions. One part dealt with non-technology issues like the nature, size and project/product type of the company, personnel characteristics and previous exposure to CASE tools. In a second part, specific questions were asked about the impact of EPOS in the different phases and activities.

A careful profile of the variety of companies and projects to be surveyed was developed, and a representative sample of EPOS installations selected. We identified the project managers, contacted them to confirm

---

[1] Evaluations of special aspects, mainly of programming environments, have been done to some extent [7], and certain user experiences have been reported (e.g., in [8]), but data on the overall effects of CASE environments on all phases and activities within a project are not widely available.

Reprinted from *Productivity: Progress, Prospects, and Payoff,* June 1988, pp. 13-19. Used by permission.

their availability and willingness to participate in a survey interview, and sent them an information copy of the questionnaire in advance. Then, in January and February 1987, personal interviews were conducted at the selected firms. Each interview took about 3 to 5 hours.

2. Characteristics of the Survey Sample

In selecting the survey participants, we considered the following objectives important:

- Respondent institutions should have medium- and long-range experience in the use of the CASE environment to give knowledgeable responses about CASE impact throughout a project's life cycle.

- The survey should include a mix of different applications to yield results of broader validity.

- Likewise, a mix of target languages would produce more exemplary results.

- Respondents should have experience in applying the environment for different phases and activities, so they could assess the widest possible range of support functions, and give informed responses about long-term impact.

Our measurements were not based on a controlled laboratory project where a software project was carried out twice, once using the CASE environment and once without it, under the same constraints like, e.g., qualification of developers (Fig. 1a below); rather, we observed productivity data from projects done with the CASE environment and compared them to data recorded before introducing the environment in the company. This means that we in fact measured the impact of the CASE environment as shown in Fig. 1b.

We assumed that experienced developers (project leaders) with a background in software projects, and experience in doing projects with and without CASE environments, would be able to estimate on the basis of their in-house data the difference between the CASE-supported project results (in terms of quality, productivity, cost, etc.) and the likely results if the same project had been carried out without the CASE environment.

Although we recognized the impossibility of obtaining real measurements, particularly in those areas which are open to more subjective evaluation, we considered the responses to contain valid information as regards overall tendencies and basic trends in the achievable benefits and acceptance levels associated with CASE environment use.

The statistics of the survey sample were as follows:

- The actual survey included 22 different projects, conducted at 14 companies in Europe, including firms like MBB, BMW, Philips, Bosch and Dornier.

- The sample showed a good mix of companies with long-range and medium-range experience in using the CASE environment. More than 80% of the sample had at least two years' experience in its use; more than 60% had EPOS for more than 3 years, about 25% had EPOS for as much as 5 years.

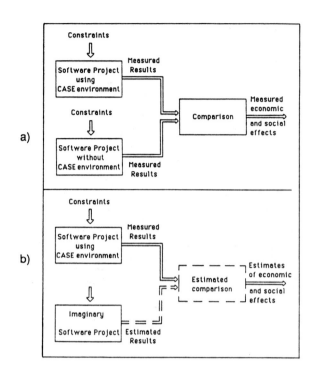

Fig.1: a) (Theoretical) controlled experiment to measure the economic and social effects of using a CASE environment.
b) Actual experiment for the CASE study to estimate economic and social impact by comparing a real CASE-aided project with an imaginary, unsupported project.

Category	Characterization	Number of projects
A	Business applications software (Banking, insurance, etc.)	0[*]
B	Systems software (compilers, operating systems, database systems, etc.)	3
C	Scientific/Engineering applications (CAD/CAM software, simulation software, etc.)	3
D	Data communications software	4
E	Hardware/software systems for communications	2
F	Real-time electronics/ avionics systems software	10
G	Hardware/software systems for industrial automation	4
H	Hardware systems (electronic hardware)	1
I	Others	3

Fig. 2: General categories describing the projects carried out using the CASE environment. (Some of the projects could not be uniquely categorized; for these, respondents check-marked two categories).

----

[*]Although EPOS can also be used for business applications, practical use in this area began too recently for any potential respondents in the field to meet the length-of-use criteria established for this survey.

- As Figure 2 shows, the sample covered a variety of applications ranging from systems software to software/hardware or even pure hardware systems, and covering most major software applications.

- A close to equally distributed range of target programming languages was achieved with about 1/3 using assembler, but 2/3 using HOL-like languages, e.g., "C" and derivatives (17%), FORTRAN (10%), Pascal, PEARL (both about 7%) and also Ada (7%). Correlating the start of a project with the programming language, we found that the majority of the projects targeting for assembly language started early in the five-year period covered by this survey; by contrast, projects using Ada have the most recent start-dates.

3. Survey Results: CASE Impact on Productivity

Instead of asking for "productivity figures" such as lines of code per man-month (the meaning of which is doubtful), the survey included questions on two effects which we considered a more realistic measure of productivity, and which at the same time were easier for respondents to estimate:

- The degree to which performance of project tasks was facilitated during the different project phases;

- The changes in expenditure resulting from CASE environment use.

As can be seen from Figure 3, the project tasks were felt to be easier in most phases when the CASE environment was used. To give an idea of the environment's corresponding support features which contributed to this result, Figure 4 summarizes important EPOS support aspects [9].

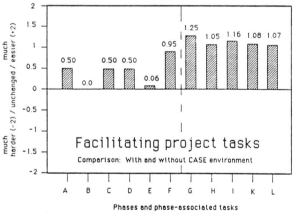

Legend:

A. Definition of requirements
B. Rough conceptual design, development of sub-system/ software requirements
C. Feasibility study
D. System design
E. Development of the software in source code
F. Program coding, integration, verification, validation & test
G. Project management and control
H. User and system documentation
I. Coordination and communication between team members
K. Control of change-related problems
L. Complexity control

Fig. 3: Degree of facilitating project tasks (indicating higher productivity)

Project Phase	CASE Support Provided by EPOS
Definition of requirements	Customizable outline template, formal definition and breakdown of requirements and constraints, glossary of terms
Conceptual design	Definition, refinement, acknowledgment of requirements and constraints, principal definition of input/output characteristics, glossary
Feasibility study (including personnel availability studies)	Specification of teammember availability and schedule constraints; definition, specification and analysis of critical details
Preliminary design	Support of seven different, most commonly used design methods, graphical* and/or textual design of modules, tasking structures, etc., including specification of interfaces, various analyses and diagram documentation
Detailed design	Graphical* and/or textual specification of functions, data structures, controlflow, etc.; comprehensive analyses and variety of graphical/ tabular/textual documentation
Coding, Integration, Test	Automatic source code generators* for Ada, FORTRAN, Pascal; coding within design objects with "code selection" for all other languages; code feedback to update design specifications after changes directly in the source code, import/export capabilities to test/debugging tools, specification and design of test software, data and results
Non-phase-oriented	**CASE Support Provided by EPOS**
Project planning*	Definition of work breakdown structure; project organization, cost and schedule planning (PERT/network computation); mapping system requirements to work packages
Project control*	Actual/nominal comparisons, controlled decentralized development, various assessments of actual project status based on evaluation of the technical part of the database
Documentation	about 20 different types of diagrams (dataflow, hierarchy, block diagram, Petri net, etc.), flexible table generator, selective documentation in user-definable forms
Quality Control	Quality requirements planning, definition of QA procedures, restrictions to structured approaches and specifications, method support, version control (constructive quality assurance), comprehensive analysis package for completeness, consistency, interface checks, etc. (analytical quality assurance)

* available in current version but not available during projects surveyed

Fig 4: Support features of the surveyed CASE environment EPOS for the different project phases and project activities [9]

One exception in making activities easier was the conceptual design phase, where no direct support of the necessary modeling process was provided by the environment used here. The other exception was the phase of coding and unit testing the software programs.[2]

Interestingly, the greatest benefits were perceived to be in the area of project management and control. This is significant since the majority of our respondents were in fact project managers, and their favorable assessment here therefore reflects their own direct perception of benefit rather than second-hand information from other members of the project team.

It is clear from the information in Figure 3 that the perceived benefits tend to be concentrated in the later phases of a project. The assistance rendered in the early phases, particularly by having a clearly defined, disciplined structure outlined from the outset, was to some degree offset by the team members' unfamiliarity with this approach, and their initial resistance to entering their ideas in pre-defined formats. Only in successive phases do the long-range benefits of such discipline become apparent.

Such concentration of benefits in the later phases was perceived not only with respect to the easing of project tasks. Figure 5 shows that, with use of the CASE environment, there was an increase in expenditures during the first phases of the projects; this was more than compensated by a decrease during the later phases, which resulted in net savings of about 9% over the entire development period.[3]

Especially interesting is the great weight attributed to savings in the subsequent maintenance phase: considering that maintenance is generally thought to account for more than 50% of the total expenditures for a software project, cost reductions of up to 69% in this area will have a major impact on full life cycle expenditures.

One specific factor which heavily influences productivity in projects is the extent to which the documentation is produced automatically by the CASE tools. The survey found that about 3/4 of the overall documentation (including progress reports, user documentation, test descriptions, etc.) was done automatically with the EPOS environment (Figure 6). Other tools used included source code pretty printer tools and CAD/CAE tools in hardware/software projects. Manual documentation was restricted mainly to special tables, sketches and circuit diagrams.

---

[2]The EPOS versions which include automatic code generation and feedback facilities had not yet been applied on a large scale at the time the interviews took place. Thus the actual coding in these projects was done using design documentation such as flow charts.

[3]The figure of 9% savings over the entire development period was not calculated from the savings in the individual development phases; rather, it results from answers to a separate question requesting estimates of cost impact during development (excluding maintenance).

Although not within the focus of this paper, other worthwhile results of the survey are briefly summarized here:

- All projects reported improvements in quality, the most substantial of which were again ascribed to improved project management/control. One particular aspect of software quality, early error detection and removal, was specifically inquired for. Figure 7 shows that 2/3 of the project managers reported detecting more errors already in the conceptual design/system specification phase, which contributed indirectly to overall project productivity.

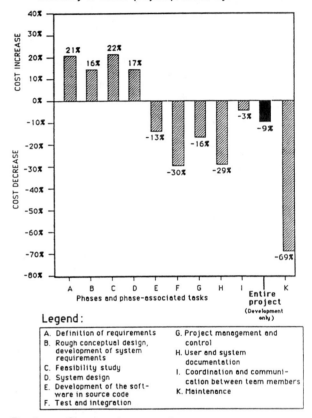

Legend:

A. Definition of requirements
B. Rough conceptual design, development of system requirements
C. Feasibility study
D. System design
E. Development of the software in source code
F. Test and integration
G. Project management and control
H. User and system documentation
I. Coordination and communication between team members
K. Maintenance

Fig. 5: Changes in expenditures through the use of the CASE environment

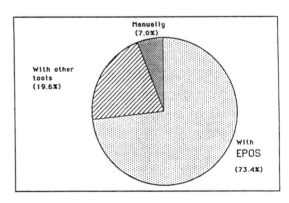

Fig. 6: Extent of automatic documentation generation using CASE tools.

The introduction of a CASE environment has different phases in which actual usage and acceptance by personnel undergoes significant changes. We monitored the projects after the training week and during initial project use, when acceptance levels declined. Later, acceptance rose again to the initial, well-received level (see Figure 8). Together with the measured impact of having especially positive pay-off effects in later phases, this suggests that careful training, including education about anticipated benefits, is necessary to ease start-up problems.

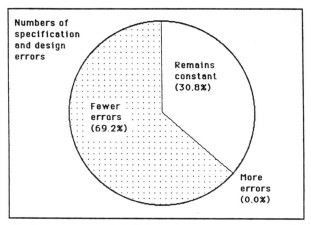

Fig. 7: Impact of CASE environment use on the incidence of specification and design errors detected late in the project.

The start-up period for using the CASE system and its methodology to its full extent can be as high as 2 months or more, or as low as 2 weeks, depending on the engineers' backgrounds and the method of introduction.

No significant correlation was measured between job satisfaction and the use of the CASE environment. However, when the surveyed projects were begun, the hardware situation differed from today's: few workstations were available, there was limited availability of graphical terminals, and fewer than 50% of the developers had a terminal "within reach." It is expected that all participants will experience increased job satisfaction when they are able to accomplish their work with increased productivity, using today's faster, more powerful computers and having more direct access to these machines.

4. Discussion of the Survey Results

In this section, we shall evaluate the survey results and try to find relations between the impact assessments made by our respondents and the CASE environment features responsible for these effects.

Looking at the most important effect - reduction of cost in the different project phases and in an entire project, as shown in Figure 5 - there are three relationships to be considered:

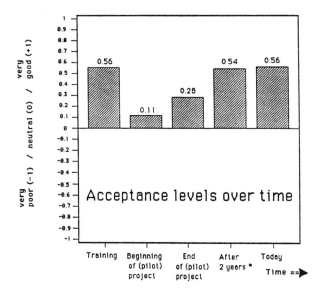

Fig. 8: Changes in user acceptance of the CASE environment over time.

* Two of the 14 companies had been using the CASE environment for less than 2 years, and thus did not answer this question.

As a disadvantage of CASE environment use, there was an increase in expenditure in the early phases of the projects, due mainly to two factors: first, the additional work of inputting textual information into the database (previously done only sketchily), and second, the enforcement of a structured approach which includes more detailed analyses in the beginning. Ultimately, of course, this results in enhanced efficiency and cost-effectiveness, and thus compensates for the initial increase in expense and effort.

There are possibilities of reducing these cost increases in the early phases, from requirements analysis to feasibility study, by introducing page readers where documentation is already available, for example from the customer. Further improvements can be achieved by changing from textual input to graphical input (including window techniques for simultaneous visualizations, as illustrated in Figure 9). However, it was clear from the survey that not all companies have this hardware in place, and that investments in state-of-the-art workstations and other hardware are necessary in many companies before high input productivity can be achieved.

The savings in program coding and unit test were estimated in our survey to be relatively low. But this was before the new automatic code generation and code feedback features [10] were introduced. Coding was done manually from flow charts and Nassi-Shneiderman diagrams. Code generation support could change the estimate for this activity substantially.

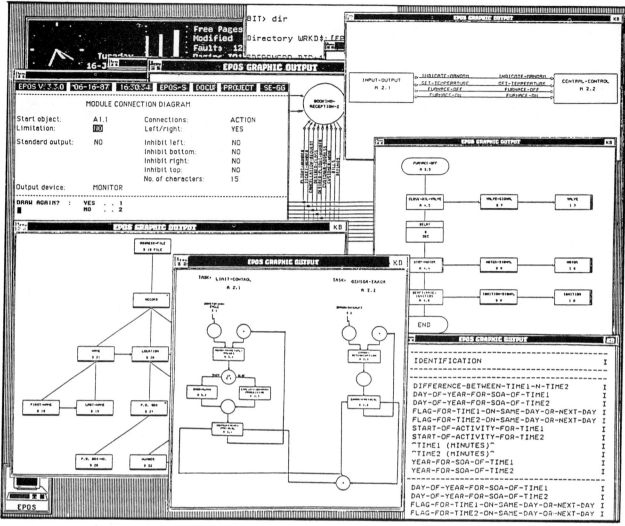

Fig. 9: Graphical input of information during systems design to reduce costs in this project phase (snapshot of EPOS on a workstation).

● Cost savings in the area of project management and control were also considered relatively low in our survey, again because the surveyed projects began years ago. With today's integrated CASE support including management support, a major additional cost reduction could be achieved in this area.

However, even if these additional effects could cause the total cost savings to change from 9% (now measured) to, say, 30% in the future, it is evident that at present the use of CASE environments provides opportunities for evolutionary rather than revolutionary development cost reductions. More dramatic improvements in cost-effectiveness might be possible in the future, by reuse of the software developed with CASE environments [11].

More significantly shown was the quality improvement achieved by use of a CASE environment. And really substantial - possibly even revolutionary - cost savings are estimated for the whole life cycle, including maintenance. The fact that the improved structuredness and documentation of the software provides the potential of more cost-effective maintenance, and the improved possibility of reusing more reliable software without first having to reverse engineer non-existing system representations [12], seem justification enough for the use of CASE environments. It should be recognized, however, that a CASE environment can still only be effective if embedded in an overall commitment to quality assurance.

7. Conclusions

The survey on the EPOS CASE environment utilization in medium- to large-scale projects showed that moderate savings throughout the development phase, considerable improvements in software quality, and revolutionary cost savings in maintenance, are achievable.

Since the sample was relatively small, and because the survey was restricted to one specific CASE environment, the results are not generally applicable to all environments in all details. Nevertheless it is felt that the trends shown here apply to other CASE environments as well. Other surveys have been started and will assemble additional reference data next year.

While our respondents might have come up with higher savings estimates if they could have drawn on experience with two or more consecutive projects using the CASE environment, it is important to bear in mind that CASE application cannot slash the costs of the development period drastically, and should not be expected to do so [13]. Nonetheless, dramatic overall lifecycle savings (considering the maintenance phase as well) are expected.

At the very least, the survey indicates that the costs of introducing CASE environments are well justified. In most cases, the initial investment in such tools should pay off over the course of the first project, and cost factors should be even more favorable with subsequent projects if the personnel is already familiar with the CASE support functions before a project is begun.

Also, it was found that introduction of a CASE environment has an impact on the style of working (towards a structured and orderly fashion). The organized information capture resulting from adherence to the environment's discipline has tremendous value for later traceability. But it is necessary to introduce such an environment slowly, with good training, to overcome acceptance problems.

Further steps in automation (application of available code generators, and use of powerful workstations) appear promising. Additional research is being done now to make (re-)use of this higher-quality software possible, so as to increase cost savings further in the long run.

For the moment, it would be desirable to achieve a greater awareness and use of CASE environments in industry, without unrealistic expectations of orders-of-magnitude productivity increases. To this end, engineers need to gain more experience in the use of CASE tools, and management needs to be educated about the anticipated changes in the life cycle cost, the necessity of sufficient computer hardware, and the possibilities and limitations of CASE environment support.

Acknowledgment:

The authors wish to thank Dr. Alex Rainer for critical review and suggestions to improve this paper.

References

[1] Alford, Mac W.: "A Requirements Engineering Methodology for Real-Time Processing Requirements." *IEEE Trans. Software Eng.*, Vol. SE-3, No. 1, 1977, 60-83.

[2] Sievert, G.E.; Mitell, T.A.: "Specification-based Software Engineering with TAGS." *IEEE Computer*, Vol. 18, No. 4, April 1985, 56-65.

[3] Softool Corp.: Softool Overview. Goleta, CA: Softool Corp., 1984.

[4] Stenning, V.: "An Introduction to ISTAR." In: Integrated Project Support Environments (ed. John McDermid), Peter Peregrinus Ltd., 1985.

[5] McClure, C.L.: "Intech's Excelerator." *Computer Consultant*, 10, 1984.

[6] Lauber, R.; Lempp, P.: "Integrated Development and Project Management Support Systems." Proc. 7th Intl. Comp. Software & Applications Conf. COMPSAC '83, Chicago, Nov. 1983. Los Angeles: IEEE Computer Society Press, 1983.

[7] Card, D.N.; McGarry, F.E.; and Page, G.T.: "Evaluating Software Engineering Technologies." *IEEE Transactions on Software Engineering*, Vol. SE-13, No. 7, July 1987, 845-851.

[8] Schuler, T.; Frank, R.S.; Kratschmer, W.: "Successes and Failures using EPOS as a Software Production Tool." IFAC Workshop "Experiences with Management of Software Projects," Heidelberg, May 1986. Proceedings publ. by Pergamon Press, Ltd., London.

[9] Lauber, R.; Lempp, P.: EPOS Overview. New York: SPS Software Products & Services, Inc., 1986.

[10] Lempp, P.: "An Environment to Promote Software Reusability at the Design Specification Level." Fifth Annual Pacific Northwest Software Quality Conference, Portland, OR, Oct. 19-20, 1987.

[11] Lauber, R.: "Automated Software Production." AIAA/NASA Intl. Symp. on Space Int. Systems, (Paper No. AIAA-87-2219). Washington, DC, June 22-23, 1987.

[12] Lempp, P.: "Software Environment Concepts for Cost-effective Transition to Ada Technology." Sixth Annual Conference on Ada Technology, Arlington, VA, March 14-17, 1988.

[13] Brooks, F.: "No Silver Bullet: Essence and Accidents of Software Engineering." *IEEE Computer*, April 1987, 10-19.

Reprinted from *IEEE Software*, Vol. 9, No. 3, May 1992, pp. 23-28. Copyright © 1992 by The Institute of Electrical and Electronics Engineers, Inc. All rights reserved.

How the Learning Curve Affects CASE Tool Adoption

Chris F. Kemerer, MIT *Sloan School of Management*

◆ *Why do some organizations buy integrated CASE tools only to leave them on the shelf? Part of the answer may lie in a misinterpretation of the learning curve and its affect on productivity.*

With the rising cost of software development, tools for integrated computer-aided software engineering offer solutions to productivity and quality problems that plague the profession. But while most software developers accept the idea that integrated CASE can help lower costs and increase productivity, the state of practice is less optimistic. Organizations tend to adopt integrated CASE only in a limited form or they abandon a good percentage of the technology soon after it is implemented.

One study shows that one year after introduction, 70 percent of CASE tools and techniques are never used, 25 percent are used by only one group, and five percent are widely used, but not to capacity. In a different survey of more than 200 leading organizations, less than 25 percent of the staff were using front-end CASE tools. In another survey of 63 leading organizations, only 24 percent were using CASE at all. Anoth-

er study reports that one organization is not using 80 to 90 percent of the CASE tool packages it purchased.[1]

Yet there is an obvious need for such tools. The already high demand for software continues to grow, and there is a shortage of qualified software developers. Indeed, one cause of quality shortfalls in delivered software could very well be the participation of marginally qualified individuals in its development. So with this relatively scarce supply of software-development labor, it makes good sense to substitute development capital in the form of CASE tools. Some think of this as software development's favorable evolution from a craft-type activity to one more closely resembling an engineering or manufacturing operation.[2]

So why aren't organizations embracing the idea of integrated CASE in more than just theory? One problem is that the first

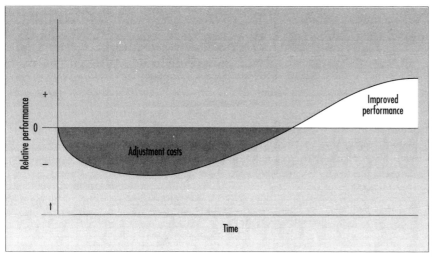

Figure 1. *Performance over time with learning effect.*

project written with an integrated CASE tool typically fails to deliver improved results. Academicians and practitioners say that the learning curve, described in the box on p. 26, can partially explain this phenomenon. But merely identifying learning as a source of the problem is not enough. Managers need more information to justify their investment in CASE technology. They need a way to predict the extent of the learning curve and data to estimate its parameters so that they can determine their return on investment or similar measures for CASE tool adoption.

Ultimately, knowing the factors that favorably influence the rate of learning, not merely the observed learning rate, will be what managers find the most useful. But a necessary first step is the ability to measure the current state of the process.

INFLUENCE OF LEARNING CURVES

Integrated CASE tools have raised the stakes of the learning issue. Because these tools cover the entire life cycle, there is more to learn, and therefore the study of learning — and the learning-curve phenomenon — is becoming especially relevant.

One interpretation of the learning curve is that initial projects are relatively more expensive than later projects and are even likely to be more expensive than projects produced under the old technology.

> The problem for CASE tool adopters is that no one agrees on how the learning curve is likely to affect tool adoption.

In a survey of more than 60 sites, W. Bruce Chew and colleagues translated this effect into the *S* curve in Figure 1.[3] The curve, which represents actual performance, dips below 0 on the relative performance scale, indicating that performance on initial projects with the new technology is worse than performance on projects with the old technology. This effect eventually wears off, but it is not what adopters of process innovations usually expect. They often project a zero increase in performance followed by a rise that eventually plateaus. Thus, they are disappointed when expected benefits do not materialize as soon as planned and may abandon the technology before realizing any net benefit.

Adding to the confusion is that CASE tools are relatively new, and there is no published data on the learning-curve effect — although a number of observers have postulated a model like Figure 1. The problem for CASE tool adopters is that no one agrees on how the learning curve is likely to affect tool adoption. For example, a model from Software Productivity Research predicts that the *S* curve for CASE tools crosses the 0 relative productivity level in about six months. A near identical graph from the Gartner Group shows the *S* curve for integrated CASE tools crossing after more than a year. A mix and match of vendor solutions reach the same level only after more than two years. On the other extreme is a survey of CASE users by CASE Research Corp.,

which found that more than one-third of all back-end (lower) CASE users claimed full proficiency in only one to two months. Finally, a report in *CASE Outlook*, while noting the absence of quantitative studies, nonetheless offers the following prediction: "... plan on a productivity reduction of 50 percent for six months, parity for the next six months, and 30 percent to 50 percent improvement thereafter [including tool-specific learning-curve effects]."[1]

Clearly, the industry has only contradictory evidence to provide CASE tool adopters — which may be part of the reason the tools aren't being adopted very quickly. (The difference may also be because time is chosen as the model's axis instead of projects, which more accurately reflects how learning occurs.) This view of learning emphasizes costs, rather than the traditional learning benefits, as the box on p. 26 describes. The goal of this article is to go beyond that view and show how learning-curve models can help managers in adopting integrated CASE tools.

ADAPTING MODELS TO INTEGRATED CASE

Although there are many learning-curve models, it is not easy to adapt them to estimating learning curves for integrated CASE tools. A number of issues — both theoretical and those having to do with implementation — present formidable obstacles to using traditional models, which were created to predict the performance of manual workers performing repetitive tasks. Users of integrated CASE tools are essentially knowledge workers performing tasks, that (at least at first approximation) are not so repetitive.

Theoretical issues. These issues include sensitivities peculiar to knowledge work, the diversity of tasks, and the confusion between tool learning curves and learning curves for supporting technologies.

Knowledge-work sensitivities. Although all the original applications of learning curves involved manual tasks, there was no reason to believe similar effects would not be found in knowledge work — tasks like system design and analysis. Such effects are

arguably stronger for tasks that are not physically constrained. Air-frame construction and printed-circuit-board assembly, for example, ultimately encounter physical constraints such as maximum speed of operation, especially if safety is a priority. So a natural assumption is because knowledge work does not have these binding constraints, traditional learning-curve models will apply at least equally well.

Unfortunately, it doesn't work out that way. Classic learning-curve models assume production categories are either

♦ large lots or batches of relatively low cost units (like semiconductors) or

♦ tens or hundreds of very large identical or nearly identical units (like airplanes or ships).

Software projects have elements of both, but fall neatly into neither. A software project can be viewed as the production of many relatively atomic units (like source lines of code or function points). However, these tend to be aggregated into units with nonuniform granularity — program size varies widely, for example — which correspond to odd-size batches. This view obviously disrupts the classic learning-curve model.

On the other hand, if the unit of analysis is the software project itself, roughly corresponding to airplanes in the second category, the units are clearly not identical. This issue of the repetitive versus non-repetitive nature of software development is receiving a lot of attention because it relates directly to software reusability. Software developers tend to treat each project as unique, when, in fact, research suggests that less than 15 percent of the code created is actually unique, novel, or specific to individual applications.[4]

An appropriate approach may be, then, to treat each project as a batch — in which the batch size is a measure of software size — and adjust the model to account for a possible wide variation in batch size. A modeling approach similar to that for a microeconomic production process may be quite suitable. In this approach, learning is merely one independent variable, which together with other variables (like the amount of input), is given equal op-portunity to influence the result.

For example, slightly modifying the model of Argote and colleagues gives you

$$\ln q_t = \alpha + \beta \ln K_{t-1} + \chi \ln L_t + d \ln W_t + \varepsilon$$
$$K_t = \lambda K_{t-1} + q_t$$

where q_t is the output in time period t, K_t is knowledge gained during t, L_t is the labor input during t, W_t is the capital input during t, and λ is a depreciation of the knowledge parameter.

In this model the effects of learning (K_t) are separable from other possible effects, such as changes in the mix of capital and labor inputs or in scale.

Task diversity. Systems-development tasks can be anything from requirements analysis to testing and documenting source code. These diverse tasks are likely to reflect different rates of learning, and be supported to different degrees by the integrated CASE tool. The issue here is how much the task mix differs from project to project. If it differs markedly and if different tasks exhibit highly different rates of learning, the results may be anomalous. There are several ways to avoid this. One is to take great care in selecting as homogeneous a set of projects as possible to model. Another is to incorporate additional variables in the model to account for this mix discrepancy. Finally, discrete tasks within the project can be modeled separately. Each of these suggestions, whether done together or separately, carries with it some practical difficulties.

Another problem is caused by how CASE tools provide different levels of support for different project tasks. For example, John Henderson and Jay Cooprider found that current tools differ significantly in their ability to support cooperative design activities.[5]

With this different level of support, plus a possible mix of activities across projects, an earlier project may be (anomalously) more productive because a particu-lar life-cycle phase or task within a phase was both significant and relatively well supported. A later project, on the other hand, might be relatively unlucky on both counts. Moreover, an earlier project may use a different version of the integrated CASE tool.

Tool versus supporting methods. The distinction between learning the integrated CASE tool and learning the underlying or supporting methodology has received some attention in both the trade press and academic writing. Texas Instru-ments' Information Engineering Facility and Knowledgeware's Information Engineering Workbench are examples of learning the tools, while information engineering is an example of learning a supporting methodology. Distinguishing types of learning is fundamental to such notions as "readiness for integrated CASE," in which developers are recommended to delay adopting integrated CASE tools until they are fully comfortable with the underlying methodology.[6]

This distinction suggests using separate models to track the individual rates of learning and to track variables relating to the training received by the staff assigned to integrated CASE projects. Although research has documented the importance of training to learning,[7] organizations tend to underinvest in training. To estimate the benefit of training, managers can adopt a version of Paul Adler and Kim Clark's model:

$$\ln \frac{q_t}{l_t} = \ln \alpha + \beta \ln X_{t-1} + \chi \ln T_{t-1} + \varepsilon$$

where q_t over l_t is productivity during time period t and T_{t-1} is the cumulative hours spent in training during $t-1$.

Implementation issues. After the functional form of the learning-curve model is established, work can proceed on empiri-

> Organizations that have already adopted integrated CASE tools are the best data-collection sites, but finding them isn't easy.

LEARNING-CURVE MODEL: A FLEXIBLE MEASUREMENT TOOL

Part of adopting an industrial process is to go through a learning curve that measures the rate at which the average unit cost of production decreases as the cumulative amount produced increases. Learning curves do not relate solely to individual learning, although some authors have attempted to restrict it in this way, using terms like "experience curves" or "progress functions" to denote group or organizational learning. But more often "learning curve" is used in the broadest sense, as it is in this article.

Learning curves are also not restricted to the measurement of low-skill labor; their effects have been observed in skills like heart surgery, for example.

Several factors contribute to the learning curve, including

♦ labor efficiency, both in production and management;

♦ improved methods and technology;

♦ product redesign, with the reduction or elimination of costly features;

♦ production standardization, with a reduction in the number of setups or changes; and

♦ effects from economics of scale.

These factors are sometimes characterized as autonomous learning (automatic gains from learning by doing) and induced learning (conscious efforts by managers to observe and improve the process).

Software development exhibits all these factors. Production standardization, for example, is exhibited by organizations that batch small maintenance changes into a few releases. This might also be interpreted as an effect from economies of scale. Greater experience with tools and applications has also been widely suggested as improving software-development productivity.

Much has been written about learning curves. Louis Yelle gives a comprehensive review.[1] Three models are the most established: the traditional model (with variants) to estimate average unit cost and more recently a model devel-

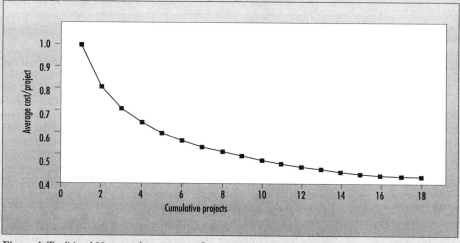

Figure A. Traditional 80-percent learning curve ($\beta = .322$).

---

cally validating models in integrated CASE settings. The three biggest tasks in implementation are locating a suitable data site, collecting the data, and validating the results.

Finding a suitable site. The best place to start looking for a site is in organizations that have already adopted integrated CASE tools. But this is no easy task for several reasons.

♦ Even if a suitable site can be found, most organizations simply do not collect the performance data necessary to quantitatively evaluate learning about integrated CASE tools. Work-hour data by project, if captured at all, may reflect sloppy or even incorrect bookkeeping. Staff members or managers may not report actual work hours if doing so will put a project over budget. Even worse, they may charge them to another project or to an overhead account, which will further compound the error if data is used for future planning.

♦ If an organization *does* keep detailed project data, it won't do much good unless

management has also kept detailed data by person or by project phase. It is easy to imagine a situation in which a new project *n* is expected to demonstrate the effect of learning but, because not enough members of project *n*–1's team are transferred to the new project, they cannot. Without data on who charged the hours (and their level of experience with the integrated CASE tool), researchers cannot readily discern this scenario.[8] Some sites may have several integrated CASE projects going on in parallel, which create multiple organizational learning curves unless management makes a significant effort to transfer the knowledge gained.

♦ Even if organizations have collected a lot of data already, other data will probably be required to carefully construct a learning curve. Practitioners are understandably concerned about demanding anything extra from an already overburdened IS staff.

Given these problems, finding a site with enough completed integrated CASE projects and a relatively similar set of team

members may seem like an impossible task. But the number of suitable sites is growing, albeit slowly, as integrated CASE catches on. Because modern technology and modern process and product measurement often go hand in hand, organizations that have adopted such tools are more likely to have modern measurement practices as well. Moreover, integrated CASE tools aren't cheap. Senior management has probably mandated the implementation of measurement to monitor the process as a prerequisite of adoption.

Thus, while practical data problems are significant impediments for most organizations to implement these models, they may prove much less formidable to early adopters of integrated CASE technology.

Collecting data. To minimize the effect on staff, researchers may have to limit the sample to a small group of hopefully representative projects. To reach a sufficient sample size, they can either use data from

oped by Linda Argote and colleagues and a model by Paul Adler and Kim Clark.

Traditional model. The earliest industrial learning curve is the Wright or cumulative-average curve, represented by

$$y = \alpha X^{-\beta} + \varepsilon \quad \beta > 0$$

where y is the average cost, α is the cost of the first unit, X is the total number of units, and β is the learning rate parameter, which can be estimated using least-squares regression after taking logarithms of both sides:

$$\ln y = \ln \alpha - \beta \ln X$$

β is sometimes expressed in percent, which reflects the percentage of decline in average cost with each doubling of cumulative volume:

$$\beta = \frac{\ln (\%)}{\ln 2}$$

Typical percentage rates observed in practice are from 70 to 95 percent. Figure A shows the curve for an 80-percent learning rate.

Smaller percentages indicate a relatively steeper learning curve, implying more rapid cost decreases. Therefore, when learning-curve researchers refer to steep learning curves, they are actually referring to a favorable event — as opposed to the popular use of the term, which implies something bad to overcome.

Recent research. The learning-curve model has been successfully used in a variety of settings and continues to be the source of significant research. Recent effort has focused on managing both the transfer and loss of learning.

The transfer of learning is the study of how knowledge gained at one site or installation is transferred to others. This transfer can be either internal, as from a pilot or leading-edge facility to the rest of the organization, or external, as in attempting to bootstrap on the efforts of other firms.

Adler and Clark describe

three types of internal learning transfer: across the development/manufacturing interface, from start-up operations to other facilities, and ongoing cooperation between facilities. In all three cases, they find evidence of sharing but also suggest that more could be done to contribute to this.

Argote and colleagues examined transfer across shipyards building Liberty ships in World War II.[2] They found that, while there was some evidence of initial learning transfer (shipyards starting later generally showed higher initial levels of productivity than earlier shipyards), no other significant learning transfers seemed to take place.

Thus both Adler and Clark and Argote and colleagues show that the transfer of learning across organizations is limited.

A topic mentioned in the learning-curve literature but rarely studied is the loss of learning, or forgetting. The literature generally assumes a

steady production process after start-up, with continuing benefits until the process is replaced. Recent experimental research conducted at Florida State University by Charles Bailey suggests that forgetting is a significant loss in procedural tasks that are interrupted for long periods. He found that the amount of forgetting was a function of the amount learned and the passage of time, but not the learning rate. The study by Argote and colleagues also noted forgetting, referring to it as the lack of persistence of learning. Their results suggest that cumulative output overstates the gains to be had from learning when the process has been significantly interrupted.

REFERENCES

1. L. Yelle, "The Learning Curve: Historical Review and Comprehensive Survey," *Decision Sciences*, Feb. 1991, pp. 302-328.
2. L. Argote, S. Beckman and D. Epple, "The Persistence and Transfer of Learning in Industrial Settings," *Management Science*, Vol. 36, No. 2, pp. 140-154.

completed projects or wait for data from future projects. The first option requires much care to ensure accurate data. Collecting historical data is often particularly problematic because many IS departments have high turnover. It is not at all unusual to begin collecting data on a completed project only to discover that the project manager or some other key individual no longer works there. Such projects may have to be excluded from analysis because records require interpretation or supplements from these key informants.

If researchers opt to use data from future projects, they should be aware that individuals collecting the data may perceive alternative uses (particularly managerial control) for it. For example, self-reported data on source lines of code or function points may be misrepresented to give the impression of high personal productivity.

Another problem in collecting future data is that the average-size firm may take a long time to generate enough new projects to make data collection meaningful. This is particularly true in evaluations of integrated CASE tools because many tools are designed to be of the greatest (perhaps any) value only on large systems. A firm is likely to do these large systems projects only infrequently, and of course, being large, they take a long time to complete.

A third problem is that the waiting period for data collection — given integrated CASE's slow adoption and relatively quick abandonment — puts research results at risk. Changes in the site's business or technology may obscure any meaningful results. As time passes, new versions of the tool will become available. These later versions may aid performance by providing more functions or greater ease of use, or they may actually hinder learning because they become more complex. Which effect dominates clearly depends on the site and tools.

An additional danger of long-term data collection is the loss of learning when tool adoption is interrupted (see box above).

Validating results. A final implementation problem is assessing the validity of the results once the research is complete. Integrated CASE tools, like other new technologies, are likely to be initiated in only one or a few specially selected pilot projects. These pilot projects may or may not be representative of systems projects as a whole.

If volunteers are solicited, there will clearly be some selection bias toward rapid technology adopters or simply staff members who are dissatisfied with their current work. Even if management selects pilot projects, the Hawthorne effect — the tendency for workers to show increased productivity under any new situation in which their performance is being monitored — may still dominate. It may, therefore be difficult to get a representative sample, and later projects may be sufficiently different to obscure learning effects.

Of course, the ultimate problem with any field study may be its external validity. Even if researchers can show the effect of an integrated CASE tool and support a causal relationship with statistical data, they cannot assume that the results will extend to other firms, even similar ones. The implementation of integrated CASE tools at one organization may have been well received by staff eager for its use, well educated in theoretical background, and gently introduced to tool mechanics through excellent training and ongoing support. The same tool at another site may have been received with hostility, with the staff feeling it had been forced on them by management.

Staff acceptance is only one example of how organizations may differ, and therefore how a tool can fail to have the same impact across sites. Differences in applications mix, technical environment, personnel, management, users, backlog, organizational structure, and history can also affect results. For example, the makeup of project team members and their experience with new technologies plays an important role. The culture of the organization — in particular, the degree of local resistance to change — is also a factor. It is important to collect learning-curve data at many sites to test the effects of differences in these environmental conditions.

Learning-curve models clearly have much to offer organizations. Besides being able to quantitatively document the productivity effects of integrated CASE tools by factoring out the learning costs, managers can use model results to estimate future projects with greater accuracy. Without this depth of understanding, managers are likely to make less-than-optimal decisions about integrated CASE and may abandon the technology too soon.

Data from the models has other, more sophisticated, uses as well, which could lead to a greater understanding of how learning occurs, what factors affect it, and how learning time can be shortened — all of which are instrumental in reducing tool-adoption costs. For example, managers can control, and to some extent anticipate, most of the benefits associated with learning.

An important research benefit would be to look at how the emerging discipline of software engineering can benefit from the knowledge these types of models provide, with emphasis on the underlying concepts of formal models developed in other, more mature engineering disciplines. Learning-curve work could provide insight into how researchers could usefully adapt concepts developed in other domains to aid the understanding of software delivery.

Another useful general outcome would be to prove the value of process measurement to software engineering. While much lip service is given to the need for and importance of measurement, its adoption has been slow and easily abandoned. But if managers continue to apply the results of measurement programs, their value will be justified and investment in them sustained. With a sound measurement base many other software-engineering process improvements may be possible. Therefore, the knowledge gained from a greater understanding of the software-technology adoption process will aid the implementation of not only integrated CASE, but also potential innovations like object-oriented technologies.

Finally, much has been written about the nationwide trend toward a service-sector economy. One related issue is the low productivity of service-sector work and the general inability to effectively measure and increase it. Software development falls in the high end of the service-sector categories, an area of increasing concern and importance for worldwide competitiveness. Increasing the understanding of software development could benefit other high-end service-sector categories as well. ◆

ACKNOWLEDGMENTS
Research support from MIT's Center for Information Systems Research and helpful comments from three anonymous referees on an early draft of this article are gratefully acknowledged.

REFERENCES
1. C. Kemerer, "Learning Curve Models for Integrated CASE Tool Management," Working Paper 231, MIT Center for Information Systems Research, Cambridge, Mass., Nov. 1991.
2. M. Shaw, "Prospects for an Engineering Discipline of Software," *IEEE Software*, Nov. 1990, pp. 15-24.
3. W. Chew, D. Leonard-Barton, and R. Bohn, "Beating Murphy's Law," *Sloan Management Rev.*, Spring 1991, pp. 5-16.
4. T.C. Jones, "Reusability in Programming: A Survey of the State of the Art," *IEEE Trans. Software Engineering*, May 1984, pp. 488-494.
5. J. Henderson and J. Cooprider, "Dimensions of IS Planning and Design Aids: A Functional Model of CASE Technology," *Information Systems Research*, Sept. 1990, pp. 227-253.
6. J. Nosek, G. Baram, and G. Steinberg, "Ease of Learning and Using CASE Software: An Empirical Evaluation," working paper, Temple University, Computer and Information Sciences Dept., Philadelphia, Mar. 1990.
7. P. Adler and K. Clark, "Behind the Learning Curve: A Sketch of the Learning Process," *Management Science*, Mar. 1991, pp. 267-281.
8. R. Banker, S. Datar, and C. Kemerer, "A Model to Evaluate Variables Impacting Productivity on Software Maintenance Projects," *Management Science*, Jan. 1991, pp. 1-18.

Chris F. Kemerer is a Douglas Drane Career Development associate professor of information technology and management at the MIT Sloan School of Management. His research interests are the measurement and modeling of software development.

Kemerer received a BS in economics and decision sciences from the Wharton School of the University of Pennsylvania and a PhD in industrial administration from Carnegie Mellon University.

He has published numerous articles on software measurement and modeling. He serves on the editorial boards of *Communications of the ACM*, *Information Systems Research*, *Journal of Organizational Computing*, *Journal of Software Quality*, and *MIS Quarterly*.

Address questions about this article to Kemerer at MIT Sloan School of Management, E53-315, 50 Memorial Dr., Cambridge, MA 02139.

How to Assess Tools Efficiently and Quantitatively

VICKY MOSLEY, *Westinghouse Electronic Systems Group*

Reprinted from *IEEE Software*, Vol. 9, No. 3, May 1992, pp. 29-32. Copyright © 1992 by The Institute of Electrical and Electronics Engineers, Inc. All rights reserved.

◆ *Over the last seven years, Westinghouse has developed a five-step method to select CASE tools. The procedure is generic, but tailorable.*

In 1984, Westinghouse purchased a tool named Use.it, but nobody wanted to use it! There were several reasons for its demise: Use.it supported a methodology that was totally unfamiliar to the engineers, was difficult to learn, was very user hostile, and hadn't been thoroughly evaluated before its introduction.

Despite an investment of more than $200,000 in purchasing, maintaining, training, and supporting this tool — all *post*evaluation procedures — Use.it was never used on any real program.

At that time, Westinghouse management decided to form a practitioners committee to help identify, evaluate, and select tools. The Software-Tools Evaluation Committee, of which I am a member, was formed in 1985. We were tasked to establish classification and evaluation criteria for software tools, primarily for VAX/VMS platforms. We created a six-page template that became the standard by which many engineers reviewed and classified tools.

In 1986, the Software Engineering Institute and Westinghouse began a joint project to develop standards for classifying and evaluating tools. I became Westinghouse's first SEI resident affiliate and helped develop the resulting tools-assessment guide.[1]

The SEI/Westinghouse guide includes

◆ A tool taxonomy that captures information like the tool name and vendor, release date, what life-cycle phases and methods it supports, key features, and the objects (like diagrams and code) it produces.

◆ Six categories of questions designed to determine how well a tool does what it was intended to do. The questionnaire comprises 140 questions divided into the categories ease of use, power, robustness, functionality, ease of insertion, and

quality of support.

When the guide was published in 1987, we were unsure how to apply the questionnaire within Westinghouse. We weren't sure if having users ask 140 questions of a prospective tool vendor would be a useful exercise or an enormous waste of time.

ON YOUR MARK

Nonetheless, the time had come to transition this instrument into use. Because the taxonomy was a subset of Westinghouse's six-page template, we decided to continue using our existing template.

We also tried to use the questionnaire, but found it not very useful in its raw form. We had no way to record our responses consistently, comprehensibly, and com-

pletely. We also tended to give more weight to questions that dealt with a tool's functionality and ease of use. So we decided to apply a 0-to-10 scoring criteria and assign a weight to *each* question, right down to the fourth or fifth decimal point. This effort took about 500 man-hours over four months.

However, when we tried to use this weighted version of the questionnaire, we were soon dismayed. It was too time-consuming and difficult to distinguish differences in scoring. What's more, assigning four- and five-digit weights to each question was overkill.

After two years, we modified our approach by minimizing the scoring to three digits and assigning the STEC's recommended weights for each category (not each question). We also tailored the method to include questions specific to

the type of tool being evaluated. Now we had a doable procedure!

GET SET

Each committee member was trained how to use the weighted assessment instrument and was assigned a set of tools to classify and evaluate. To make sure the assessments were fair, we assigned several engineers to the same tool. To establish credibility, we applied the tools on scaled-down versions of real projects, thus obtaining a more realistic assessment of what the tool could actually do.

READY

Far too often, tools assessments are completed by the product's vendor or by someone who:

♦ just scans the brochures and user manual,

♦ is unfamiliar with the tool's methods,

♦ lacks an understanding of the project or user requirements, or

♦ uses the tool for a 30-day trial on useless examples that fall short of testing the tool's functionality.

The STEC tried to avoid all these circumstances. If the tools were unavailable, we acquired evaluation copies. Our motto is "We don't believe it unless we see it!" We used only senior practitioners as evaluators — engineers who understood the methods the tool supported, how it could be applied on the project, and how it would meet their customer's requirements.

By 1988, we had set up a ShowCASE Lab in a central Westinghouse facility. The lab is open to all employees for product demonstrations, training, and evaluations of potential products. The lab promotes the "try before you buy" philosophy and, unlike the ill-fated Use.it, many projects use it!

GO!

By 1990, the STEC had evolved a five-step process.

1. Classification
2. Brief evaluation

WESTINGHOUSE TOOL CATEGORIES

CASE tools are continuously evolving. We started with about six categories in 1985 and now use 12; we plan to add a reuse category soon. With this classification scheme, you don't have to pigeonhole tools into one category or another. An evaluator can simply check off all boxes that apply. The current classification categories used at Westinghouse and some sample tools are

♦ *System simulation and modeling*: Architecture and dataflow modeling, algorithm simulation, sizing and timing tools, animated displays.

♦ *Requirements traceability*: Editors, database-management systems, and applications running on top of DBMSs.

♦ *Requirements analysis*: Context and dataflow diagrams, data dictionaries, and object-oriented analysis tools.

♦ *Design*: Structure charts, module specifications, pseudocode, code generators, and language-sensitive editors.

♦ *Code and unit test*: Compilers, language-sensitive editors, languages, code formatters, cross-compilers, linkers, and source-level debuggers.

♦ *Test and integration*: Test drivers, coverage analyzers, regression testers, and test benches.

♦ *Documentation*: Desktop-publishing systems, form-management systems, documentation templates, and overhead preparers.

♦ *Project management*: Tools in three major categories — planning and scheduling, tracking and status reporting, and costing and sizing.

♦ *Configuration management*: Mechanisms for access and version control, product baseline, and file and change management.

♦ *Quality assurance*: Checklists, histograms, graphs, charts, and tables.

♦ *Metrics*: Line counters, code-quality measures, cyclomatic-complexity measures, management measures, and other standard measures.

♦ *Other*: Reuse, data management, communication, spreadsheets, and electronic bulletin boards.

3. Quantitative assessment
4. Tailored summary
5. Consultation service

Step 1 is always completed. Whether or not any or all of the remaining steps are performed depends on the nature of the evaluation, the time and resources available, and the requirements of potential users.

Classification. Step 1 generally involves the *what* of the tool: what platform(s) it runs on, what additional software or hardware it needs, what method or techniques it supports, and what function or functions it performs. Because tools are continuously changing and evolving, it is also a good idea to capture the version or release date of the tool. To help identify a tool's *whats*, we have developed the 12 categories shown in the box on the facing page.

The 1980s witnessed a proliferation of requirements traceability, analysis, and design tools. The 1990s will witness the era of WYSIWYG documentation tools with live-link capabilities, automated test tools, metric-collection tools, reuse tools, and a new suite of reverse-engineering tools. We have also witnessed the evolution of "big tools," with smaller tools being grouped into tool sets that support a broader spectrum of uses across multiple categories. And many tools and tool sets are evolving into more of what we need — integrated environments. We will continue to modify our categories as the technology evolves.

Brief evaluation. Step 2 generally involves identifying *how well* the tool performs. This brief narrative highlights the tool's good and bad points and includes comments about the nature of the evaluation and any pertinent, crucial points about the product or vendor. Step 2 is done when time constraints preclude a detailed evaluation or when a credible, expert user can effectively summarize the tool's usefulness or uselessness.

Quantitative assessment. Step 3 is the core of the process. It is performed when we need a detailed or comparative analysis of one or more tools. The assessment instru-

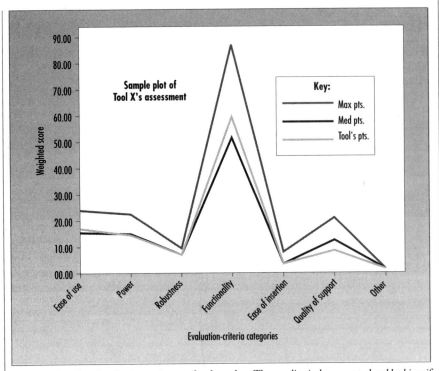

Figure 1. *Sample tool evaluation against a tailored template. The gray line is the score a tool could achieve if it received the maximum points allowed on each question in each category. The black line is the score a tool could receive if it obtained the median points allowed on each question in each category. The light gray line is the tool's actual score.*

ment is the generic set of 140 questions and a tailored set of functional questions specific to the type of tool being evaluated. The number of tailored questions can vary from 30 to 100, depending on the tool category.

We also added a seventh category to include questions omitted from the original questionnaire (such as tool cost, standards compliance, and specific user requirements). Thus, an evaluation template will have between 170 and 240 questions.

Each category is assigned a weight based on the user's requirements to, for example, emphasize functionality over power. The STEC provides a recommended weight for each category on the basis of our experience over the last seven years. We recommend, for example, that tool functionality be weighted 30 percent and power 10 percent.

A practitioner then evaluates each tool against its respective tailored template. We allow only three scores for each ques-

tion to limit the amount of subjectivity. The results are plotted as a line graph, like the one in Figure 1, to provide a pictorial representation of the overall result.

Figure 1 shows that Tool *X* scored a little above the median in ease of use, robustness, ease of insertion, and "other." It scored below the median in power and quality of support. It scored 59.40, well above the median of 51.30, in functionality, but fell far short of the maximum score of 87. In this case, the assigned weights clearly show that functionality is the top priority, followed by ease of use. However, we strongly caution against selecting a tool solely because of its score's pictorial representation.

Tailored summary. In this step, the evaluator takes the results of the assessment, extracts the critical and essential characteristics according to the user's requirements, and completes a tailored summary of what the score really represents. Table 1

TABLE 1
TAILORED SUMMARY OF TOOL X

Category	Maximum points	Median points	Points for Tool X	Comments
Ease of use	24.00	15.20	16.80	Has good user interface, but keys can't be tailored …
Power	22.00	13.60	13.00	Takes five minutes to start up and performance is slow …
Robustness	9.00	5.40	6.00	There is compatibility between versions
Functionality	87.00	51.30	59.40	Supports the methodology well, but does not do …
Ease of insertion	5.00	3.00	2.85	Has good installation procedures, but is available only on …
Quality of support	19.00	11.40	6.90	There is maintenance, but no hotline or customer-support number…
Other	1.25	0.75	0.85	Cost is extremely high; complies with X11/Motif standard …

shows the tailored summary of Tool X in an abbreviated format.

Consultation services. In Step 5, the evaluator takes the results of either the brief evaluation or the assessment and recommends the top one to three tools to potential users. But the consultation does not end here.

The STEC often assigns a trained evaluator to work with a project member to evaluate a product hands-on so that potential users can get more experience with and exposure to the recommended tool or tools. After this phase, a tool is selected. But the consultation does not end here either.

The STEC helps the project members acquire and install the tool, monitors the tool's use, and provides feedback about the tool to other projects as well as to the vendor. The feedback loop is extremely valuable because it gives the organization an opportunity to capture metrics on tool use and provides important information on the successes and failures of actually using the tool on real projects.

Tool evaluation is only the tip of the iceberg! Transitioning the tool into actual use is the rest of the iceberg.

To date, the Westinghouse STEC has classified more than 500 tools. We have compiled brief evaluations on about 25 percent of them (many of them published),[2] quantitative evaluations on the best 10 percent, and — in response to the requirements of a few projects — completed comparative evaluations on about one percent.

Our tool-evaluation process continues to evolve as the tools continue to mature and the technology advances. The process, its techniques, the tailorable templates, and its weighted criteria are very flexible.

We have presented our process to both the SEI and the Software Technology Support Center at Hill Air Force Base in Salt Lake City. The STSC is looking to leverage the Westinghouse process as it evolves into the US Defense Department's central facility for tool classification and evaluation. Both Westinghouse and the STSC seek to advance the state of the practice in using good tools for systems and software engineering and to establish standards by which we can accomplish this. ◆

REFERENCES
1. R. Firth et al., "A Guide to the Classification and Assessment of Software Engineering Tools," Tech. Report CMU/SEI-87-TR-10, Software Eng. Institute, Pittsburgh, 1987.
2. *Softwhere Newsletter*, V. Mosley, ed., 1986-1992.

Vicky Mosely is a principal engineer in the Aerospace Software-Engineering Division at Westinghouse, where she chairs two technology groups: the Software Tools Evaluation Committee and the Environment Working Group. She is a guest lecturer in tool technology at Johns Hopkins University's Applied Physics Laboratory.

Mosely received a BA in mathematics from Towson State University, Baltimore, and an MA in computer science from Johns Hopkins University.

Address questions about this article to Mosley at Westinghouse Electronic Systems Group, PO Box 746, MS 499, Baltimore, MD 21203; Internet mosely@swars.bwi.wec.com.

A Case Study of SREM

Paul A. Scheffer and Albert H. Stone, III
Martin Marietta Denver Aerospace

William E. Rzepka
Rome Air Development Center

This methodology can improve the integrity of a large software system description, but it is labor-intensive and hard to learn.

In 1979 the Rome Air Development Center, Griffiss Air Force Base, New York, initiated a program to investigate whether the Software Requirements Engineering Methodology could specify and analyze software requirements for the embedded computers that are a part of US Air Force Command, Control, Communications, and Intelligence (called C^3I) systems.[1] SREM had been developed in 1977 by TRW, Inc., under contract to the US Army Ballistic Missile Defense Advanced Technology Center. It had been specifically designed to describe and analyze real-time, stimulus-response requirements of single-computer, missile-defense systems.[2] By 1979, the question had arisen whether SREM could be applied to the man-machine interfaces, large databases, and multi-computer, distributed networks that characterize large, C^3I systems.

A C^3I system is a heterogeneous collection of people, procedures, and equipment organized to perform a mission. The specific purpose of the C^3I system is to provide the decision maker with the kind of information he or she needs to effectively manage the mission resources. Equipment typically includes aircraft, sensors, communications circuits, computers, software, shelters, etc. Primary missions include

- *Command and management.* The World Wide Military Command and Control System and North American Air Defense Command Cheyenne Mountain Complex are examples of systems that assimilate information from many sources and process it into a form high-level decision makers can use.

- *Communications.* The Strategic Air Command's Automated Total Information Network is an example of a packet-switching network that connects many military installations.

- *Surveillance and control.* The Joint Surveillance System performs peacetime surveillance of United States and Canadian air space; the Ground-Based Electro-Optical Deep Space Surveillance system is a multi-computer network for telescope-signal processing of space objects.

- *Intelligence.* The Tactical Information Processing and Interpretation system is an intelligence gathering system that involves the collection, processing, and interpretation of large information databases.

To answer the question about SREM's potential for describing C^3I systems, the Rome Air Development

Reprinted from *Computer*, Vol. 18, No. 4, April 1985, pp. 47-54.

Center effort used SREM to specify the software requirements for a small C³I subsystem. This work reached two conclusions.

First, SREM in its current state could adequately specify software requirements for command and control systems. This was demonstrated for critical C³I elements such as the man-machine interface, database, and communications. But, in addition, the evaluation uncovered some aspects of SREM that were not completely responsive to command and control system needs; and the evaluation did not seriously address the performance of the SREM system software, the effectiveness of the SREM training materials, and the utility of the user interface to the SREM tools.

These results led to the second conclusion: further evaluation of SREM on large C³I systems was needed. This effort would be a technically thorough evaluation of the capabilities of SREM for specifying and analyzing command and control software requirements, and would recommend improvements based on the evaluation. The comprehensive investigation was contracted to Martin Marietta Denver Aerospace in the fall of 1980 and was completed in the spring of 1983.[3] This article describes that work.

Background

In recent years SREM has been the focus of several studies that have either characterized its functionality with respect to some problem domain or attempted to assess the effectiveness of its procedures, specification language, and tools relative to other techniques. Stainer performed a feature comparison of SREM and PSL/PSA[4] that described strong and weak points of each technique.[5] Salwin compared SREM and PSL/PSA in the context of a Navy system for analyzing weapon system readiness data.[6] Slegel examined SREM's ability to validate requirements for maintenance and diagnostic software in a real-time command-and-control system.[7] A McDonnell Douglas group evaluated

SREM in the real-time, ballistic-missile-defense context.[8] Its report described SREM's capabilities for displaying requirements and detecting consistency errors and tool costs. Alford has reported the status of SREM's requirements development procedures, requirements specification language, support software, transfer to user organizations, and planned extensions and improvements.[9] Celko compared the specification properties and error-detection capabilities of SREM, PSL/PSA, and IORL[10] as a result of applying these techniques to an Army management information system; he concluded that using any automated tool is superior to manual validation of requirements.[11]

Scope

SREM is a formal, integrated approach to requirements engineering activities. It begins when the system requirements analysis has identified system functions and functional interfaces between subsystems and system operating rules, and the top-level system requirements have been allocated to the computing resource. It is designed to induce certain qualities often lacking in the specification of many large software systems, including internal consistency, explicitness, testability, and traceability.

In addition to the step-by-step requirements engineering techniques, SREM includes a machine-processable, "English-like," Requirements Statement Language and a Requirements Engineering and Validation System to automatically process the requirements statements and to perform a wide range of analyses and simulations on its centralized database. REVS constitutes the automated-tools part of SREM. It uses a relational database (called the Abstract System Semantic Model) to capture requirements processed from RSL.

Functionally, REVS consists of six software components that create the ASSM and examine its contents:

- *RSL (RSL translator)*. Translates requirements and creates the ASSM;
- *Rslxtnd (RSL extend)*. Augments/extends the RSL language elements;
- *Radx (analysis/data extraction)*. Extracts information from the ASSM for analysis and documentation, identifies ASSM subsets for consistency/completeness, and analyzes ASSM content for dataflow;
- *Simgen (simulation generation)*. Builds a simulation package;
- *Simxqt (simulation execute)*. Performs the simulation exercises; and
- *Simda (simulation data analysis)*. Analyzes and documents the simulation.

In the evaluation of SREM that we describe in this article, the primary mechanism consisted of applying it to two typical Air Force systems through the existing specifications that defined these systems. With this exercise, three evaluation aspects could be examined:

- The ability of SREM to describe the software requirements of C³I systems;
- Where SREM can best be applied in the Air Force software life cycle; and
- The quality of SREM training.

We focus on the first and second evaluation aspects, and discuss each using a common format: assessment goals, evaluation methods, derived results, and recommendations. We address training from the perspective of important evaluation issues.

Applying SREM to C³I systems

Goals. To determine SREM's applicability to C³I systems, two areas were examined: specification scope and requirements analysis capabilities.

The first addressed SREM's ability to describe all characteristics of C³I systems. The characteristics of C³I systems that distinguish them from other systems and the ones that the evaluation project tried to express in RSL are

- Real-time and near real-time processing;
- The ability to present data to an analyst and react to his decisions;
- The ability to deal with real-world objects that simultaneously are users of C^3I data, providers of C^3I data, and objects about which the C^3I system maintains data;
- The ability to manipulate static data, such as cartographic or hypsographic information, as well as such dynamic data as tank position or sensor status;
- Distributed processing; and
- Communications processing.

The second area of concern was SREM's capacity to automatically detect such specification errors as requirement ambiguities, requirement inconsistencies, and specification incompleteness.

Methods. SREM was applied to two systems: the Communications Switch Interface Development system and the Advanced Sensor Exploitation system. CSID is an interactive system for compatibility analysis of communications switching system interface data that is currently operational at the Rome Air Development Center. It is described in a design specification.[12] ASE is a distributed C^3I system responsible for gathering, correlating, and disseminating sensor information. The ASE is described in a software requirements specification.[13] The SREM technique was used to interpret requirements, produce an ASSM, and analyze each system's specification. Functional simulations were only applied to selected ASE subsystems.

The initial input to SREM is a system specification that is translated into RSL and interpreted to determine the interfaces with the outside world, the messages across these interfaces, and the required processing relationships and flows (Figure 1). Next, the details

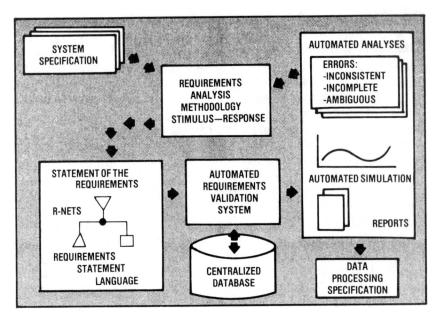

Figure 1. Software Requirements Engineering Methodology.

of the functional requirements, including all of the input/output data relationships, their attributes, maximum and minimum values, allowed ranges for non-numeric data, and the processing steps, are completed. RSL is used to input these requirements, described as Requirement Networks, or R_nets, into the REVS, which in turn builds the centralized database called the Abstract System Semantic Model. The automated static analyzer, Radx, is executed to check for errors in element attributes or relationships between elements. When all information has been input and all errors corrected, the result is a formal functional requirements specification.

Before the requirements specification can be considered complete, a system simulation is needed to verify that the envisioned system's interfaces and processing relationships behave as required. Simple functional models are created in Pascal for each of the processing steps that have been identified. These models are embedded directly in the RSL and used as input to a simulation generation function to create a behavioral model of the functional requirements.

When the processing relationships have been verified, performance re-

quirements must still be specified for the functional requirements so that system performance constraints can be tested. Each performance requirement will constrain a processing path within the system. This method of establishing performance requirements allows the traceability of requirements and highlights the system structure for review.

If it is also necessary to verify that the requirements specification is analytically feasible, one more simulation step, called the analytical feasibility demonstration, is performed. This simulation uses actual algorithms of the intended system instead of simple functional models to establish that the identified software requirements can be tested.

All REVS components were used in evaluating SREM. The RSL translator function was used to construct an ASSM for both applications, ASE and CSID. The Radx function served three purposes: first, the Radx analysis capabilities were employed to verify the consistency of the ASSM by examining the attributes associated with the ASSM elements, tracing detected errors to one of two places, either the RSL description or the originating requirements documentation; second,

Table 1. RSL production data.

SPEC	DOCU-MENT SIZE (PAGES)	MAN-HOURS [1]	TIME (MONTHS)	ASSM SIZE				
				LINES RLS	NUMBER ELE-MENTS[2]	PERCENT DATA[3]	PERCENT PROC[4]	PERCENT OTHER[5]
CSID	196	7498	10	10353	1109	53	40	7
ASE	515	11277	20	35550	3016	46[6]	8.8[6]	44.9[6]
Total	711	18775	30	45903	4125	-	-	-

NOTES:
1. Engineering hours to translate and analyse specification.
2. RSL elements such as data, R__net.
3. Messages, Data, Entity__Classes, etc.
4. R__nets, Subnets, Alphas, etc.
5. Sources, Originating__Requirements, etc.
6. Averaged over six subsystems (last three columns only).

the same analysis capabilities determined the completeness of the formal specification by examining the relationships between elements; and third, the Radx capabilities for user-defined analysis were used to produce a document approximating a MIL-STD-490 type B-5 functional requirements specification. The language extension function, Rslxtnd, of REVS enhanced data requirements descriptions. The Simgen function was used in conjunction with the Simxqt and Simda functions to exercise the dataflow logic. Models of the R_net processing steps were added to allow the Simgen function to construct a simulation program executed by Simxqt with the results analyzed by Simda.

Results. Table 1 shows, for each system studied, the size of the specification used, the time spent creating the ASSM databases, and the size of the ASSMs produced. The following statistics can be derived from the table:

- Approximately 19 lines of correct RSL were produced per eight-hour workday;
- Approximately 1.8 correct RSL element definitions were produced per eight-hour workday;
- While error-occurrence data were not kept for CSID, about 100 specification errors were found when applying the SREM (not necessarily REVS) to ASE, resulting in about 120 man-hours

expended per error discovered; and

- A significant disparity occurs in the composition of the databases (Figure 2); in particular, the amounts of information required to describe control flow (40 percent versus 9 percent) and overhead activities, such as configuration management, traceability, and commentary (7 percent versus 45 percent), varied significantly between specifications examined.

The learning curve for the RSL must be considered as well. While RSL was produced at approximately 11 lines per day initially, experienced analysts were able to achieve about 25 lines per day. A similar difference was experienced in the production rate of RSL element definitions (1.2 versus 2.1 elements per day).

Analyst effort needed to achieve these productivity rates averaged 26.4 man-hours per page of specification. Since the project consisted of only the CSID and ASE data points, this average is not considered a reliable predictor of validation effort.

A detailed analysis of specification flaw exposure was done for the ASE system. Table 2 shows error classes and how they were found. Clearly evident here is that the strength of SREM is its methodology as opposed to its automated validation tools. The structure of the methodology guides the analyst to an understanding of the re-

quirements through an iterative learning process that exposes requirement flaws.

In examining the ASE error data and its associated analyst ($372,000) and computer ($20,400) costs, we can conclude that the cost to detect each error was approximately $4785. This result appears to have been influenced by several factors. First, many of the textual descriptions in the ASE system specification were generated from DeMarco dataflow diagrams, resulting in a high-quality specification with relatively few errors. Second, the analysts reported that not all of the errors detected (about 10 percent) were documented. Third, in arriving at the cost/error figure, it was assumed that all of the man-hours (and hence costs) associated with the ASE evaluation were devoted to error detection. However, a significant portion was expended on other activities, such as configuration management, traceability, and textual descriptions. A final perspective from which to view this data is the total cost of developing the ASE system. Approximately $7.5 million has been invested in the design and implementation of the ASE. Hence, the cost of using SREM to specify and analyze the ASE system has been about five percent of the total system development cost.

Caution must be used in comparing the raw error-correction costs from the SREM study to other cost studies published in the literature. The instability of dollar-values over time, and hence labor cost, is a significant variable, as is the influence of two techniques (that is, manual and SREM) since one may pre-expose errors to the other. Moreover, it is not possible to determine how many errors each technique misses. The conclusion that can be reached from these data is that the application of a disciplined methodology like SREM is a cost-effective means of analyzing software requirements.

All of the attributes that characterize C^3I systems were contained in one or both of the specifications. The real-time and near real-time phenomena present throughout the ASE specification proved very difficult to express because many timing requirements spanned several R_nets. RSL is limited to describing such requirements only along control flow paths within an R_net. Decision-making characteristics proved difficult to express when applied to man-machine interfacing in prompt-driven systems. Throughout translation of the CSID specification, the project team found it necessary to add state flags and their related conditional data to describe and correctly associate the CSID user's reply to the prompt that evoked the reply. The additions severely reduced the clarity of the requirements in the ASSM.

C^3I real-world objects were easily transformed into RSL with the element types ENTITY_CLASS and EN-TITY_TYPE. The data requirement characteristics were described easily by attributes associated with the element types DATA and FILE. RSL is capable of describing only distributed processing and parallel processing requirements in which the sequence is not important. This generality in processing structure precludes detailed description of distributed and parallel processing situations where time sequences are important, and so SREM is most appropriately used for software requirements analysis or high-level design activities. Communications characteristics are easily described with appropriate RSL attributes of specific element types (for example, value range); detailed information (for example, baud rate) can be associated with the characteristics by appropriate extensions to RSL using the language extension function (Rslxtnd).

Recommendations. The sample application of SREM to these test systems clearly demonstrated the benefit of disciplined techniques in requirements analysis. A formalized scheme uncovers many problems and questions that help improve the integrity of the system description. But this is true of any disciplined approach to requirements analysis: benefits

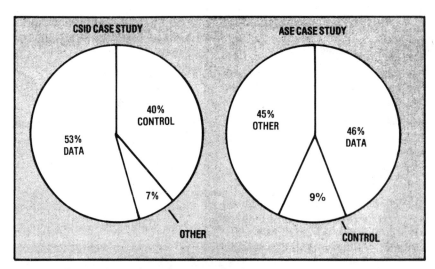

Figure 2. Comparison of requirements databases.

outweigh costs because flaws are detected early and are not permitted to permeate the system.

The major recommendations that relate specifically to C^3I applicability concern parallel processing and distributed processing capabilities. For appropriate detail, the RSL must be modified to explicitly describe parallel and distributed processing. The RSL modifications would in turn require the modification of Radx to extract and analyze the new information, as well as the modification of Simgen so parallel and distributed processing can be portrayed within the simulations.

Role of SREM in the software life cycle

Goals. The goal here was to determine in which phase or phases of the software life cycle SREM is most appropriate. This goal was approached from three directions:

- Assessment of the methodological technique prescribed for using SREM;
- Evaluation of the ability of the REVS software tools to support SREM; and
- Determination of the best placement of SREM within the software life cycle used by the Air Force.

The term "software life cycle" is used to identify the processes that occur in the development of software systems from initial conception to final realization in an operational environment. The following phases and associated processes are considered.

- *Conceptual.* The need for a system to solve a particular set of problems is identified, with feasibility assessments, tradeoff studies, and analyses being performed. Requirements for computer resources are allocated. The description of the system takes the

Table 2. ASE error data summary.

CLASS	NUMBER	% OF TOTAL	HOW EXPOSED
Inconsistency/misuse	30	36	80% by analyst; 20% by REVS
Ambiguity/lack of detail	17	21	100% by analyst
Incompleteness/non-use	35	43	100% by analyst
	82	100	

form of an initial system specification.

- *Requirements definition.* Requirements are defined for system functions, interfaces, performance, and such non-functional issues as safety, human factors, and reliability. A data dictionary is produced.

- *Design.* The specification for the system envisioned in the requirements phase is transformed into an overall design of how the system is to accomplish its goals. The transformation involves the allocation of system functions to hardware and/or software, a description of the objects the system is to operate on, and a description of the algorithms to be used in operating on those objects.

- *Coding-and-checkout.* The design is translated into a computer language. It is then executed to evaluate its performance.

- *Test-and-integration.* The resulting program is tested to ensure that the software performs as intended, and the system, as implemented, fulfills all system requirements.

- *Operational.* The system is in operation and must be maintained. The maintenance process is invoked to correct problems not previously encountered or to change the system as the needs of its users change.

Methods. As its name suggests, SREM is intended specifically for requirements analysis. Requirements analysis involves functional specification and data description that occur in both the requirements-definition and design phases of the life cycle. The first part of the methodology evaluation addressed whether SREM was an effective technique for defining unambiguous and testable requirements. The second part was a comparative one, to determine whether the requirements produced were of sufficient quality that derived designs would be

of higher quality than those produced without the benefit of SREM. Hence, SREM was evaluated by

- Examining the consistency and completeness of the requirements produced;
- Examining the REVS tools products for information content, tool maturity, and utility; and
- Comparing designs produced from both the original specifications (CSID and ASE) and from the translations of those specifications into RSL.

To place SREM correctly in the requirements-definition and design phases of the software life cycle and to identify how well it supported requirements analysis, the completed requirements databases (ASSMs) were using as the basis for validating the original specifications. Databases were built for the CSID system and three ASE subsystems (ASE, C³I, and NELS). Simultaneously, designs were produced in a conventional fashion by top-down decomposition expressed through Nassi-Schneiderman charts by using only the software specification documents. Figure 3 shows this comparison scheme. The resulting designs were compared on common bases of design walkthroughs, McCabe's complexity measures and Myer's reliability measures,[3] and by subjectively determining if the design characteristics of hierarchical construction and levels of abstraction and information hiding were adequately supported by SREM.

Results. The SREM proved to be of great value for the task of requirements analysis. This structured approach aided the requirements analyst in identifying inconsistencies and ambiguities in the specification as the methodology progressed through all of its steps. However, SREM utility appears to lie within a fairly narrow range of the life cycle. It was developed to specify software requirements after the system requirements analysis phase has been completed, but before any detailed processing algorithms have been formed. The consensus of the

analysts using SREM was that its strengths are defining, correcting, or analyzing software-specific requirements of the system.

The RSL Translator cannot adequately recover from a syntax error and continue its error-detection process as if the previous error did not occur. As a result, the phenomena of RSL syntax errors being produced by a previous error was prevalent throughout the entire specification-translation process and caused the project team to become very sensitive to the quality of the RSL syntax being entered into the ASSM.

The Simgen function of REVS was applied to two of the ASE subsystems. The Simgen function itself will automatically run an ASSM data analysis (Radx) every time a simulator generation is attempted. Valuable time and resources may be unnecessarily expended if no significant changes are made to the simulator definition. Moreover, Simgen does not maintain any kind of "error status" flag on the results of the Radx analysis, so that the simulator generation will be run to completion even though the preceding Radx step was in error.

The evaluation of the designs produced from both RSL specifications and the original specification documents (Figure 3) showed no clear advantage for either technique. Both sets of designs were approximately equal in complexity and modularity according to the measures used. However, a controlled experiment was not intended, and the same design team was used for both versions, which certainly influenced the result.

Recommendations. For designs produced directly from specifications or RSL, controlled experiments must be performed to collect sufficient data and to draw conclusions. We recommend that such experiments be conducted.

While the SREM technique itself proved to be valuable in identifying specification problems, REVS left much to be desired. The RSL translator was inefficient and performed error recovery inconsistently; both of these problems should be corrected before REVS is released for general use. Radx has similar problems. Dataflow analysis should be decoupled for Simgen and placed under user control. When a simulation's dataflow has been analyzed once, and as long as it is not modified, the simulation should be executable without another dataflow analysis.

In general, REVS needs to be made more efficient in terms of the computer resources used and convenience. Several basic structural changes would improve the REVS package. The changes to consider are

- Partition the predefined Radx analyses into smaller executable pieces so the Vax version is comparable in modularity to the CDC version.

- Further investigate Vax multitasking to accomplish more parallel activities (expand on simple foreground-background concept).

- The DBMS technique should not use its own paging scheme, which encourages thrashing in a virtual memory system.

- REVS initialization requires inordinate time, indicating extensive processing at each startup. Table-driven or other predefined structures could reduce resource consumption.

- The command language facilities would be improved with a hierarchical Help structure, more detailed prompting levels (indicating which subsystems are available, providing requests for needed input, signaling when a function is complete), and elaborating numeric error codes with meaningful messages.

- Decoupling RSL processing from database creation (syntax-only check) to reduce the time and costs associated with RSL translation.

Training evaluation issues

Training is an important element in the successful integration of any methodology into the infrastructure of

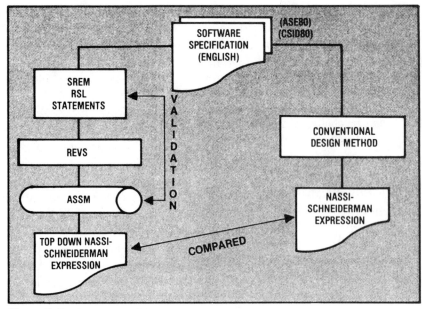

Figure 3. System comparison scheme.

a software development organization. The organization must determine its availability and quality prior to committing to its routine use. To help in making this determination, it should consider at least three aspects of training. First, the planning and logical structure of the course must be examined with respect to

- *Audience considerations.* What is the target audience and does the course address its needs? Can the course material be reasonably covered in the time allowed?

- *Course overview.* Are the objectives of both the methodology and the training clearly stated?

- *Planned activities.* Do the class exercises support the material covered in the lecture? Is sufficient hands-on experience included?

- *Progress evaluation.* Are criteria given so student progress may be evaluated? Are the criteria related to observable student behavior?

- *Course summary.* Is provision made for summarizing or reviewing difficult concepts?

Second, course execution must be considered, including

- *Teaching methods.* Is the quality and amount of instructor-student

interaction adequate? Are discussions encouraged? Are examples used to clarify difficult concepts?

- *Environment.* Are the conditions under which the course is taught comfortable and conductive to learning?

Third, course materials must be evaluated for utility in both learning and using the methodology.

Data gathered during the ASE case study provides some interesting insights into the nature of the requirements engineering process using the SREM model:

- The work of requirements analysts is predominantly the definition, description, and configuration management of data. Process (control flow) descriptions amount to only nine percent of the specifications produced.

- Analyst productivity was 19 lines of formal specification language per day. This is about the same as some higher order programming languages, but is only about half of the productivity rate of Fortran. The rate is probably attributable to the large amount (45 percent) of descriptive information contained in the specifications.

- The cost of learning formal requirements engineering techniques is significant. Analyst productivity during the learning period (first specification) was only one-half of its rate while generating a second specification.

- Requirements engineering, like software development, is highly labor intensive. Computer analysis costs accounted for only five percent of budget.

The evaluation showed that SREM is a viable approach for specifying C^3I software requirements. As with any new and complex technology, however, problems have been encountered. The evaluation team has recommended changes to the SREM specification language, analysis tools, and training.

Since the time of this evaluation, TRW has made several improvements to the internal organization and implementation of REVS, such as a complete reorganization and recoding of the database management system, reportedly improving performance by a factor of 70. Also, RADC has initiated an enhancement effort to improve the "user friendliness" of REVS. R_nets graphics, electronic-forms entry of RSL and REVS commands, user Help facilities, improved error detection, recovery and diagnostics, and requirements documentation generation tools will be available in the fall of 1985. A users group is being organized to distribute and maintain the enhanced REVS software. □

Acknowledgments

The authors wish to thank the following people for their diligent efforts and assistance during the SREM evaluation: Roger Weber of RADC; Chris Beall, Bev Castor, Jim Fullerton, Dave Hartschuh, and Susan Madison of Martin Marietta Denver Aerospace.

References

1. W. E. Rzepka, "Using SREM to Specify Command and Control Software Requirements," technical report RADC-TR-82-319, Rome Air Development Center, Griffiss AFB, NY, Dec. 1982.

2. M. W. Alford, "A Requirements Engineering Methodology for Real-Time Processing Requirements," *IEEE Trans. Software Engineering,* Vol. SE-3, No. 1, Jan. 1977, pp. 366-374.

3. A. H. Stone et al. *"SREM Evaluation, Final Report,"* RADC technical report, contract F30602-80-0272, Apr. 1983, 2 vols.

4. D. Teichroew and E. A. Hershey, "PSL/PSA: A Computer-Aided Technique for Structured Documentation and Analysis of Information Processing Systems," *IEEE Trans. Software Engineering,* Vol. SE-3, No. 1, Jan. 1977.

5. H. M. Stainer, "An Evaluation of PSL/PSA and RSL/REVS—Two Computer-Assisted Software Requirements/Specification/Description Tools," technical report FS-76-205, Fleet Systems Dept., Johns Hopkins University, Applied Physics Laboratory, Laurel, Md., Oct. 1976.

6. A. E. Salwin, "A Test Case Comparison of URL/URA and RSL/REVS," technical report FS-77-161, Fleet Systems Dept., Johns Hopkins University, Applied Laboratory, Laurel, Md., July 1977.

7. R. C. Slegel, "Applying SREM to the Verification and Validation of an Existing Software Requirements Specification," *Proc. Compsac78.*

8. "SREM Evaluation Results Summary," technical report, McDonnell Douglas, Huntington Beach, Calif., Oct. 1978.

9. M. W. Alford, "Software Requirements Engineering Methodology (SREM) at the Age of Four," *Proc. Compsac80,* Oct. 1980, pp. 366-374.

10. "IORL Language Reference Manual Version 2," technical manual, Teledyne Brown Engineering, Dec. 1982.

11. J. Celko, J. S. Davis, and J. Mitchell, "A Demonstration of Three Requirements Language Systems," *Sigplan Notices,* Vol. 18, No. 1, Jan. 1983.

12. *CSID Interpreter Software Requirements Document,* Harris Corporation, 1980.

13. K. Lubbes et al., *The Advanced Sensor Exploitation (ASE) Analysis/Design Report,* Pattern Analysis and Recognition Corporation, 1980.

Paul A. Scheffer is manager of software engineering research at Martin Marietta Denver Aerospace, where he has been leading the design and development of an integrated software engineering environment. In addition to research and development in software techniques and tools, he has led other application software development projects, been involved in the Ada effort, and served as program manager for various government agencies. Prior to joining Martin Marietta, he worked for Planning Research Corporation, MITRE, and the federal government.

Scheffer is an IEEE member and received a BS degree in mathematics and an MS in computer science from Purdue in 1964 and 1971, respectively.

Albert H. Stone III is now with the Computer Languages Section of the Software R&D Laboratory at Hewlett Packard's Fort Collins System Division. His primary interest is in the understanding and application of advanced software engineering techniques to the software development process. Prior to joining H-P, he worked at several aerospace companies, where his interests included the development of metrics for measuring and predicting facets of the software development process, as well as tools for modifying that process. He has taught courses at Metropolitan State University and has participated in the IEEE Software Reliability Standards Working Group. He received an IEEE Computer Society outstanding paper award at the Seventh International Conference on Software Engineering. Stone received his Bachelor's degree in Mathematics from San Jose State University in 1976, and is pursuing a Master's degree in Computer Science at Colorado State University.

William E. Rzepka is a guest editor of this issue of *Computer.* His photograph and biography appear on page 12.

Questions about this article can be directed to Paul A. Scheffer, Martin Marietta Denver Aerospace, Mailstop S8030, PO Box 179, Denver CO 80201.

How To Lose Productivity With Productivity Tools

Elliot J. Chikofsky
Index Technology Corporation

Productivity tools are only part of the solution to achieving productivity in system development. Management practices of the user organization regarding the use of tools have to be as effective at fostering productivity as the tools themselves.

Organizations introduce software tools, methods, and Computer-Aided Software Engineering (CASE) environments to improve productivity and to enhance their ability to deliver meaningful, consistent, and complete projects in a timely manner. But many organizations have found that these tools require more effective management approaches to achieve these objectives. Without reviewing their management practices, organizations unknowingly lose the very productivity benefits they strove to achieve.

Misconceptions and Pitfalls

There are many common misconceptions and pitfalls which impede the effectiveness of tools and methods. Most of them are caused by an organization's explicit and implicit management decisions surrounding the use of tools. Together, these pitfalls form a strategy for losing the productivity gains that the organization thinks it has achieved:

• Underestimate the Effort Required

Tools tend to take a lot more time and effort than we initially think they do. There are many examples of organizations failing to comprehend and allocate the resources required for successfully introducing the tools and scaling the learning curve.

© 1987. Index Technology Corporation.

• Introduce a Savior

Tools have often been brought in as the salvation of projects in crisis - the worst possible scenario for tool introduction. Projects which are already projected to be overdue and over budget are unsuitable candidates for new technology, a fact which is all too often ignored.

• Apply the Same Tool in the Same Way to All Projects

Tools in place are often applied to every problem - without examining whether they are really appropriate solutions. The adage "if you have a hammer in hand, every problem begins to look like a nail" is particularly true of the recent history of software tools.

• Fail to Customize the Tool to the Need

Tools are often introduced without adequately tailoring them to the organizational environment. The existing facilities of the tool may never have been examined to choose appropriate defaults for the project at hand, and to select project management options. Further, the tool may not have been constructed for adaptation. There may, in fact, be another model or variation which would be more appropriate.

• Presume Organizational Stasis

Having chosen the right tool for the job, an organization may have failed to notice that the job has changed.

• Have the First Student Train the Rest

Training of users is given insufficient support, often treated as overhead or holiday boondoggles. In many organizations, the first person to attend a training class is expected to come back to the office and teach everyone else.

Reprinted from *Productivity: Progress, Prospects, and Payoff*, June 1988, pp. 1-4. Used by permission.

• Ignore the Tool's Intended Purpose

The reality of the intended job in the organization may match the apparent purpose of the tool, but may not match the developer's intended purpose of the tool. Many copies of early analysis and design tools have been put to use as over-qualified word processors, with little regard to their analytic facilities.

• Fail to Re-Examine Tools in Use

Without periodic re-examination, many user practices become the accepted or "proper" way to use the tool, without regard for their overall impact on productivity.

• Blame the Tool

No matter what happens, it's the tool's fault. Tools are easy scapegoats and get blamed for a lot of management inattention.

• Fail to Define Productivity

Most tools are promoted and acquired based upon objectives dealing with productivity, yet most organizations have not considered what they mean by productivity. Without a viable definition of the organization's productivity objective, effective measures of progress are not possible. As the Cheshire Cat said to Alice, if you don't know where you want to go, which direction you go doesn't matter.

• Fail to Recognize Economics

It is important to keep in mind the economic incentives for tool use: the profit motive. A productivity tool's purpose is to allow the user to do more with the same or less resources. More might be measured in volume, quality, or shortened time.

In deciding to introduce the tool, someone concluded that the benefits outweighed the costs. The costs for introducing tools are most often very visible: software, training, computer facilities. Benefits are less visible, less tangible. They may be in terms of savings; improvement in quality of products; improvement in productivity; the ability to tackle otherwise unmanageable problems. Benefits are usually harder to measure than costs, and clearly take much more time to accumulate.

Organizations often have only vague notions of the benefits to be achieved. In examining the use of existing tools, it is useful to ask some key questions: Is management still waiting for the benefits to be realized? Who is expecting the benefits: specific users, first-level management, top-level management? Are those benefits still applicable to the continued use of the tool?

Failure Begins in Tool Acquisition

Many of the problems of tool use are direct results of an organization's approach to the introduction of tools. There are five key factors which characterize the acquisition of productivity tools:

• Organizations often shop for methods and tools without well-defined goals.

Many organizations have "Tool Finder" as an explicit or implicit job role, charged with acquiring technology. This has resulted in the large number of organizations which have "at least one of everything" in the way of software tools, and has been responsible for the long advertised lists of well-known corporate clients. Unfortunately, many of the organizations with tool finders have not assigned responsibility for the successful introduction of discovered tools into user projects. Thus, many of the acquired methods or tools have never made it beyond the initial evaluation phase. Many of those which have gone beyond initial evaluation have ended up in pilot projects with insufficient support from management or with inadequate interest from, and interaction with, the real potential users.

By contrast, the transition-successful tool finder relies on a well-defined set of objectives, often the result of corporate strategic, or project management tactical, planning efforts. Pilot projects are most successful when planned with the informed and interested participation of users and management.

• Methods and tools work well in the small but have had difficulty in the large.

New methods and tools are introduced with astounding frequency, and often receive fanfare in the literature well before they have been tried on real-life projects. The pressure for researchers, particularly in academic environments, to create and publish new approaches as soon as they can adds fuel to the fire. But organizations have often found that methods which work well on small examples, or "in the lab", need to be reconsidered and revised to meet the needs of large projects in the field.

Through the use of well-planned pilot projects, organizations can identify the correct scope in which new methods and tools can succeed, and where they need to be engineered to the appropriate scale.

• Organizations don't adopt methods, they adapt them.

For a method to be accepted in an organization, it must adapt to the corporate culture. This adaptation occurs in several ways. The project management procedures of the organization provide a framework into which the products of the method must be fit. The contractual obligations of the organization constrain, and often mandate, the deliverables of the development process.

Many organizations looking to acquire methods have not been satisfied with implementing the methods in "off the shelf" form. Instead, they have selected what they consider to be the best and most applicable aspects of several methods, often covering different life cycle phases or different modeling perspectives, and have welded them together into a new corporate method. (For an example of a corporate integration of methods, see Kathleen Mendes' article "Structured Systems Analysis: A Technique to Define Business Requirements" in the Summer 1980 edition of the Sloan Management Review.)

The adaptation of methods means that tools to support methods must be able to adapt to be successful. The best tools are able to evolve with the organization's needs without extensive intervention by the tool developer.

• Organizations and people do not like drastic change.

Methods which require analysts or project groups to work in a manner which departs significantly from their experience and understanding have been harder to introduce and get accepted. This implies that it will be quite difficult to change to better methods which are more demanding, recognizing the uphill effort needed to gain acceptance.

By designing new methods to better capitalize on familiar aspects and procedures of the potential audience, it should be possible to improve the implementation process and aid their acceptance.

• The abundance of diverse tools encourages "acquisition gridlock".

With so many alternative approaches (and lack of consensus) regarding software engineering tools and methods, management finds itself without reasonable criteria to make informed decisions. This is further compounded by the lack of identified goals discussed above. The drive to examine each and every tool on the market for the "best" solution has caused many organizations to go into a form of acquisition gridlock. Another new tool entering the marketplace causes a new round of deliberation.

Organizations which have broken the cycle early and have chosen some initial tool set, knowing full-well that it was not a perfect choice, have better handled the technology introduction hurdle. These organizations are now better prepared to receive and utilize second- and later-generation tools.

Failing the Learning Curve

Most people view the learning curve as something the organization goes through once to achieve productive efficiency.

Many organizations keep repeating the learning curve. By not having mechanisms in place to preserve and exchange expertise between project teams or departments, they implicitly encourage projects to cover the same ground again. In such cases, the organization never quite attains the productivity benefits it should expect from the effort put in.

The Learning Curve

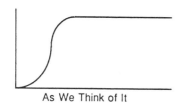

As We Think of It

As Many Organizations Practice It

The learning curve is not a rise to a plateau. Organizations can lose the productivity they've gained by allowing what they've learned to decay over time.

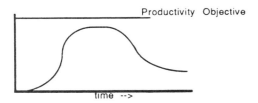

Productivity Objective

time -->

There are, however, various techniques which organizations have used effectively to manage the Learning Curve and stop reinventing the wheel:

- Providing meaningful support to new projects and users, regardless of political boundaries.

- Tailoring training to the user audience; including meaningful problems, examples.

- Explaining standards and conventions; providing "how to" documentation.

- Making the materials from prior projects accessible.

- Applying the tool in levels with new users - matching features of the tool to the needs and levels of expertise of the new users.

- Avoiding the presumption that someone who has been to one class can train the rest of the new users.

- Revising conventions and standards to reflect real project experience.

Conclusions

There are many ways in which an organization can unknowingly fail to realize the benefits expected from productivity tools. Operational issues, the tool acquisition process, and the treatment of the learning curve each contribute to a potential loss of productivity. By periodically re-examining its explicit and implicit management decisions regarding tools, organizations can be sure that they are getting the value they need out of tool technology.

This presentation is based in part on a paper entitled "Issues in the Transfer of Software Engineering Tool Technology" from the November 1987 IEEE/ACM/SEI Workshop on Transferring Software Engineering Tool Technology.

Biography

Mr. Elliot Chikofsky is Director of Research & Technology at Index Technology Corporation, maker of the Excelerator line of CASE products. He also teaches graduate courses in Software Engineering and Database Management Systems at Northeastern University.

He was guest editor of IEEE Software's March 1988 issue on CASE, and is the General Chair of the upcoming 2nd International Workshop on CASE (in cooperation with the IEEE Computer Society). From 1981 through 1983, he chaired the Productivity Tools and Technology Committee of the IBM user group Share. He has been a consultant in the area of applying software engineering tools since the late 70's.

Elliot J. Chikofsky, Index Technology Corporation, One Main Street, Cambridge, MA 02142; (617) 494-8200 x552

BIBLIOGRAPHY

(arranged alphabetically by principal author)

1. *Agents of Change: Managing the Introduction of Automated Tools,* B. Bouldin, Prentice-Hall, Englewood Cliffs. N.J., 1989.

2. *Information Systems Development: Principles of Software Engineering,* A.F. Case, Prentice-Hall, Englewood Cliffs, N.J., 1986.

3. *Software Engineering Environments,* R.N. Charette, Intertext/McGraw-Hill, New York, N.Y., 1986.

4. *Peopleware,* T. DeMarco and T. Lister, Dorset House, New York, N.Y., 1987.

5. *Computer-Aided Systems Engineering,* H. Eisner, Prentice-Hall, Englewood Cliffs, N.J., 1988.

6. *CASE: Using Software Development Tools,* A.S. Fisher, John Wiley & Sons, New York, N.Y., 1988.

7. *CASE: The Methodologies, The Products, and The Future,* C. Gane, Prentice-Hall, Englewood Cliffs, N.J., 1990.

8. *Analyzing Systems,* J.A. Kowal, Prentice-Hall, Englewood Cliffs, N.J., 1988.

9. *CASE is Software Automation,* C. McClure, Prentice-Hall, Englewood Cliffs, N.J., 1989.

10. *Three Rs of Software Automation: Reengineering, Repository, Reusability,* C. McClure, Prentice-Hall, Englewood Cliffs, N.J., 1992.

11. *Transferring Software Engineering Tool Technology,* S. Przybylinski and P.J. Fowler, eds., IEEE Computer Society Press, Los Alamitos, Calif., 1988.

12. *Software System Design: Description and Analysis,* W.E. Riddle and J.C. Wileden, IEEE Computer Society Press, Los Alamitos, Calif., 1980.

13. *Software Design: Concepts and Methods,* W. P. Stevens, Prentice-Hall, Englewood Cliffs, N.J., 1991.

14. *CASE: Concepts and Implementation,* L.E. Towner, McGraw-Hill, New York, N.Y., 1989.

15. *Software Development Environments,* A.I. Wasserman, ed., IEEE Computer Society Press, Los Alamitos, Calif., 1981.

16. *Decline and Fall of the American Programmer,* E. Yourdon, Prentice-Hall, Englewood Cliffs. N.J., 1992.

17. *Proceedings: Fourth International Workshop on CASE,* IEEE Computer Society Press, Los Alamitos, Calif., 1990.

18. *Proceedings: Fifth International Workshop on CASE,* IEEE Computer Society Press, Los Alamitos, Calif., 1992.

19. *Proceedings: Symposium on the Assessment of Quality Software Development Tools,* IEEE Computer Society Press, Los Alamitos, Calif., 1992.

ABOUT THE AUTHOR

ELLIOT CHIKOFSKY chairs the IEEE Computer Society's Technical Committee on Software Engineering and is a member of the Computer Society's Board of Governors (1993-1995). He is a consultant on information systems development, methods, tools, and the application of CASE and reengineering/reverse engineering technology. He is also a lecturer in industrial engineering and information systems at Northeastern University in Boston, where he has taught graduate courses in software engineering and database management since 1987. Most recently, he was director of CASE development at Progress Software Corporation, a maker of distributed client/server 4GL/RDBMS products, where he was an industry speaker on CASE and 4GL in downsizing and distribution.

From 1986 to 1991, Chikofsky was director of research and technology at Index Technology Corporation, maker of the Excelerator line of CASE products. Before joining Index, he was vice president and cofounder of ISDOS Inc., a research and development spin-off from the University of Michigan in the fledgling CASE industry of the early 1980's. From 1976 through 1985, he was responsible for the commercial development of PSL/PSA and related software engineering tools.

He currently serves as secretary of the International Workshop on CASE (the technical meeting of the CASE field), and was its founding president. A senior member of the IEEE, he has been an active contributor in many Computer Society activities. He was Associate Editor-in-Chief of IEEE Software magazine from 1989 to 1992 and was founding editor of its software management column. He has been a vice chair of TCSE since 1989, and also serves as secretary of TCSE's reverse engineering subcommittee. He chaired the first three industry/research Reverse Engineering Forum conferences, and will cochair the reverse engineering workshop at the International Conference on Software Engineering in 1993.

He received his BS in computer and communications science (1975) and his MS in industrial and operations engineering (1978), both from the University of Michigan. This is the second edition of the author's IEEE Computer Society Press technology series edition on CASE. He is also the author of two IEEE CS Press videotape tutorials — *CASE Technology,* and *Reverse Engineering*.

IEEE Computer Society

IEEE Computer Society Press Publications

Monographs: A monograph is an authored book consisting of 100-percent original material.

Tutorials: A tutorial is a collection of original materials prepared by the editors, and reprints of the best articles published in a subject area. Tutorials must contain at least five percent of original material (although we recommend 15 to 20 percent of original material).

Reprint collections: A reprint collection contains reprints (divided into sections) with a preface, table of contents, and section introductions discussing the reprints and why they were selected. Collections contain less than five percent of original material.

Technology series: Each technology series is a brief reprint collection — approximately 126-136 pages and containing 12 to 13 papers, each paper focusing on a subset of a specific discipline, such as networks, architecture, software, or robotics.

Submission of proposals: For guidelines on preparing CS Press books, write the Editorial Director, IEEE Computer Society Press, PO Box 3014, 10662 Los Vaqueros Circle, Los Alamitos, CA 90720-1264, or telephone (714) 821-8380.

Purpose

The IEEE Computer Society advances the theory and practice of computer science and engineering, promotes the exchange of technical information among 100,000 members worldwide, and provides a wide range of services to members and nonmembers.

Membership

All members receive the acclaimed monthly magazine *Computer*, discounts, and opportunities to serve (all activities are led by volunteer members). Membership is open to all IEEE members, affiliate society members, and others seriously interested in the computer field.

Publications and Activities

Computer **magazine:** An authoritative, easy-to-read magazine containing tutorials and in-depth articles on topics across the computer field, plus news, conference reports, book reviews, calendars, calls for papers, interviews, and new products.

Periodicals: The society publishes six magazines and five research transactions. For more details, refer to our membership application or request information as noted above.

Conference proceedings, tutorial texts, and standards documents: The IEEE Computer Society Press publishes more than 100 titles every year.

Standards working groups: Over 100 of these groups produce IEEE standards used throughout the industrial world.

Technical committees: Over 30 TCs publish newsletters, provide interaction with peers in specialty areas, and directly influence standards, conferences, and education.

Conferences/Education: The society holds about 100 conferences each year and sponsors many educational activities, including computing science accreditation.

Chapters: Regular and student chapters worldwide provide the opportunity to interact with colleagues, hear technical experts, and serve the local professional community.